AGING AND THE CRIMINAL LEGAL SYSTEM

LINDSEY E. WYLIE
EVE M. BRANK

AGING AND THE CRIMINAL LEGAL SYSTEM

COMMUNITY SERVICES, COURTS, CORRECTIONS, AND POLICY

AMERICAN PSYCHOLOGICAL ASSOCIATION

Published by
American Psychological Association
750 First Street, NE
Washington, DC 20002
https://www.apa.org

Order Department
https://www.apa.org/pubs/books
order@apa.org

Typeset in Meridien and Ortodoxa by Circle Graphics, Inc., Reisterstown, MD

Printer: Vicks Printing, Yorkville, NY
Cover Designer: Beth Schlenoff, Bethesda, MD

Library of Congress Cataloging-in-Publication Data

Names: Wylie, Lindsey E. author | Brank, Eve M. author
Title: Aging and the criminal legal system : community services, courts, corrections, and policy / Lindsey E. Wylie, Eve M. Brank.
Description: Washington : American Psychological Association, 2025. | Series: American psychology-law series | Includes bibliographical references and index.
Identifiers: LCCN 2024051001 (print) | LCCN 2024051002 (ebook) | ISBN 9781433843006 paperback | ISBN 9781433843013 ebook | ISBN 9781433849206 Web PDF
Subjects: LCSH: Criminal justice, Administration of | Victims of Crime—Legal status, laws, etc. | Older prisoners—Legal status, laws, etc. | Older people—Crimes against | Correctional law
Classification: LCC K5001 .W95 2025 (print) | LCC K5001 (ebook) | DDC 345/.00846—dc23/eng/20250130
LC record available at https://lccn.loc.gov/2024051001
LC ebook record available at https://lccn.loc.gov/2024051002

https://doi.org/10.1037/0000469-000

Printed in the United States of America

10 9 8 7 6 5 4 3 2 1

CONTENTS

SERIES FOREWORD

Monica K. Miller

As series editor of the American Psychology–Law Society (American Psychological Association's [APA's] Division 41) book series, it is my pleasure to introduce the book titled *Aging and the Criminal Legal System: Community Services, Courts, Corrections, and Policy*. The book is written by Lindsey E. Wylie, JD, PhD (National Center for State Courts and University of Nebraska Omaha) and Eve M. Brank, JD, PhD (University of Nebraska–Lincoln).

Through its book series, the American Psychology–Law Society (AP-LS) seeks to (a) advance and disseminate the science of psychology and law; (b) advance the practice of psychology in legal contexts and establish contemporary best practices; (c) promote human rights, dignity, and justice in our multicultural, pluralistic society; and (d) actively encourage mentoring in the profession through knowledge dissemination and the publication process.

The AP-LS Book Series seeks proposals from authors and editors across the broad spectrum of psychology and law, both science and practice. The editorial team is particularly focused on books authored by and edited volumes from (a) traditionally underrepresented authors and editors, (b) collaborating psychologists and lawyers/legal scholars, and (c) collaborating veteran and early-career scientists and/or practitioners. The editorial team hopes its published volumes will inform scholars and practitioners as to the current state of the science on their chosen topics. In doing so, the series is intended to encourage unbiased science and best practices that promote well-being and prevent discrimination and injustice.

The goal of the editorial team is to commission state-of-the art volumes covering a wide range of topics at the nexus of psychology and law—ones that will be of interest to both practitioners and researchers. As series editor,

I'm delighted that this book will be the first of my editorship. The topic of aging and the criminal legal system is a critical area of study and, as such, is a fitting topic for this book series. The authors have thoroughly described the psychology and the law (and their intersection) related to older people in a way that will be understandable to many audiences.

The population of older adults in the United States is growing rapidly. By 2030, all Baby Boomers will be over 65, and by 2034, the number of people past retirement age will surpass the number of children for the first time in history (U.S. Census Bureau, 2018). These data make this book timely and relevant to a large part of the population.

The criminal justice system, like every other system in society, must make changes to adapt to this shift in the country's age demographics. In many areas of law, policymakers have ignored developmental differences regarding older adults—even, at times, borrowing from the law as related to juveniles. Sometimes laws, policies, and procedures are built on ageist stereotypes. Systems such as prisons are often unable to provide for the needs of older adults. This book addresses some of these issues head-on. It summarizes the law and psychology related to older adults when they become victims, witnesses, and perpetrators of crime. It discusses issues of forensic assessment and determining the appropriate sentences for older adults. The authors identify ways in which the law should or should not, and does or does not, consider the specific abilities and circumstances of older adults.

The psychology of aging in the criminal legal system has become a topic of much interest to practitioners and academics. As such, there is a need to summarize and synthesize what the field has learned thus far. This volume accomplishes just that, in exemplary fashion, providing unique, comprehensive coverage of the state of the science concerning the psychology of older adults in the criminal justice system while focusing on relevant psychological and legal foundations. With a basis in both law and policy, this book has potential to have a significant impact both on future academic work and on legal practice and policy.

In closing, I would like to end by thanking the two members of the editorial board who do the work of recruiting and reviewing proposals for the series: Jemour Maddux and Monique Bowen. They represent leading scholars in psychology who have graciously donated their time to help advance the field. I would also like to thank Chris Kelaher, senior acquisitions editor for APA Books, who guided us through the entire process. Without all of you, this book would not have become reality.

PREFACE: PURPOSE AND BACKGROUND OF THIS BOOK

Why did you pick up this book? Whether driven by personal interest or coursework, you likely have a curiosity about older adults in our criminal legal system. Why is that? Are you inclined toward topics in criminal behavior, or are you more focused on issues related to older adults generally? Perhaps you are drawn to both topics. Regardless of your reasons, we hope that by the time you reach the final chapter, you will have gained new insights into how older adults interact with the criminal legal system. Although, as Jimmy Buffett commented, "growing old is not for sissies" (France, 2023), most of us will grow old. Our goal as authors of this book is for readers to realize that the issues facing older adults are everyone's issues. Most important, we hope you discover new research questions or legal areas you wish to examine, drawing from familiar research methods and topics or exploring new ones.

Our own interests in older adults within the legal system began when the second author, Brank, started her career as a new assistant professor in the Department of Criminology, Law and Society at the University of Florida. With much of her practical experience and research work during graduate and law school focused on children and families, Brank was eager to explore new areas within law and psychology.

Brank's interest in older adults stemmed from a combination of things. A general curiosity and never-quenched desire to do something different drove her, as did learning vicariously through her husband's medical school coursework about the rapid increase in the number of older adults in our society. These factors, combined with conversations she had with people through church and work who were informally caring for their older family members, shaped her perspective. It did not take Brank long to realize that there were not that many law-psychology researchers who had or were currently focused on older adult issues. At the same time, the American Psychology–Law Society (AP-LS) created a new grant mechanism to encourage interdisciplinary work beyond the law and psychology fields. As 2006 awardees, Brank and two medical professionals received $5,000 in AP-LS grant funding to explore families navigating informal older adult caregiving. Armed with graduate student research on termination of parental rights (Brank et al., 2001) and public support for holding parents responsible for the behaviors of their children (Brank & Weisz, 2004), Brank traversed the separate, yet related, legal landscape of how legal systems work with children, families, and older adults.

One year after Brank was awarded the AP-LS interdisciplinary grant, the first author, Wylie, joined Brank at the University of Florida. Wylie was delighted to return to her undergraduate alma mater after completing her master's degree at John Jay College of Criminal Justice and research internships with Policy Research Associates and the Center for Court (now Justice) Innovation in New York City. Building on her personal experiences in the legal system and then research surrounding court treatment programs, Wylie was looking forward to studying how the legal system unintentionally impacts vulnerable and resilient populations that it intends to protect or (re)habilitate.

As with Brank, aging and law issues were not at the forefront of Wylie's ideas for a program of research as a budding graduate student, and she was more familiar with juvenile law issues than older adult law issues. Nonetheless, when Brank handed Wylie the (actual) box of printed materials and ideas for the AP-LS interdisciplinary grant project and beyond, Wylie quickly understood the vast inattention paid to older adults in the law, which offered an important opportunity to focus on an underserved population in research generally. Although Wylie's plans for doctoral education at the University of Florida were rerouted when Brank accepted a position with the University of Nebraska–Lincoln law-psychology program, Wylie excitedly agreed to transfer graduate programs. Sharing a vision for taking the road less traveled, they continued to explore how aging interacts within the law, now at Brank's graduate alma mater.

The time was ripe. As experimental social psychologists, both Brank and Wylie were intrigued by the growing field of empirical legal studies. During both Brank and Wylie's graduate school years in the 1990s and early 2000s, scholarship on American elder law started to formalize, with development of legal theory and the "rise of . . . empirical elder law" (Doron, 2020, p. 14) to study the impact of the law with quantitative statistical analysis and more rigorous empirical methods. Simultaneously, behavioral science theories gained interest among researchers to explain behavior and outcomes specific to legal settings. For instance, the therapeutic jurisprudence doctrine suggested the law itself can be a therapeutic agent, for which legal rules, procedures, and actors can be social forces that produce therapeutic or antitherapeutic consequences for individuals (Wexler, 2001; Wexler & Winick, 1991; Winick, 1997). Likewise, researchers applied procedural justice theory and focused on how legal systems and actors influence perceptions and behaviors of legal system consumers (Tyler & Lind, 2001). These emerging theories with an interdisciplinary lens differed from their predecessors and sought to explain how legal professionals and legal environments could be modified to improve outcomes for legal consumers, instead of vice versa.

Funded by the AP-LS interdisciplinary grant, Brank and Wylie's first project tested community dyads—older adults and cohabitating family members—on their understanding of concepts around legal responsibilities when providing care to an aging and infirm adult, as generally defined in state criminal abuse and neglect laws. The paper "Assuming Elder Care Responsibility: Am I a Caregiver?" was presented at the Third Annual Conference on Empirical Legal Studies at Cornell Law School in 2008 and published by the *Journal of Empirical Legal Studies* the following year (Wylie & Brank, 2009).

Recruiting the study's sample and collecting data with community-dwelling older and infirm adults was challenging and fulfilling—both metaphorically and physically! During one dyad interview, Wylie and (then undergraduate research assistant and now) Professor Christopher King sat down to homemade rhubarb pie and whipped cream at a respondent's home. In another session, interviews were held at a Village Inn restaurant during coffee and free pie Wednesday. The research participants not only opened their kitchens but also shared their unique concerns and difficulties. On one memorable occasion, Wylie sat on the edge of the bed of a dying man in hospice care who was living with his adult daughter. He was weak and tired but wanted to respond to her interview questions. Later in the interview with his adult daughter, she indicated how thrilled he was to share his experiences with researchers. Even more than the presentations and publications, the thank-you notes and verbal expressions of gratitude received from older participants for including them in research further encouraged this work.

As described in the Introduction, scholarship within elder law has traditionally focused on a narrow scope of issues, mostly civil law issues relevant to a subset of older adults with more resources or wealth, such as end-of-life planning (e.g., wills, estate planning), and topics from the perspective of a vulnerable older adult in need of protection (e.g., guardianship, abuse and neglect). Conversely, there had been little consideration of issues touching on aging across various roles and stages within the criminal legal system.

Near the end of Wylie's doctoral program, however, issues central to aging and the criminal legal system gained media and policy attention nationally. Also, within Wylie's and Brank's home state of Nebraska as federal and state governments grappled with identifying solutions to the consequences of prison overcrowding and the rising health-related expenses of older and infirm people in prisons. After Nebraska state data revealed a substantial increase in the proportion of older adults residing in prisons from 1983 to 2012, the Nebraska State Penitentiary took proactive and innovative approaches to screen older adults at prison intake for any functional impairments requiring accommodations from the prison. After prison staff noted that admission screening results quickly became outdated for some older adults and failed to identify ongoing accommodations after admission, University of Nebraska Omaha (UNO), gerontology professor Julie Masters and Wylie worked with the prison to revise the screening process.

As the department chair in gerontology, Masters asked Wylie whether she would be interested in developing a class on aging and criminal law issues. Wylie questioned Masters, "Is there enough material to warrant its own course?" Masters's expression indicated she was not concerned. As a gerontologist studying the physical, mental, and social changes as people age, Masters was keenly aware "that as people age, the challenges or the issues that they might face tend to be a little more complicated" (UNO, 2017). Surely the same holds true, if not more, in the criminal legal system. Wylie first taught the course, Aging and Crime, at UNO in 2014 and continued for six semesters, always with a full class of more than 20 undergraduate and graduate students across several disciplines: gerontology, criminology, social work, and psychology.

In the years since Wylie first taught the Aging and Crime course, scholarship surrounding these issues has burgeoned in the fields of gerontology, social work, and forensic psychiatry but less so in disciplines that study behavior in criminal contexts (e.g., law-psychology, criminology). This book aims to remedy this shortfall.

AGING AND THE CRIMINAL LEGAL SYSTEM

Introduction

Aging and the Law: Theoretical Foundations

Think about an older person. Do you think of your grandmother or grandfather, who is kind and wise but at times slightly forgetful? Or your retired neighbor, who is distant and spends hours each week manicuring their lawn? Or are you like Bernard Baruch (1870–1965), American financier and elder statesman, who famously said that "old age is always fifteen years older than I am" (Baruch, n.d.). Maybe you even thought about yourself. After thinking of this older person, what are your feelings toward this person and how might it influence your interactions with them?

Although several factors influence how people think, feel, and behave toward older adults, psychological theory and research show that in modern industrialized countries, especially in the United States, individuals hold both positive and negative thoughts and attitudes toward older adults. According to social psychologists, these mixed perceptions explain why some older adults are viewed as "doddering, but dear" (Cuddy & Fiske, 2002, p. 4), and others are viewed as admirable, but aloof. More specifically, studies have documented that when people have stereotypical beliefs that older adults are less competent, are less competitive of resources, and have poor physical and cognitive health, it prompts feelings of pity and protective behavior toward the older adult. However, this generalization shifts when older adults are in high-status positions. Instead, research finds that when people hold stereotypical beliefs that older adults are highly competent and competitive of resources, this prompts feelings of envy and adversarial behavior toward the older adult

https://doi.org/10.1037/0000469-001
Aging and the Criminal Legal System: Community Services, Courts, Corrections, and Policy,
by L. E. Wylie and E. M. Brank

(Cuddy et al., 2005; Fiske et al., 2002; Löckenhoff et al., 2009). These mixed perceptions help to explain the muddled role older adults have in contemporary society.

Now, think about an older person in the context of the criminal legal system. What is their role? Do you think about a judge, a victim of financial abuse, or a person engaging in criminal behavior? Are there any societal assumptions about an older adult who is in this role? Older adults interact across several points—as legal professionals, such as police officers or judges, and as nonprofessionals, such as an older victim of a crime, an older eyewitness to a crime, or an older perpetrator of a crime. As discussed within the forthcoming chapters of this book, how an older person experiences the legal system is dependent on their intersectional role (e.g., judge, parolee). The field of elder law is remarkably diverse, encompassing a wide range of legal topics. Its scope is defined not by restrictions on subject matter but rather by its focus on serving the needs of older adults. In other words, any legal issue that affects seniors falls within the purview of elder law (Kohn, 2020a).

Although older adults have countless interactions as they navigate legal systems, traditionally, research and practice have considered only civil issues within the scope of legal aging scholarship (i.e., guardianship and alternatives, estate and advance legal planning, and Medicare planning). Recently, legal scholars recognized this deficit and called for an expansion into other areas of the law and the development of multidisciplinary research and theory (Doron, 2020; Kohn, 2020b). As a response to their call, this book bridges research and theory from behavioral sciences and law to criminal legal issues relevant to older adults. Although theory in legal scholarship seeks to explain normative legal responses and their exceptions under a rational actor model, legal theories typically do not account for the role of human behavior in legal responses. As such, theory and research from behavioral sciences can inform legal theories by further accounting for human experiences and behavior, and employing statistical techniques to predict deviations from normative legal responses (Monahan & Loftus, 1982).

AGING IN AMERICA

In some sectors of society, older adults have been displaced from places of authority and autonomy (Butler, 2009), making old age something to be feared (Brank, 2011) and fought (T. D. Nelson, 2002). However, this was not always the case historically. A notable example, Sparta, was an ancient Greek city-state and exemplar of a true formalized gerontocracy—a society led by sexagenarians. Although not a democracy, the Spartan government had something similar to the U.S. Constitution and a governing body akin to a supreme court and legislature called the Gerousia, which was composed of 30 members—28 men over 60 years old and two kings, who could be under 60 (Kingman, 2017). Although the media has commented that the United States is governed by the "exceptionally old" (D. Smith, 2023), a true gerontocracy requires leaders to be substantially older than the population median age. Likely, Spartan society revered elders because military requirements and related physical hazards meant reaching 60 years old was not common (Kingman, 2017), and surviving into older age indicated that a person was capable of fierce leadership.

Unlike in Sparta, where older adults were chosen as that society's primary decision makers, the United States was established with much younger leaders in mind. The U.S. Constitution minimally requires the president to be 35 years old (U.S. Const. art. II, § 1), Senate members to be 30 years old (U.S. Const. art. I, § 3), and House members to be 25 years old (U.S. Const. art. I, § 2), with no minimum age to be a Supreme Court justice. Nonetheless, at the time we wrote this book, older adults hold some of the most powerful decision-making positions in government and have significant political power. The two most recent U.S. presidents are in their 70s (Trump and Biden), the median ages of the 118th Congress House of Representatives and Senate are 58 years old and 65 years old, respectively (Blazina & Desilver, 2023), and the average age of the presiding U.S. Supreme Court justices is 63 years old (Supreme Court of the United States, 2024).

Even as powerful decision makers in the United States, individuals in political positions still face societal assumptions about chronological age and abilities. For instance, in his 80s, President Joe Biden "drew attention to his status as the oldest person ever to occupy the Oval Office, with opinion polls showing Americans worried he [was] too old" (S. Holland, 2023, para. 1) for the presidential reelection in 2024. In response to those "who worry he is too old for the rigors of the White House," (S. Holland, 2023, para. 3) President Biden deflected with "humor" (para. 3) about his age and attempted to "convince voters that his age and experience over a half-century in public life [was] an asset in tackling America's problems" (para. 3). President Biden later withdrew from his reelection campaign following increased concerns regarding his health. As Chapter 2 (this volume) explores in greater depth, the age of political candidates often becomes a focal point during elections, potentially diminishing support for the older population. Indeed, individuals who live long enough will likely experience such instances of stereotyping, prejudice, and discrimination based on age (Palmore, 2015).

CULTURAL HISTORY OF OLDER AGE

All known societies have a named social category for old age and associated beliefs about older age. However, societies for most of recorded history have wavered in how to conceptualize old age. Some historical periods have considered people in their 40s to be in old age, with other periods considering much later ages (Thane, 2003) or suggesting separate definitions for men and women (Covey, 1992). Categorizations such as these provide efficiency—a sort of shorthand—for determining how a person should behave and what rights and responsibilities they should have (Eglit, 2004). For example, the ancient Greek philosopher Hippocrates divided old age into stages, with the first beginning at 56 years of age and the final stage beginning at 90 years of age (Covey, 1992). The Old Testament of the Bible describes very old figures who reached 900 years of age, yet also describes old age as around 70 to 80 years old (Covey, 1992, referring to stories in Genesis and Psalm 90:10).

Some believe the reason older adults are less valued today than they were in centuries past is due to economic shifts from agrarian societies (e.g., growing their own food) to industrialized ones focused on manufacturing (Löckenhoff et al., 2009) to the present digital economy. For example, geriatrician William Thomas (2004) detailed how early hunter-gatherer lifestyles necessitated a lack of care for the old or infirm. As Thomas noted, if a child struggled to keep up with the speed at which the tribe was moving, the child could be carried, but an older person had to be left behind. Even in societies that were not nomadic yet still relied on a subsistence (i.e., survival) economy, members who were considered weaker were believed to be burdensome. Contrast this to the United States in the 18th century, which held admiration for aging. During this time, the United States was a developing agricultural society with bountiful food storage and fewer survival needs, which allowed for more resources to care for others. By the mid-1700s, men powdered their hair gray or wore wigs to appear older (Eglit, 2004) as they shaped a new country (W. Achenbaum, 1978). Reaching older age in the colonial era was rare given high mortality rates (Fleming et al., 2003) not solely explained by higher rates of infant and child deaths (Covey, 1992).

As historians have explained, as industrialized factory work became more prevalent between 1865 and 1914, the perceived worth of older adults was again questioned by society because the work most valued was physically challenging for aging bodies (Hareven, 1976). Common stereotypes persisted that older adults were "ugly and disease-ridden" (W. Achenbaum, 1978, p. 39) and unable to contribute to the workforce, generating discrimination in the form of social and physical distance (M. S. North & Fiske, 2012). Following industrialization, the workforce became more sedentary in nature, and physical differences between older and younger workers were less relevant when jobs no longer required physical labor to perform them. As jobs have become more cognitively demanding than physically demanding in the modern digital era, common stereotypes around older workers have shifted from physical limitations to assumptions about cognitive limitations and ability to learn new technology.

Although cultural history may explain how the majority population experienced aging through shifts in the U.S. economic system, some scholars dispute the modernization theory as overly simplified and devoid of attention to cultural differences (Hendricks, 1982). For example, modernization theory does not account for unequal aging and intersectionality with other group membership, such as race, ethnicity, and gender (Holman & Walker, 2021); the impact of ageism (De Tavernier et al., 2019); or individualized experiences of aging based on social and biological factors (Hall, 2014). Acknowledging the diverse theories of aging, the following sections summarize various perspectives on how older Americans experience the aging process. The first section describes biological processes in aging, including normative (i.e., typical) processes in physical aging and cognitive aging. This is followed by some examples of pathological and diseased (i.e., atypical) aging processes most relevant to the criminal legal system, including physical limitations, mental health and substance use disorders, and dementia-related disorders.

BIOLOGICAL PROCESSES IN AGING

The aging process is a riddle, "one of the central mysteries of biology" (Rando & Chang, 2012, p. 46), because of the boundless environmental and genetic factors that contribute to the process. Physical aging is a complicated phenomenon influenced by genetics, the environment, epigenetics (i.e., how behaviors and environment influence genetics), and other factors determined by chance (Rodríguez-Rodero et al., 2011). Still, biological and cognitive research is clear that some developmental changes are inevitable in aging, although changes are not consistent across individuals (Jylhävä et al., 2017), and there is a wide range of functional abilities among older adults as they age (Mast et al., 2022). Some older adults function similarly to or better than their younger counterparts, but as a group, older adults proportionally face greater deficits in physical and mental capabilities (Frolik & Barnes, 2015). Everyone's aging process involves some normative, age-related changes, but worsened aging patterns are represented by pathological disease, dysfunction, and decline (Wilson et al., 2020).

Normative or Typical Aging

Physical and sensory changes common in the typical aging process may be easily visible and nonpathological. For example, these changes can include decreased skin elasticity, graying hair, stooping posture, loss of muscle tone (sarcopenia), and increased adiposity (Boss & Seegmiller, 1981; Schoenborn et al., 2006). As many readers may have already experienced, eyesight generally weakens with age (National Institute on Aging, 2021), as does hearing (Schoenborn et al., 2006). Other typical aging processes may lead to increased risks of injury, illness, and death (Boss & Seegmiller, 1981; R. A. Miller, 1999). For instance, bone mass generally decreases with older age, which weakens bones and makes them more susceptible to breaking (Demontiero et al., 2012). Older populations are also more vulnerable to infection due to depressed immune function (Oh et al., 2019). Furthermore, because older adults experience normative reductions in most body systems, if pathological diseases are present, these can exacerbate normal aging processes. For instance, aging can contribute to issues in cardiovascular health (B. J. North & Sinclair, 2012);

lung, kidney, and other organ performance; and cognitive functioning (da Costa et al., 2016). Liver and kidney systems work less effectively with advancing age, which means they metabolize and excrete drugs (both legal and illegal) less efficiently (Bhutto & Morley, 2008; Boss & Seegmiller, 1981).

Intelligence and Cognition

Despite developmental changes that do occur, intelligence does not decline with age. One helpful way to differentiate age-based intelligence is to consider the distinction between fluid and crystallized intelligence. Although the ability to solve novel or complex problems (i.e., fluid intelligence) generally declines with age, the accumulated knowledge a person has (i.e., crystallized intelligence) improves or at least remains stable (Zaval et al., 2015). Cognitively, normative aging is associated with minor declines in processing speed (Wilson et al., 2020). In the absence of disease, older adults can compensate for these small deficits so they generally do not contribute to impairment. Researchers indicate that older adults are highly adaptable compared with younger adults (Lowe et al., 2022), and they benefit from their life experiences in a way that younger people cannot (Glück & Scherpf, 2022).

Mental Health and Substance Use

Whereas declines in physical and cognitive health are more widely discussed and understood, less attention has been paid to older adults and concerns associated with mental health and substance use. In 2012, Congress recognized a hidden problem affecting older adults: mental health disorders and substance use disorders (SUDs). To address this issue, they commissioned a report from the Institute of Medicine (IOM; Edens et al., 2012). The report's objectives were to document the prevalence of these conditions among older adults and to project the behavioral health workforce needs for this population. The report acknowledged data were not available for definitive percentages but estimated approximately 14% to 20% of older adults had a mental health disorder or SUD. Furthermore, the IOM reported poorer outcomes, such as higher hospitalization rates and emergency department visits, for older adults with physical illness and mental health disorders than for those with a physical illness alone.

Historically, mental health services accounted for only 1% of Medicare expenditures (Edens et al., 2012), in part because the older generation during the study period was unlikely to seek professional services (Mackenzie et al., 2008). In more recent decades, Americans have become more willing to seek treatment for mental health (Mojtabai, 2007) as perceptions of mental illness have become less stigmatizing (Baral et al., 2022). The American Association for Geriatric Psychiatry (n.d.) has an estimated membership of approximately 2,000 but professionals in the field warn the supply of providers may fall short of the demand for services (Bartels & Naslund, 2013).

Per the most recent edition of the *Diagnostic and Statistical Manual of Mental Disorders* (5th ed., text rev.; American Psychiatric Association, 2022), SUDs are diagnosed along a severity continuum based on the number of symptoms experienced from substance use. A systematic literature review (M. H. Taylor & Grossberg, 2012) spanning the years 1960 to 2011 ($n = 26$) found that contrary to society's expectations, drug use among older adults had increased from previous decades. Identifying that older adults who use substances have a unique profile compared with younger adults, the review also noted that most of the research focused on illegal drug use and not legal alcohol or prescribed drug use. Alcohol remains the most common substance that older adults use. Longitudinal data from the National Survey on Drug Use and Health indicated that approximately 20% of adults aged 60 to 64 and approximately 11% over age 65 reported current binge drinking (Ghantous et al., 2022). Data also presented an increase in the use of heroin and cocaine and the misuse of stimulants among those aged 50 and older. Studies suggest that SUDs among older adults are underdiagnosed because treatment seeking is lower in this group (Mackenzie et al., 2008), and medical professionals are more likely to address physical or cognitive issues first (B. Han et al., 2009). Both underutilization of treatment and lack of attention from health care providers perpetuate misconceptions that older adults do not have SUD needs (Kuerbis et al., 2014). Several factors could account for substance use trends within the older adult subpopulation: physical vulnerabilities to substances, unknown prescribed medication interactions, prescription misuse, chronic pain and opiate use, and increased acceptance of medical marijuana (National Institute on Drug Abuse, 2020).

Dementia-Related Disorders

Although 30% to 40% of adults over age 85 display symptoms of dementia, dementia-related disorders are not part of typical aging (Alzheimer's Association, 2024). Rather, dementia is caused by an underlying pathology, such as Alzheimer's disease or other cognitive-related disorders. With data from the U.S. Census Bureau and Medicaid/Medicare, the IOM (Eden et al., 2012) reported approximately 5.1 million people aged 65 and older presented with dementia, or 12.7% of the population aged 65 and older. To date, there has been little research examining dementia and the criminal legal system (Arias & Flicker, 2020; Cipriani et al., 2016), with most studies conducted in nonforensic settings such as hospitals or nursing homes (e.g., Eastley et al., 1993; M. O'Connor, 1987). As described in Chapter 5 (this volume), the criminal legal system is experiencing the impact of deteriorating cognitive disorders, and the American Bar Association (ABA) advocates for systematic screening across all system points in the criminal legal system (ABA Commission on Law and Aging, 2022). Although data are not yet available in the United States as to the number of individuals who are system involved with dementia, some preliminary figures outlined in Chapter 5 indicated a noteworthy overlap (21%)

of dementia-related disorders in a sample of first-time arrestees (65 and older) in Israel (Barak et al., 1995). Utilizing a unique and valuable data system that compares South Carolina's dementia-related disorders database with the prison database, researchers found a 1% overlap of individuals who appeared in both databases over a 24-year period. Importantly, though, these data cannot determine whether dementia symptoms were present before or after incarceration (ABA Commission on Law and Aging, 2022).

SOCIAL DETERMINANTS OF AGING

The longer a group of people live, the more diverse that group becomes. Social factors play a significant role in the aging process, making each person's aging process idiosyncratic. Aging is natural and lifelong and, though universal, is not uniform. How people age is shaped by their social and physical environments, including personal experiences within the family into which they were born and their community. Research on the social determinants of aging have found that aging patterns are predicted by factors such as sex, race, education, social activity and networks, and lifestyle (Brinkley-Rubinstein, 2013; Dannefer, 2003; Kelly et al., 2017; Merkt et al., 2020; Rodríguez-Rodero et al., 2011). Socioeconomic status also plays a role; a person's zip code is a strong predictor of their life expectancy (Petrow, 2019). As proposed by the weathering hypothesis (Geronimus, 1992), a lifetime of social and economic disadvantage can lead to accelerated declines in physical health (Forde et al., 2019).

Intersectional Group Membership

The individualized aging process is further characterized by the intersectionality of aging and membership in another population subgroup. Intersectionality focuses on how discrimination explains inequality as it is concerned with social differences and relationships of power, privilege, and oppression (Holman & Walker, 2021). Intersectionality, a concept introduced by Crenshaw (1989), was initially formulated to elucidate the experiences of Black women in the criminal legal system. This framework helps explain subgroup inequalities that might otherwise be overlooked. By focusing on membership in more than one group as a distinct subpopulation, intersectionality seeks to direct social justice attention toward subgroups who face disadvantages that may otherwise be invisible (Crenshaw, 2016). Intersectionality research has focused mostly on sex and race. For example, studies on stereotypes found that Black Americans were perceived as lazy and unintelligent (Krieger, 2014). However, when these stereotypes were examined by subgroups, Black women were specifically viewed as "mammies, matriarchs, and welfare recipients," (Krieger, 2014, p. 651) whereas Black men were seen as criminals and rapists. Gerontologists have considered the interaction between ageism and other forms of discrimination, most often sexism. Compared with the breadth of research on individual and structural ageism, however, there are far fewer studies on the interplay between ageism and other forms of discrimination, making it an important area of future research (Chang et al., 2020).

Generational Factors

Sociostructural age dynamics are quickly changing in the United States. The characteristics of those considered older will also ultimately change, and demographic shifts are important to consider for policy and practice. For example, most older adults in the current era have been married, which may not be true in future generations of older adults (A. W. Roberts et al., 2018). Furthermore, with each generation, the United States becomes more racially and ethnically diverse. Unfortunately, research has not addressed the intergenerational consequences of ageism and seldom attributes generational differences to discrimination. Nonetheless, the rapid growth of the older population and a potential "new old age" adds ambiguity to the traditional pattern and dynamics of intergenerational interdependence (M. S. North & Fiske, 2012).

EXPLANATIONS FOR LEGAL RESPONSES TO AGING IN LAW AND PSYCHOLOGY

As stated by elder law legal scholar Nina A. Kohn (2020b),

> age discrimination is so central to the law that rules which treat people differently on the basis of their age—even when the rules prejudice certain people based on their age—are often not even regarded as notable, let alone concerning. (p. 202)

Even the concept of elder law as a separate area of law, some argue, may be controversial because of paternalistic and perpetrating ageist assumptions that older adults need protection (Hall, 2009). As we discuss throughout this book, the legal system typically uses categorical distinctions for older age, which are based on chronological age and regard older adults as a discrete category. To illustrate, the following are some laws and policies that distinguish older adults from others as a separate class: being required to retire from public service, being a vulnerable adult in abuse and neglect crimes, being exempt from jury service, being eligible for compassionate release from prison, or receiving more frequent parole hearings.

Legal Theories in Aging and the Law

The study of elder law has grown rapidly in the past few decades, especially since the first issue of the *Elder Law Journal* in 1993. Scholarship within elder law historically focused narrowly on issues relevant to the clinical legal practice of elder law, which limited elder law's contribution to multidisciplinary research and development of legal theory ripe for empirical research (Doron, 2020; Kohn, 2020a). To complement the practice of elder law, prominent legal scholars called for robust multidisciplinary and theoretically informed research at the intersection of law and aging (Brank, 2007; Doron, 2020; Kohn, 2020a). Written by international experts, a collaborative landmark text *Theories on Law and Ageing* edited by Israel Doron (2009b) discussed several legal theories broadly defined as "any construction of explicit explanation that accounts for [legal] reality" (p. vi). These models focused mostly on legal realities within civil legal systems; however, aging issues also often intersect with criminal legal systems. Furthering theory and research on aging and criminal law issues can similarly assist policymakers in addressing current and incoming challenges to prioritize goals in the U.S. criminal legal system.

Most of the legal theories presented in Doron's (2020) text describe a singular theoretical perspective to systematize the "how" and "why" behind the legal system's response to the "what"—termed by Doron as "legal realities"—including court rulings, legislation, administrative law, and policies older adults experience. As described by Doron, during the first rise of elder law in the 1990s, legal scholarship focused on civil practice issues common with older adults, such as advance planning, through preeminent elder law scholar Lawrence Frolik's later-in-life perspective (Doron, 2020; Frolik, 2009). In light of the significant contributions that aging and the law has made within state guardianship laws, a therapeutic jurisprudence model was also presented to explain the legal system's realities as a means to protect the rights and psychological, physical, and financial well-being of older adults (Kapp, 2009). Commenting that therapeutic jurisprudence within aging and the law is paternalistic, a scholar offered a mental health law perspective that presented aging as a "social deviance" (Schmidt, 2009, p. 124) from the norm of having capacity and free will, and legal systems as a means for socially controlling those who are aging. A disability law perspective identified similarities because both fields span multiple domains of substantive law and focus on assessing the law's impact on members of the specialized group (Surtees, 2009). An equity theory acknowledged the social (exclusion and ageism) and personal (one's own aging process) vulnerabilities of aging individuals as a legal justification for legal protections, as opposed to a per se categorization by chronological age, such as children. Having a distinct category in law, the theory states that elder law is "inherently paternalistic" (Hall, 2009, p. 107) and contributes to the internalization of ageism.

A central question in elder law is consistently asked: Should the field "revive and reenergize the classic [elder law] debate over what role—if any—chronological age should play in establishing rights or benefits" (Kohn, 2020b, p. 195) or whether socially constructed determinants are more appropriate? Although chronological age can be necessary for determining cutoff points for categorization, theorists propose that age is a social construct and should not be based on chronology (Giles & Reid, 2005; Hall, 2014; S. R. Levy & Macdonald, 2016). Professor of Applied Legal Studies Margaret Hall (2014) expanded on her equity theory to describe a critical theory of aging and the law, which views old age as a complex construct in which "social identity is iteratively entwined with embodied experience" (p. 2). Hall reasoned that, like other theories based on socially constructed identities, as seen through a critical lens (e.g., race, gender), being old impacts those whose identity is defined by their older age. Different from other identities, however, social identity based on oldness is both biologically and socially created through the "physiological experience of aging, and the special vulnerabilities attendant on that experience" (p. 2). The embodied experience of aging and becoming an "old person" is individualized by "material, social, and relationship contexts" (p. 11), which are "intimately experienced and seen/responded to by others" (p. 13).

Nevertheless, as argued by Doron's (2009a) own pluralistic model in *Theories on Law and Ageing*, "the only way to fully grasp the richness and diversity of elder law is through a multidimensional model, which connects different functions and targets that law wishes to achieve" (p. 59). Doron's multidimensional model of aging and the law represents five types of legal responses to older adults, and the model explains the varied, sometimes seemingly inconsistent legal responses to older adults (see Figure 1). At the center of the multidimensional model of aging and the law are the core legal principles (the "juristic core"), which are the primary procedural and substantive legal responses. In the United States, which is governed by the Constitution, many core legal responses are based on constitutional protections, such as due process and equal protection (see Chapter 1, this volume). Core legal responses can also come from statutory, regulatory, and common law court rules. The core legal principles are intended to be universal—applicable across events and responding to a range of legal issues. Importantly, a core legal response has its advantages and its disadvantages when it comes to the legal rights of older

FIGURE 1. A Multidimensional Model of Elder Law

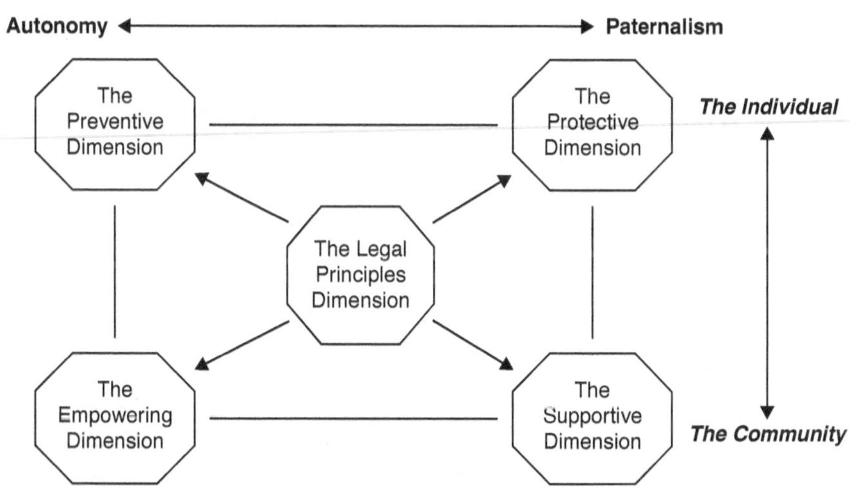

Note. From "A Multi-Dimensional Model of Elder Law," by I. Doron, in I. Doron (Ed.), *Theories on Law and Ageing: The Jurisprudence of Elder Law* (p. 60), 2009, Springer (https://doi.org/10.1007/978-3-540-78954-3_5). Copyright 2009 by Springer. Reprinted with permission.

adults. Although universal legal responses protect older adults along with the entire population, normalize aging as integral in society, and promote equality values among citizens, such responses fail to recognize any individualized biological and social needs specific to each person (Doron, 2009a). From Doron and Kohn's (2011) perspective, "the juristic core is a blunt tool for protecting the rights of older persons" (p. 4), and laws developed under core legal principles may be insufficient to address problems that arise for special sectors of the population, such as older adults.

As modifications to core legal principles, the other four dimensions reflect other types of legal responses (the "what") to explain variations in how the legal systems respond to older adults. The multidimensional model of aging and the law proposes that legal responses may be classified into four categories: (a) preventive responses, (b) protective responses, (c) supportive responses, and (d) empowering responses (Doron, 2009a). When classified to one of the five dimensions, each response can be explained according to where it falls on the two axes: its underlying philosophical approach on the x-axis (the "why"), labeled autonomy and paternalism, and its underlying policy objective on the y-axis (the "how"), labeled as individualized and community/societal. More specifically, Doron and Kohn (2011) provided examples that fall within each legal response type within civil law issues impacting older adults. For instance, preventive legal responses consist of tools and systems for older adults to plan for an independent future (autonomy and individualized), such as incapacity planning (e.g., power of attorney), government-incentivized individual retirement accounts, and reverse mortgages. Responses within the protective dimension include legal responses aimed at protecting older adults as a vulnerable population (paternalism and individual), such as elder maltreatment laws and guardianship. Supportive legal responses focus on the social context, including policies that provide formal and informal support networks of individuals who provide care or services to older adults (paternalism and community), such as the federal Family and Medical Leave Act of 1993 and filial responsibility laws requiring certain family members to support relatives if the older person is indigent (Wylie & Brank, 2009). Last, empowering responses are designed to promote older adults realizing their rights and entitlements for improving the status of older adults (autonomy and community), such as the federal Supporting Older Americans Act (2020; a reauthorization of the Older Americans Act of 1965) that provides states with financial resources so that older adults have access to legal resources or advocates such as *guardian ad litems* in guardianship hearings.

Although well-meaning and usually necessary, responses outside of the juristic core carry assumptions about the needs and wants of older adults and may further aging biases and discrimination (Doron & Kohn, 2011). With use of the multidimensional model of aging and the law, legal system responses can be mapped to each dimension to describe and understand how systems are addressing issues for older adults. This mapping exercise can reveal whether law and policies specific to older adults are disproportionately focused on autonomy, paternalism, individual responsibilities, or external support systems. As a model formulated only to explain legal responses, Doron's (2009a) multidimensional model does not account for the influence of human behavior in the underlying philosophies and objectives of laws and policies, nor does it account for how human behavior is influenced by legal responses to aging (i.e., Do they foster ageism?).

To wholly conceptualize how older adults interrelate with legal systems, psychology theory and research can augment existing aging and the law theory to include explanations about human behavior. Theory and research on self- and intergroup perception can explain legal responses toward older adults in the United States by the older person's role in the legal system (the "who"), the context of the legal system response (the "where"), and any environmental cues to explain why a legal response may deviate from what is expected based on its hypothesized underlying philosophy and objective (the "when"). Moreover, whereas Doron's (2009a) multidimensional model was formulated to explain legal responses within elder civil law, the model is also intended to be applicable to other areas of law and can be extended to map criminal legal system responses in the United States (the "what").

Psychological Theories in Perceptions and Experiences of Aging

Social psychology theory and research in self- and intergroup perception focuses on understanding how individuals perceive themselves and others in social contexts to understand complex human social behavior. This area of psychology explores how people form impressions of themselves, including their self-concept and self-esteem, and how these perceptions influence their behavior, attitudes, and interactions with others. Additionally, researchers study how individuals perceive and categorize members of different social groups based on group membership (e.g., race, ethnicity, gender, age). Research in this area examines biases, stereotypes, and prejudice that may arise from intergroup comparisons as well as the processes underlying self-identity and social identity formation.

Biases Toward Older Adults

Specifically, theories in social psychology seek to explain commonly held stereotypical beliefs and how people internalize those beliefs into prejudicial attitudes to explain institutional, interpersonal, and internalized discrimination (S. R. Levy et al., 2022). Overall, research indicates that older adults are described with both positive and negative stereotypes (Barrett & Cantwell, 2007; Cuddy et al., 2005), with endorsements of negative stereotypes being more prevalent (Chasteen et al., 2002; Hummert, 1993; Kite & Wagner, 2002; Nelson, 2002).Whether positive or negative stereotypes are elicited in a given situation is dependent on many factors, including the person's perceived appearance (Chonody & Teater, 2016) as well as environmental cues and context (e.g., Hummert, 2011). For instance, terror management theory (Greenberg et al., 2002) explains that younger people engage in ageist behaviors because older adults provoke cues about death, which produces a younger person's own fear of mortality. Furthermore, studies show that collectively, research participants indicate preferences for older adults who exhibit stereotype-consistent behaviors rather than for older adults who exhibit stereotype-inconsistent behaviors (Cuddy et al., 2005).

Variations in how older adults are perceived are also conditional on contextual factors (Castelli et al., 2004; Schaller et al., 2003) that facilitate either desirable or undesirable stereotypes. According to the role congruity theory, biased responses develop from the interaction of stereotypic beliefs about the target and the context in which the target is evaluated (Diekman & Hirnisey, 2007; Eagly & Karau, 2002). When a group's stereotype is mismatched to valued social roles, then individual perceivers have emotional responses that generate prejudicial feelings and subsequent discriminatory behavior—or ageism. Much like Hall's (2014) critical theory of aging and the law, intergroup perception theory explains the embodied experience of aging based on one's perceived social identity (Tajfel & Turner, 1979, 2004) and whether one sees oneself in the outgroup or the ingroup (Chonody & Teater, 2016).

As depicted in Figure 2, if someone perceives an older adult as an "other" from the outgroup, then the stereotype content model (SCM) further explains whether the older adult will be perceived according to positive or negative stereotypes. The SCM of intergroup relations, first conceptualized by Susan

FIGURE 2. The Stereotype Content Model

		Competence	
		Low	High
Warmth	High	**Paternalistic stereotype** low status, not competitive (e.g., housewives, elderly people, disabled people)	**Admiration** high status, not competitive (e.g., ingroup, close allies)
	Low	**Contemptuous stereotype** low status, competitive (e.g., welfare recipients, poor people)	**Envious stereotype** high status, competitive (e.g., Asians, Jews, rich people, feminists)

Note. Adapted from "A Model of (Often Mixed) Stereotype Content: Competence and Warmth Respectively Follow From Perceived Status and Competition," by S. T. Fiske, A. J. C. Cuddy, P. Glick, and J. Xu, 2002, *Journal of Personality and Social Psychology, 82*(6), p. 881 (https://doi.org/10.1037/0022-3514.82.6.878). Copyright 2002 by the American Psychological Association.

Fiske, suggests that discriminatory behavior is rooted in power relations, justifying the status quo, and assigning desirable traits to others who do not have competing goals (Fiske, 1993; Glick & Fiske, 2001). These complex attitudes and emotions explain inconsistent discriminatory behaviors that can be benevolent, indifferent, or actively harmful (Cuddy & Fiske, 2002). Similar to Doron's (2009a) multidimensional model of elder law, the SCM asserts that people are perceived according to two dimensions that help to explain discrimination: warmth/likability (e.g., are they trustworthy?) and competence/ability (e.g., do they have the capacity or skill to compete?). Where a target group falls along each dimension determines the content of the stereotypical beliefs and attitudes toward the group. The SCM predicts that individuals perceived as having powerful status will generate assumptions that they have high competence, but individuals perceived as lacking status and therefore a low competition of resources will generate assumptions that they are warm (Fiske et al., 2002).

Studies in this area have demonstrated that "elderly people" are typically perceived as low status and low competition, warm, but incompetent, which elicits emotions of pity (Cuddy et al., 2005, p. 881). When associated with these mixed warm–incompetent stereotypes, older adults can be targets of the most common form of ageist behavior, benevolent ageism, which results in overhelping and other protective behaviors (Bugental & Hehman, 2007; Cuddy et al., 2005). Take, for example, senior discounts at stores and restaurants. These special practices stem from the belief that older adults are in need of protection because they are not in the workforce, yet today, on average, older adults have more wealth than do younger adults (A. Achenbaum, 2015). On the other hand, when older adults are perceived as high status and competitive of resources, categorized as low warmth and high competence, this instead brings about feelings of envy and dislike. Instead of leading to protective behavior, interactions with older adults perceived as high status result in hostile and isolating behaviors toward them.

Age Discrimination

Similar to racism and sexism, ageism refers to stereotyping, prejudice, and discrimination based on age (Palmore, 2015), but unlike other forms of bias, ageism presents a distinctive issue in that most of the ingroup (the young) will eventually become part of the outgroup (the old), or at least hope to be one day. That is, if you do not die young, you will be old. In contemporary American society, it is socially accepted to hold biased views against older adults (Weir, 2023). Indeed, antiaging is a billion-dollar industry (Perls, 2004) that draws from these biases. Within government and legal decisions, although legal policies based on race and gender have become less legally acceptable in contemporary law, age is still a commonly accepted factor in policies that affect legal rights, legal responsibilities (Eglit, 2004; Kohn, 2020a), and segregation of groups (Hareven, 1976).

Such complicated perceptions contribute to assumptions people have about the character, behavior, and abilities of older adults—perceptions that bear on the law's response to aging and, correspondingly, how the law bears on the experience of aging—in the forms of institutional, interpersonal, and internalized ageism (World Health Organization, 2021). Institutional ageism occurs through systems or institutions via policies and actions, such as a company policy that unfairly privileges younger adults over older adults. Interpersonal ageism takes place in social interactions such as when an older adult is treated as unimportant or out of touch because of their age. Finally, ageism can be directed inward as internalized ageism, wherein an older adult internalizes ageist beliefs about themselves and harbors negative feelings about their abilities because of their age (B. Levy, 2009). For example, an older adult may believe that because older adults are generally not good with technology, they cannot learn a new computer program.

Throughout this book, ageism is described as a social determinant of chronic disease (J. O. Allen, 2016; World Health Organization, 2021). Recurrent experiences with negative stereotypes combined with discrimination may make ageism a chronic stressor in the lives of many older adults. Although ageism is not experienced over the lifespan, repeated exposure to chronic stressors associated with aging stereotypes and discrimination may increase chronic disease risks, mortality, and adverse health outcomes (J. O. Allen & Sikora, 2023). In an important emerging area, experiences of ageism also depend on the intersectionality in membership in any other groups (Holman & Walker, 2021). Factors including sex, race, education, social activity and networks, and lifestyle contribute to cumulative (dis)advantage, are highly predictive of aging patterns (Brinkley-Rubinstein, 2013; Dannefer, 2003; Kelly et al., 2017; Merkt et al., 2020; Rodríguez-Rodero et al., 2011), and lead to accelerated decline in physical health (Forde et al., 2019).

STRUCTURE OF THE BOOK

Building from scholarship on the biological and social determinants of aging, this book bridges theory and research from psychology and law to the study of aging and the law. As part of the American Psychology–Law Society (AP-LS; American Psychological Association Division 41) book series, this book aims to educate the psychology and legal professions and the public on important and emerging topics in psychology and law. The mission of AP-LS is to "enhance well-being, justice, and human rights through the science and practice of psychology in legal contexts" (AP-LS, n.d., para. 2). We hope this book serves as a primary resource and catalyst for students, researchers, clinicians, service providers, lawyers, and other legal professionals to innovate new areas of inquiry and practice within aging and the law. In the time since the second author published *Elder Research: Filling an Important Gap in Psychology and Law* (Brank, 2007), scholarship focused on older adult legal issues has evolved and grown—even rebranding from "elder law" to "aging and the law."

Although research and practice have advanced the understanding of older adult legal issues, as this book describes, there is still so much to do. Therefore, in the spirit of aging stereotypes, this book aims to "jog your memory" and "speak louder" to the readers: Now is the time to expand scholarship to emergent older adult issues in traditional and innovative areas of research and practice in law-psychology.

Aging and the Criminal Legal System presents a multidisciplinary perspective that is divided into 10 chapters to explain and describe the legal responses to older adults interacting within the criminal legal system. The chapters summarize theory and research from our areas of social psychology and law but importantly also include scholarship from law, gerontology, geriatric psychiatry, social work, nursing, clinical psychology, medicine, and public health. The chapters in Part 1 discuss legal responses to older adults under various criminal legal system roles: Chapter 1 introduces key psychology and legal issues relevant to older adults. Chapter 2 examines legal decision makers (e.g., attorneys, judges, elected officials, jurors); Chapter 3, older victims of crime; Chapter 4, eyewitnesses to crime; and Chapter 5, perpetrators of criminal behavior. Next, the chapters in Part 2 discuss the criminal legal system stages and processes that generate legal responses for older adults who are involved in the criminal legal system, with Chapter 6 describing legal responses from law enforcement, community agencies, and the courts; Chapter 7 describing forensic evaluation; Chapter 8 describing issues relevant to older adults who are incarcerated; and Chapter 9 describing legal responses to the increase in older prison population and corresponding expenses. The concluding chapter calls to the reader—the future researcher (and future older adult)—to extend practice and research with older adults in the criminal legal system. We hope this book stimulates interest in the topic and energizes scholarship within the field of law-psychology to direct legal responses within aging and criminal law.

I

ROLES OF OLDER ADULTS IN THE CRIMINAL LEGAL SYSTEM

1

Issues in Aging and the Criminal Legal System

Old age is not a disease—it is a strength and survivorship, triumph over all sorts of vicissitudes and disappointments, trials and illnesses.

—Maggie Kuhn, "Seeking Change"

More than 50 years ago, Maggie Kuhn founded the Gray Panthers, which staged "rowdy public protests, political lobbying, and grassroots organizing" (S. J. Douglas, 2020, para. 6) fighting ageism alongside younger activists on issues ranging from health care to racial justice. Enraged by forced retirement at age 65 following 25 years of employment at a church and even more irritated with receiving a sewing machine as a retirement gift, Kuhn took on ageism in the 1970s (S. J. Douglas, 2020) at a time when older people were expected to withdraw from society, explained by the gerontological disengagement theory (Cumming, 1964; Hochschild, 1975). Kuhn's activism highlighted a persistent problem: most modernized societies focus on declines in old age, rather than the remarkable adaptability of older adults as they experience physical and cognitive changes (P. A. Thomas, 2011).

Kuhn insisted that issues facing older adults should be part of any social reform and wanted to "shatter every stereotype" about older people, especially older women (S. J. Douglas, 2020, para. 3). Despite the ubiquity of ageism, these underlying beliefs are often false (Weir, 2023). As noted in the Introduction and throughout this book, even though some cognitive functioning does deteriorate in aging, a great deal of research shows that most older adults

https://doi.org/10.1037/0000469-002
Aging and the Criminal Legal System: Community Services, Courts, Corrections, and Policy, by L. E. Wylie and E. M. Brank

maintain good health and cognitive functioning—with some areas that improve as one ages, such as creativity, happiness, and overall positive mental health (M. L. Thomas et al., 2016).

By the late 1970s, the Gray Panthers had more than 100,000 members across 30 states tackling accessibility in mass transportation, budget reductions to Social Security and Medicare, abuse in nursing homes, universal health care, and, most notably, in 1986, pushing Congress to ban mandatory retirement based on age. Central to their mission, the Gray Panthers and Kuhn promoted activism and intergenerational collaboration on issues that impact all age groups: housing, health care, racial equality, economic justice, and the environment. The Gray Panthers' motto—"age and youth in action"—was exemplified by involvement of younger advocates called "panther cubs" and objections that age groups should not be segregated from each other or pitted against each other, as is common in media portrayals. Kuhn's approach to combating ageism involved engaged community activism focused on broader social justice issues that affect all age groups (S. J. Douglas, 2020). In contrast, modern antiageism movements promote positive messages emphasizing the importance of successful or active aging. For instance, the interest group AARP (2024) promotes "personal fulfillment" for Americans ages 50 and older.

Some argue, however, that in doing so, law and policy will overemphasize independence, self-reliance, and individual responsibility, further dividing social power relationships. Combining both Kuhn's and modern perspectives, law and aging scholar Israel Doron (2018) instead encourages *ageivism*, which promotes and protects aging rights from the lens of older adulthood as a distinct socially constructed group. Doron's ageivism approach suggests that when individuals willingly identify themselves as older adults and embrace their life experiences, the impact of legal responses based on age-related assumptions may be reduced; ultimately reducing institutional, interpersonal, and internalized ageism.

This chapter introduces the reader to concepts relevant to aging and the criminal legal system and serves as a reference for technical terms and legal language presented in the remaining chapters. We describe instances in which older adults have been considered a subset of the population requiring *per se* special treatment as a classified group under legal doctrine and the difficulty in defining old age for the purposes of the law. Next, we summarize key concepts in criminal law and, following that, the sources of law that make up the U.S. criminal legal system responses impacting older adults. Throughout, we provide the relevant behavioral science research.

BEHAVIORAL SCIENCES AND AGING

The population is continuing to age. The raw and relative number of older adults is increasing, given longer lifespans and recent birth rate decreases (United Nations Department of Economic and Social Affairs, 2019). Globally, the World Health Organization (WHO, 2022) predicts the world's population of adults over 60 years old will double between 2022 and 2050. The U.S. Census described older adults as the fastest growing subpopulation in the United States for most of the 20th century, except during the 1990s when the relatively smaller Depression Era cohort reached age 65 (A.W. Roberts et al., 2018). A 100-year trend analysis illustrated that from 1920 to 2020 (see Figure 1.1), the population of adults aged 65 and older grew almost five times faster than the population. Between 2010 and 2020, the 65 to 75 years old subpopulation experienced the most growth when the Baby Boomer generation turned 65, and by 2030, the same trend is expected when the Baby Boomer generation ages into the next age category (Caplan, 2023; Hoyt, n.d.). The aging population trend is evident across society, and the justice system is no exception—there's a growing presence of individuals who exceed conventional age thresholds throughout legal institutions.

FIGURE 1.1. U.S. Census Population 65 Years and Over by Size and Percentage of Total Population: 1920 to 2020

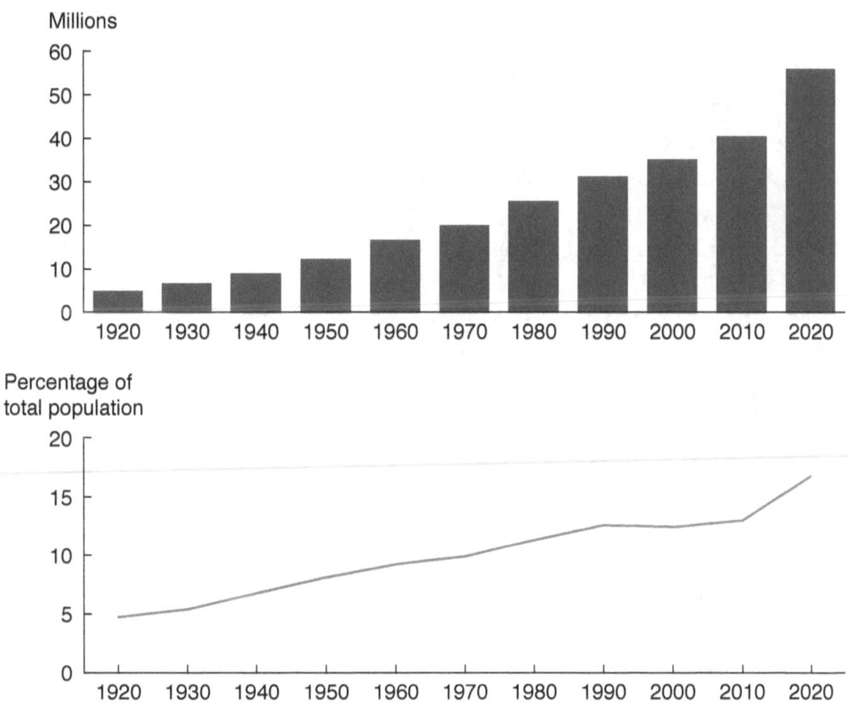

Note. Data are from "2020 Census Demographic and Housing Characteristics File (DHC): 2020 Census of Population and Housing," by the U.S. Census Bureau, 2023 (https://www2.census.gov/programs-surveys/decennial/2020/technical-documentation/complete-tech-docs/demographic-and-housing-characteristics-file-and-demographic-profile/2020census-demographic-and-housing-characteristics-file-and-demographic-profile-techdoc.pdf). In the public domain. For information on data collection, confidentiality protection, nonsampling error, and definitions, refer to U.S. Census Bureau (2023).

Despite demographic trends, behavioral science research with older adults in the criminal legal system has been remarkably limited by the samples included, the theories applied, and the research methods employed. Within law and behavioral science research, studies have narrowly focused on older adults in the role of victims of crime, with little attention to other roles in the legal system as legal decision makers and perpetrators of criminal behavior (Holzer et al., 2022). A comprehensive review of all published *Law and Human Behavior* articles from 1977 to 2016 identified that fewer than 0.1% of study samples included older adults, compared with 11.6% of study samples that included children under age 18. In the few studies with older adult samples, topics focused on eyewitness memory (usually as a victim–witness) and mental health (typically on issues of capacity or competency). Furthermore, if older adults were included in samples, it was due to their professional role in the legal system as a judge or expert witness (Wylie, Hazen, et al., 2018). In writing the current book, we scanned for additional articles published after 2016 and identified two with samples of older adults: one on eyewitness memory (Nyman et al., 2019) and one on risk assessment tools and sentencing (Monahan et al., 2017).

In the book *Children, Social Science, and the Law,* Bottoms, Kovera, and McAuliff (2002) noted that researchers in law-psychology have an "obligation to understand child-relevant law and policy so that they are prepared to conduct research that is useful to courts, policy makers, and practitioners. Legal professionals and practitioners must then understand and use that research" (p. 1). We agree with their sentiment. Law-psychology researchers and practitioners must be prepared to conduct research that is useful to legal systems (Brank, 2007) and appropriately respond to the influx of older adults with "alteration, accommodation, and innovation" (Eglit, 2004, p. 2). The next two sections provide an overview of the legal structures and legal theories that govern the U.S. criminal legal system to aid the reader in understanding pertinent topics ripe for meaningful research.

OLDER ADULTS AND CRIMINAL LEGAL SYSTEM RESPONSES

To extend Doron's (2009a) framework, the legal responses for older adults within the U.S. criminal legal system include factors such as their role within the criminal legal system as well as interactions with legal realities such as court rulings, legislation, administrative law and policies, and local rules. Although in simplest terms civil law provides remedies for individuals, and criminal law punishes people for offenses committed in violation of criminal laws (Scheb & Sharma, 2023), these two systems do intersect. Even when individuals are involved in criminal legal cases, some decisions or proceedings are civil matters couched within or adjacent to a criminal case (e.g., competency evaluations) or are included because they uniquely affect legal professionals (e.g., mandatory retirement). Thus, although the goal is to shed light on U.S. criminal law issues, the current book is not exclusive to criminal law. Throughout this book, we reference policies that an older person may encounter and illustrate examples from different sources of law and from both the federal and state legal systems.

The U.S. Constitution established a federal democratic republic with three distinct branches: legislative, executive, and judicial. As such, the laws and policies that govern criminal law in the United States are a mixture of doctrines that were created under the Constitution, enacted by the legislative branch, interpreted by the judicial branch, and enforced by the executive branch. Throughout this book, we reference law and policy from both federal and state jurisdictions. For instance, we discuss federal and state statutes created by Congress and state legislatures as well as case law shaped by judicial court decisions, which at times interpret a federal or state statute or constitutional issue. In addition, we reference regulations within executive branch agencies under administrative law that have the same authoritative power as legislative statutory law has.

Criminal legal system responses to older adults take place within criminal legal system roles, system points, and processes and develop from laws and policies that are intended to apply universally to all citizens. Policies are laws, regulations, procedures, administrative actions, incentives, or voluntary practice of governments and government agencies. Although the U.S. Constitution defines the minimum constitutional requirements that governments must follow within their criminal legal system laws and policies, because criminal law is mostly formed under state governments and agencies, core criminal legal responses can vary across the United States and are further localized by factors such as the county, court and judge, administrative agency, and even service provider and program (e.g., drug testing policies). In addition, policies are constructed through mechanisms such as resource allocation in federal and state legislative budgets and administrative agency budgets. To name just a few examples, policies originate from law enforcement agencies regulating how police officers interact with citizens under various circumstances, from court systems setting criteria for exemption from jury service, and from pretrial services setting the criteria and conditions required to release a defendant from jail.

DEFINING OLDER AGE IN LEGAL SYSTEMS

More people are reaching ages that have traditionally been considered old (Caplan, 2023; Frolik & Barnes, 2015). Longer lifespans contribute to the increase in the raw number of older adults, but lower birth rates mean that the relative number of older adults, as compared with younger adults, is also increasing (United Nations Department of Economic and Social Affairs, 2019). If the WHO (2022) predictions are correct, the world will look very different by 2050. Every aspect of life, including the criminal legal system, has seen and will continue to see an increase in the number and proportion of older adults involved (American Bar Association Commission on Law and Aging, 2022).

Nonetheless, there is no single agreed upon nor commonly applied definition of old age. In general, age is measured along a continuous scale by years since birth but is often conceptualized into stages (i.e., infancy, childhood, adolescence, middle age, and old age); however, there are no standardized ranges for some of the life stages (Kratcoski & Edelbacher, 2016). Unlike childhood and adolescence, which have relatively clear age and development milestones, older age is a moving target, making it challenging to define (Brank, 2007), especially because aging is a complex biological process that involves both genetic predispositions and environmental factors (McHugh & Gil, 2018). The definition of when old age begins depends on who you ask and for what purpose. Research shows that people of various ages and generations define old age differently (Chopik et al., 2018).

Age Defined by Chronology

Although the legal system has embraced various descriptors for old age over time, such as *elderly, senior,* and, more recently, *older adult,* regardless of the terminology used and chronological value attached, old age in the United States has significant legal meaning (Hall, 2014). However, as Kohn (2020b) questioned, "should the law permit differential treatment based on chronological age anytime it is not arbitrary, or should differential treatment be permitted only when there is a robust—perhaps even compelling—justification?" (p. 194). Despite legal policies using chronological age as a proxy for designating older adults as a *per se* group requiring special protections, scholars argue that categorical legal designations for eligibility or ineligibility for a legal policy should be based on social and personal vulnerabilities (Hall, 2014) or measures of individualized functional capacities (Surtees, 2009) while considering the cumulative nature of experiencing ageism and its intersection with other subgroup membership inequalities (Holman & Walker, 2021).

Legal policies may designate a chronological age for the purpose of triggering entitlement to some form of benefit. A person at 62 can collect early Social Security benefits but can only collect their full benefits at age 65. The age of eligibility for Social Security benefits is also a moving target and is subject to change; the federal Social Security Administration notes that the age for collecting benefits will gradually increase from 65 to 67 years old for those born in 1960 and later (Social Security Administration, n.d.). To make a claim of employment age discrimination, the Age Discrimination in Employment Act of 1967 requires employees to be 40 years old. The original Age Discrimination in Employment Act (ADEA)limited age discrimination claims to employees between 40 and 65 years old, but in the ADEA Amendments of 1978, the maximum age was extended to 70 years old as employees began working beyond their eligibility for Social Security benefits. In the ADEA Amendments of 1986, the maximum age limit was eliminated (Willis, 2020), in part through efforts by Maggie Kuhn and the Gray Panthers, who refused to keep "out of the way, playing bingo and shuffleboard" (S. J. Douglas, 2020, para. 5).

A person's chronological age indicates only how long they have lived, which may not be informative of their current health and life expectancy. Whereas one 70-year-old may be experiencing very little mental or physical impairment, another person of the same age may be experiencing a series of comorbid mental and physical ailments. One solution is to shift the focus away from how long a person has lived to the person's life expectancy. Demographers Sanderson and Scherbov (2019) argued that a person should be categorized as old when they have 15 years or fewer of remaining life expectancy. Although useful for life insurance actuarial tables, that level of individualization is difficult to apply to the law, which often requires a clear bright-line rule for categories. Furthermore, this approach has obvious difficulties because life expectancy can be impacted by any number of individual experiences of aging, as discussed in the Introduction, such as physical activity level, tobacco use, and access to health care. Whether chronological age should be a factor for legal responses and whether legal professionals should be required to retire at a certain age is further discussed in Chapter 2. Chapter 3 examines how state elder maltreatment laws use chronological age as a threshold to determine whether an older adult is considered vulnerable under the statute. In Chapters 8 and 9, which discuss incarceration-related issues, chronological age is again presented as a criterion for eligibility for early release from prison.

Age Defined by Functional Abilities

Gerontological literature commonly measures aging according to activities of daily living (ADLs) and instrumental activities of daily living (IADLs). ADLs are those functional activities required to manage one's basic physical needs, including personal hygiene or grooming, dressing, toileting, transferring or ambulating, and eating. IADLs include more complex activities related to the ability to live independently in the community, such as managing finances and medications, food preparation, housekeeping, and laundry. Individuals can have diminished abilities in any of these domains, all of them, or none of them. When discussing whether someone has functional ability, difficulties in ADLs and IADLs are used to describe ability to function independently (Edemekong et al., 2023) and make decisions about the level of care needed. Aging people have different preferences for where they want to live at the end of their lives, and gerontologists use the term *aging in place* to describe the preference for older adults to live autonomously and independently (Davis, 2022; Fetterman, 2023) according to their functional abilities.

Each of these concepts is associated with how older adults will interact with the criminal legal system responses. In Chapter 3, on victims of crime, ADLs and IADLs are important when considering who is providing care and the level of care needed for older adults to prevent elder abuse and self-neglect. Chapter 4 discusses eyewitness memory, a topic that elucidates assumptions about older adults' vision and memory. In Chapters 5, 6, and 7, topics center on whether an older adult has the mental and physical capacity to participate in the relevant legal proceeding. In Chapter 8, about older adults living in jails and prisons, we discuss the application of ADLs and IADLs to prison ADLs and issues faced by correctional facilities to accommodate the needs of older adults.

Although aging in place is feasible or desirable for some older Americans, many older adults may cohabitate with their adult children (possibly in a different state or country), reside in Medicaid-covered nursing homes, or live in isolation or even unhoused. Chapter 3 describes older victims of crime and how fear of abuse or neglect influences housing options. Chapters 5 and 6 describe events that can occur when older adults engage in antisocial or criminal behavior or interact with law enforcement, which may differ by whether they are community- or facility-dwelling older adults. Chapter 9 discusses older adults returning from incarceration who face challenges with housing when they reenter their communities, many of which have few resources or options for individuals with serious criminal convictions.

LEGAL CONSTRUCTS IN AGING AND THE LAW

In the next sections, we draw attention to and briefly summarize legal constructs that are foundational threads woven through the chapters that follow. In the current chapter, we introduce these legal constructs generally and indicate the forthcoming chapters in which each is applied or justified as a source of law in aging and the law. We encourage readers to note any competing notions within legal realities and legal responses, which appear to protect older adults as a vulnerable separate group (i.e., as the law does with juveniles), as compared with underlying notions of independence or active aging, self-determination, and personal responsibility.

Parens Patriae, Autonomy, and Paternalism

An overarching tension underlying aging and the law is between autonomy and paternalism and the government's interest in protecting its citizens who cannot protect themselves, under the legal doctrine *parens patriae*. Under the *parens patriae* principle—translated from Latin as "parent of the country or homeland"—government authorities carry the responsibility for protecting citizens and ensuring their well-being. A person with autonomy is independent and free from external control—meaning they have freedom of choice and likely need less care. Older adults perceived as more autonomous will likely be treated with person-centered approaches (Brownie & Nancarrow, 2013). In contrast, older adults may be treated more paternalistically when perceived as in need of care. Paternalism is characterized by overprotection, overrestriction, and superiority over the older adult (Fernández-Ballesteros et al., 2019). Although studies reveal that honoring an older adult's autonomy improves their perceived quality of life (Ford et al., 2000), assumptions about an older adult's competence for the task at hand generate tensions surrounding legal responses to aging.

The tension between these two approaches, autonomy versus paternalism, is present in several of the following chapters. For example, in Chapter 2, we discuss mandatory retirements at certain ages for some careers, which suggests as a society we need to restrict employment for some rather than treating them as autonomous individuals who can decide when it is best to retire. In Chapter 3, we discuss self-neglect and the possibility that an older adult is making an autonomous decision to stop caring for themselves even though many state statutes will paternalistically require intervention. Similarly, we discuss the role of autonomous decision making as it is related to what can be characterized as foolish legal decisions even though older adults may have very different views of money.

Moreover, when older adults are victims of crime, ageist beliefs and fear of harm or neglect can encourage paternalistic behavior by caregivers as discussed in Chapter 3 (this volume; Brank & Wylie, 2016), by legal professionals as illustrated in Chapter 4 (this volume; Wylie, Brank, & Bornstein, 2015) or, when an older adult is suspected of criminal behavior, by law enforcement or other community agencies, as shown in Chapter 5. Additional legal professionals and legal decision makers, such as attorneys, judges, forensic evaluators, jurors, corrections officers, and parole board members, may also similarly rely on assumptions that older adults are less competent to perform the tasks before them. Indeed, Chapters 7 through 9 of this volume describe several challenges that courts and correctional facilities face in balancing autonomy and paternalism when capacity and legal competency are at issue (Mast et al., 2022).

Capacity and Legal Competency

In ordinary plain language outside of legal contexts, capacity and competency are sometimes used interchangeably to mean the same thing; indeed, Merriam-Webster (n.d.) lists "legal competency" as the first definition for the noun *capacity*. However, in the U.S. legal system, competency has a distinct legal meaning and refers to a judicial decision of whether a person meets the state's definition of *incompetency*. In arriving at their decision, judges consider evidence presented by medical and clinical experts as to the person's capacity (or diminished capacity) to "adequately make a specific decision, such as financial decisions, or perform a specific task, such as driving" (Darby & Dickerson, 2017, p. 4). Capacity is fluid; in one moment an individual may lack the capacity required for a decision or task but may regain the requisite capacity at another time. In view of this, capacity is assessed specifically to a moment of time, which could be for present matters or for past matters requiring a retrospective assessment. One's capacity is highly context specific (American Bar Association Commission on Law and Aging & American Psychological Association, 2021); thus, diminished capacity in one decision-making area (e.g., financial) does not mean diminished capacity in another area (e.g., voting).

Within the law all adults are presumed to be legally competent, meaning they have the capacity to understand and appreciate the consequences of their actions. In other words, there is no set age when an older adult automatically becomes legally incompetent. Contrast this to young people; there are age-based permissions for young people to participate in some decisions. For example, although the traditional age for earning one's driver's license is 16 or 17 years old, no state disallows a driver's license solely based on older age. Instead of a specific age when someone no longer has a driver's license, some states have created special requirements wherein older adults must have more frequent vision and driving exams than younger adults must. Another example is the decision to marry. Although minor age is a barrier to marriage and will create a void marriage (Brank, 2019), advanced age by itself is not a determining factor in marriage validity (*Matter of Nunziata v. Nancy K.*, 2021).

Despite political calls for mandatory cognitive tests for older individuals in response to "electing two of the oldest men ever to occupy the White House" (Greenwood, 2023, para. 3), diminished capacity is not the expectation as someone ages. As described in the Introduction sections on biological and social aging processes, advanced age by itself is not predictive of decisional incapacity (e.g., Boettger et al., 2016), and assuming such furthers negative aging stereotypes that older adults have diminished mental and physical functioning. Although issues of capacity and legal competency are relevant to all age groups, both the typical aging process and stereotypes of older adults as senile (Cuddy et al., 2005) have made the practice and study of legal competency a hallmark issue in aging and the law scholarship (Doron, 2020).

As described in Chapters 6 and 7, if there are concerns of diminished capacity, attorneys, judges, and other legal professionals initially screen for suspected incompetency, and then a medical or clinical professional performs a full assessment. A capacity evaluation is concerned with the individual's ability to effectively make decisions based on the appreciation of choices and weighing of subsequent consequences (Grisso & Appelbaum, 1998). Hence, determinations of legal competency are determined on a case-by-case basis, and there are no *per se* chronological age cutoffs after the age of majority for determining competency (Brank & Wylie, 2021). Similar to other legal standards, legal competencies are determined by statute and case law but rely on mental health professionals to assist the courts in formulating their decision (Grisso, 2002) on whether the individual's impaired mental capacity limits their ability to make a legally relevant decision or action (Darby & Dickerson, 2017). In criminal justice contexts, legal competencies refer to an individual's physical, mental, and social vulnerabilities impacting their ability to participate in the investigative process (Grisso, 2002; Gudjonsson & Grisso, 2008). A psychiatric or medical diagnosis is not sufficient to determine competency; the demands and environmental context of the individual case should be considered (Gudjonsson & Grisso, 2008). Although most case examples illustrate mental capacity issues, physical capacity may also be at issue for older adults (see Box 1.1 for an example of medical incapacity).

It may be challenging for judges to decide case outcomes according to a binary "competent" or "not competent" because they are presented with medical evidence that reports capacity along a continuum and as fluid across time

BOX 1.1 | EXAMPLE OF PHYSICAL INCAPACITY FOR TRIAL: THOMAS DORAN, AGED 57

In addition to a defendant's mental capacity, courts have recognized distinct and separate grounds for incompetency to stand trial for physical disorders that make "trial excessively painful or risky" (*United States v. Doran*, 1971). In a 1964 indictment, the defendant Thomas Doran was charged with conspiracy to defraud the government for offenses that occurred 10 years prior when he was 47 years old. The question before the federal court was whether the now 57-year-old defendant's medical problems rendered him unfit for trial. The federal district court's opinion acknowledged that competency could include both mental and physical capacities but commented that in this case, the defendant's mental competency was not at question despite some memory loss and mental health problems. In the judge's words,

> The more compelling factor in the interrelated aspects of the unitary human being before us is the danger that stress will cause him severe trauma and possible death. Nobody has attempted the absurd task of "quantifying" this risk. All seem to agree—the court finds, in any event—it is "substantial." How "substantial" a risk of this kind should bar trial of a duly returned indictment? The question is a hard one, susceptible of no neat answer usable from case to case. (*United States v. Doran*, 1971)

Physical competency to proceed with trial examines whether the defendant's medical condition or physical ailments would be exacerbated by subjecting them to trial. Similar to mental competency, there is no *per se* age for physical incompetency, but it is instead based on functional evaluation. In Doran's circumstances, while his case was pending for 2 years, he had a stroke. When a cardiovascular specialist and neurologist evaluated him, they indicated "an alarming array of symptoms—hypertension, weakness of the right extremities, a limp, difficulties of speech and expression, pathological obesity, evidences of a history of gouty arthritis, insomnia, problems of memory, emotional instability and easy fatigability" (*United States v. Doran*, 1971). To assess for physical fitness to proceed, the court considered several medical factors, related evidence of activities outside of court (i.e., work or play), any remedial measures to minimize the defendant's health risk, the permanency of the condition (see Aprile, 2012), and the seriousness of the case to public interest and safety. In a prior case on a similar issue, the court weighed the older person's health problems and any remedial measures, such as shortened trial days, medication, medical equipment, and medical personnel (*United States v. Sweig*, 1970). Both doctors concluded he was unable safely or competently to stand trial, nor did they see him being fit in the "foreseeable future." The government evidently agreed, and the trial was postponed.

and context (Arias, 2013; Moye & Marson, 2009). Although viewing capacity as graduated and fluid is medically accurate, the legal system's bright-line rules that are necessary for deciding case outcomes often fail to meet such intermediate determinations. Accordingly, judges must determine where along the capacity continuum a person should be considered incompetent and whether a person is incompetent in some or all areas of decision making (Arias, 2013).

Competency is a critical issue at every stage of a criminal case, from initial police interaction through investigation to initial charges; diversion, disposition, and sentencing; and incarceration, reentry, and, in some instances in which the sentence is death, execution. In the forthcoming chapters, we discuss how issues of capacity and legal competency arise for the highlighted subgroup and the sources of law that govern each. For instance, at the federal jurisdiction level, competency to testify as a witness is presumed by the rules of evidence for that jurisdiction (e.g., Federal Rule of Evidence 601, 28 U.S.C. App, 1975), whereas competency to participate in court proceedings as a defendant is tested using Supreme Court case law, the *Dusky* standard (*Dusky v. United States*, 1960). Each state has adopted some versions of each of these rules.

Criminal Responsibility

Criminal responsibility is a legal concept that applies when someone commits a criminal offense with intention, recklessness, or negligence. In criminal cases, the prosecution has the burden of proving a defendant's guilt beyond a reasonable doubt, which is the most rigorous legal test for determining responsibility (as opposed to lesser standards in civil law). Unlike with state juvenile justice systems, there are no age restrictions for older adults that would automatically assign them to a different criminal legal system (Brank & Wylie, 2021). Of course, as discussed in the preceding section on defining older age, within the legal system are several examples of age-specific thresholds for older adults. In adult criminal procedure, whether someone is legally responsible for the alleged criminal behavior cannot be determined by age alone, as it can in the juvenile justice system. In recent decades, juvenile justice systems have embraced research in adolescent neuroscience that demonstrates young people do not have the same decision-making capacity as do adults, which has served as an anchor for assigning criminal responsibility in juvenile sentencing cases (e.g., *Miller v. Alabama*, 2012). No equivalent body of research or area of the law similarly addresses diminished criminal responsibility based on older age (Brank & Wylie, 2021).

Criminal responsibility is decided retrospectively and examines the person's fault at the time of the alleged offense. In determining criminal intent, it is not sufficient for the government to solely prove the defendant's *actus rea* (they committed the "bad act") to have a *prima facie* case that meets all the required elements outlined in statute for a given offense. The government must also prove the defendant's *mens rea* (they had a "guilty mind") at the time of the offense. To hold someone responsible for criminal acts, the government must make sure the person was aware of their misconduct, but this does not mean they need to know the behavior is illegal to be guilty. When defendants offer an affirmative defense, such as an insanity defense, they acknowledge committing the offense (*actus rea*) but argue that due to a lack of *mens rea* at the time, they did not possess the guilty mind required for conviction.

Each state's criminal statutory code outlines the test for fact finders—judges or juries—to determine whether a defendant had criminal responsibility at the time of the offense. More than half the states use the *M'Naghten* test (Legal Information Institute, 2020), followed by the next most common, the American Law Institute (1962) Model Penal Code test (§ 4.01). States also differ in whether they allow for an insanity defense and rules around testimony and evidence presented. Four states do not allow an insanity defense (Kansas, Montana, Idaho, and Utah). Although the specific legal standards and procedures vary by jurisdiction, forensic mental health professionals play a crucial role in evaluating defendants' mental states across all systems. Chapter 7 introduces forensic evaluation in criminal court and further describes the legal standards for criminal responsibility and the very limited research about criminal responsibility and older adults.

CONSTITUTIONAL ISSUES AND LEGAL TESTS

Amendment X to the U.S. Constitution states that any powers not retained by the federal government are provided to the states and the people. The federal government has relatively limited powers under the Constitution, including taxation, regulating interstate and foreign commerce, waging war, and making treaties (Farnsworth, 2010). Each state has a three-branch government modeled after the federal government; however, state governments have some powers to create law and policy that are modified from the federal systems. This is especially true for criminal law and procedure, as long as the law or policy is constitutional. States have their own constitutions, which can provide additional constitutional protections to people but cannot provide fewer protections than does the U.S. Constitution. Most often, when referring to a constitutional issue in subsequent chapters, we are referring to the U.S. Constitution, but it is good to keep in mind that states may provide stronger protections in their state constitutions.

Equal Protection

Amendment XIV to the U.S. Constitution is central to the protection of civil rights, making it unlawful for the government to deny a person equal protection under the state's laws, and has been interpreted by the Supreme Court as limiting discrimination toward different groups of people, termed *classes*. In a discrimination case, the Supreme Court's legal analysis depends on the plaintiff's categorization into one of three broad classes: (a) suspect classes (race, national origin, and religion), (b) quasisuspect classes (gender and birth illegitimacy), and (c) nonsuspect classes (all others). With groups that are categorized as a suspect class, the government must meet the test of strict scrutiny—meaning the state has to prove that a law or policy is narrowly tailored to the state's interest (Legal Information Institute, 2024). Issues of equal protection arise when testing whether state laws are discriminatory, such as in Chapter 2 when we discuss age discrimination and Chapter 6 when we discuss sentencing structures that are based on age.

Due Process

Due process is a legal requirement, within both civil and criminal matters, that guarantees individuals are treated fairly and that legal matters are resolved according to established rules and principles. Amendment V to the U.S. Constitution applies to the federal government, and the due process clause of Amendment XIV applies to the states. The due process clause also guarantees that before depriving a citizen of life, liberty, or property, the government must follow fair procedures. In other words, the government cannot just act in accordance with a given state or federal law; citizens are also entitled to fair procedures. Action denying the process that is due would be unconstitutional. The due process clause protects many of our "cherished—and most controversial" rights (Chapman & Yoshino, n.d., para. 1), such as procedural protections (e.g., sufficient notice during competency hearings), individual rights in the Bill of Rights (e.g., criminal procedures in investigation and trial, right to bear arms; U.S. Const. amend. I–X), and fundamental enumerated rights not explicitly stated (e.g., right to marry). The due process clause is the source of law for most criminal procedures throughout a criminal investigation (see Chapter 6, this volume), procedures that outline the trial process (see Chapter 6), and sentencing guidelines (see Chapter 9).

Cruel and Unusual Punishment

Amendment VIII to the U.S. Constitution forbids the federal government from imposing unduly harsh penalties on criminal defendants at any point in an individual's case, from decisions for pretrial release to the type and length of punishment after conviction. It states, "Excessive bail shall not be required, nor excessive fines imposed, nor cruel and unusual punishments inflicted" (U.S. Const. amend. VIII). The cruel and unusual punishment clause is the most argued against in criminal procedure, in part because the phrase "cruel and unusual" is not definitive and can change over time according to shifting cultural views on punishment. Court case law is only clear that barbaric methods of punishment are not allowed; courts have disagreed on whether the clause applies to sentencing generally, forbidding punishments that are disproportionate to the seriousness of the crime, or whether the clause applies only to the appropriateness of the death penalty (Stevenson & Stinneford, n.d.).

The forthcoming chapters address legal realities older adults experience in sentencing, especially sentences for life in prison and death sentences. In particular, Chapter 6 presents example case law and research on how aging may impact sentencing, and Chapter 9 addresses topics related to whether it is cruel and unusual punishment for older infirm adults to remain in prison.

CONCLUSION

In Kohn's (2020b) "A Framework for Theoretical Inquiry Into Law and Aging," she argued for "fruitful" scholarship that challenges common assumptions that pose barriers for generating robust theory of law and aging—namely, that aging and the law is not a single unified field, but rather the topics addressed in the practice of elder law are merely a small subset of issues at the heart of the academic study of elder law. She argued that despite its "antidiscrimination ethos," elder law scholarship often advocates for policies that give preferential treatment to older adults, which itself is discriminatory. She further suggested that the field would benefit from acknowledging that old age is not a universal human experience but rather one limited to those who live long enough to reach that stage. Perhaps the true comparison is not whether older adults are being treated preferentially, as compared with younger adults, but whether they are being treated preferentially as compared with their deceased cohort members.

Encouraged by Doron's (2009a) multidimensional model of aging and the law, we identify the varied legal responses to older adults in the criminal legal system to describe the possible underlying philosophies (Is this legal response based in assumptions of paternalism or autonomy?) and objectives (Is this legal response aimed at an individual older adult or older adults collectively as a community?). To better understand the role of ageism, we further evaluate the criminal legal system responses according to the content of underlying stereotypical beliefs about older adults' capabilities (Is this person able to do what is required of them?) and perceived cooperativeness (Is this person trustworthy and likable?). Because environmental cues may also impact legal responses, especially responses directed to individual older adults in a given situation, psychological theory and research in person perception explains when legal responses deviate from what prescriptive legal theories hypothesize. Clearly, it is important to consider an individual based on their own personal experiences and historical contexts (Hayes, 2017).

2

Older Adults as Legal Decision Makers

Outwardly I am eighty-three, but inwardly I am every age, with emotions and experience of each period.

—Elizabeth Coatsworth, *Personal Geography*

Dr. William Osler gave a speech in 1905 when he was leaving his employment at Johns Hopkins for a prestigious position at Oxford University. He stated,

> Take the sum of human achievement in action, in science, in art, in literature—subtract the work of the men above forty, and while we should miss great treasures, even priceless treasures, we would practically be where we are today. . . . The effective, moving, vitalizing work of the world is done between the ages of twenty-five and forty. (Bliss, 1999, p. 323)

At the time of this speech, Osler was an author, professor, esteemed physician, and 55 years old; he went on to remark on "the uselessness of men above sixty years of age, and the incalculable benefit it would be in commercial, political and in professional life if, as a matter of course, men stopped work at this age" (Bliss, 1999, p. 323). Osler's speech, complete with an allusion to the euthanasia scheme from Anthony Trollope's (1882) novel, *The Fixed Period*, was meant to cleverly reflect humility for his own work and critique the status of universities that hired faculty for life (Bryan, 2018). Unfortunately, his sarcasm and subtleties were missed by much of the media reporting on his farewell

https://doi.org/10.1037/0000469-003
Aging and the Criminal Legal System: Community Services, Courts, Corrections, and Policy, by L. E. Wylie and E. M. Brank

address, and soon some older Americans feared being "Oslerized" (Brank, 2011; Bryan, 2018).

Why was there such a response to these comments that were meant to be tongue-in-cheek? Perhaps Osler said what many silently believed and felt about older adults in the workplace (Butler, 2009). If Osler made his same speech today, and it was taken at face value, it would likely create some backlash given that 40 is popularly referred to as "the new 30" (Tierney, 2004), and it is common for people to start new careers at 40 years of age or older. In the current chapter, we first detail the legal responses to workplace older age discrimination and court case examples drawn from employment discrimination law. Next, we describe instances of age discrimination, broadly defined as any time a legal response aims to differentiate older age, either through chronological *per se* categorizations, as found in age discrimination law wherein the eligibility for protection from age discrimination begins at 40, or through individualized methods, such as mandatory retirement of a judge based on tests for diminished capacity instead of chronological age. Although it is limited, we summarize the research conducted with legal professionals as older adults based on the varied types of legal responses they encounter as they age. For example, as detailed below, police officers have received considerable legal attention regarding mandatory retirement policies under the Age Discrimination in Employment Act of 1967 (ADEA), and many states have statutes that allow older adults to opt out of jury service (statutory upper age limits range from 65 to 80 years old).

LEGAL RESPONSES TO AGE DISCRIMINATION

Given that much of our attention in this chapter is on employment discrimination law, we discuss civil cases in which the outcomes include civil damages rather than criminal responsibility. As decision makers within the criminal legal system, older adults in these professions have distinct "embodied experiences" (Hall, 2014, p. 2) that may influence legal responses to aging, perceptions of other older adults within the system, and whether they perceive themselves as older adults. Moreover, legal professionals likely experience ageism differently than do the nonprofessionals discussed in the remaining chapters, considering factors known to predict ageism, such as appearance and demeanor, whether job functions require skills stereotypically associated with aging (e.g., physical, cognitive), additional contextual and environmental cues (e.g., a badge, a robe, the jury box), and intersectional group membership (e.g., female judge, Black lawmaker).

The Age Discrimination in Employment Act

In the United States, discrimination based on someone's older age in employment settings is unlawful, pursuant to the ADEA in decisions related to hiring, promotion, compensation, and other job-related determinations for employees 40 years of age or older. During the civil rights movement, the ADEA was drafted 3 years after Title VII of the Civil Rights Act of 1964 made it unlawful to discriminate based on race, color, religion, sex, or national origin (Van Ostrand, 2009). At a time when more than 60% of nonskilled industrial jobs had age limits between 35 and 49 years old (Bessey & Ananda, 1991; Graebner, 1984), and mandatory retirement at designated ages was quite common (Frolik & Barnes, 2015), the ADEA addressed older adults' disadvantage in finding, retaining, and regaining employment. Moreover, Congress believed that arbitrary discrimination based on age further interfered with commerce and the free flow of goods. As such, they hoped the ADEA would reduce unemployment and deterioration of skills for older workers as well as increase older Americans' morale. If an age-eligible employee believes they have experienced a "material adverse employment action," the employee can either file their case with the U.S. Equal Employment Opportunity Commission (EEOC), the agency that enforces employment discrimination laws, or bypass the administrative route and file the case with the courts (EEOC, n.d.). To bring a case for age discrimination in employment settings, the older worker must prove either intentional discrimination called *disparate treatment* (i.e., the law is discriminatory on its face) or unintentional discrimination called *disparate impact* (i.e., the law is not discriminatory on its face but has a negative impact on older workers).

Although the ADEA was drafted similarly to Title VII of the Civil Rights Act of 1967, protections based on older age under the ADEA were intentionally drafted as separate from protections under Title VII. In fact, Congress chose not to include age with the other protected classes within Title VII (Eglit, 1986) and later passed the ADEA following a report by William Willard Wirtz (1965), then secretary of labor, on the problems of age discrimination. Secretary Wirtz detailed in his report that, unlike racial discrimination, age discrimination was not based on hatred or dislike of older workers. Instead, Wirtz argued that age discrimination was based on faulty assumptions about older persons' abilities. From its inception, the ADEA was not meant to address malicious employment policies commonly believed to be the underlying basis for racial and gender discrimination (Crosby & Dovidio, 2008) but rather was meant to address incorrect societal beliefs about growing old.

There are some exceptions to the ADEA. First, the ADEA is *per se* categorical protection for employees 40 and older but does not include protection for employees younger than 40. In effect, employers can favor an older worker, but an employee aged 39 would be ineligible to file a claim under the ADEA. Second, to protect smaller businesses, the ADEA applies to employers with 20 or more employees, although many states have discrimination laws that include all or most employers. Third, the ADEA permits age discrimination in situations when age is a bona fide occupational qualification (BFOQ). A BFOQ must be closely related to the job tasks necessary to perform typical business functions and is most often permitted when the job is in a public safety role (e.g., commercial plane pilots). Fourth, employers may provide the defense that their practices are nondiscriminatory and based on reasonable factors other than age (known as the RFOA defense). Fifth, not all employers are required to follow the ADEA, and certain types of employers can require mandatory retirement at a specified age for employees who are "bona fide executives" or in "high policy making positions," as well as through mandatory retirement ages for firefighters and law enforcement.

The legal analysis for ADEA cases applies a similar Title VII-type causation analysis, with notable and possibly consequential differences. Although the intent of both acts was to reduce discrimination, as explained previously, Congress drafted the ADEA and Title VII of the Civil Rights Act into separate laws. As the U.S. Supreme Court has interpreted discrimination cases under each act based on specific case facts, the legal analyses have caused further divergence between the two acts (Van Ostrand, 2009; Wiener & Farnum, 2016). Notably, the legal standard for older workers to prove that an employer's action was because of age discrimination has a more challenging threshold than does a similar discrimination claim under Title VII protecting race, color, religion, sex, or national origin (42 U.S.C. § 2000e-2(m), 1991). The decision for the sex discrimination case *Price Waterhouse v. Hopkins* (1989) indicated that the legal standard for cases brought under Title VII uses a mixed-motive theory. In practice, this standard allows discriminatory practices as long as the employer can also prove there was an additional, legitimate reason for the discriminatory employment action and evidence showing they would have reached the same conclusion even if the illegitimate reason (i.e., protected class membership) was not considered. In 1991, Congress codified the case's decision and included the mixed-motive test in Title VII.

However, the same legal analysis test did not carry over to ADEA discrimination cases, despite similar language in the ADEA that discrimination is not allowed "because of such individual's age" (29 U.S.C. § 623(a), 1967; Van Ostrand, 2009; Wiener & Farnum, 2016). In contrast to the legal analysis under Title VII, older workers under the ADEA as interpreted in *Gross v. FBL* (2009) must show that age was not just a contributing factor but also a determinative factor for discriminatory employment action. Unlike cases brought for other protected classes, plaintiffs alleging age discrimination must show that "but for" their older age, the adverse employment action would not have occurred, but any legitimate reasons will prevent older plaintiffs from proving the employment action was discriminatory. Writing the majority opinion for *Gross*, U.S. Supreme Court Justice Clarence Thomas stated that if Congress had intended the ADEA to have a mixed-motive legal test like Title VII did, then Congress would have also amended the ADEA, which Congress has not yet done. In this evolving area of case law, subsequent Supreme Court cases held that the same "but for" standard is applied to age discrimination retaliation claims (*University of Texas Southwestern Medical Center v. Nassar*, 2013). Most recently, in *Babb v. Wilkie* (2020), the Supreme Court ruled that plaintiffs could bring a mixed-motive theory to prove a discriminatory adverse action within federal employment settings, essentially lowering the burden of proof for older workers in federal government positions. However, the court ruled that the "but for" causation test will still be applied in determining the appropriate remedy, such as compensatory damages or other relief related to the employment decision.

The Equal Protection Clause

Although ADEA claims are much more frequent, an employee is entitled to claim age discrimination based on the equal protection clause of Amendment XIV to the U.S. Constitution, which, as described in Chapter 1 (this volume), is the constitutional amendment that prohibits states from discrimination based on age. Constitutional discrimination claims apply a different legal test, which is based on the plaintiff's group membership and the legal classification designated to that group. For instance, the Supreme Court has designated membership based on race, national origin, and religion as suspect classes because there are no justifiable reasons for different treatment, and their constitutionality is tested under *strict scrutiny*. Groups designated as quasi-suspect classes, sex and legitimacy of birth (as well as sexual orientation in U.S. District Courts), and laws alleged to be discriminatory are tested under *intermediate scrutiny* because there may be fact-based biological reasons for unequal treatment. For any remaining groups, which includes group membership based on factors such as age, wealth, political preference, and criminal convictions, the government need only have a rational basis for disparate treatment, meaning the government must have a reasonable and logical reason for treating these groups differently. Because older adults are not a suspect class, and the rational basis test would apply, proving age discrimination is more challenging under state and federal equal protection clauses, and claims have rarely, if ever, succeeded (Kohn, 2020a).

Forced and Mandatory Retirement

The idea of retirement is relatively new and was not particularly widespread until the 19th century (Willis, 2020). Before then, employers tended to accommodate older workers, in the rare instances when workers lived into their old age. The legal response to aging professionals in the form of mandatory retirement was a product of industrialization and pension programs. In the sections that follow, we address how the legal system specifically responds to the aging legal workforce, which has affected law enforcement officers and judges with lifetime appointments.

Law Enforcement

Law enforcement agents, such as local police officers, are given great latitude in how they approach protecting citizens and enforcing laws. With that duty comes an expectation that they may need to engage in activities that require them to be both physically and mentally fit to perform their job functions

(Capitano, 1986). As such, many—though not all—law enforcement agencies set both required retirement ages and maximum ages for law enforcement recruits. Early retirement for law enforcement agents, when first imposed, was considered a privilege because of the difficulty and danger of the job (Schiff, 1993). The Civil Service Retirement Act of 1930, amended in 1947, allowed for voluntary retirement as early as age 50 for Federal Bureau of Investigation officers who had served 20 or more years (U.S. Office of Personnel Management, n.d.). The early retirement benefit was extended to all federal employees who were performing investigative or arrest duties, air traffic controllers, and firefighters, with the aim of employing young and vigorous staff in the interest of public safety (Schiff, 1993). Early retirement federal policies were allowable, as long as they were voluntary and not mandatory and did not conflict with the ADEA as passed in 1967.

In 1978, however, this changed when Congress made significant adjustments to the structure of the ADEA by enacting a mandatory retirement age of 55 (currently 57) for federal law enforcement officers and firefighters and then extending the definition of an employer to include local and state employers. Interpreting this extension, the petitioner in *EEOC v. Wyoming* (1983), who was forced to retire at age 55 from the state fish and game department per state statute, filed with the EEOC that the mandatory retirement extension violated the ADEA. The Supreme Court held that the extension to state and local governments was allowed under the ADEA, which left state and local agencies to case-by-case BFOQ analysis (Schiff, 1993) and generated several cases arguing that the government age limitations violated EEOC requirements (W. R. Nelson & Roberts, 1986).

Later in 1978, after a Supreme Court ruling effectively held that the ADEA did not prohibit mandatory retirement related to a particular pension plan issue (*United Air Lines, Inc. v. McMann*, 1977), the ADEA was amended to raise the upper age limit eligibility to age 70, eliminate mandatory retirement for most federal employees, and prohibit benefit plans from requiring or permitting involuntary retirement. This meant that employers could not impose minimum retirement before the worker reached age 70 (Barker & Clark, 1980). Then in 1986, Congress removed the upper age limit for eligibility completely, which removed any local or state agency's ability to enforce mandatory retirement.

Lawmakers continued to introduce bills so that state and local agencies could decide their own police and firefighter mandatory retirement exemptions based on BFOQs. Congressional testimony emphasized public safety considerations for both state police and firefighters as well as disavowed age discrimination generally and support for the ADEA amendment, including from the AARP (Nelson & Roberts, 1986).

Opponents argued that as opposed to requiring *per se* mandatory retirement based on chronological age, employers could instead conduct physical or cognitive exams. However, these arguments failed to provide a viable test alternative to an age qualification (Willis, 2020). In support of bills allowing for mandatory retirement based on age, proponents presented medical testimony, stating "medical science and testing have simply not advanced to the point where we can safely eliminate age limitations and rely exclusively on individual testing" (*Exemptions for Police and Firefighters Under the Age Discrimination in Employment Act*, 1986, p. 2). Ultimately, Congress granted temporary exceptions for police, firefighters, and tenured university faculty until the end of 1993. In 2021, President Biden signed the First Responder Fair RETIRE Act, an accelerated retirement system for first responders whose positions are listed in Section 6c of the act, which established a mandatory retirement age of 57.

Notably, medical science advancements have been made since the ADEA was first passed and since the subsequent hearing in 1986. For example, one advancement involves artificial intelligence and machine learning in early prediction of coronary disease, without invasive procedures (Alizadehsani et al., 2019; Chen & Hengjinda, 2021). As evidenced by the shifting case law in both ADEA and mandatory retirement, technological advances may again place these legal responses to an aging workforce back on the desks at the U.S. Supreme Court.

Judges

According to legal scholar and federal judge Richard Posner, "The judiciary is the nation's premier geriatric occupation" (1995, p. 180). As a lifetime appointee, in 2020 Ruth Bader Ginsburg was the third sitting Supreme Court justice in 15 years to die while still actively a member of the court, which in part invigorated public support for maximum age limits for U.S. Supreme Court justices to serve on the bench (Gramlich, 2023).

A lifetime appointment for U.S. Supreme Court and federal judges is intended to separate the judiciary from the election cycles of the legislative and executive branches. Indeed, the average age of federal judges recently reached a record high of 69 years of age (Thomsen et al., 2023) due in part to their lifetime appointments (Administrative Office of the U.S. Courts, n.d.-a). Mandatory retirement for judges has been considered a legal response to the aging judicial workforce. In one such instance, Judge Pauline Newman, born in 1927 and appointed to the bench by President Ronald Reagan in 1984, was barred in 2023 from hearing new cases for 1 year or until she underwent court-ordered medical examinations (Brittain & Raymond, 2023). In making the decision to bar Judge Newman from hearing cases, the judicial council and chief judge said they based their decision on evidence that suggested Judge Newman was not fit to perform her duties (El-Bawab, 2023). Judge Newman countered that the adverse employment decisions were based on age discrimination and motivated by rejection of her contrary views.

State-level trial and appellate courts have a blend of appointed and elected judicial processes, and more than half of the states impose mandatory retirement ages for state court judges—most commonly 70 years old (Raftery, 2023). Of note, North Dakota does not impose a mandatory retirement age, but if a judge does not retire by age 73, they waive all earned retirement benefits

FIGURE 2.1. Mandatory Judicial Retirement: Appellate

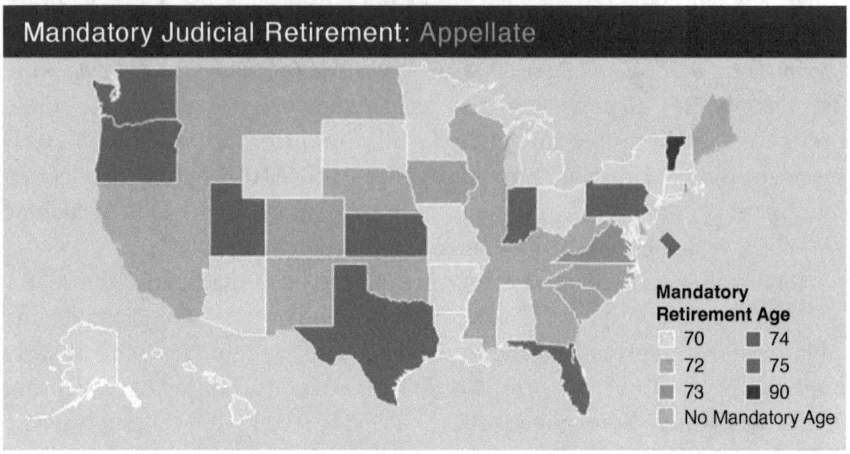

Note. From *State Judicial Retirement Plans*, by National Center for State Courts, 2023 (https://www.ncsc.org/salarytracker/special-reports/retirement-map-and-states).

(N.D. Cent. Code § 27-17-01, 2023). Data collected by the National Center for State Courts are available online and include a map of the United States that displays each state's statutory judicial mandatory retirement ages, if any, and judicial retirement plans for both state trial and state appellate court judges (National Center for State Courts, 2023). Figure 2.1 displays the states with mandatory retirement for appellate judges, but data are also available for trial court judges. Although there are no mandatory retirement ages for federal judges, the Rule of 80 provides a retirement incentive to them (Administrative Office of the U.S. Courts, n.d.-b). If the judge's age and years of service add up to 80, a judge may obtain senior status.[1] For example, a judge who is 70 years old with 10 years of service or is 65 years old with 15 years of service can enter senior status, which allows the judge to retire and receive their pension.

In 1991, the Supreme Court upheld the state's ability to create its own retirement age policies after two Missouri state judges challenged their state constitution's requirement that state court judges must retire at age 70 as violating the ADEA (*Gregory v. Ashcroft*, 1991). According to the court's opinion, judges fit within the ADEA exception that mandatory retirement is allowed for "appointees on the policymaking level" (ADEA of 1967, 29 U.S.C. § 631). Legal scholars question this opinion, however, elucidating that the judiciary is the "least answerable to the people" and is supposed to interpret fixed rules without political ideation (Hullinger, 2020), the underlying rationale for judicial lifetime appointments.

[1]The Rule of 80 was part of a 1984 amendment to 28 U.S.C. 17, codified in 1948. See Title 28, Judiciary and Judicial Procedure (1948) and Retirement on salary; retirement in senior status (1984).

Empirical research has investigated whether age limits in legal professions are achieving their desired results. Legal scholars challenge the court's characterization of judges as policymakers, noting that the judiciary is the "least answerable to the people" (Hullinger, 2020, p. 157) and is designed to interpret established rules independent of politics—a principle reinforced by lifetime appointment. However, not all research supports this conclusion. An analysis of U.S. Supreme Court longevity and terms of service found that productivity decreased as measured by the number of cases the court accepted for review and the frequency of opinions per court term (Teitelbaum, 2006). Given the number of law clerks who perform legal research on behalf of their assigned judge, it is difficult to make definitive conclusions about the impact of mandatory retirement policies on judicial performance (Shen, 2020). Although judges may receive help, a judgeship also requires working among peers and managing a team of law clerks, which requires social and planning skills (Ash & MacLeod, 2020). It is also important to note that judges, by the nature of their legal duty, are always reacting to the cases brought before them rather than proactively deciding issues, which means their demographic characteristics may not be as relevant as those of the other parties in a case or, at the very least, cannot be considered alone (Eglit, 2005). Although not yet conducted, quasi-experimental methods may shed light on judicial performance given the presence of mandatory retirement by comparing naturally occurring policy practices across states or comparing before and after policies were implemented (Schachter, 2013).

Besides judicial performance, researchers have sought to evaluate whether older age influences case outcomes. An older study that measured whether demographic characteristics of judges influenced their decisions concluded that older judges were more likely to sentence individuals to incarceration and for longer terms but that the punitiveness was not directed at any particular subgroup of defendants (Myers, 1988). According to research on moral decision making, there may be an age-based shift in moral reasoning as one ages, which may account for this finding. In an experiment that compared older (63 to 90 years old) and younger (21 to 39 years old) adults on how they arrived at a moral judgment about harmful behavior, older adults were more likely to rely on the harmful outcome as opposed to the intent of the person (Margoni et al., 2018).

Legal scholars have proposed that an individualized approach to judiciary retirements would be superior to the current *per se* age-based mandatory system. This suggestion is based on recent advances in neurocognitive science, which now make it more feasible to conduct periodic assessments of judicial capacity. Such an approach would address concerns about aging judges more effectively (Shen, 2020). Others suggest a combination of term and age limits (Opeskin, 2015). Of course, for appointed judges, such as those on the federal bench, including the Supreme Court, there are political reasons for wanting a judge to retire. For example, Democrats questioned Justice Ruth Bader Ginsburg's decision to stay on the bench through President Obama's presidential term (C. R. Barber & DeChalus, 2022). Her death at age 87 while a sitting justice meant then-current Republican president Donald Trump could appoint his choice of a more conservative justice to the already politically unbalanced court. Indeed, President Trump appointed Justice Amy Coney Barrett, which shifted the balance of the court to a more conservative-leaning court.

Attorneys

Despite the primary role that attorneys play as legal decision makers in the legal system, few legal responses are aimed at older attorneys, and little is known about the impact of aging on their careers and their performance (Collins et al., 2017; Eglit, 2004). Most attorneys work for private law firms, and about half of the largest American law firms (ranging from 50 to 1,598 attorneys) have mandatory retirement policies, most specifying ages 63 to 68; almost 80% reported offering special financial incentives to encourage older attorneys to retire, and some have reduced-work-for-reduced-pay arrangements available for older attorneys (Dau-Schmidt et al., 2009). The career of an attorney has been described as a "late peak, sustained" (Posner, 1995, p. 180) activity, with litigation work specifically being more demanding and less sustainable as one gets older.

Several decades ago, political scientists Nagel and Gagliano (1965) tested the impact of attorney demographic characteristics, including attorney age, on performance measured by case outcomes in a sample of 100 cases. After dividing the sample of attorneys at the mean age of 47 years, they found that older attorneys were more likely to win their cases than were attorneys in the younger category. Upon further examination, the researchers divided the attorneys into three groups: 35 years and younger, 36 to 54 years old, and 55 years and older. The middle-aged attorneys were the most successful. In another study that employed quasi-experimental methods, the longer an attorney had been a public defender, the shorter the incarceration sentence that their clients received (Abrams & Yoon, 2007). Still, the legal profession, like all of society, has more older members than ever before, but the demand for senior attorneys has not similarly increased (Dau-Schmidt et al., 2009). For example, the largest age group for the Vermont Bar Association is 50 to 59, and there are more members in their 80s than in their 20s (Barnes, 2008).

Similar to the exception for those deciding policy, the ADEA (29 U.S.C. § 631) has an exemption that allows laws to have age-based employment policies specific to executives that could apply to attorneys. A *bona fide executive* is any employee who meets certain qualifications (e.g., salary), whose primary duties include management and supervision, and who has authority in hiring and firing (Willis, 2020). When attorneys become managing partners in a law firm and are no longer considered employees entitled to discrimination law protections (*Von Kaenel v. Armstrong Teasdale, LLP*, 2019); the Supreme Court has similarly relied on the amount of control the person holds at the firm as the legal test for determining whether they are entitled to receive protection (*Clackamas Gastroenterology Associates, PC v. Wells*, 2003). However, in some instances law firm partners are protected under the ADEA (*EEOC v. Sidley Austin Brown & Wood*, 2002). In 2000, the EEOC began investigating the law firm Sidley, Austin, Brown, and Wood (hereinafter referred to as "Sidley") for potential age discrimination because 32 partners were told they had to downgrade their positions at the firm or leave to provide younger firm members more opportunities. Sidley also reduced their mandatory retirement age from 65 years of age to a range from 60 to 65 years of age. A federal judge approved a $27.5 million settlement in which the Sidley law firm will compensate 32 former partners who, according to the EEOC, were forced to leave the firm due to age discrimination (EEOC, 2007).

As in other business sectors, the justification for mandatory retirement for attorneys was traditionally based on career development ethos for midcareer partners who would replace senior partners in retirement. Thus, in this context, the legal response to aging attorneys is based on perceptions of finite resources and can perpetuate fear that younger workers should compete with older workers for resources, an underlying explanation for ageism. Beyond forced or encouraged retirements, older attorneys report day-to-day age discrimination or bias in the workplace. In a survey of North Carolina attorneys, 38% indicated that they believed they had been treated unfairly because of their age (Collins et al., 2017). As stated by a former judge in opposition to forced retirement, "there are plenty of ways to get someone off the court or from law practice" (Barnes, 2008, para. 14). Others, however, recognize that cognitive-related disorders such as dementia are difficult to identify in their early phases and even more difficult to address (Barker, 2021).

Elected Political Officials

The legal responses to older adults in elected positions differ from those previously discussed, which are based on public and officer safety. In the sections that follow, we address how the legal system specifically responds to the aging legal workforce of elected political positions, which instead are based on public opinion and the voting booth.

State and Federal Lawmakers

Contrary to first responders and judges, individuals who create American laws do not have a maximum age to which they can serve in state legislatures or the U.S. Congress. As described in the Introduction, although the U.S. Constitution establishes minimum age requirements for Congress members—age 25 for the House of Representatives and 30 for the Senate—the United States has not set maximum ages or required retirement policies for those roles. Indeed, in 2023 the United States had the oldest Senate and the second-oldest House of Representatives (Tutella, 2023). During the congressional sessions in 2023, only 10 of the 100 members are younger than 50 years old, with 34 members 70 years or older (Blazina & Desilver, 2023). Many older members continue to run for reelection well past the average retirement age for other careers (Karni, 2023). In September 2023, Senator Dianne Feinstein, who represented California, died as the-then-oldest sitting U.S. senator at the age of 90 after serving 31 years in the Senate. At the time of her death, she was still a sitting senator, though she had been absent from serving for part of the year due to health issues, and many called for her to resign given concerns about her cognitive abilities (Lutz, 2022). Kentucky Senator Mitch McConnell was the longest-running Senate leader when he stepped down at age 82 in 2024, presumably at the urging of his political party to "make way for a younger" leader (Alvord, 2024, para. 2).

Unlike other legal professions discussed thus far in this chapter, all state and federal lawmakers are voted in by their local communities. However, some public opinion research demonstrated that respondents preferred younger candidates (Eshima & Smith, 2022; D. C. Roberts & Wolak, 2022), suggesting that in practice, younger candidates might be elected at higher proportions if more were available (Stockemer & Sundström, 2023). Moreover, despite many politicians staying in office well beyond the average retirement age, most Americans favor maximum age limits for elected officials (Gramlich, 2023). Because legal professionals are elected by American society, legal responses to aging for older lawmakers are based on voter perceptions and prone to the stereotypical assumptions society holds about older workers.

Are there bona fide occupational reasons to limit the service terms of lawmakers by age? After all, as we described in the Introduction, advanced age does not automatically mean they have diminished capacity to perform their job functions. Perhaps there is fear that, like Senator Feinstein, an elected official may vacate the seat they were elected to only to be replaced by a governor-appointed replacement or that older lawmakers may not represent the interests of younger voters (Sevi, 2022). Researchers in political science evaluate how a legislator's age influences both the types of legislation they propose and their voting patterns on bills becoming law. More specifically, Curry and Haydon (2018) gathered data on all bills introduced to the House of Representatives from the years 2005 to 2008, including who introduced the bill and whether the bill had an aging focus. The analysis compared the age of the legislator and the number of "senior issue" bills they introduced, defined as bills that addressed policies and programs primarily affecting older adults (e.g., health care reform, prescription drug coverage). Although age was not associated with the senior issue bills, the researchers found that older legislators introduced less publicly controversial bills, such as those focused on assistance for the disabled and handicapped. In light of these findings, older lawmakers may choose to focus on introducing widely agreeable nonpartisan bills. This approach could help them remain productive and potentially increase their chances of retaining their positions.

The President of the United States

It is not just Congress that is aging; the leader of the executive branch has also been historically older. At the time of the writing of this book, President Biden was the oldest ever sitting president, and just before him, former President Trump was the oldest sitting president when he was elected in 2016 (Snell, 2023). In an experimental study conducted in the earliest part of the 2020 election cycle, political scientist Sevi (2022) listed the top six Democratic party candidates during the February primary elections and tested whether each candidate was likely to defeat President Trump in the upcoming election based on their age. To test this, in light of previous research that voters are less likely to support older candidates when age is a salient campaign issue, Sevi randomly assigned the study participants to receive either the control condition that mentioned their previous career or the experimental condition that mentioned their age. The age priming manipulation did not impact the respondents' assessments of how well the potential candidates would do in the general election. Sevi concluded that the age manipulation may not have influenced respondents because candidate ages were already salient given the media attention to candidate age, and participants may have already solidified their opinions of the candidates.

Exclusion From Jury Service

The previous sections addressed employment issues for older individuals who are professional legal decision makers in the criminal legal system. Jurors are another group that includes older individuals. Jurors, however, are not impacted by employment law. Instead, many state statutes provide that older adults can opt out of jury service. For example, in Mississippi a person 65 years of age or older is exempt from jury service (Miss. Code § 13-5-25, 1972). South Carolina recently introduced a bill to raise their exemption age from 65 to 75 years of age (S.C. Gen. Assemb., 2023). Ironically, the opt-out age for jurors is below the age of many judges (Faklis, 2018).

Psychologists O'Connor and Evans (2020) examined what potential jurors thought of these juror age exemptions and whether age impacted desire and capability to serve on a jury. As expected, the study found that older participants (mean age = 73.41 years) expressed significantly greater willingness to serve on a jury in the upcoming year than did the younger participants (mean age = 20.03 years). The older adults said they wanted to serve on a jury because it was their civic duty. The younger adults were more likely, compared with the older adults in their sample, to agree with the age-based opt-out option for older adults to avoid jury service. Older adults in their sample who believed they would make good jurors thought so because of their life experiences, whereas the younger adults felt the older adults would not make good jurors because of assumptions about older adults' poor health and biased beliefs, which demonstrated general ageist beliefs among the younger adults in the sample.

Schachter (2013) argued that the BFOQ exceptions under the ADEA may be seeping into the jury selection process and may foster ageist stereotypes that older adults are not qualified for jury service. Indeed, although attorneys are not permitted to use their peremptory strikes based on race (*Batson v. Kentucky*, 1986) or gender (*J.E.B. v. Alabama*, 1994), no similar restriction prevents attorneys from dismissing a juror based on their age (Rothman et al., 2000). Because of assumptions that older adults will be more punitive, research suggests that prosecutors are more likely to exclude younger jurors, whereas defense attorneys are more likely to exclude older jurors (Anwar et al., 2014).

Having an age-diverse jury is important not only for constitutional purposes but also to add value and depth to the deliberations (Boni-Saenz, 2022), even though most research suggests that juror age has a limited impact on verdicts (Eglit, 2005; Higgins et al., 2007). Furthermore, most states fail to keep records of jurors' ages (Boni-Saenz, 2022), which makes it difficult to do archival research in those states regarding real jurors' ages and corresponding trial outcomes. Some jury research does demonstrate differences based on juror age. For example, lie-detection abilities decrease with age (A. M. O'Connor et al., 2019). In particular, older adults (mean age = 73.41 years), as compared with younger adults (mean age = 20.03 years), were less accurate in detecting children's lies when watching child interview recordings (A. M. O'Connor et al., 2022). However, it should be noted that although older adults achieved on average only 25% lie-detection accuracy, younger adults achieved only 47% lie-detection accuracy—slightly worse than chance (A. M. O'Connor et al., 2022). Older adults are also more likely to blame victims (Adams-Price et al., 2004) but also more likely to convict (Anwar et al., 2014) compared with younger adults. As noted in the previous section about judges, older adults in experimental studies tend to focus on outcomes instead of intentions when making moral judgments about harmful behaviors, which means the seriousness of offenses may be more important for older adults than for younger adults (Margoni et al., 2018).

To understand why older jurors may have distinct methods for reaching a verdict, Dix (2021) conducted a qualitative telephone study with five older jurors who recently sat on a jury for a criminal trial (age 55 or older, mean age of 68 years). Each juror sat on a different trial that included the crimes of assault, attempted murder, and murder, with both guilty and not guilty verdicts represented. Using the story model (Pennington & Hastie, 1992) and the director's cut model (Devine & Caughlin, 2014), Dix highlighted three themes from the interviews. The older adults interviewed reported arriving at their verdict according to three themes identified by the researcher: feeling sorry for the defendant, feeling sorry for the victim, and their general feelings toward the criminal justice system. As Dix noted, her research was not experimental and included a very small sample; however, her work could be useful in future research that experimentally isolates potentially important factors to determine whether juror age differentially affects verdicts and reasons for verdicts.

CONCLUSION

As law professor Howard Eglit (2004) noted in his text *Elders on Trial*, population changes necessitate legal responses in the form of new legislation, accommodations, and innovations. According to Eglit, the rise of the aging population could bring unfair treatment to older workers due to our culture's pervasive ageism, but also, as older adults are more prevalent as decision makers in the legal system, ageism could be directed toward younger people. Although today ageism is pervasive in the American legal and political system, older adults hold a great deal of political power, and vast amounts of money are expended for the benefit of older adults through social programs. For instance, 24% of the U.S. budget in 2024, or $1.6 trillion annually, goes to pay Social Security benefits, with the greatest percentage going to retired workers (Center on Budget and Policy Priorities, 2024). Medicare, a health insurance for those over 65 years of age or those who have disabilities, annually costs the United States $848 billion (Center on Budget and Policy Priorities, 2024). Of course, employees pay in to both Social Security and Medicare while working, so some may argue that these are repayments rather than payments. However, Urban Institute calculations indicate that a hypothetical worker who contributed to Social Security and retires in 2025 will receive more financial benefits than they paid into the program (Steuerle & Smith, 2022). As such, we sit in the tension of history, not sure whether older adults will lose or gain more social standing.

Although definitions, perspectives, and legal responses to older age may change throughout time and across context, aging continues. No matter how it is understood, addressing the criminal legal system's response to older adults in decision-making positions is an important topic to consider. Of course, as discussed in the Introduction to this book, aging stereotypes generally ascribe negative qualities to older adults, either about their abilities or about their demeanor. Consequently, in employment contexts, supervisors may mistakenly perceive older adults as having diminished capacities, not because of actual limitations but because of societal stereotypes about aging (Schachter, 2013).

The legal responses in this chapter focused on approaches that limited or forced older adults to exit or avoid their public service decision-making role. In this area of aging and the law, the sources of law protect older adults from age employment discrimination, require retirement from positions with public and officer safety concerns (law enforcement) and lifetime appointments for which cognitive declines may affect important legal decisions (judicial), and excuse older citizens from jury service. Each of these responses are directed at older adults as a group, and each applies *per se* age requirements that designate the age criteria for eligibility into the group. In legal responses to address age discrimination, perhaps the specified age criteria are an attempt to eliminate subjectivity in who considers themselves eligible (or not), reduce reliance on ageist beliefs in case outcomes, and/or reduce potential internalized ageism produced by legal responses that impact an older person's autonomy.

3

Older Adults as Victims of Crime

Between 2017 and 2022, Pennsylvania experienced a drastic increase in older adult deaths following maltreatment complaints—from a reported 120 deaths in 2017 to 1,389 in 2022 (M. Levy, 2023). What was the cause? Marc Levy from the Associated Press reported that officials from the Pennsylvania Department of Aging offered possible reasons, including the increase in the number of people over 65 years of age and the impact of COVID-19. A problem with the Pennsylvania data, however, is that when someone dies following an abuse or neglect case, there is no way to indicate the cause of death. Caseworkers entered only why a case was closed, with one of the options being death. The Pennsylvania statistics—and their lack of clarity between allegations and later death—serve as just one example of the complications in addressing older adult abuse and neglect. Without data to understand the etiology of elder maltreatment and risk factors, adult protective services (APS) agencies and policymakers do not have the information necessary to respond with legal interventions for the problem. Relatedly, limited data reduce the ability for community agencies to provide effective care and limit the ability for researchers to assist in developing data-driven legal responses to protect older adults (Fettig et al., 2024).

Vice President Hubert Humphrey once said,

> The moral test of government is how that government treats those who are in the dawn of life, the children; those who are in the twilight of life, the elderly; those who are in the shadows of life, the sick, the needy and the handicapped. (Knight, 2016)

https://doi.org/10.1037/0000469-004
Aging and the Criminal Legal System: Community Services, Courts, Corrections, and Policy, by L. E. Wylie and E. M. Brank

Unfortunately, as the current chapter details, older adults are sometimes maltreated by their families and the professionals paid to care for them. Sometimes, they even neglect themselves. Although a competent adult has the right to withhold necessities of life for themselves, questions should be raised to better understand why and when. Older adults can be the victims of any kind of crime, but legislation, policy, and research have mostly addressed the victimization of older adults in the form of elder maltreatment. Because it is the most discussed area of victimization for older adults, we briefly summarize a contextual theory of elder maltreatment within legal systems and the involvement of legal professionals who work with older victims. Then, we dedicate the remainder of the chapter to describing issues in elder maltreatment, which includes acts of commission and acts of omission within formal and informal caregiving situations as well as self-neglect. Although some legal systems have addressed the needs of older adults, specifically older victims, much work is left to do, especially to disentangle the legal responses present in the child protective system from the legal responses appropriate in the adult protective system.

TYPES OF OLDER ADULT VICTIMIZATION

As illustrated in the Venn diagram in Figure 3.1, elder maltreatment is distinguishable from, yet overlaps with, other harms against older adults (Jackson, 2018). Although there is lack of consensus on the definition of elder maltreatment (Roberto, 2016), there are five generally accepted types: physical abuse, psychological abuse, sexual abuse, financial exploitation, and neglect (Lachs & Pillemer, 2015). The diagram in Figure 3.1 includes "abuse in later life," differentiated by its focus on violence and sexual assault in domestic or intimate partner relationships (Crockett et al., 2015). Although there is some overlap with elder maltreatment, "crimes against older adults" are distinguished because of stranger perpetrators, as opposed to a trusted person (Policastro et al., 2015). "Abuse of vulnerable adults" is based on statutorily defined vulnerability, which includes a *per se* age criterion to include anyone over 18 years of age (Hughes et al., 2011). Self-neglect is mutually exclusive from elder maltreatment because there is no perpetrator. Bearing in mind that these are distinct but overlapping constructs, we discuss fear of victimization and crimes against older adults generally, recognizing that older adults represent a relatively smaller proportion of victims generally and are less likely to be the victims of violent crime.

With respect to general crimes against older adults, figures published by the Bureau of Justice Statistics in 2022 indicated that older adults make up a smaller but substantial proportion of individuals victimized (A. Thompson & Tapp, 2023). With regard to violent victimization (rape or sexual assault, robbery, aggravated assault, and simple assault) by demographic age group, those aged 50 to 64 represented approximately 17% of victims, and those aged 65 and older represented approximately 11%, based on rates per 1,000 individuals.

FIGURE 3.1. How Elder Abuse Is Distinguishable From, Yet Overlaps With, Other Harms Against Older Adults

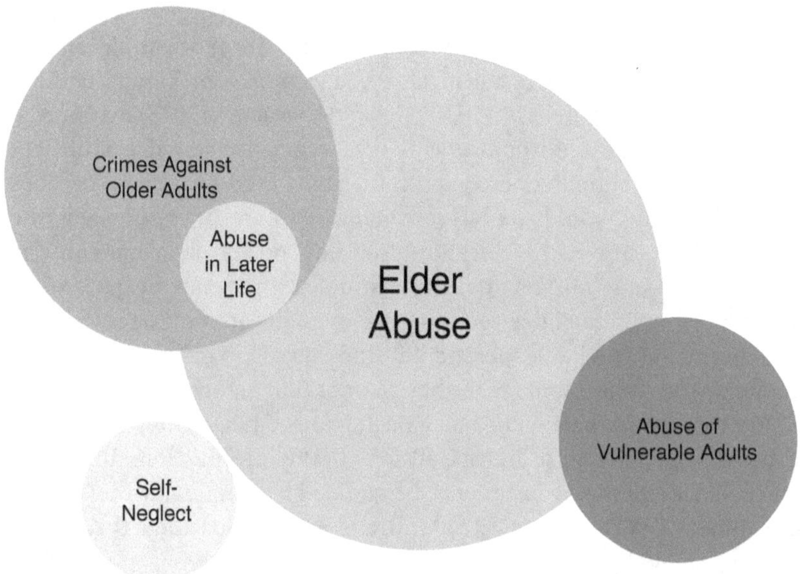

Note. Based on definitions in Heisler (2015). From *Understanding Elder Abuse: A Clinician's Guide* (p. 10), by S. L. Jackson, 2018, American Psychological Association (https://doi.org/10.1037/0000056-000). Copyright 2018 by the American Psychological Association.

If simple assault is removed, the rates decrease to 8%, based on rates per 1,000 individuals. Research has estimated that approximately one in three community-dwelling older adults has contact with the police as complainants, witnesses, or perpetrators of crime (Lachs et al., 2004). Of those, more than half are contacts with first responders as victims of a crime.

Only recently have data been available to estimate the prevalence of elder maltreatment (Jackson, 2016). APS, the U.S. agency responsible for investigating maltreatment claims and providing supportive services to adults aged 18 and older who have functional or mental impairment, receives more than 1.3 million claims of maltreatment per year (U.S. Administration for Community Living, 2021). It is estimated that 17% of the world's population 60 years of age have been the victim of some form of maltreatment (World Health Organization, 2017), either as a single or repeated act or a lack of action that occurs within a trusted relationship (Jackson, 2016). Other research has estimated its prevalence from 2% to 30% of the population (Burnes et al., 2015; Dong & Simon, 2011; Hamby et al., 2016), and a meta-analysis across studies from 28 countries found an overall prevalence rate of 15.7% (Yon et al., 2017). Variability in incidence rates stems from the way the maltreatment is categorized. Describing and categorizing older adult maltreatment is complex, given the multiplicity of contributing factors to the maltreatment (A. Clarke et al., 2016), and was made more complex during the COVID-19 pandemic (S. D. Han & Mosqueda, 2020).

FEAR OF VICTIMIZATION AND REPORTING VICTIMIZATION

In criminology research, the victimization–fear paradox refers to the finding that older adults, compared with younger adults, are more afraid of being a victim of crime despite their statistical risk of victimization being significantly lower (Weinrath & Gartrell, 1996). Kappes and colleagues (2013) explained that this paradox could stem from the way researchers asked older adults about their fears. For example, one common question used for several decades to measure fear was "Would you feel safe being out alone in your neighborhood after dark?" Of course, this question does not specifically ask about crime. An older adult may answer that they would not feel safe because of their own physical vulnerabilities such as poor eyesight or bad knees. When the researchers conducted an experimental study aimed to differentiate between situational and dispositional fear, they did not find an age-related difference. Another concern for older adults may be due to age-related vulnerabilities (see the discussion of biological and social aging in the Introduction, this volume). As such, older adults may experience heightened fear, especially those who are more vulnerable (Chu & Kraus, 2004; Greve, 1998) or perceive themselves as more vulnerable (Hall, 2014).

Older adults may also be less likely to disclose victimization, whether it be general crimes or due to maltreatment, usually in hopes that they will not be perceived as vulnerable, needy, or having diminished capacity. Reporting general physical assault or financial exploitation to law enforcement or even adult children or others in their lives may signal to others (and themselves) that these adults are now old and in need of protection. This can feel paternalistic and not in accordance with their self-identity as older (or not). Older adults may fear losing their autonomy if others view their current living situation as unsafe. This fear often stems from concerns about being moved to institutional care or a family member's home, contradicting their desire to age in place—a preference supported by gerontological theories (see the Introduction).

Nursing professors studied how older adults personally defined physical abuse and why they may be reluctant to report actions (Ziminski Pickering & Rempusheski, 2014). After reading short scenarios describing situations including hitting, burning, medication misuse, and restraining, respondents (mean age 74 years) decided if the actions constituted abuse and whether they would be likely to report such actions. Although the respondents mostly agreed on what constituted physical abuse, they lacked consensus on restricting movements; only one in four thought it was physical abuse to lock the door to a basement pantry to prevent an older adult from falling down the stairs. Reflecting a difference between institutional and informal care, actions from a paid caregiver were perceived as more abusive than were the same actions by an adult child. Most participants responded that they would be reluctant to report the abuse if the alternative were institutional care, their adult child was the abuser, they had limited resources, and they were dependent on their adult child for support.

CONTEXTUAL THEORY OF ELDER MALTREATMENT

Elder maltreatment, also referred to as elder mistreatment or elder abuse (Dong, 2015), like all victimization, occurs within a contextual frame. Figure 3.2 provides a pictorial depiction of the contextual theory of elder abuse (Bolkan et al., 2023; Roberto & Teaster, 2017). As the authors of this theory noted, risk factors and opportunities for intervention exist at each level. For example, as described in the Introduction (this volume), ageism is prevalent and pervasive. When it comes to older adult maltreatment, ageism represents a societal level context. Negative societal attitudes about aging and older adults interfere with

FIGURE 3.2. Contextual Theory of Elder Abuse

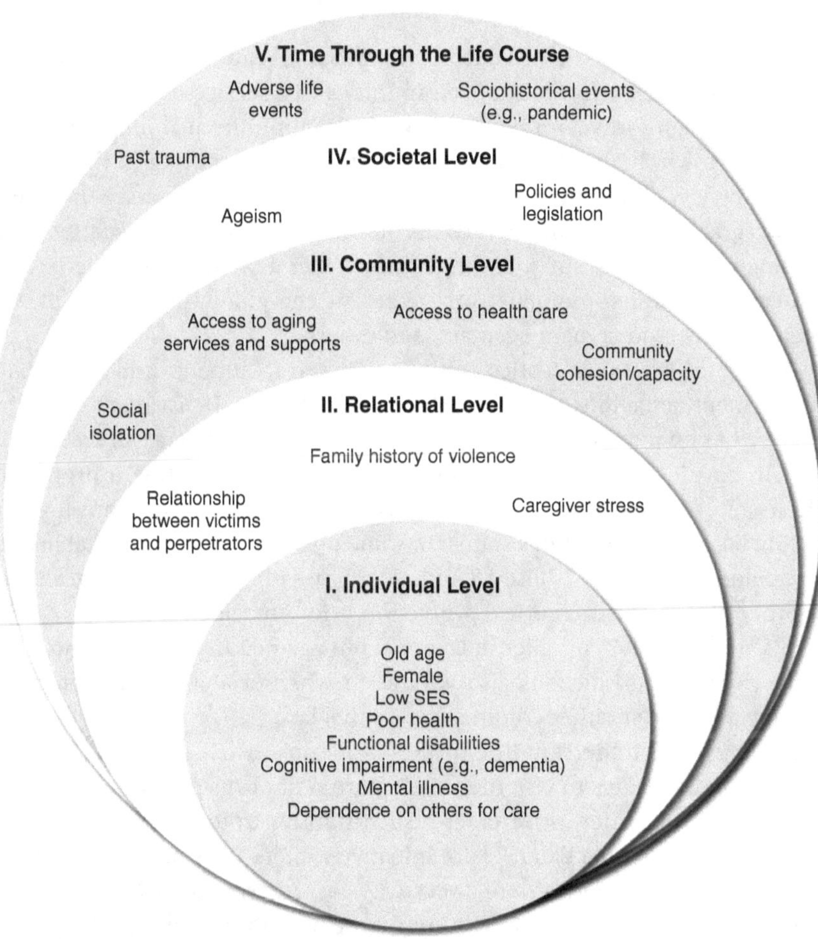

Note. SES = socioeconomic status. From "The Context of Elder Maltreatment: An Opportunity for Prevention Science," by C. Bolkan, P. B. Teaster, and H. Ramsey-Klawsnik, 2023, *Prevention Science, 24*(5), p. 914 (https://doi.org/10.1007/s11121-022-01470-5). Copyright 2023 by Springer Nature. Reprinted with permission.

appropriate funding and resources being devoted to elder maltreatment prevention. Little is known, however, about how community-level factors contribute to a person's risk of abuse (Fettig et al., 2024). The theory clearly demonstrates the complexity of the issue and the need for multifaceted approaches to understand and address elder maltreatment. One step toward better understanding the issue is understanding who the perpetrators are likely to be and the settings in which the maltreatment is likely to occur. The next section describes the legal responses to elder maltreatment in the United States. We describe federal legislation to support states in expanding community support agencies as well as legal responses to protect older adults from maltreatment in institutions, guardianship, and informal caregiver supports.

LEGISLATION AROUND OLDER ADULT VICTIMIZATION

In 1965, Congress passed the Older Americans Act, reauthorized most recently in 2020, in response to a lack of community social services for older persons, establishing authority to provide grants for community planning and social services, research and development, and personnel training in the field of aging. The law established the Administration on Aging to oversee the newly created grant programs and to serve as the federal focal point on matters concerning older persons. In addition to these federal laws, states have laws to protect older adults from elder maltreatment and guide the practice of APS agencies, law enforcement agencies, and others.

As part of the Elder Justice Initiative, aimed to support and coordinate enforcement and efforts to combat elder abuse, the U.S. Department of Justice website has an interactive list of legislation, and website users can search and review statutes by jurisdiction and by the type of maltreatment protected. These statutes vary from state to state, with states having variations for protection based on the victim's status. In some places, the law is applicable only for "vulnerable adults" (those 18 and older but with functional impairment); in other places, the categorical protection is for an "elder person" or "older adults" (e.g., aged 65 or older in Georgia, but aged 62 in Delaware and 60 in Pennsylvania). Jurisdictions also vary as to whether abuse and neglect are unallowable under either criminal law or civil law.

For a greater understanding of the variations across the United States, we encourage readers to visit the U.S. Department of Justice website (https://www.justice.gov/elderjustice/elder-justice-statutes-0) to review a few of the state statutes under the Elder Justice Initiative section. Does the statute include all five types of abuse that were discussed? Does the statute include any types of language or definitions different from those used in the current book? Does the statute define the subgroups of victims who trigger abuse or neglect, and is age an eligibility criterion? Does the statute mention self-neglect, and why might it not? The statutory landscape of elder maltreatment, especially financial exploitation, has constantly shifted as elder maltreatment has come to the forefront of public awareness. This is especially true as internet fraud and other fraudulent behavior perseveres in the digital age. The National Conference of State Legislatures tracks and reports bills that are submitted to each state legislature by topic. In 2023, for example, 34 states and Puerto Rico introduced legislative bills, and 17 states adopted laws to address financial crimes against older adults, focusing on such issues as mandatory reporting, criminal penalties and efforts to raise awareness, and prevention techniques and resources (National Conference of State Legislatures, 2023).

As discussed, elder maltreatment often goes under- or unreported. In response, each state has laws to protect vulnerable populations from abuse by requiring mandatory reporters (e.g., medical professionals) to report elder maltreatment if suspected, justified under the state's *parens patriae* power (see Chapter 1). Proponents of mandatory reporting laws believe they are necessary to detect maltreatment for older adults who are too scared to report the abuse (Velick, 1995). Expressing the possible patronizing causes and effects of mandatory reporting, some have argued that empowering older adults to report is a more autonomous approach to combating elder abuse (Brank et al., 2012).

CAREGIVER MALTREATMENT: NURSING HOMES, GUARDIANSHIP, AND INFORMAL CARE

Maltreatment can occur in any relationship or along the continuum of care options, whether the older adult is living in a skilled nursing facility, in the community with a guardian, or with someone informally for care. Any form of maltreatment can be perpetrated by any person, but we focus on caregiver maltreatment in this chapter because it offers a situation rife with complexities in the study of aging and the law. Although legal responses aimed at formal caregiving situations, such as nursing homes and guardianship, have received public attention for elder maltreatment, it is also important to examine legal responses within informal caregiving.

Further complicating the elder maltreatment legal landscape, state statutes differently define who constitutes a caregiver and their legal responsibilities as a caregiver. For example, Illinois defines a caregiver in two statutory places in civil and criminal codes. First, the state's Adult Protective Services Act (2013) states a caregiver is a "person who either as a result of a family relationship, voluntarily, or in exchange for compensation has assumed responsibility for all or a portion of the care of an eligible adult who needs assistance with activities of daily living." Second, the Criminal Code of 2022 (720 Ill. Comp. Stat. 5, Sec. 12-4.4a(e)) additionally details a caregiver as a

> person who has a duty to provide for an elderly person or person with a disability's health and personal care, at the elderly person or person with a disability's place of residence, including, but not limited to, food and nutrition, shelter, hygiene, prescribed medication, and medical care and treatment.

These varying definitions across statutes between civil and criminal codes within a single state highlight the complexity and potential inconsistencies in legal approaches to elder maltreatment, underscoring the need for clearer, more uniform standards in caregiver identification and responsibility.

Skilled Nursing Facilities

Skilled nursing facilities, also known as nursing homes, provide institutional care for aging adults who need the highest level of care. Generally, this is when a person is unable to perform their activities of daily living, such as toileting, bathing, feeding, dressing, and moving around. Older adults are the largest proportion of the population living in institutional medical facilities. The Nursing Home Reform Act of 1987 imposed federal requirements of care on nursing homes that receive Medicaid or Medicare and created individual rights for nursing home residents. States also have responsibilities to regulate and license the nursing homes in their state. Despite the legislated rights of residents, systematic reviews of research suggest that elder maltreatment in nursing homes is quite high, with 64% of staff reportedly engaging in behaviors classified as elder abuse within the past year (Yon et al., 2017) and coresident abuse also occurring frequently (Myhre et al., 2020).

Nursing home staff face various risk factors that may contribute to the abuse of residents. Many nursing homes are staffed by nursing assistants who receive low wages and feel they are expendable by management (Conlie Shaw, 1998). Furthermore, compared with at-home living situations, nursing homes offer a potential ease of using chemical restraints. Chemical restraints are the use of medications to subdue residents for discipline or convenience purposes (Braun & Frolik, 2000). Overuse or misuse of medications interferes with a resident's autonomy and can create a myriad of health consequences. For example, some psychotropic medications can increase the fall risk because they interfere with a resident's gait and balance. Of course, a fall for an older adult can have severe and negative outcomes. Before the Omnibus Budget Reconciliation Act of 1987, which contained the Nursing Home Bill of Rights, nursing homes were relatively free to use chemical restraints with their residents. Under the Nursing Home Bill of Rights, residents have the right to be protected from misuse of medications used to chemically restrain as discipline or at staff's convenience. Nursing home staff may prefer residents to be medicated so that they will not create more work for the staff, particularly if the resident is someone who requires care or is viewed as difficult. Unfortunately, minimal research exists to clearly differentiate when nursing home staff are using medications in appropriate versus inappropriate ways (Robins et al., 2021).

There are often financial incentives for holding nursing homes responsible for elder maltreatment. Colloquially referred to as having "deep pockets," nursing homes are in a categorically different financial situation than is an individual maltreating an older adult because of the nature of being a business and having large insurance coverage (Brickley et al., 2022). Therefore, attorneys are financially incentivized to represent a nursing home abuse victim in a way they are not when the perpetrator is an individual.

Assisted Living Facilities

In recent decades, assisted living facilities have become a more popular living arrangement option, representing a preference for less medical care and more independence (Kohn, 2020a). Unlike skilled nursing facilities, assisted living facilities vary in the services provided because there is no federally defined standard. States also differ in how they define what an assisted living facility provides. Given their great variability, it is difficult to provide a clear picture of what services will be provided at a particular assisted living facility. For the most part, they provide private or semiprivate living arrangements and some assistance with activities of daily living, but some are staffed by medically trained personnel, and others have no medical staff at all. Such lack of clarity with the level of care a person will receive can lead to role ambiguity and unclear expectations for care, which can contribute to the potential for neglect of an older adult.

Guardianship

In contrast to an older adult moving into a facility, families wanting to formalize the caregiving relationship at home can embark on a guardianship process. Guardianship law is state based; that is, there are no national standards for defining guardianship (E. L. Greene, 2008). With a guardianship, a judge, usually with the help of a psychological capacity assessment (Rothke et al., 2019), determines whether the older adult is no longer competent to manage their affairs and that someone needs to be appointed to do so (Gavisk & Greene, 2007). If a person has planned for this, then they will likely have a power of attorney or a living trust established that will spring into effect when the older adult is determined to be incompetent. Either way, both processes involve a clear designation of a person who is responsible for the older adult. Although a limited guardianship with a focus on certain tasks and abilities would often make more sense, most guardianships are full, which means legally the older adult has no decision-making powers (Jameson et al., 2015). Acknowledging the potential for abuse inherent in guardianship situations, especially full guardianships, elder law scholars advocate for supported decision making whenever feasible. This approach aims to preserve as much autonomy in decisions for older adults as possible, thereby reducing vulnerability to exploitation (see https://www.eldersandcourts.org/guardianship_conservatorship/resources-for-courts for resources).

If a guardianship is implemented, it clarifies both that the older adult is a person in need of care and that the guardian is the person responsible for that care (Falk & Hoffman, 2014). In last-resort situations, the court appoints a public guardian—a public official or publicly funded organization that serves as a legal guardian in the absence of any family or friends willing or able to do so (Teaster & Chamberlain, 2020). Usually, the older adults are living in nursing facilities when they are under a public guardianship, but there are still opportunities for the public guardian to inflict abuse on the older adult, especially financial exploitation, as we describe more fully later in the section on types of maltreatment.

Informal Domestic Caregiving

The caregiving task becomes even more complex for informal caregivers outside of formal nursing or assisted living facilities because of role ambiguity and lack of clarity about when caregiving responsibilities begin. In contrast, for parents who bring home a newborn baby or adopt an older child, it is clearer that the parents are expected to provide care for the child. There are countless books describing the developmental milestones, online resources for checking those milestones against the child's own progression, and plenty of relatives and friends ready with advice. The child will usually require less and less care as they age to the point that they will move out of the parents' home and survive on their own. Indeed, the law imposes certain age-based restrictions on the child that prompt the parents to know what their child is competent to handle. For example, most states set 16 as the legal driving age, so before that age, with some exceptions, the child will not be able to legally drive an automobile.

In contrast to caring for a child, caring for an older adult (in the absence of a formal guardianship assignment) often develops gradually and without a clear defining shift between the older adult helping the family to needing care themselves (Wylie & Brank, 2009). Most informal caregivers are spouses or adult children who are caring for their family member many hours per week for several years (Wolff et al., 2018). Because there is no age-based definition for when an adult becomes incompetent—and clearly, many older adults will never lose their competency—an informal caregiver is faced with determining when they should begin providing care for their family member. In other words, when does simple helping transition into caregiving? For many older adults, it is a slow progression with increasing caregiver burden (Lindt et al., 2020). Even for those who experience a serious injury or event that pushes them immediately into needing care, the older adult—and the family caregiver—can still hope that the older adult will get better, heal, and no longer need the same level of care.

Some maltreatment is clear, like that described in the case of *State v. Rodriguez* (2021) in which an adult son whipped his 82-year-old father with the cord of a clothing iron and then stole and used his father's credit cards. Other situations are less clear, especially when the case involves informal caregiver neglect. An adult daughter caring for her father at home said she believed she was following medical advice with her father's feeding and believed her father would have told her, as he had before, if his bedsores were hurting him and causing him serious harm (*GF v. Department of Human Services*, 2017).

Several years ago, we conducted a study to determine how well potential caregivers (mean age 41 years) and care recipients (mean age 72 years) matched their plans and views about older adult caregiving using vignettes that described a vulnerable older adult who had moved in together with an adult daughter while another adult child lived 10 minutes away (Brank & Wylie, 2016). We manipulated the randomly assigned vignettes to describe the older woman as being either autonomous (i.e., able to care for her daily needs) or not autonomous. In addition, the vignettes were manipulated to describe the older woman as welcoming help or being unwilling to accept help from the older adult child. Across all conditions, participants viewed the caregivers described in the vignettes as having more abilities than the potential caregiver participants thought they would have in the situation depicted. The sampled groups of potential caregivers and care recipients also disagreed on how much decision-making responsibilities the older adult should have. Taken together, the results demonstrated how unclear the roles are for informal caregiving situations.

In addition to role ambiguity, studies have documented that informal caregiving may lead to psychological distress (Lindt et al., 2020) and adverse physical health of the caregiver (Fenequito et al., 2023; Schulz et al., 2020). Caregivers of older adults face complex and emotionally taxing decisions about how to provide appropriate care. On top of that, caring for an aging person comes with financial (both short- and long-term), physical, social, and emotional burdens (National Academies of Sciences, Engineering, and Medicine, 2016). Although caregiver burden was once believed to be the primary reason why caregivers abused older adults, research has demonstrated that there are a multitude of reasons for maltreatment (Brandl & Raymond, 2012). Indeed, focusing on caregiver stress as a reason for abuse can unintentionally place blame on the older adult for creating a burden and overshadow the abuser's characteristics that may be predictive of abuse. No matter the underlying reasons for the abuse, we know it is occurring and can cause great harm. The following sections describe the different categories of abuse, beginning with types of maltreatment.

SPECIFIC TYPES OF ELDER MALTREATMENT

Research on the prevalence of each type of maltreatment suggests that psychological abuse is the most frequent type of maltreatment (Jackson, 2016), but data from APS agencies indicate that many older adults (30% to 40%) experience multiple types of maltreatment, referred to as *polyvictimization* (Teaster, 2017). Research on elder maltreatment is generally limited, with an even greater scarcity of studies focusing on diverse subgroups of older adults. Scholars hypothesize that the experiences of minoritized groups likely differ from those of the general older adult population typically represented in existing research. This gap in knowledge underscores the need for more comprehensive and inclusive studies to better understand the nuanced experiences of elder maltreatment across various demographic groups (Jackson, 2016).

Psychological Abuse and Neglect

Whereas some cases of abuse are obvious (e.g., *State v. Rodriguez*, 2021), others are less clear-cut, and that is especially true when the case involves psychological abuse or caregiver neglect. Psychological abuse harms the older adult using words or nonverbal means such as threatening to put the older adult in a nursing home, isolating the older adult from others, or giving the older adult the silent treatment (Conrad et al., 2011). Neglect, which can be intentional or unintentional, occurs when the older adult's needs are not met (American Psychological Association, 2024). As discussed, how needs are defined and who should be meeting those needs can be more complex than a casual observer might suspect.

Physical Abuse

Physical abuse is an intentional use of force that results in some sort of physical pain, harm, or injury and includes such actions as slapping, hitting, use of physical restraints, or an inappropriate use of medications (Weissberger et al., 2020). Old age can create physical vulnerabilities that increase risks of injury and death when an older adult is physically abused (R. A. Miller, 1999). Chronic disease and medications can also lead to unexplained bruises, bone fractures, and abrasions, which makes it difficult to differentiate simple aging from abuse (L. M. Young, 2014). Research consistently demonstrates that when an older adult is physically abused, the perpetrator is most frequently their adult child, a partner or spouse, or some other family member who lives with the older adult (Friedman et al., 2011). Physical abuse often co-occurs with other forms of abuse (Weissberger et al., 2020), yet it is dramatically underreported (Acierno et al., 2010), for the reasons we described earlier.

Sexual Abuse

Older adult sexual abuse is usually explained by three different theories (Chopin & Beauregard, 2021). First, the anger and control theory suggests that the abuse occurs because of the perpetrator's anger and desire for control rather than sexual motivation. In contrast, the gerontophilia theory posits that the abuse is sexually motivated. *Gerontophilia* is the term used to describe sexual attraction toward an older person. A third theory is founded on opportunity, such that the abuse occurs because a motivated perpetrator had an opportunity with an unprotected and vulnerable victim. For example, this could describe a sexual assault that occurs during a burglary of an older adult.

In general, older adults have clearly reached the age of majority for consenting to sexual activity. Unlike the lower age limit for children and adolescents, there is no upper age limit restricting consensual sexual activity. Although our society commonly desexualizes older adults (Risen, 2016), many still report desiring and experiencing sexual fulfillment (DeLamater, 2012; Dominguez & Barbagallo, 2016). As discussed in the Introduction and later in Chapter 7 of this volume, competence is task specific, which means that an older adult may not have the capacity to decide complex legal issues but could be completely competent to decide whether they would like to engage in sexual activities. Although it can be complicated and confusing for the older adult's adult children, all sexual activity by an older adult cannot be assumed to be abuse.

Of course, there are also issues around an older adult's ability to consent if the older adult is legally incompetent to do so. For example, can an older woman with dementia consent to have sex with her husband? Such cases are difficult to prosecute, with one study noting that zero out of 39 cases were brought to trial for alleged spousal elder sex abuse (Burgess & Phillips, 2006). Research suggests that stranger rape is much more common among older adult victims than among younger victims, and older adults, as compared with younger populations, are more likely to be sexually assaulted in their own homes (Budd & Liddic, 2021; Burgess et al., 2007). As with physical abuse with older adults, sexual abuse with older adults, in particular postmenopausal older women, results in greater injury than is likely with younger adults because of preexisting age-based frailties (Muram et al., 1992).

Financial Abuse and Exploitation

Financial abuse is likely the most common type of elder maltreatment (Weissberger et al., 2020) perpetrated by both family and nonfamily (Acierno et al., 2010) and comes in many different forms (Gibson & Greene, 2013), with some estimates suggesting that more than 5% of older adults living in the community experience financial fraud each year (Burnes et al., 2017). AARP estimates that $28.3 billion per year is stolen from older adults over the age of 60 (Gunther, 2023). Because families are apt to comingle their finances and often fail to keep detailed records, familial fraud can be especially difficult to detect (Setterlund et al., 2007). Residential exploitation is another form of financial abuse that involves a person putting an older adult's home in jeopardy by misusing the home for the benefit of someone other than the older adult (DePrince et al., 2020). This could include using the home to store or sell illegal substances, pressuring the older adult to obtain a reverse mortgage to create a cash flow not for the benefit of the older adult, or living with the older adult without paying a fair share of the expenses. Despite growing awareness among lawmakers, policymakers, and the public about the potential risks of financial exploitation, few national studies have examined this form of abuse. This lack of comprehensive research mirrors the overall scarcity of representative data on older adult maltreatment. Several methodological challenges contribute to this gap in knowledge. These include underreporting of incidents, small and biased sample sizes, inconsistent definitions of financial exploitation, and infrequent or unsystematic data collection (Stamatel & Mastrocinque, 2011).

Some research demonstrates that when financial exploitation occurs alone versus in conjunction with another form of abuse (e.g., physical abuse), the victim is often less healthy, and the abuser is more likely to be the older adult's caregiver (Jackson & Hafemeister, 2012). Therefore, when the abuse is financial abuse alone, the appropriate response is one of education about fraud and enacting appropriate safeguards around the older adult's finances. In contrast, when financial abuse occurs in tandem with other forms of abuse, the interventions need to be all-encompassing.

Another complication with older adult financial abuse is the natural developmental change in a person's attitudes and priorities as they age. Renowned developmental psychologist Erik Erikson is widely recognized for his theory on older adults' tendency to engage in life review during their later years. According to Erikson, this stage involves reflecting on one's past, reevaluating meaningful relationships, and potentially reprioritizing goals and values for their remaining time (Erikson & Erikson, 1998). Empirical research confirms this age-based priority shift, such that a person nearing the end of their life may be inclined to move away from valuing financial resources the way they may have in their middle years. Imagine an older adult who has amassed a great deal of wealth through their hard work and dedication to their career. As they are approaching the end of their life, they begin to devalue monetary possessions and focus more on relationships. Accordingly, they competently (assuming they have not been found to have diminished capacity) give their neighbor, friend, or a new love interest a substantial financial gift. Adult children of the older adult may view this gift (and the perceived loss of their expected inheritance) as suspect and out of character for their parents who may have previously valued money more than relationships. However, this may be reflective of an older adult's priorities developing appropriately (Brooks, 2022). Furthermore, it is important to remember that just as a younger person's bad decisions do not equal incompetence, neither do an older adult's bad decisions—no matter how subjectively defined. Eccentricity is allowed at any age of adulthood (Frolik & Barnes, 2015), but such eccentricities or developmental changes can create real challenges in determining whether an older adult has simply grown into new values or they are experiencing financial exploitation.

Self-Neglect

Adult maltreatment statutes were modeled after child protection statutes (Lu & Shelley, 2021). Florida law provides one of the clearest examples of this, with the statutes being identical except "elderly person" is substituted for "child" (Wells et al., 2020). Although using the same language is efficient for the legislative committees drafting the bills, several important issues make doing so inappropriate. Importantly, APS agencies cannot require an older adult to accept their services or interventions unless the older adult has a cognitive impairment that renders them unable to make their own decisions (Lu & Shelley, 2021). This is not an issue for child protective services given the minority status of all children, which means that children do not have a choice regarding whether they want to participate in the legal intervention for suspected maltreatment.

This distinction between children and older adults is especially important on the topic of self-neglect. Self-neglect occurs when an older adult is not providing for their own basic needs (Dong, 2017); however, there is no universally accepted definition of self-neglect, given the wide variations of what cultures and socioeconomic classes determine are necessities (Pavlou & Lachs, 2008). Self-neglect does not automatically mean that a person is legally incompetent. A competent adult has the right to choose not to bathe, eat, socialize, and attend doctor's appointments. However, once that person is in the care of another person, that caregiver then can be held legally responsible for harm if they do not ensure requisite care.

This complicates matters because a person may refuse to take care of themselves and refuse to accept care from their caregiver (Yu et al., 2023). In the aforementioned vignette study with potential caregivers and care recipients, we experimentally tested whether the older adult's refusal of care impacted caregiving decisions. The neutral third-party participants paternalistically interpreted that refusal as meaning that the older adult needed more help. In other words, when the participants read that a presumably competent older adult refused help from a caregiver, the participants seemingly denied the older adult's autonomy and assumed they needed more care (Brank & Wylie, 2016).

Homicide

Although older adult victims of homicide do not represent a large proportion of homicide victims, when older adults are victimized, they may present characteristics unique from other forms of homicide. Rogers and Storey (2019) conducted a systematic review of research on all forms of elder homicide across almost 4 decades, finding 33 articles written on the topic. Rogers and Storey found that past research focused on victim characteristics, offender characteristics, victim–offender relationship, and offense characteristics. However, research in this area is still relatively recent and scant, which means that in some instances there are only a handful of studies examining a particular facet. For example, only three studies in the review examined whether the homicide victims had also been victims of elder abuse, neglect, or intimate partner violence. It is impossible to draw strong conclusions with so little research on the topic. Furthermore, Rogers and Storey (2019) noted that in addition to the studies reviewed using different age cutoffs for inclusion, the studies also did not focus on nuanced risk factors for elder homicide beyond basic demographic characteristics. Epidemiology researchers Shawon and colleagues (2021) examined U.S. homicides reported in the year 2018 for people aged 60 and over. These homicides represented 9% of all homicides for that year, with firearms being the most common weapon used, men most commonly the victims, and most homicides occurring in the victim's home.

Cases in the media demonstrate the complexities the statistics overlook. For example, Gerald Adams, age 80, shot and killed his wife, Donna Adams, age 79, in their home in November 2023 (Robinson, 2023). Donna had numerous medical issues, and although Gerald's family thought he may have been feeling overwhelmed by his caregiving role, there were no signs of an argument or struggle before the shooting (Hastings, 2023). Shortly after, Adams was charged with murder, and investigators were still collecting evidence to determine whether Adam's intent was for homicide or assisted suicide.

REMEDYING OLDER ADULT VICTIMIZATION

As noted, older adults can be reluctant to report abuse (Snow et al., 2023) when the abusers are their caregivers; for some older adults, the fear of no care is worse than abusive care (Mion & Momeyer, 2019). Furthermore, services and systems lack appropriate screening tools, training on the signs of abuse, and clear reporting procedures for professionals working with older adults or people who suspect abuse (Gallione et al., 2017). Some suggest that even the terminology could be interfering with older adults engaging in the system because they may be more willing to accept that they have been mistreated rather than abused (Smyth, 2011). Scholars fear that the COVID-19 pandemic likely increased older adult abuse given the isolation and the increased dependency of older adults on others (S. D. Han & Mosqueda, 2020).

Another complicated factor for some family caregivers is their own experience of childhood abuse from their parents who now need care. One study found that 26% of current caregivers reported childhood abuse at the hands of those for whom they were now providing care (Kong, 2018). There are potential interventions that can help stop the cycle and allow the caregiver to heal from their own trauma. One aspect that can help is for the caregiver to ensure that they engage with decision making and boundary setting around taking on the caregiving role and that it is not just a presumed role they accept (Kong et al., 2021).

When an older adult chooses to address abuse through formal intervention, the most likely options are engaging law enforcement for possible criminal prosecution or pursuing some form of civil action. Because the perpetrators are often family members or caregivers, many older adults do not want to engage in these legal options. The older adult may have conflicting emotions about getting their family member in trouble. Moreover, if their family member who is the abuser is enabling the older adult to remain living independently or semi-independently, then the older adult likely fears losing that independence if they report the maltreatment (McNeal & Brown, 2019).

Criminalization of elder maltreatment is a relatively new phenomenon that began to occur in the 1990s. Initially, APS agencies were the primary intervention because it was generally believed that maltreatment occurred as a result of caregiver stress, similarly to how child abuse can occur (Jackson, 2016). Research in the late 1980s began suggesting that rather than caregiver stress, older adult abuse was more often the result of the perpetrator's psychopathology rather than the result of the victim's vulnerability (Anetzberger, 2005; Burnight & Mosqueda, 2011; Jackson, 2016). This change shifted the research focus from thinking about elder maltreatment like child maltreatment and instead aligned older adult maltreatment with other forms of intimate partner and domestic violence that were well within the criminal justice system purview. Still, as noted previously, many state statutes to protect older adults remain modeled after statutes to protect children, demonstrating that the law has not shifted as the research has.

PREVENTIONS AND INTERVENTIONS

Although prevention and interventions for older adult maltreatment are still lacking, several methods for both exist. Preventing older adult maltreatment mostly focuses on advocacy, education, support, and services. For example, caregiver helplines or training are meant to provide support and educate caregivers so that they will not resort to abuse (Bolkan et al., 2023). Interventions to stop elder maltreatment generally fall into three categories targeting (a) professionals to improve their ability to detect abuse, (b) older adults who are experiencing abuse, and (c) caregivers who are perpetrating abuse (Ayalon et al., 2016).

What should a police officer do if they are called to investigate a potential elder maltreatment situation? This is a situation in which criminal justice and older adult health intersect (Brown et al., 2014). In one study, Brown et al. examined knowledge of aging-related health among officers in the San Francisco Police Department. The officers self-rated their knowledge of working with older adults and provided descriptive responses to questions about age-related health issues such as dementia and hearing impairment and how those can impact their interactions with older persons. Virtually all the officers (89%) reported interacting with older adults at least monthly; only 32% rated themselves as knowledgeable or very knowledgeable about aging-related health issues. Furthermore, whereas police work often requires quick decision making, police participants in this study noted the need to slow down when working with older adults because of aging-related health issues such as hearing impairment or mobility impairment.

Several states have specific training for their law enforcement agents around how to interact appropriately with older adults (Bourns, 2000). For example, Milwaukee, Wisconsin, has what is referred to as the Gray Squad, an anticrime unit in which all police personnel within the unit receive specialized training in how to interview older adults and are more knowledgeable about community resources available for older adults. Research on this specialized unit demonstrated that it increases positive attitudes toward the police for those older adults who have interacted with the specialized unit as compared with police not within the Gray Squad (Zevitz & Gurnack, 1991). See Chapters 4 and 6 (this volume) for lengthier discussions of how some law enforcement departments are engaging with agencies focused on aging and related issues, such as the Alzheimer's Association, to design the most effective legal responses for older adults in contact with law enforcement agents.

JURY RESPONSES TO OLDER ADULT ABUSE

Although rare, older adult abuse can reach the courts and be tried in front of a jury. As we described in the Introduction, older adults are stereotyped, generally, as being high warmth and low competence in the stereotype content model (Fiske et al., 2002, 2007). Psychology researchers Syme and Cohn (2020) examined whether those stereotypes impacted mock juror decision making related to an older adult maltreatment case, using research materials describing an actual case, in which a husband was charged with sexual abuse for having sex with his wife with dementia who was living in a nursing home. The participants read either instructions that were general legal guidelines for sexual consent or specialized instructions about her age and residential status. All participants were instructed that the prosecution bore the burden of proving the wife's inability to consent to sexual activity. Although the different instruction options did not impact guilt ratings, pity was the most endorsed attitude toward the scenario. Moreover, levels of pity toward the victim predicted lower guilt ratings for the perpetrator, which confirmed the warm–incompetent implicit age bias.

Psychologist Golding and his colleagues (2004, 2005) have examined how mock jurors interpret and decide cases involving older adult maltreatment based on factors such as age and cognitive or physical health. In one study (Golding et al., 2004), undergraduate student mock jurors read criminal trial summaries of an older adult neglect case. The victim was described as either 76 or 86 years old and as having either a cognitive deficit or a physical disability. Mock jurors were significantly more likely to find the defendant guilty of maltreatment when the victim was described as having a cognitive deficit but less likely when they were described with a physical disability. The age of the victim did not impact guilt ratings. In a follow-up study (Golding et al., 2005) with two experiments, the researchers further manipulated victim age and then gender, but neither impacted guilt ratings. Instead, participant gender impacted guilt ratings, such that women believed the described victim more than did men and rendered more guilty verdicts.

Juror decisions are also influenced by older adults who testify in court as victim–witnesses and the type of evidence they offer. A community sample of mock jurors rendered significantly more guilty verdicts for the defendant when a 45-year-old witness testified with indirect hearsay, compared with the 75-year-old's direct and indirect hearsay testimony (Dunlap et al., 2007). In a study that focused on aging stereotypes rather than chronological age, the researchers manipulated whether the victim's health status was described as healthy, frail, or confused. However, the victim's described health status did not influence verdicts; most respondents rendered guilty verdicts across all three conditions. When mock juror participants did not render guilt, they most often cited a lack of intent by the accused to cause harm (Kinstle et al., 2008). More recent mock juror research has found that victims may be believed more in civil than in criminal cases (Le Grand et al., 2021; Wasarhaley & Golding, 2017). Together, the research on how mock jurors interpret elder maltreatment demonstrates the complexity and number of factors that can be important in these cases.

CONCLUSION

It is hard to think about anyone being mistreated, especially near the end of their lives. As Vice President Humphrey's quote alluded to, how we care for our oldest adults speaks to our society. Although we have seen exponential legal responses to increase spending, attention, and intervention for other areas of family and domestic violence, legal responses to older adult maltreatment have garnered less attention (Dong, 2015; Lachs & Pillemer, 2015; Lu & Shelley, 2021). Due to poor data collection, there is limited national longitudinal research on older adult maltreatment (Dong, 2015) and comparable data across states (Lu & Shelley, 2021). New developments in reporting data on adult maltreatment are promising for designing and evaluating policy and programming to address elder maltreatment while balancing individual civil rights of older adults and reducing any unintended effects policies have on aging biases. The National Adult Maltreatment Reporting System was initiated in 2016 and is the first national reporting system for APS programs to collect quantitative and qualitative data on APS practices and policies as well as information about maltreatment case outcomes for older adults and adults with disabilities. The goal of the National Adult Maltreatment Reporting System is to provide consistent national data on the exploitation and abuse of adults, but the program is still early in implementation (U.S. Administration for Community Living, 2024).

Although elder maltreatment receives less attention compared with other sources of violence, legal responses to older adults as victims of maltreatment are one of the more multidimensional areas of aging and the law and include legal responses that are protective, preventive, supportive, and empowering. The core legal response when someone harms another person falls under general assault and battery criminal law statutes applicable to all adults. When older adults are victims, however, U.S. legal responses have special protections for older adults as "vulnerable" who may need APS protection from self-neglect. There have also been protective responses such as mandatory reporting of abuse and neglect by certain reporters, which assumes an individual older adult is not competent to report the maltreatment themselves but is perceived as likable to warrant such help. These legal responses aim to protect and prevent against harm but rely on paternalistic assumptions that an older adult lacks capacity. Such legal responses may facilitate interpersonal ageism between older adults, mandatory reporters, and agencies such as APS as well as internalized ageism in which the older adult believes they are less capable.

At the community level, supportive responses such as quality regulations for state-funded nursing homes ensure older adults have regulated formal care that makes them safer from maltreatment, and empowering legal responses are available through the Older Americans Act, which was amended in 1992 to include legal advocacy services for older adults who may be victims of maltreatment. Although well-meaning, these supportive and empowering responses put the responsibility on older victims to pursue assistance themselves, which, as discussed in this chapter, is not always something they are able or willing to do. Still, there are reasons to be hopeful that older adult maltreatment will receive similar consideration soon. World Elder Abuse Awareness Day began in 2006 to spotlight the topic of abuse and neglect of older adults and to bring better understanding to it (United Nations Department of Economic and Social Affairs, 2023). Every June 15, the day is commemorated with events such as Take Your Grandparent to Work Day, resource fairs, or academic conferences. In the United States, the White House Conference on Aging has been held once per decade since 1961 (last held in 2015) and focused on public health challenges (White House Conference on Aging, 2015).

4

Older Adults as Eyewitnesses

Imagine you are watching or reading the local news, and the story of an 84-year-old woman robbed at gunpoint shortly after sunset is featured. Thankfully, the woman, Betty, was not injured in the robbery, but the robber snatched her purse with all her cash, credit cards, and checkbook inside. The police are looking for a suspect that Betty described as "a White male about 6 feet tall with dark brown hair and tattoos on his arms." Now imagine that the story instead involves a 34-year-old woman named Emma who was robbed; are you more confident in Emma's or Betty's memory? When you think about these two victims, who do you think is more accurate in what they remember? Which victim is more likely to provide enough detail to further the investigation? Who would be more confident in their memory or description? If Betty and Emma were each asked to come down to the police station for additional questioning or a suspect lineup, would their experiences with investigators be similar? Should they be? If the case goes to trial, which of these two victims would be more believable to a judge or jury?

This chapter briefly summarizes memory and eyewitness research, particularly as it relates to whether legal responses for older witnesses should consider age-related vulnerabilities as they do with children (Snow et al., 2023). In addition, we discuss aging biases as they relate to eyewitness-memory–specific tasks in recognition, recall, confidence in their memory, and testimony in court. If you are like many people, you may have assumed that Emma would make a better eyewitness than Betty. After all, as discussed in the Introduction and

https://doi.org/10.1037/0000469-005
Aging and the Criminal Legal System: Community Services, Courts, Corrections, and Policy, by L. E. Wylie and E. M. Brank

throughout this book, declines in cognitive and physical abilities required for seeing, hearing, and remembering are typical in aging. However, as the research in eyewitness memory and aging detailed later in this chapter reveals, assumptions about the abilities of older eyewitnesses do not always hold true. Moreover, legal responses that unintentionally elicit ageist beliefs in older adults may impact their performance in stereotype-consistent ways—possibly confirming aging stereotypes of older adults. The sources of law in this chapter include the legal standards and best practices that developed from the research conducted on eyewitness memory. Criminal legal systems have embraced the recommendations that research has developed to improve the collection and use of eyewitness memory evidence.

EYEWITNESS MISIDENTIFICATION

Law enforcement investigators and prosecutors rely heavily on eyewitnesses in criminal investigations and convictions (Godsey, 2017). Likewise, eyewitness research has contributed enormously to improving the criminal legal system's use and handling of eyewitness forensic evidence (Wixted & Mickes, 2022). The extensive area of eyewitness research dates back more than 100 years to Hugo Münsterberg's (1908) book, *On the Witness Stand*, which describes the fallibility of eyewitness memory. In fact, he described his own eyewitness mistakes that he made while providing testimony under oath about a burglary that had occurred in his own home. He concluded that his "illusions" (Münsterberg, 1908, p. 41) were not due to any general memory deficits but rather a combination of confusion, suggestion by police, and forgetting. He then gave a call for the new field of psychology to provide its research results to the courts and to do more applied research relevant to the law. It took some time for the scientific community to respond, but the law-psychology research community has responded in abundance with more than 40 years of laboratory, field studies, meta-analyses (e.g., Wylie, Hazen, et al., 2018) and two American Psychology–Law Society (AP-LS) scientific review papers (Wells et al., 1998, 2020) focused on various aspects of the reliability of eyewitness evidence for law enforcement and courts.

LEGAL STANDARDS FOR EVALUATING FAIRNESS AND RELIABILITY

The Due Process Clause of Amendment XIV to the U.S. Constitution protects defendants against an unnecessarily suggestive eyewitness identification. In 1977, the Supreme Court established the modern test for evaluating the fairness and reliability of eyewitness identification evidence in *Manson v. Brathwaite*. The test asks two questions: Did police use suggestive identification procedures? If so, can any suggestiveness be excused based on reliability factors? The Supreme Court has also outlined five conditions to consider when evaluating

BOX 4.1 | STATE LEGISLATION BASED ON BEST PRACTICES IN EYEWITNESS INVESTIGATION

To protect against eyewitness misidentification, Minnesota signed a requirement into law for law enforcement to adopt statewide best practices in lineup procedures. A professor local to Minnesota at Augsburg University and a nationally recognized expert on eyewitnesses, Dr. Nancy Steblay, provided testimony on the scientific evidence of eyewitness identification in support of the bill (Innocence Project, 2020). The law, which passed just prior to the murder of George Floyd by law enforcement in Minneapolis, Minnesota, in May 2020, required the statewide model policy for collecting evidence from eyewitnesses to include best practices (Wells et al., 1998) on four key issues for reducing contamination and increasing eyewitness evidence reliability: administering lineups, instructing witnesses during lineups, selecting nonsuspects in lineups, and documenting the eyewitness's level of confidence at the first identification (Minn. Stat. § 626.8433, 2020).

eyewitness identification evidence. The Manson criteria include the witness's opportunity to view the criminal at the time of the crime, the length of time between the crime and the identification, the level of certainty demonstrated by the witness, the accuracy of the witness's prior description, and the witness's degree of attention during the crime. In 2012, in *Perry v. New Hampshire*, the Supreme Court ruled that a trial judge cannot exclude witness identification based on suggestive circumstances, unless there was improper police manipulation of the identification. In light of eyewitness memory research, states have passed laws to improve the collection and use of evidence from witnesses. For an example of state legislation related to eyewitness identification, see Box 4.1.

EYEWITNESS IDENTIFICATION SCHOLARSHIP

Eyewitness identification research has focused on two broad categories of factors that may contribute to eyewitness misidentification. These include system variables and estimator variables. *System variables* are those factors that can be controlled by the criminal legal system that relate to the accuracy of eyewitness identification; they include how the lineup is structured and administered, the way the investigator asks witnesses questions, and securing a confidence statement from a witness at the time of identification (Wells et al., 2020; Wilford & Wells, 2013). *Estimator variables*, on the other hand, are outside the control of the criminal legal system; they include factors about the incident, characteristics about the perpetrator, and characteristics about the eyewitness. As system variables are within the control of legal actors and criminal legal systems, research attention, as well as policy and procedure recommendations, have largely focused on system variables that can be manipulated or changed to increase eyewitness reliability (Wells et al., 1998, 2020). Experts in eyewitness identification acknowledge that "despite the fact that there are many powerful [system] variables that affect the reliability of eyewitness identification evidence" (Wells et al., 2020, p. 6), it is important that investigators note these factors because they can influence the quality of a witness's memory (Meissner et al., 2007) at each stage of the memory process.

THE STAGES OF MEMORY AND EYEWITNESS MISIDENTIFICATION

Cognitive psychologists have identified three stages in memory processing: encoding, storage, and retrieval. Errors in eyewitness memory can occur at any of these stages. The encoding process converts sensory material into information to be remembered. Our minds take data we bring in from our senses—for example, something we see—and encode it to our memory system as something we can remember. How well information is encoded into memory is impacted by the quality of our sensed material and the length of time we experienced the sensed material. After the information is encoded, the next stage is to store it in one of our memory systems: working memory, short-term memory, or long-term memory (Cowan, 2008). The most temporary memory storage system—working memory—holds brief information for immediate use only, such as limited information remembered while engaging in a short cognitive task such as math problems (Baddeley & Hitch, 1974; G. A. Miller et al., 1960). Short-term memory serves as a temporary storage system for information needed in the near future. It holds a limited amount of easily accessible data for specific, immediate purposes. For example, it might store a brief list of ingredients you mentally rehearse while heading to the grocery store (Cowan, 2008). As its name suggests, the long-term memory system—episodic memory—stores what we traditionally call our memories. These include our personal memories from our childhood—how our grandmother's cookies smelled or the name of our first cat—but also more recent personal memories such as the details of a crime incident or perpetrator. Once these are encoded and stored, the final stage in the memory process is retrieval, or accessing the encoded and stored information.

Generally, eyewitness memories are long-term episodic memories. To accurately describe an incident, a person must retrieve the long-term memory and then articulate it well to investigators. Because memory is a series of stages, problems at each stage may cumulate through each stage. Although theoretically limitless, long-term memory storage is impacted by how well the information was encoded into memory and whether the memory was encoded into a memory storage system that can be accessed. After all, it is impossible to store a correct memory if a correct memory was not encoded, and it is consequently impossible to retrieve and describe a correct memory. Even if an accurate memory was encoded and stored, memories are further impacted by postevent information, such as conversations with other witnesses, the news, or even how investigators interact with witnesses. Any inaccurate postevent information can contaminate memories and lead to the incorporation of inaccurate information into memory, known as the misinformation effect (Loftus, 1975).

For example, at the beginning of this chapter, you read about a woman who was either 84 or 44 years old. Relying on your memory without looking back in the chapter, identify the character who was described as 44—was it Betty or Emma? If you answered Emma, you responded similarly to many participants tested in research conditions—but your response is wrong. Emma was actually described as 34 years old in the opening paragraph of the chapter. The question introduced misinformation, and if the inaccurate age of 44 was what you retrieved when asked, then your behavior exhibited Loftus's (1975) misinformation effect. If we had not drawn your attention to misinformation planted in the question and if you were later asked to explain the chapter's opening example and you misremembered Emma's age as 44, then you would have experienced a memory retrieval error of false information.

OLDER ADULTS AND EYEWITNESS IDENTIFICATION

Older adults may be more likely to become victims or witnesses of certain types of crime. As discussed in Chapter 3, older adults can be victims of abuse, whether from caregiver maltreatment in nursing homes, through guardianship, or within informal care by a family member or friend. Older adults can be reluctant to report abuse (Snow et al., 2023), especially when the abusers are their caregivers (Mion & Momeyer, 2019). Studies examining statistics on the frequency of police interactions with older adults have found that interactions between older adults and police are common (Brown et al., 2014), with the most frequent interactions falling into the following categories: older adult victimization (Lachs et al., 2004), calls to nursing homes for resident assault (Lachs et al., 2007), noncriminal issues such as traffic or medical incidents (Liederbach & Stelle, 2010), and dementia-related behaviors such as wandering, suicidal threats, and needing help (Liljegren et al., 2018). As such, it is important that legal professionals and investigations understand older adults and the various reasons older adults may be involved in investigations.

A person's eyesight or hearing can impact how well they can acquire information, possibly impacting the encoding of memories (Fozard & Gordon-Salant, 2001). Older witnesses with poorer eyesight or auditory processing, therefore, may be less likely to gather necessary details from external stimuli to create a memory during encoding. The length of time between each stage may also differently affect older adult memory systems. For instance, eyewitness memory research has found that with longer intervals of time, older adults are less accurate in what they encode and retrieve, as compared with younger adults (Memon et al., 2004; J. H. Searcy et al., 2001). Research with older adults in a laboratory memory study indicated some losses in the ability to remember specific details of past episodes almost immediately after encountering them, but given the right retrieval cues in short-term memory, older adults can successfully remember some specific details of a recently encoded episode as well as younger adults can (N. R. Greene & Naveh-Benjamin, 2022).

Studies comparing the brains of older and younger adults during encoding and retrieval suggest age differences based on different brain activation in each group (Grady et al., 2005). Research has specifically observed age differences in cognitive tasks that require fast processing, working memory, or transforming information for decision making. So, although cumulative knowledge and experiential skills are maintained in advancing age memory, typical degeneration in the neurological system can cause deficits within each stage of memory (Murman, 2015). Different brain systems exhibit varying levels of neuronal loss, making complex cognitive representations (such as crime scenes) become more fragmented during retrieval (Fisk & Sharp, 2003), while simpler cognitive tasks such as recognizing a face in a spread of photographs result in greater accuracy because the task involves fewer cognitive resources (Yarmey, 2001).

Although memory loss is inevitable, declines in memory exhibited by differences between younger and older adults may be inflated by the methods used in research studies or in practice. To illustrate, studies relying on self-report measures of confidence in eyewitness studies have found that older adult participants were significantly less confident than were younger participants about their abilities, even when they were correct in the memory task (Parkin & Walter, 1992). Eyewitness procedures that require older adults to make quick decisions may produce more inaccurate results (Fisk & Sharp, 2003) because of declines in processing speed, working memory, or executive cognitive function (Murman, 2015). Environmental cues or societal messages that reinforce negative stereotypes about aging can influence older adults' performance as eyewitnesses. For example, a police officer's patronizing tone or oversimplified questions might trigger an older person's internalized belief that their memory is unreliable due to age. These cues, whether from the immediate interview setting or from past experiences, may lead older adults to question their own cognitive abilities, potentially affecting the accuracy and confidence of their eyewitness testimony (e.g., A. K. Thomas et al., 2020). See Box 4.2 for more discussion about techniques shown to be effective with older adults.

In 2020, the AP-LS, Division 41 of the American Psychological Association, updated the 1998 scientific recommendations developed through collaborative effort of six national experts in eyewitness identification evidence, AP-LS members, and the legal community (Wells et al., 2020). Although nearly 40 years of research was discussed, there was no mention of how legal systems and actors should accommodate and work with older adults. Importantly, the scientific recommendations in the paper were intentionally focused on system variables because they are procedures or methods that are within the control of legal systems, whereas estimator variables such as age of eyewitness are not within the control of the system. Although research on older adults is not

BOX 4.2 | **INVESTIGATIVE TECHNIQUES WITH OLDER ADULTS**

A blog post by Matthew Sharps, a psychology professor at California State University, Fresno, described his experience as an investigative psychologist applying psychology to the criminal investigation process. He described the speed of a criminal investigation and interview and how investigators could accommodate older adults:

> We tend to value speed in communication, especially in the time-sensitive context of a criminal investigation. Law enforcement interviews with eyewitnesses are often conducted in a rapid-fire manner that doesn't allow much leisure for contemplation.
>
> With the aged witness, this is exactly the wrong approach to take. The older witness should be interviewed in a comfortable environment, preferably one which offers minimum perceptual and cognitive distractions. The pace of the interview, contrary to the rapid communication preferences of many detectives and investigative psychologists (sadly, including myself) should be leisurely, with plenty of gaps between questions, and plenty of time for the older adult to frame and consider answers. (Sharps, 2021)

mentioned, the scientific recommendations do mention children. The scientific review paper noted that children are "particularly susceptible to suggestion" (Wells et al., 2020, p. 9; see also Ceci & Bruck, 1995) and referred to a "robust literature" on "effective, evidence-based protocols for interviewing children" (Wells et al., 2020, p. 9; see also La Rooy et al., 2015). In contrast, older adult eyewitnesses were not mentioned even though older adults have unique needs that, if accommodated, could make them more credible and reliable eyewitnesses.

SYSTEM AND ESTIMATOR VARIABLES

Differences in eyewitness memory accuracy for younger and older adults could be due to several factors, including cognitive declines in processing complex or novel stimuli due to aging (estimator), how investigators ask questions during interviews (system), whether the photo array has the actual offender present (system), the amount of time that has passed from the event to interview (estimator), or whether a weapon was present during the event (estimator). Older witnesses, either through typical or pathological cognitive change, differ from younger witnesses in how accurately they remember the events of a crime, but these differences appear only under specific conditions of eyewitness identification. Although witness age is itself an estimator variable, a better understanding of how aging affects eyewitness performance can lead to improved investigative practices that accommodate these differences through system factors. As such, most of the research attention with or about older eyewitnesses has been devoted to system variables and determining the ideal conditions for older eyewitnesses' memory and confidence using different types of eyewitness tasks.

Type of Memory Task

Studies comparing older and younger adults on eyewitness identification tasks have found that older adults are less accurate when tasks ask them to freely recall information without the help of additional contextual information (Coxon & Valentine, 1997) but may be just as accurate as younger adults when the eyewitness memory task involves recognition that includes additional contextual information for comparison (Bartlett & Memon, 2007; R. A. Wilcock et al., 2007). Consider a practical example: Imagine a person of authority asked you to tell them the names of all the capitals of the states in the United States, in alphabetical order—how many would you identify correctly? If instead you were given a list of capital cities and asked to match each one to its state, how many would you get right under those conditions, with contextual information to help structure your memory? Being asked to freely recall the U.S. capitals in alphabetical order is much like being asked to recite the details of a crime in chronological order and requires much more cognitive energy than does having multiple-choice options. Whereas photo arrays and lineups are recognition-based tasks in which the person is being asked to identify a person among several options, interview questions about specific details of an event or asking someone to "tell me everything, from the beginning, in order"—a common phrase used in cinematic investigation scenes—are recall-based tasks.

Target-Present and Target-Absent Lineups and Photo Arrays

In contrast to smaller differences in recognition tasks in which older and younger adults have been shown to correctly identify the alleged perpetrator (target) in a lineup task (termed a *hit*), older adults have a higher rate than do younger adults of falsely choosing a filler lineup person that the researchers know is not the suspect (termed a *foil*; Bartlett & Memon, 2007). In other words, when presented with a lineup of people or photographs, older adults are less likely to refrain from choosing an innocent suspect or foil (Valentine et al., 2003; R. Wilcock & Bull, 2014). Of course, when making an identification in a real crime, it is not known with certainty whether the actual suspect is present in the lineup or photo array. However, when using experimental eyewitness identification methods, researchers know the identity of the true "suspect," typically an actor in a live event or video, which allows for these age comparison studies.

Simultaneous or Sequential Lineups and Photo Arrays

Another factor impacting lineup or photo array performance is the way the photos are presented to the eyewitness. Historically, and likely in many jurisdictions still, law enforcement presents suspects simultaneously, with photographs lined up on a table or individuals standing side by side. This type of memory retrieval uses relative judgment, in which participants can make relative comparisons among suspects, and increases the likelihood of selecting a false positive suspect (i.e., foil). Adjusting this method to present the photos sequentially—one at a time—results in fewer false positive identifications (e.g., Steblay et al., 2001). Nevertheless, Erickson and colleagues' (2016) meta-analysis demonstrated that using a sequential lineup for older adults does not have the same beneficial effect. Recent research comparing sequential and simultaneous live lineups with children and older adults revealed several key findings. Both children and older adults with weaker facial recognition abilities showed an increased tendency to choose a suspect, demonstrating a choosing bias. The study also found that younger children and the oldest adults tended to select the first person presented in sequential lineups more often than they selected people in other positions, indicating a first position selection bias. On the basis of these results, the researchers advised caution when using sequential lineups with younger children or older adults (Nyman et al., 2020).

Duration and Distance

Eyewitnesses have no control over how long they will be exposed to the target when they are witnessing an actual crime, but memory research demonstrates that memory accuracy generally increases as exposure duration increases. One estimator variable that researchers consider when studying older adults is how the duration of exposure to a suspect affects their ability to make an accurate identification. Unsurprisingly, in light of what we know about the encoding process, both younger and older adult eyewitnesses who experience longer exposures to the target are more accurate in their identifications (Memon et al., 2003). Given known visual declines with age, studies have examined how distance affects eyewitness accuracy in older adults. Research shows that older adults are less accurate than are younger adults when identifying targets at greater distances (Nyman et al., 2019). In one study, older adults made more errors in estimating the perpetrator's gender when the target was farther away (Nyman et al., 2019).

Race and Age of the Witness and Suspect

One important demographic factor that interacts with age is the cross-race effect, also known as own-race bias. This well-established phenomenon, which shows that people are generally better at identifying individuals of their own race (Meissner & Brigham, 2001), is also present with older adults (Wylie, Bergt, et al., 2015). Likewise, some research has also demonstrated an own-age bias such that eyewitnesses are better at remembering people from their own age group (Rhodes & Anastasi, 2012), but a meta-analysis on the same topic determined that there does not seem to be an own-age bias for older adults (Erickson et al., 2016).

Presence of a Weapon

Another factor that occurs at the time of encoding is what has been called the weapons-focus effect (Loftus et al., 1987). Eyewitnesses are less likely to correctly identify a perpetrator if there was a weapon (or some other unusual object; see Pickel, 1998) because cognitive resources were attuned to the weapon (or other unusual object). Although the specific weapons-focus effect for older adults has not received much research attention, García-Bajos et al. (2012) examined low- versus high-typicality scripts and found that when the participants viewed a high-typical script, there were no differences between the older and younger participants. However, when the participants viewed the low-typicality script, the older adult participants had significantly worse recall of the events as compared with the younger adults, which suggests that the impact of the weapons-focus effect could be even stronger with older adults.

MISINFORMATION AND SOURCE MEMORY

As discussed earlier, eyewitnesses may receive intentionally or unintentionally inaccurate information, or misinformation, from other witnesses or investigators during or after an event. Decades of research have demonstrated that when a person receives misleading information, it can distort the memory of the original event so that during retrieval, the false memory is pulled from storage (Loftus et al., 1978). This misinformation effect is generally studied by exposing participants to an event, presenting them with some inaccurate information about the event that is intended to mislead about specific details, and tested for their memory of the original event. Research on age differences in the misinformation effect has found varying results, with some studies showing that older adults are more susceptible (e.g., Aizpurua et al., 2011; Karpel et al., 2001; Mueller-Johnson & Ceci, 2004; Roediger & Geraci, 2007), others showing no difference (e.g., Bornstein et al., 2000; Chan et al., 2009; Coxon & Valentine, 1997; Dodson & Krueger, 2006; Searcy et al., 2000), and some showing that younger adults are more susceptible (West & Stone, 2014).

Studies and meta-analyses have aimed to examine the potential theoretical and methodological reasons for these diverging effects. A stronger misinformation effect in older adults has been explained by declines in their ability to remember the source of information in memory (Aizpurua et al., 2011; Cohen & Faulkner, 1989; K. J. Mitchell et al., 2003). Retrieving the source of a memory requires individuals to retrieve the circumstances in which it was encoded, with specific details such as the time, spatial context, or task in which it was encountered (Stampacchia et al., 2019). Source monitoring refers to judgments about the source of the memory, less so about the content of it

(Johnson et al., 1993). Accordingly, because older adults have known challenges in identifying the source of memory, the misinformation effect may be more pronounced because they confuse the source of the event information with the source of the postevent information more often than do younger adults.

Others have sought to examine whether the conditions under which an event is coded may impact differences in how we encode as we age. For instance, Robin West, who studied the psychology of memory and aging at the University of Florida, and medical doctor Kevin Stone compared the misinformation effect in older and younger adult participants using a live event stimulus during which a confederate to the study interrupted the study session, and misinformation was embedded for half the sample during a cued recall task (West & Stone, 2014). To test whether age-group differences in the misinformation effect are due to learning strategies at encoding, the research study also varied whether participants were told to remember the interruption (i.e., intentional encoding) or not told anything about the interruption (i.e., incidental encoding). As in some other studies, older and younger adults made the same number of misinformation errors when they were intentionally told to remember the event—much like studies that tell participants to watch a video with a task to follow (Roediger & Geraci, 2007). Yet, when the groups were not told to remember the event, younger adults made more misinformation errors. The authors concluded that because of overall declines in the ability to recall information from the original event generally, older adults may be less prone than are younger adults to report false information at testing if they are not even encoding or retrieving the misinformation in the first place (West & Stone, 2014).

In illustrating the importance of defining "older adult" and not assuming homogeneity among older adults, we conducted a meta-analysis of 23 studies using misinformation methods comparing younger and older adults without cognitive decline (Wylie et al., 2014). The meta-analysis combined the statistical effects across all identified studies that identified an overall small to medium effect size for differences by age groups, concluding older adults were more susceptible to misinformation. Given that older and younger adults encode, store, and retrieve information differently, the meta-analysis examined several procedural moderating factors to test whether differences in study results were due to procedures that could affect memory systems; however, the only factor that explained differences across studies was the average age of the older adult sample—when the sample age was higher, the differences between older and younger adults were more pronounced. The nonsignificant procedural moderators included how the original event was presented (i.e., video, photograph, live event, or audio), how participants were misinformed (i.e., cued recall, narrative, photographs, confederate, or audio), timing from event to misinformation and then retrieval, and the types of memory that are tested during the study (i.e., free recall, cued recall, or recognition). Although none of the procedural moderating factors significantly explained differences, the meta-analysis was limited by the number of studies with diverse types of procedures.

At the time of the meta-analysis, only one published study (Mueller-Johnson & Ceci, 2004) had used a live event in their research. This scarcity of live event studies is significant because the nature of the event being witnessed could impact how older adults encode, store, and recall information as well as their ability to remember its source. Live events, as opposed to video recordings or written scenarios, may produce different effects on memory processes in older adults.

In summary, research shows clear differences between older and younger adults in their ability to recall versus recognize memories accurately. However, when it comes to the misinformation effect, meta-analysis found no significant age-related differences. This suggests that susceptibility to misinformation does not explain the memory differences observed between age groups.

ACCOMMODATING OLDER WITNESSES

Studies examining law enforcement perceptions indicate that most do not feel prepared to work with older adults. To achieve competence in this area, substantial additional training would be necessary (Snow et al., 2023; Wright & Holliday, 2005). Similarly, other legal professionals can expect to encounter older adults in various circumstances but lack official guidance on information gathering with older adults (Snow et al., 2023). Furthermore, there is a need for screening tools, training on the signs of abuse, and clear reporting procedures for professionals working with older adult witnesses (Gallione et al., 2017).

Research has identified ways to improve eyewitness accuracy and confidence. For example, one well-established finding is that investigators should tell eyewitnesses that the perpetrator may or may not be present in the lineup. This instruction has been shown to enhance the reliability of eyewitness identifications. When investigators do not say this, eyewitnesses are significantly more likely to choose someone, whether the perpetrator is present or not (Steblay, 1997). One study found that adding a "mystery man" (i.e., a silhouetted image) to a lineup resulted in older adults more successfully rejecting a target-absent lineup and had no impact on the target-present lineup. The researchers speculated that the mystery man lowers the expectation that the perpetrator will be present in the lineup in a more concrete and memorable way than only the investigator saying so (Havard et al., 2017).

Increasing Contextual Information

During interviewing, techniques may be used to increase the contextual information provided during questioning, such as cognitive interviewing techniques (e.g., Mello & Fisher, 1996), visually distinctive memory aids, and interviewing at a lower speed to allow time during retrieval (Fisk & Sharp, 2003). Holliday and colleagues (2012) demonstrated a positive impact for using the Modified Cognitive Interview (Holliday, 2003) with older adults, which is an enhancement of the traditional Cognitive Interview (CI; Geiselman et al., 1986), which focuses on the eyewitness mentally recreating the environment at the time of the witnessed event. Holliday and colleagues' enhancement focuses on having the eyewitness reporting all remembered details regardless of their potential relevance, which can alleviate older adults' internalized ageism about memory performance. However, studies comparing the CI with children and older adults suggested that across multiple retrieval stages of the CI, the final retrieval stage is much less effective for older adults relative to younger adults at eliciting prior unreported information; therefore, investigators have much less to gain from older adults than they do from younger adults with repeated inquiries (during the same session) of a witnessed event (Dodson et al., 2015).

Another potentially positive intervention for older adults is the Self-Administered Interview, which is fully self-administered and was developed for immediate harvesting of episodic information and therefore is likely to avoid demand characteristics that could be present with the CI (Gawrylowicz et al., 2014). Additionally, research has found promising impact for the Self-Administered Interview with a Sketch Reinstatement of Context (Dando et al., 2020). Wilcock and Bull (2014) suggested that future research on older adult eyewitnesses should focus on how to enhance their abilities given what is known about the developmental deficits.

Legal and Procedural Rules

Legal scholars have also argued that adversarial trials, which are structured on the assumption that in-person cross-examination is the most revered type of evidence, may disproportionally exclude older adults from providing eyewitness testimony (Love, 2015, 2019). Physical and cognitive problems produce risk in a witness's ability to provide reliable and credible evidence at trial, including attrition prior to trial (e.g., death or progressive illness), declines in abilities in memory discussed above, mobility issues in accessing courts, or limitations in communication that present as impairments to credibility while testifying even if competent (e.g., speech issues following stroke). Witnesses are questioned and then cross-examined by the other attorney or party (if representing themselves) using an oral presentation, and any statements made outside of court (hearsay evidence) are presumptively nonadmissible. Witness credibility is dependent on the judge's assessment of testimonial factors—that is, the witness's ability to observe, recall, and recount the event in the courtroom. Any physical and cognitive problems present are likely to influence these factors. To accommodate older adults as witnesses, trials can be expedited; pretrial testimony can be preserved; testimony can be provided from outside of the courtroom using remote or televised hearings; other evidence can assist with in-court testimony; and a principled approach to hearsay, in which statements can be entered if *sufficiently necessary and reliable*, can meet the needs of witnesses who are no longer able to testify (Love, 2015, 2019).

AGING BIASES AND EYEWITNESS MEMORY

All memory stages—encoding, storing, and retrieving—can impact eyewitness identification and confidence. So too, the natural aging process comes with changes in sensory perception and attention, memory, and processing speed (Murman, 2015). Likewise, all stages of memory are impacted by typical and pathological aging symptoms. Although it is well understood that aging is associated with loss of memory, generally, the conditions under which memory loss occurs and for whom are complex and can occur at any stage of the memory process. Before we describe the biological factors that can contribute to age-related performance on eyewitness-memory-related tasks, it is important to draw attention to social–psychological factors in aging biases and their contributory role in eyewitness memory accuracy and confidence.

If a young parent loses their car keys, others will likely assume an external reason for losing their keys, such as a lack of sleep or distraction. Alternatively, if an older grandparent loses their car keys, others are more likely to assume that they lost their keys because of memory loss or dementia. Research has demonstrated this attributional double standard, even though the research landscape on memory and aging is more complicated and nuanced than our aging stereotypes and attitudes may suggest. For example, it is well documented that memory fades with time, but societally we also hold certain biased stereotypes about older adults. One prominent such stereotype is that older adults have poor memories. Research has shown that older adults are often perceived according to negative stereotypes (Cuddy et al., 2005) about their cognitive and memory abilities (Hertzog et al., 1999; Kite & Johnson, 1988; B. Levy, 2009). When a young person shows a lapse in memory, the behavior is attributed to a lack of effort or attention with an explainable external reason. In contrast, when an older adult shows a lapse in memory, it is attributed to a decline in internal systems such as memory or a lack of competence (Erber, 1989; Erber et al., 1992, 1993).

Perceptions of Older Adult Eyewitnesses

Under Rule 601 (1975) of the Federal Rules of Evidence, all witnesses are presumed competent to be a witness, there are no specified "mental qualifications," and lack of capacity is seldom sufficient to deny a witness the opportunity to provide testimony. This was not always the law; prior to Congress adopting these rules in 1975, some states had statutes that *per se* made some categorical groups incompetent to testify based on age, mental capacity, and other factors. The rules abolished the restrictions in criminal law but allowed states to adopt their own standards in civil cases. In criminal cases, whereas the judge determines the witness's competence to testify—that is, whether they can give an oath of truthfulness and whether they can give an accurate account—the factfinder (jury or judge) assesses the witness during testimony to make determinations of their credibility and the credibility of their testimony

(American Bar Association Commission on Law and Aging & American Psychological Association, 2021). Both competency determinations and credibility assessments can be influenced by aging biases.

As discussed in previous chapters, older adults are often perceived according to "warm" and "incompetent" stereotypes and pity-motivated overhelping behavior (Cuddy & Fiske, 2002). How could these beliefs and attitudes contribute to law enforcement or attorneys' trust of older adults' eyewitness identification in an investigation or trial? Just as research on the perceptions of older adult victims is scarce, so is research on perceptions of older adult eyewitnesses and how they affect relevant case outcomes. It does seem clear that the older adult stereotypes described in a preceding section influence how people view older eyewitnesses. In general, an older eyewitness as compared with a younger one is seen as less accurate, similar to the "incompetent" stereotype; however, the older eyewitness can also be perceived as more honest or trustworthy, similar to the "warm" stereotype (Kwong See et al., 2001; Mueller-Johnson et al., 2007; Ross et al., 1990).

Wright and Holliday (2005) surveyed police officers in the United Kingdom to examine their perceptions of older witnesses. Survey results revealed that more than half believed older witnesses were less reliable and thorough than were younger witnesses. Studies using mock jurors have similarly found that older adult eyewitnesses are perceived as less credible (e.g., Brimacombe et al., 1997), resulting in fewer guilty verdicts, especially the more stereotypically old the eyewitnesses appear (Nunez et al., 1999). More recent research with Japanese participants suggests that it may not be age that influences perceptions of credibility but rather the content of the testimony and whether it appears consistent (Iida & Itsukushima, 2021). Furthermore, studies have found that in addition to age, other demographic factors such as accent, class status, and race interact with the credibility perceptions of eyewitnesses (Frumkin & Stone, 2020).

Negative Aging Stereotype Activation and Memory

Not only could these stereotypes affect perceivers such as police officers or jury members, but they also may affect memory performance for older adults themselves. A meta-analysis examining 32 studies and 82 effect sizes revealed a small to medium impact of age-based stereotype threat on older adults' performance (Lamont et al., 2015). The analysis found that stereotype-based stimuli caused stronger performance declines than did fact-based stimuli when used to activate stereotypes. The effect was most pronounced when cognitive performance was tested. Additionally, the impact was greatest when outcomes were measured shortly after stereotype activation. These findings highlight how age-related stereotypes can significantly influence older adults' cognitive performance in testing situations. Basic science research has employed social cognition experimental laboratory methods, in which stereotypes are activated using priming methods such as words (e.g., Hess et al., 2004), and stereotype threat literature (Steele, 2010), in which stereotypes are activated using stereotype-relevant tasks that make the stereotype salient (e.g., S. J. Barber et al., 2019). In these studies, older adults' performance on memory tasks declined following conditions presumed to activate negative stereotypes about aging. Inversely, others have found that older adults' susceptibility to false memories in a word recall paradigm decreased when negative aging stereotypes associated were de-emphasized (A. K. Thomas & Dubois, 2011). Several explanations for these effects have been given. Some research has found connections between poor performance and biological measures related to anxiety such as skin conductance, blood pressure, and heart rate (B. R. Levy et al., 2000), and others have found personality differences such as the self-relevance of the stereotypes to participants (O'Brien & Hummert, 2006).

The effects of age-based stereotypes on behavior are not consistent across all studies. Their impact depends on how aging stereotypes are presented and how memory is tested. A meta-analysis revealed that stereotype threat effects were significant only under specific conditions (Armstrong et al., 2017). These effects appeared when the method of activating stereotypes matched the type of memory being tested. For example, blatant statements about older adults' poor memory performance affected episodic memory tasks. In contrast, subtle manipulations, such as testing older adults alongside younger ones, influenced working memory tasks. The analysis also found that stereotype threat significantly affected free recall but not cued recall or recognition tasks. Additionally, these effects were observed only when memory was tested immediately after stereotype activation.

Other research has sought to test the behavioral effects of negative aging stereotypes using laboratory settings and complex events and eyewitness memory paradigms. In these studies, older and younger participants watched a video that depicted a crime, had some kind of presentation of misinformation (e.g., in the synopsis or in cued recall questions), and then tested their ability to accurately remember the information from the video (actual crime scene) and reject the misleading information presented to them after the video (Henkel, 2014; A. K. Thomas et al., 2020; Wylie, Brank, et al., 2015). The studies, however, varied in how they activated aging stereotypes in the experimental condition, each aiming to more realistically simulate an actual eyewitness situation for activating negative aging stereotypes and test memory using typical eyewitness memory paradigm tasks, such as accuracy, confidence, and susceptibility to misinformation.

One study that we conducted examined eyewitness instructions by a confederate actor law enforcement investigator (a modifiable system variable; Wylie, Brank, et al., 2015). The study manipulations aimed to activate aging stereotypes at retrieval through a well-known phenomenon called "elderspeak" whereby individuals of all ages speak to older adults in speech similar to baby talk (Ryan et al., 1986). Another study activated aging stereotypes through feedback after participants' memory was first tested after the video, regardless of actual accuracy, with specific negative feedback about their memory performance, general information that most people their age did poorly on the memory test (stereotype threat), or simple requests to answer the questions again (Henkel, 2014). Two additional studies used the same short 300-word fabricated research articles about memory declining with age (high threat) or memory not declining with age (low threat) to activate each condition (A. K. Thomas et al., 2020; A. K. Thomas & Dubois, 2011). Even though older adults demonstrated less accuracy on general recall, under more controlled processes at retrieval, the stereotype activation condition did not contribute to declines in accuracy and susceptibility to misinformation (A. K. Thomas et al., 2020; Wylie, Brank, et al., 2015). The findings from Wylie and colleagues (Wylie, Brank, et al., 2015) suggested that a subtle manipulation such as using patronizing language in episodic memory may not produce stereotype threat effects for all participants; however, participants who perceived and believed they would be subjected to age discrimination were more suggestible.

Various conclusions have been proffered to explain these findings. It may be that when negative stereotypes are activated prior to retrieval, older adults may approach a memory test in a more cautious manner or use more strategies for memory than when threat is not activated (A. K. Thomas et al., 2020) or when they experienced increased vigilance toward errors and signs of failures under stereotype threat (Mazerolle et al., 2021). It is possible that older adults in these studies may not internalize the general feedback that people of their age group tended to do poorly in the stereotype threat condition (Henkel, 2014). Alternatively, as Armstrong and colleagues' (2017) meta-analyses revealed, as eyewitness memory is in the long-term episodic memory system, blatant stimuli may be best to affect that type of memory, given that studies using more basic science methods that are testing working memory are producing more robust effects.

CONCLUSION

The scientific findings for eyewitness memory and investigation techniques are some of the most well-developed areas of research within the discipline of psychology and law, generating two scientific review papers with recommendations based on scientific evidence dating back to the 1970s (Wells et al., 1998, 2020); however, only a small proportion of that research has involved older adults. Although this area of psychology and law research is more inclusive of older adults than are other areas in that field (Wylie, Hazen, et al., 2018), compared with the breadth of research on eyewitness interviewing techniques generally, or with children (Wells et al., 2020), there has been comparatively less research attention on interviewing older adults as witnesses (Snow et al., 2023). Although Bartlett and Memon (2007) declared that "research on the older eyewitness is in its infancy" (p. 311), just recently Snow and colleagues (2023) indicated that while "several dozen" papers on aging memory capabilities were produced in 15 years, "research on topics like motivations for disclosure and police training needs are minimal" (p. 2) and has not yet matured.

Given the demographic shifts we discussed throughout previous chapters and the increased attention on older adults as victims we described in Chapter 3, it is concerning that professionals know so little about how to work with older eyewitnesses relative to general procedures. Even though law-psychology has contributed so much to the scientific recommendations for handling eyewitness evidence, studying older eyewitnesses may not be as legally meaningful. Perhaps this is due to the assumption that the most reliable evidence comes in the form of in-person cross-examination of witnesses; nonetheless, many assume that older adults are less credible witnesses, which limits practical reasons to study older adults as witnesses. Alternatively, legal scholars have proffered that attorneys do not want to rely on an eyewitness who may not be healthy enough or live long enough to testify at trial, and the rules of evidence and procedure (e.g., hearsay rules, adversarial testimony) inadvertently exclude older adult testimony (Love, 2019). Older adults may also be understudied in eyewitness memory research because the types of crimes older adults witness do not generally receive much attention from legal systems (e.g., abuse or neglect, petty theft), and practically (reflecting our own experience) recruiting older adults for social–cognitive laboratory studies is methodologically challenging (see Chapter 10).

Normative and pathological aging processes contribute to declines in the abilities that are associated with eyewitness memory and testimony. However, as discussed in this chapter, older adults do not always show differences in tasks based on memory and recall, and the behavior of the legal professionals could contribute to stereotype-confirming behavior for older adults. Researchers have found that legal responses to older eyewitnesses that modify traditional investigative techniques have successfully minimized age-related differences between older and younger adults. When legal responses are modified for older adults, especially those perceived as accommodating stereotypical age-based incapacities, such responses may further perpetuate interpersonal ageism between investigators and the older adult, impacting older eyewitnesses' performance on tasks presumed to be challenging for them.

5

Older Adults as Perpetrators of Crime

In 2011, at age 80, Doris Payne was found guilty of two counts of theft and sentenced to 5 years behind bars for stealing jewelry from a department store. She was released 3 years later because of prison overcrowding and has since been arrested multiple times for pilfering jewelry, including in 2013 when she lifted a 12-carat white gold ring worth $22,000 from a boutique in Palm Desert, California. Nicknamed the "Granny Gem Thief" and "Diamond Doris," Doris Payne has made headlines as a career international jewel thief. Payne's life is the subject of the documentary *The Life and Crimes of Doris Payne* (Marcolina & Pond, 2013), which depicts 7 decades of a catch-me-if-you-can criminal career that included 32 aliases, millions of dollars' worth of stolen articles, and time in jails and prisons (Rasmussen, n.d.). In addition to her age and lengthy criminal career, Payne's motive, demeanor, and methods for stealing fueled her infamy. As the daughter of a poor coal miner in racially segregated West Virginia and a nurse, Payne explained she stole millions of dollars' worth of merchandise across the world to uplift her position in life and help her mother (D. Payne, 2019). She was described as charming and attractive, and her perceived trustworthiness facilitated her thefts (Marcolina & Pond, 2013). In her memoir, Payne stated that she was exceptionally proud of being the opposite of what is expected (D. Payne, 2019).

One reason that Doris Payne's story is of interest is because her behavior does not match what we expect for her age; we infrequently associate aging with criminal behavior. In nearly every article written about the story, Payne's

https://doi.org/10.1037/0000469-006
Aging and the Criminal Legal System: Community Services, Courts, Corrections, and Policy, by L. E. Wylie and E. M. Brank

age is either in the headline or one of the first facts mentioned in the opening sentence. As illustrated in the Introduction (this volume), older adults are generally perceived as "warm, but incompetent," with an inverse relationship between the two. An older adult who is perceived as more likable is often perceived as less competent, and conversely, an older adult who is perceived as more competent will typically be perceived as less likable (Cuddy et al., 2005). Despite her intersectional challenges as a Black woman, Payne's pleasant demeanor likely influenced perceptions of her criminal aptitude and reform potential.

This chapter is the first of several that focus on older adults as system-involved individuals and the criminal legal system responses to them. First, we introduce well-established criminological theory of age and crime, noting that older age is one of the strongest predictors of reduced criminal behavior. Then, we describe statistics on the rates of crime for older adults, including longitudinal research aimed at predicting whether there is evidence of geriatric crime waves. Although older adults are generally responsible for just a small proportion of offenses as the age–crime curve predicts, it is important to examine the underlying explanations for why some older adults do engage in anti-social or criminal behavior. We focus on explanations for older adults engaging in criminal behavior, summarizing available research on social lifespan issues, mental health and substance use, and neurobiological deficits. Next, we discuss the types of offenses that older adults most often bring to the attention of the criminal legal system. Even though they are more likely to be arrested for minor and substance-related crimes than for serious ones, we also describe research that has focused on older adults and serious crime—homicide and sex offenses. Addressing an emerging area, the final section explores gun ownership among older adults, illustrating some of the concerns with diminished capacity, firearms, and unfortunate shootings by individuals with dementia-related disorders.

Although a geriatric crime wave remains unfounded, legal concerns about dementia underscore the need to study older adults in early criminal justice processes (American Bar Association [ABA] Commission on Law and Aging, 2022). As discussed in this chapter, there are no legal responses with *per se* categorizations wherein older adults are treated preferentially; any adult aged 18 and older will enter the same adult system. For instance, there is not a separate elder legal system that begins at a specific age and treats older adults distinctly (see Chapter 1), but as discussed in other chapters, older adults may be provided leniency by law enforcement or judges based on their perceived age, on a case-by-case basis (see Chapter 6).

THE AGE–CRIME RELATIONSHIP

Theory in criminology shows that age is a strong predictor of criminal behavior. The age–crime curve illustrates that the prevalence of criminal behavior peaks in the teenage years, declines quickly, and then decreases more gradually as individuals get older (Farrington, 1986; Hirschi & Gottfredson, 1993). According to the initial theory formed by Hirschi and Gottfredson (1983), the age–crime curve is universal and applies to all demographic and socioeconomic categories and across all offenses. In part because of this peak, most developmental lifespan research has focused on age and criminality in juveniles and younger to middle-aged adults who are the perpetrators of most violent and nonviolent crime. In this chapter and several that follow, we bring attention to issues that ensue when older adults are the perpetrators of crime. Although statistics show that the proportion of older adults committing crimes has not dramatically increased, administrative data reveal dramatic growth in the number of older adults in state and federal prisons (see Chapters 8 and 9). Contrary to earlier age–crime curve research, the precise age at which crime peaks depends on a variety of characteristics and conditions and does vary by type of offense (e.g., Fagan & Western, 2005). Despite its infrequency, studying criminal behavior in older adults is warranted because there are unique explanations and risk factors for why older adults engage in criminal behavior. With known differences in the reasons for criminal behavior and desistance due to age, there may be sufficient rationale for legal responses to be modified for older perpetrators.

In the book *When Crime Waves*, the author Vincent Sacco (2005) visually described a wave, shown in Figure 5.1, and suggested that a hypothetical crime wave has a rise, a peak, and a decline. He described the movement of the wave as natural, with crime rates increasing and decreasing over time, often with no explanation other than public rhetoric on the social problem the crime wave is targeting. He argued that crime waves are social constructs that get labeled, not to any particular acts or people but instead to social episodes. Sacco argued that although crime rates do fluctuate, crime waves are often manufactured

FIGURE 5.1. Standard Crime Wave

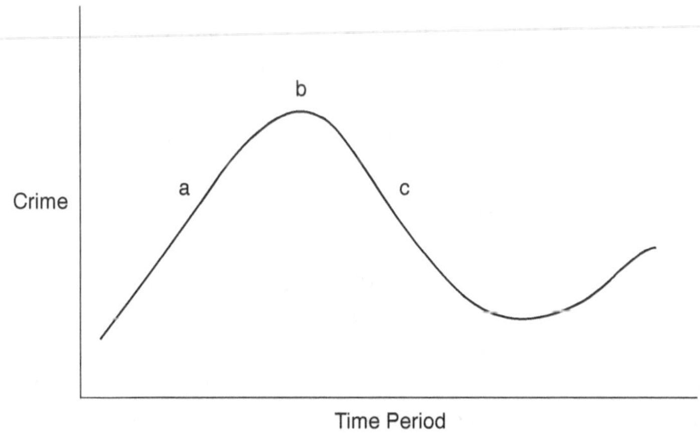

Note. From *When Crime Waves* (p. 15), by V. Sacco, 2005, Sage Publications (https://doi.org/10.4135/9781483328799). Copyright 2005 by Sage Publications. Reprinted with permission.

by those who benefit from the resulting public concern and reactions. As Sacco (2005) contended, "There is a crime wave when there exist widely shared perceptions that a crime wave is under way" (p. 9). A familiar example took place in the 1990s with juveniles and the label "super predator" (Kapler, 1996). During the same period, punitive criminal justice policies were enacted nationwide (see Chapter 6 subsection entitled Issues in Sentencing) and toward juveniles. When crime waves are announced, Sacco encouraged asking "Who benefits from the wave?" whether the benefit is actual or perceived.

In the 1970s and 1980s, theories emerged predicting a geriatric crime wave post-2000, based on projected Baby Boomer population growth (Bachand, 1984; Shichor, 1985). In the early 2000s at the predicted time, media reported a rise in serious and violent crime committed by older adults (e.g., Evans, 1998; Feldmeyer & Steffensmeier, 2007; Marquart et al., 2000) based on data incorrectly analyzed by researchers. Although typically the stereotype of the aging offender is a needy, isolated shoplifter (Sacco, 2005), the prediction of a geriatric crime wave aimed to present a tougher aging offender and conjure rhetoric that older adults were committing more serious crimes (Steffensmeier & Harer, 1987). Media portrayals were incorrectly based on gross national arrest figures; however, once statisticians applied age-standardization methods to arrest count data (to account for population growth in each age group), the so-called geriatric crime wave was dismissed. More specifically, criminology and life-course researchers indicated little change in the rate in both violent and nonviolent crime committed by older adults from 1980 to 2004 (Feldmeyer & Steffensmeier, 2007).

SEQUENTIAL INTERCEPT MODEL

Criminal legal system involvement can be conceptualized using the sequential intercept model (SIM); see Figure 5.2. Initially the SIM was designed to illustrate how people move through each system point to show opportunities for more therapeutic interventions, including prearrest crisis services, multiple points for diverting out of the legal system, and court programs such as specialty courts or connection to other services (Munetz & Griffin, 2006). Since its development, the SIM has become a community planning tool with which researchers assist jurisdictions to map their current practices, policies, and available resources to the needs of system-involved individuals with behavioral health needs in the community to identify gaps and required modifications (Substance Abuse and Mental Health Services Administration [SAMHSA], 2024). As with any group interacting with the legal system with mental health and substance use needs, older adults as a subpopulation will encounter any of the six intercepts (0 through 5) that are depicted (ABA Commission on Law and Aging, 2022).

Although some have speculated that older adults are likely diverted at Intercept 0 (crisis services) or 1 (law enforcement), data are limited for individuals

FIGURE 5.2. Sequential Intercept Model

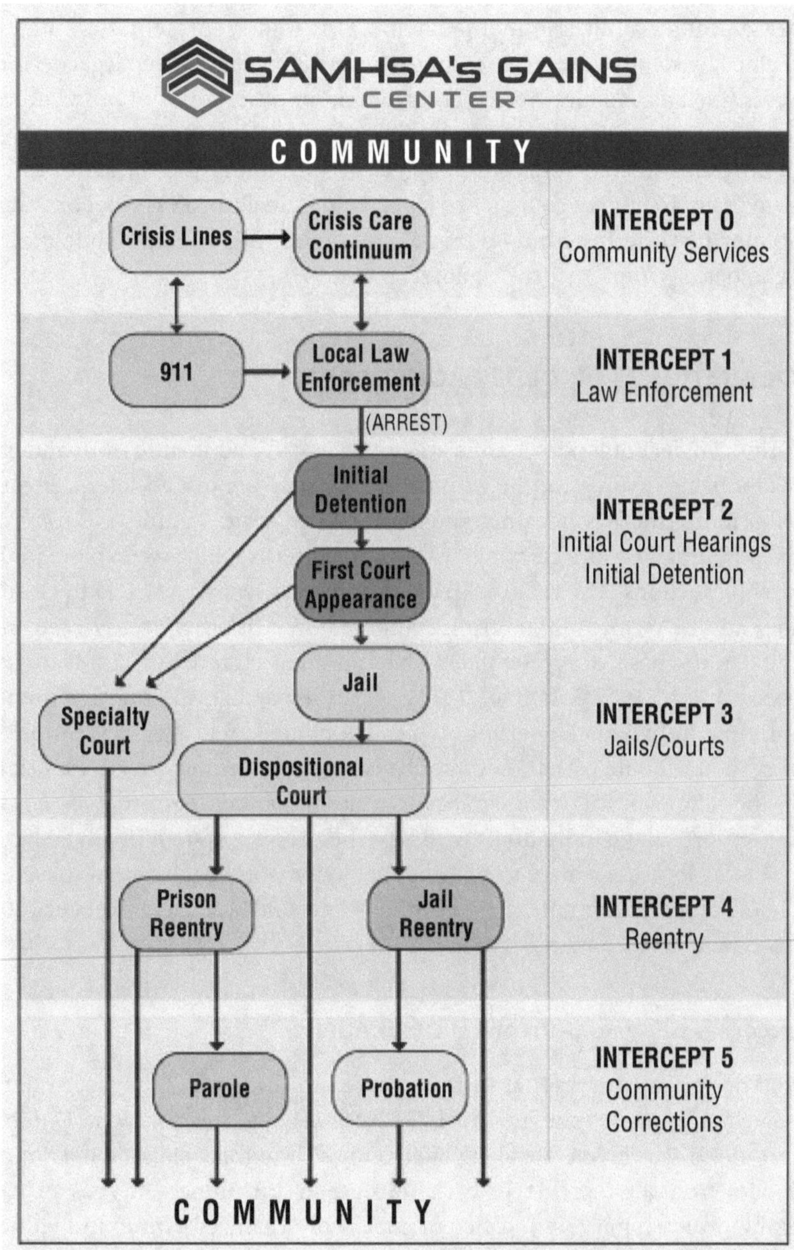

Note. From *The Sequential Intercept Model (SIM)*, by the Substance Abuse and Mental Health Services Administration, 2024 (https://www.samhsa.gov/communities/criminal-juvenile-justice/sequential-intercept-model). In the public domain.

in contact with early-system points, making it challenging to identify opportunity for intervention or diversion to more appropriate placements (ABA Commission on Law and Aging, 2022). This also means that reports on trends in older adult crime may use statistics based on official reports that may underrepresent older adult criminal behavior. This underrepresentation may be explained by some of the legal responses by law enforcement and legal decision makers, such as leniency by law enforcement or other forms of prosecutorial discretion (Cutshall & Adams, 1983), diversion for older offenders (e.g., diversion programs, therapeutic courts such as driving-under-the-influence courts and veterans' treatment courts), and inability to formally process older offenders who may be suffering from issues of competency due to neurobiological or psychological symptoms (see Chapters 6 and 7).

EXPLANATIONS FOR OLDER ADULT CRIMES

Clearly, all older adult perpetrators are not the same, and their reasons and patterns for being involved in the criminal legal system are just as heterogeneous. Furthermore, there is not one type of offense that older adults are committing, although there are certainly trends and patterns which we explore in the following sections. The criminal legal system uses its own criteria to classify "older adults," which differs from standards used in other areas of law and aging. On the basis of accelerated aging and other cumulative disadvantages (Forde et al., 2019; LaVeist et al., 2011), expert researchers in aging and mental health in criminal justice settings typically define people aged 50 or more as older. The rationale is that older adults who are system involved, especially over their lifespan, will have significant health disparities (Parrott et al., 2019). Furthermore, aging individuals who have been or are system involved likely experience legal responses to criminal behavior from legal systems based in intersectional discrimination as "criminal" and "old" (Angus & Reeve, 2006; Crenshaw, 1989; Holman & Walker, 2021).

Typologies of System-Involved Older Adults

Based on length of criminal history, there are three typologies of system-involved older adults: the *inveterate*, the *relapsing*, and the *first timer* (Fattah & Sacco, 1989). The inveterate aging offender has chronically engaged in criminal behavior from adolescence or early adulthood, including subtypes such as lifelong professional criminals or members of organized crime, individuals chronically homeless and/or using substances, habitual misdemeanants, individuals with antisocial personality disorder, or chronic sex offenders. The next type is the relapsing older offender, which includes older adults who were thought to have been rehabilitated but who relapse into crime after a long period of successful adjustment and staying crime-free—possibly triggered by some life crisis or changes brought about by old age. A relapsing offender may be monomorphic, engaging in similar crime later in life, or polymorphic, engaging in different types of crime later in life. The third type, the first timer, is the most atypical and is characterized by having no prior delinquency or criminal history. The first timer may become criminally involved because of psychiatric or behavioral changes caused by atypical or pathological aging (i.e., loss of judgment, inhibitions, or sudden mistrust), dementia symptoms, drug or alcohol abuse, personality changes from aging, or environmental changes (i.e., placement in assisted living or nursing home).

Social Lifespan Issues

Although there is a breadth of research on the age–crime curve (Hirschi & Gottfredson, 1993) and onset of criminal behavior, which typically occurs in early adolescence, life-course criminologists have noted that less is known about why some people desist and no longer engage in criminal behavior, whereas others persist with criminal behavior over their life course (Sampson & Laub, 2003). Life-course criminology researchers Sampson and Laub (2003) studied 500 system-impacted boys and men ranging from age 7 to age 70, seeking to identify whether there were characteristics (e.g., individual differences, childhood characteristics, family background) that could predict whose delinquent behavior would continue as they aged and whether there is a distinct group whose crime rates remain stable even as they age. In sum, this seminal longitudinal research found no distinct groups or pattern of factors that predicted a stable crime rate over one's life but instead that "desistance processes are at work" (Sampson & Laub, 2003, p. 301) even among those who engage in criminal behavior into adulthood. In other words, almost everyone stops committing crimes at some point in their lives.

Older adults do not necessarily have the same motivation, opportunity, or ability to commit some types of crime as do their younger counterparts. With age, there is a decline in physical strength and energy as well as psychological drive. For older adults, therefore, it may be that even if they have the motivation to commit the crime, they may not have the opportunity or ability to do so. This likely explains why property offenses, such as shoplifting and minor theft (Kratcoski & Edelbacher, 2016), as well as drug or alcohol-related offenses (Butts, 2019; Feldmeyer & Steffensmeier, 2007) are the most frequent crimes committed by older adults. They are crimes that older adults still can commit. Low-level property offenses are typically motivated by financial need, are most likely committed during the day, and require little physical ability. Lifestyle adaptations that accompany increased age mean that older adults encounter fewer opportunities for engaging in crime. Unlike young adults, aging adults are not typically in situations that are high crime risks, such as spending time with a group using drugs or alcohol late at night. As more cognitively matured adults, older adults may be deterred by legal sanctions, as they more fully appreciate that time is a diminishing, exhaustible, and increasingly valuable resource (Shover, 1996; Steffensmeier & Allan, 2000; Tittle & Paternoster, 2000).

Aspirations and goals also change as adults age. Whereas younger people may engage in crime for status within a group, older adults are less likely to strive for material fulfillment or recognition. The major sources of reinforcement for criminal behavior (e.g., desire for money, sex, or status; resentment; antisocial peer pressure) are absent or relatively weaker for older adults (Ulmer & Steffensmeier, 2014).

Mental Health and Substance Use

As described in the Introduction (this volume), the behavioral health of older adults in the criminal legal system is an "area of major concern for researchers, practitioners, policymakers, and advocates" (Maschi, Sutfin, & O'Connell, 2012, p. 163). Although data suggest that as many as half of adults aged 50 and older in prison are diagnosed with some type of mental health issue, including serious mental illnesses, such as major depression, schizophrenia, and/or dementia-related disorders (James & Glaze, 2006), there is a shortage of research detailing criminal legal system responses and associated experiences of adults aged 50 and older. In a systematic review of studies published between 1988 and 2012, 31 studies were published on aging and mental health in the criminal legal system. Of those, most were conducted in secure prison care settings ($n = 16$) or a forensic psychiatric hospital or forensic psychiatric units ($n = 8$). Of the 31 studies, the most widespread diagnoses were schizophrenia, major depressive disorder, dementia, and substance use disorder. Consequently, very little is known about the mental health issues of older adults involved in early and later legal system points (Maschi, Sutfin, & O'Connell, 2012; Parrott et al., 2019) depicted by the SIM—including at the point of arrest (Intercept 1), pretrial detention (Intercept 2), court processing (Intercept 3), probation, and parole or community supervision (Intercepts 4 and 5).

Alcohol and substance use can also contribute to antisocial or criminal behaviors, especially for those who already have neurobiological or other mental health problems. For instance, Kratcoski (1990) found that 44% of older adults who committed homicide (and 40% of the victims) were under the influence of alcohol—not acute intoxication, but behavior caused by cerebral damage from alcohol abuse. Yarnell and colleagues (2020) indicated that older adults are using illicit drugs and meeting the diagnostic criteria for substance use disorders (SUDs) at a higher rate than are previous geriatric cohorts. When data are available, they are often limited by prevalence of mental health issues or SUDs, with little published research on treatment or treatment outcomes (Parrott et al., 2019). According to the Survey of Inmates in Local Jails, last administered in 2002, the rate of using substances significantly differed by age group in the jail sample. Individuals aged 25 to 44 had the highest rate of SUDs (7 in 10), and individuals aged 55 or older had the lowest rate, which was still 5 in 10 individuals who are detained (Karberg & James, 2005).

There are two patterns of aging substance abusers: early-onset, those with a history of substance abuse who continue into old age, and late-onset, those who develop substance abuse habits as older adults (Roe et al., 2010). Early-onset illegal substance use is a complex phenomenon, with ample research discussing the etiology of early substance abuse from genetics, adverse childhood experiences, social pressures from peers, and so on. The factors that contribute to sustaining substance use into older adulthood are less well-understood, but researchers hypothesize that positive outcomes for reducing substance use in later adulthood include effective treatment and family support, whereas negative predictors include crime involvement, social pressure, availability of substances, or comorbid psychiatric disorders (Ruiz et al., 2007; M. H. Taylor & Grossberg, 2012). Late-onset illegal substance use is less common and accounts for less than 10% of older substance users as compared with early-onset illegal substance use (Wu & Blazer, 2011). Some associated factors include medical factors such as physical ailments, self-medication, and the development of psychiatric disorders (e.g., depression, anxiety, dementia and other cognitive impairments), and social factors similar to those of younger adults, such as grief, social isolation, financial problems, and poor support systems (Ghantous et al., 2022; M. H. Taylor & Grossberg, 2012).

Neurobiological Deficits

Research has long sought to understand biological factors that contribute to criminal behavior (e.g., Cipriani et al., 2016). An early publication by Cesare Lombroso (1876/2006) identified physical abnormalities of those "born criminal" (see Knepper & Ystehede, 2012), and later work by Raine pointed to the structural and metabolic changes in the frontal lobes and other brain structures of those who commit murder (Raine, 2002; Yang & Raine, 2009). A body of research demonstrates that complications with certain parts of the brain, specifically the limbic system (i.e., the amygdala) and temporal lobes, contribute to poor emotion regulation and potential subsequent violent behavior (Delgado, 1982; Mark & Ervin, 1970). For instance, people with traumatic brain injury to the frontal lobe tend to show more aggressive and violent behavior than do those with nonfrontal lobe head injuries or no head injury (Grafman et al., 1996). Similarly, patients with dementia symptoms who have frontal predominance often react impulsively to environmental cues and may be physically aggressive as a result of misperceptions and delusions (Mendez et al., 2011). Nevertheless, more is known about antisocial behavior caused by acute neurobiological predictors, such as strokes and head injuries, and much less is known about the role of dementia-related disorders in antisocial behavior (Mendez et al., 2011).

As our population increases and the awareness of cognitive impairment among older adults increases, multiple issues related to the interface between persons with dementia-related disorders and the criminal legal system need to be addressed. Medical ethics scholars argue that current criminal legal system responses fail to address the challenges that criminal law and criminal procedure are facing, which can lead to unconstitutional and inappropriate detention and incarceration (Arias & Flicker, 2020). Comprehension of the role of dementia in the legal system is in its infancy, and national organizations are just starting to explore how individuals with neurobiological deficits and the legal system interact. The ABA published a report in 2022 identifying the limitations of the criminal legal system's response to age-related brain changes in prosecution or the correctional system (ABA Commission on Law and Aging, 2022). Following the ABA report, a year later in February 2023 the ABA passed a resolution urging

> all federal, state, local, territorial, and tribal legislative bodies, as well as governmental agencies to adopt laws, policies, and practices to recognize and address the complex issues associated with persons involved in the criminal justice system who are living with dementia. (Godfrey, 2023, para. 1)

The resolution further urges training for legal professionals across the system on recognizing and screening for dementia and education to "understand its impact on an individual's understanding, behavior, decision making, communication, and judgment" (ABA, 2023, subsec. a).

To date, very little is known about the prevalence of dementia-related disorders in the criminal legal system because systematic data are not readily available (ABA Commission on Law and Aging, 2022; Arias & Flicker, 2020). In part, this is because dementia is a heterogeneous syndrome caused by several possible pathologies, including Alzheimer's disease, frontotemporal lobar degeneration, vascular disease, and Lewy body dementia, and it presents differently across individuals, varying by disease progression and symptoms (see Arias & Flicker, 2020).

Although clinical research has demonstrated that people with dementia-related illnesses can exhibit behavioral and psychological symptoms that may prompt criminal behavior, there has been little research specifically examining dementia with older adults (Arias & Flicker, 2020; Cipriani et al., 2016). Most studies have been conducted in nonforensic settings such as hospitals or nursing homes (e.g., Eastley et al., 1993; M. O'Connor, 1987), meaning that the results may not necessarily generalize to a forensic population of older adults. Of the few studies with system-involved older adults, they often include very small samples, further limiting their generalizability and conclusions. As study findings have indicated, there may be significant overlap between dementia and older adults who are system involved as first-time offenders (D. Miller, 2011).

One study conducted clinical interviews with 28 first-time offenders in Israel, aged 65 and older, and found that 21% had dementia (Barak et al., 1995). In another study, Mendez and colleagues (2011) evaluated 33 patients with dementia who engaged in antisocial acts (i.e., acts or events that violated sociomoral norms not during delirium or confusion) to better understand the etiology of antisocial behavior in people with dementia. Participants were referred to the clinic by family or physicians to assess cognitive and behavior changes using neurobehavior evaluation, laboratory assessment, and neuroimaging. Their findings generated two groups based on the patients' antisocial behavior and impulsivity. The largest proportion ($n = 22$) included individuals in contact with the law for committing impulsive but nonviolent antisocial acts, such as sexual disinhibition and pathological stealing; this group tended to have frontal lobe illnesses such as frontotemporal dementia or Huntington's disease. The second group ($n = 11$) included individuals who committed non-impulsive acts, such as physical assaults, assaults with a weapon, or stalking with homicidal behavior; this group's behavior stemmed from agitation, aggression, delusional beliefs, aphasic paranoia, and advanced memory or cognitive impairments.

Why might some people with dementia exhibit antisocial behavior whereas others do not? One proposed explanation is that preexisting antisocial personality traits emerge once the person has dementia symptoms (M. O'Connor, 1987), but this explanation fails to consider that individuals diagnosed with dementia-related disorders typically do not have a criminal history to exacerbate (B. L. Miller et al., 1997). Instead, evidence suggests that dementia-related disorders can alter a person's personality and make them angrier and less tolerant of others and increase their sexual disinhibition (Hindley & Gordon, 2000). With people living longer, there is a higher statistical probability that aging Americans will be diagnosed with a dementia-related disorder (National Academies of Sciences, Engineering, and Medicine, 2018). The intersection of dementia, older age, and criminal procedure has become an extremely important constitutional due process issue. Robust research is needed to inform how law enforcement interacts with suspects (see Chapter 5), issues associated with forensic evaluation and restorability to legal competency (see Chapter 6 and 7), disease progression and determining criminal responsibility (see Chapter 8), and whether an individual's sentence is no longer justifiable (see Chapter 9).

Availability of Data Impacting Trends in Older Adult Crime

Historically, crime statistics could not provide much information, other than the number of individuals in a subgroup who were arrested for a crime. As law enforcement agencies and others recognized the importance of collecting data, federal agencies have worked to improve national-level data collection and presentation on crime statistics. Pre-2021, law enforcement submitted only aggregate monthly crime totals, limiting analysis of trends across factors or subgroups. The updated incident-based reporting system, which was previously limited to reports of crime rates, allows for a more detailed picture of criminal behavior and the intersectionality of subgroups (e.g., older White men, older Black women). Although not yet nationally representative, the Uniform Crime Reporting program collects incident-based national data collected by the Federal Bureau of Investigation's National Incident-Based Reporting System. This new data collection effort, to which the Bureau of Justice Statistics transitioned completely in January 2021, allows for identifying characteristics and associations between variables to better understand criminal behavior. For those interested in exploring these data, Chapter 10 provides additional information on where they can be accessed.

TYPES OF OFFENSES

By examining the trends and patterns that emerge in the following sections, the reader will gain a better understanding of the complexities of criminal behavior among older adults, which may require diverse legal responses. Although there is no singular type of offense in which older adults engage, statistics and research reveal that they are more likely to be arrested for less serious crimes rather than for those more severe in nature.

Minor Offenses and Substance-Related Offenses

The reader may be able to picture the older adult who is system involved for less serious crimes such as shoplifting from the grocery store due to confusion on payment or for trespassing and public intoxication because they are unhoused. However, very little is known about the subpopulations of older adults who may become system involved for misdemeanors or violations. Due to the well-established research conclusion that criminal activity decreases with age (Farrington, 1986; Hirschi & Gottfredson, 1993), there are relatively few studies in which older adults are the primary focus. Generally, criminological and public policy research focuses on issues associated with more serious crimes, whereas older adults are more likely to be associated with less serious crimes.

In general, minor offenses often stem from problems with cognitive deficits or lack of resources. From statistics presently available, older adults were more likely to be arrested for minor offenses and alcohol violations than for serious offenses (Feldmeyer & Steffensmeier, 2007). Although older adults comprise the fewest total number of drug arrests compared with other age groups, illegal drug use arrests have substantially increased for older adults in recent years. For instance, one report found that even though drug-related offenses were lowest for those aged 50 and older, the rate had increased by 92% between 2000 to 2018 (Butts, 2019). As described in the Introduction, data indicate that a substantial proportion of older adults suffer from alcohol and SUDs and that there is a rise in older adults using illegal drugs (Edens et al., 2012).

Serious Offenses

This section describes the research on older adults and more serious offenses such as homicide and sexual offenses as well as violent crime stemming from older adult gun ownership. Despite data demonstrating that older adults commit less serious offenses, in-depth research with aging adults has focused mostly on legal responses to serious offenses, such as rape/sexual assault, assault, larceny, and burglary (Carson & Sabol, 2016)—offenses typically subject to sentences to jail or prison. Such a focus presents an unbalanced perspective on the legal responses for older adults. However, because the incarceration of older adults is one of the biggest challenges for correctional facilities, it is important for the reader to understand the circumstances contributing to when older adults also commit more serious crimes that are punishable to incarceration. Moreover, these types of offenses are more likely to engage scholarship and media attention because of the seriousness of these crimes and the ability to study individuals who are incarcerated (versus those who commit less serious offenses and are more likely to be community dwelling). In other words, there is a research advantage to studying more serious offenses because they are less likely to be dismissed (due to age or otherwise) by law enforcement or prosecutorial discretion (see Chapter 6 for further discussion of sentencing).

Homicide

Relatively few homicides and violent crimes are committed by older adults; as such, there is very little research about the characteristics of older adults who commit these types of offenses—with most of the research examining the characteristics of older adults as the victims of homicide (see Chapter 3). In a systematic literature review of older adults who were arrested for homicide aged 55 years and older that was published in the journal *Psychiatry, Psychology and Law*, researchers Nguyen and colleagues (2021) identified 15 studies meeting their inclusion criteria for analysis. As older adults have been discussed as a heterogenous group spanning many ages and aging processes, not surprisingly, researchers found that reasons and risk factors for committing homicide were different for older adults than for younger adults (Nguyen et al., 2021) and also varied within the older adults studied (Block, 2013). In general, older adults who commit homicide are usually White males in the context of their home, toward people they know, following a quarrel—often with alcohol and/or firearms involved (Block, 2013; Kratcoski, 1990; Nguyen et al., 2021). Studies have also found that the majority of older adults who commit homicide do not have a prior violent criminal record (Block, 2013; Kratcoski, 1990) but may have a nonviolent record (Block, 2013), with common characteristics that included social maladjustment, performing a caregiver role, physical and mental health problems, and problematic substance use (Nguyen et al., 2021).

There is often media attention around spousal homicide and/or spousal homicide–suicide for older adults, but data show the phenomenon is not that common overall. For instance, researchers have examined the intersection of age and sex, using data from the Chicago Homicide Dataset from 1965 to 2000. One study analyzed data including 476 older adults aged 60 and older (or 11.3% of those who were arrested for homicide) and concluded that the proportion of women who committed homicide declined with each older age group, so that younger women were more likely to commit homicide than were older women (Block, 2013). Moreover, women who committed homicide were much less likely to have a violent criminal background than were men who committed homicide. Another study that focused on victims found that 9 in 10 homicides included a known victim, and of those cases with a known victim, in half of the cases the victim was an acquaintance; in only a quarter, spouses; and in the remaining quarter of cases, a relative (Kratcoski, 1990). Although these longitudinal data indicated that men over 60 were more likely than men between 25 and 59 to kill an intimate partner (Block, 2013), only a small proportion of cases overall are homicide–suicide cases. Within the relatively small group, all cases of homicide–suicide involved a husband committing suicide after killing his wife, but there were no cases of wives killing their husbands (Kratcoski, 1990).

In Finland, research examined older adults arrested for homicide (60 and older) for psychopathic traits as well as other mental and physical health markers compared with younger adults arrested for homicide (Putkonen et al., 2010). Those aged 60 and older were less often diagnosed with drug use disorders and personality disorders (including psychopathy) but more likely to be diagnosed with dementia-related disorders and other physical illnesses. In a systematic review of homicide and dementia, Sundakov-Krumins and colleagues (2022) examined 13 studies, finding that in community settings, men typically victimized their spouses, but in institutional settings, they usually targeted other male residents. Although data on the specific type of dementia were not always available, the presence of dysexecutive syndrome was prevalent. Dysexecutive syndrome refers to some form of frontal lobe damage that interferes with executive functioning (Godefroy et al., 2010), and it is thought to be an important factor in understanding older adult homicides when there is the possibility of a dementia-related disorder (Richard-Devantoy et al., 2010).

Sex Offenses

Among serious offenses committed by older adults, sex crimes are both more easily imagined by the public and better understood by researchers (E. Taylor, 2011). For instance, when people think about older adults who commit sexual offenses, the term "dirty old man" is an image often conjured (Crookes et al., 2022; Hart, 2008) even though most sex offenses are committed by younger men (Hanson, 1997; Hanson & Bussiere, 1998; Hart, 2008), and studies demonstrate that sexual arousal and libido decrease with age (Barbaree et al., 2003; Booth, 2016). It may be easier to think of older adults committing sex crimes because although the commission of most types of crimes significantly declines with age, the commission of sex offenses appears to decline at a slower rate (Booth, 2016). In addition, sex offenses are a type of crime that older adults can continue to commit or start committing in older age, especially when the crime involves less physically capable victims (e.g., children; using the internet). Studies link several aging-related factors that predict sex offenses, such as physical sexual inabilities, declines in felt and perceived masculinity, social isolation, biological changes, and psychological/neurocognitive deficits (Hanson, 2002; Hart, 2008). Prison statistics suggest that when individuals were sentenced later in life as an older adult, they were most likely to be sentenced for a sex offense (Curtice et al., 2003; Fazel et al., 2002; Fazel & Grann, 2002) and were often first-time offenders (E. Taylor, 2011).

The rate of older adults arrested for sex offenses is relatively low compared with other age groups. National data on the number of older adults registered as sex offenders are unavailable, in part because sentencing and registration requirements differ considerably across jurisdictions. For example, a study (Ghossoub & Khoury, 2021) including one jurisdiction's registry found that 1.3% (n = 194) of individuals registered during the study period were 65 and older. Within this age group, approximately 88.7% were first-time offenders, all were male, most were White, and the mean age at the time of the offense was 68.6 years old.

Despite more being known about older sex offenders than about older people who commit other types of crime, research on older sex offenders in the United States is sparse, with most of the extant research conducted with European samples (e.g., Chua et al., 2018). A systematic literature review by Chua and colleagues (2018) examined research studies and case reports that compared older and younger first-time incarcerated sex offenders to better understand the reason for late-life onset of committing sexual offenses. Only seven studies (two research studies and five case reports) met criteria for inclusion in the systematic review, and these studies were limited in both clinical and sociodemographic data. Overall, the review identified two types of older sex offenders—those who had committed sexual offenses previously but were not detected and those were likely true first-time offenders with a neurocognitive disorder that contributed to sexual offending later in life.

A study of another state's sex offender registry revealed that among community-dwelling older adults involved with the justice system for the first time, 87% waived their right to trial (Ghossoub & Khoury, 2021). Of these, 60% received probation with a suspended sentence. It is likely that first-time older adults with neurocognitive disorders comprise the larger proportion of the individuals who receive probation with the possibility of resentencing and that those with a longer criminal history are the individuals who are sentenced to incarceration before being released and registered in the community as sex offenders (ABA Commission on Law and Aging, 2022). Ghossoub and Khoury (2021) speculated that their sample may have included individuals with neurocognitive disorders known to contribute to problematic sexual behaviors, but data were not available to test this hypothesis.

Overall, research is mixed on the association between criminal sexual offenses and dementia-related disorders or other psychiatric problems. Chua and colleagues' (2018) systematic review concluded that dementia-related disorders were the most common diagnosis but cautioned about the studies' collective limitation of not reporting information related to conducting assessments for cognitive or dementia symptoms. On the other hand, studies have found that most older sex offenders do not have neurocognitive issues (Clark & Mezey, 1997; Fazel et al., 2002; Rodriguez et al., 2017). In comparing the psychiatric and personality disorders of older adults who committed a sex offense with those of older adults who committed a nonsexual offense, Fazel and colleagues (2002) found few differences between the groups. Both age groups had a similar psychiatric and personality profile. They were both low in dementia (1%), psychotic disorders (7%), and depressive disorders (7%) but higher on the prevalence of personality disorders (33%). The only differences between the two groups were personality traits—namely, the older sex offenders had a higher rate of personality traits that were schizoid, obsessive–compulsive, and avoidant than had older adults who committed other offenses. This suggests that older adults convicted of sex-related offenses have more disorganized and pathological traits than do older adults committing other offense types.

Some think the reason older individuals are more likely to commit sex offenses compared with other crimes is because some sex offenses require less physical effort, including passive types of sexual crimes such as possession or distribution of child pornography (Hart, 2008). Although this assumption seems to make intuitive sense, the data suggest otherwise. First-time older adult offenders are typically charged with active crimes requiring physical effort, often targeting vulnerable individuals including minors (Chua et al., 2018; Ghossoub & Khoury, 2021), such as neighbor children (Clark & Mezey, 1997) or grandchildren; people with intellectual disabilities; and other more vulnerable older adults (Chua et al., 2018). Overall, Ghossoub and Khoury (2021) found that most offenders in this sample were convicted of nonpassive offenses (80.8%), most commonly child molestation (36.5%), with a smaller proportion convicted of the more passive offense of pornography, mostly possession of child pornography (16.3%).

A common concern with sex crimes is public safety and the likelihood perpetrators will recidivate with additional sexual offenses. Studies generally support low recidivism rates for first-time older sex offenders, especially when they are released later in life. Using a 15-year follow-up for recidivism, research demonstrated that approximately 26% of those under 50 years old sexually recidivated, whereas only 12% of sex offenders aged 50 and older sexually recidivated (Harris & Hanson, 2004). Recidivism rates depend on the population sampled. In a U.S. sample of 194 first-time sex offenders aged 65 and older, only 3 (1.7%) recidivated with a sexual offense within 4 years from release (Ghossoub & Khoury, 2021). Studies, including a meta-analysis of 21 studies across 6,969 offenders (Hanson & Bussiere, 1998), suggest that individuals who are released at an older age are less likely to recommit sex crimes (Fazel et al., 2006; Lussier & Healey, 2009; Nicholaichuk et al., 2014).

Recidivism rates also depend on the type of sexual offense conviction (Fazel et al., 2006; Hanson, 2002). For instance, the statistical correlation between age and recidivism was strongest for more violent offenses (i.e., rapists) but less strong for other types of offenses, such as incest and extrafamilial child molestation (Hanson, 2002). A Swedish study by Fazel and colleagues (2006) examined risk factors to identify whether any would indicate differences between older and younger individuals who commit sex offenses. The researchers compared the risk factors of sexual or violent recidivism of four age groups (under 25, 25–39, 40–54, and 55 and over) who were released from prison ($N = 1,303$); the vast majority (95%) were convicted of penetrative offenses (e.g., rape, sexual coercion, child molestation). Recidivism rates significantly decreased in the older sex offender age groups, especially for those aged 55 and older. Indeed, for the most part, older adults show a low base rate for sexual reoffending, regardless of their risk level when convicted, except for a small group of persisters who have lengthy criminal histories (Nicholaichuk et al., 2014).

Gun Ownership

Research indicates that older adults are more likely to use sharp instruments or blunt objects than firearms in violent crimes (Overshott et al., 2012). However, the issue of older adults and firearms is gaining attention, particularly regarding competency to own guns. This topic is emerging alongside other ethical and legal questions about violence and gun ownership in later life (see Box 5.1). Since 2007, Gallup (2020) has periodically surveyed households on gun ownership and reported very little change over time, with approximately one in three American adults saying they personally own a gun and just under half (44%) reporting that they live in a household with a gun. Individuals aged 65 and older have the highest rates of all the groups of personally owning a gun (36%) and living in a household with a gun (48%). As reported in *The New York Times,* "The attachment to guns often dies hard for older people. Even after dementia develops, relinquishing guns can feel almost like an

BOX 5.1 | EMERGING AREA OF FIREARMS AND GUN OWNERSHIP

In April 2023, two news stories involving older men and guns made national headlines with similar circumstances. In both stories, an older White man shot and killed a young person who mistakenly entered their property. In rural New York, 65-year-old Kevin Monahan shot and killed a White 20-year-old who turned in Monahan's driveway. In Missouri, 84-year-old Andrew Lester shot and killed a Black 16-year-old who rang the doorbell looking for his younger sibling. Both defendants mentioned their age and/or fearful feelings as reasons for the shootings. Monahan's attorney claims several vehicles revving their engines that night caused alarm for the "elderly gentleman" and "elderly wife," and Lester cited living alone and being "scared to death" of being physically harmed when the boy came to the front door. Both men were described by neighbors as the type who were concerned with trespassers and worried about crime near their homes (Bosman et al., 2023).

amputation" (Span, 2018). Although most of the concern around older adults owning guns centers on the potential for suicide (Mertens & Sorenson, 2012; Saadi et al., 2020), gun ownership by older adults has also been linked to other violent behavior, such as intimate partner violence, homicide (Cipriani et al., 2017; E. Greene et al., 2007), and homicide–suicide (Kratcoski, 1990; Tapp & Coen, 2024). Notably, compared with a person living in a home with no firearm, the adjusted odds ratio for homicide was 1.41 times more likely for a home where a gun was present (Wiebe, 2003).

In some situations, it may be that the older adult was licensed to purchase a gun when they were younger or that a spouse owned the gun but has since died, leaving the widow or widower in possession of a gun that was not originally theirs. Still, a significant proportion may choose to purchase a gun later in life due to fear of victimization, and firearm companies have adapted guns (Mertens & Sorenson, 2012), such as the Palm Pistol, designed to be ergonomic and "intended for seniors, disabled or others with grip limitations due to hand strength, manual dexterity or phalangeal amputations" (Constitution Arms, 2024).

Although studies are limited, research has centered on the connection between cognitive disorders (e.g., dementia, Alzheimer's disease), aggression, and diminished capacity for older gun owners (Cipriani et al., 2017; Polzer et al., 2022; Schwertner et al., 2021). With these concerns, some have called for "firearm retirement," a notion similar to giving up one's driver's license (Norton et al., 2022) or extending gun violence restriction orders (i.e., red flag laws or extreme risk protection orders) to cover dementia. This would allow families and law enforcement and, in some states, health care professionals and educators to petition the court for the temporary removal of firearms from people who may be a danger to themselves or others (Galluzzi & Warner-Maron, 2018; Kohn, 2020c; Saadi et al., 2020). Unlike other behavioral domains in which age-related declines pose significant risks (e.g., driving, flying as a pilot), there are few legal responses for regulating older firearm owners or ensuring that they can use a firearm safely (E. Greene et al., 2007). Similarly, although there is a minimum age one must be to purchase a gun, there is no maximum age limit to do so. As with other areas of capacity, older adults demonstrate diminished capacity at varying rates (see the Introduction to this volume), if ever at all, and Amendment II to the U.S. Constitution has been interpreted to mean that individuals have a right to own a gun (*District of Columbia v. Heller*, 2008).

The most relevant regulation is the federal Gun Control Act of 1968, an amendment to the National Firearms Act (1934), which forbids gun ownership for anyone who has been adjudicated "mentally defective or has been committed to any mental institution." Applying the NFA to older adult gun ownership, however, presents some problems. Although research shows that older adult firearm owners support policies for restricting access to guns for someone who is a danger to self or others or who has dementia or confusion (Carter et al., 2022), such legal responses may have practical constraints. Individuals may not have a formal adjudication indicating incompetency and may not have spent time in a mental health facility, as required under the NFA. Often, competency is not an issue when impairment is mild and until the individual poses a risk to themselves or others. Additionally, the NFA applies to the purchase of guns but not the ownership of them (E. Greene et al., 2007).

Other policymakers have proposed solutions such as increasing the role of health professionals in counseling patients and caregivers regarding the implications of firearms in the home (Cipriani et al., 2017). In a probability-based web survey of older adults (aged 50 to 80), most respondents found health care screening and safety counseling acceptable; however, only a small proportion of respondents had been asked about gun safety by a health care provider in the past year (Carter et al., 2022). Another, more restrictive option is initiating guardianship through the courts. The use of guardianship in probate courts can be a means to remove the right to have a firearm from those who have diminished capacity to handle owning a gun. Supported under the legal doctrine of *parens patriae*, in adult guardianship proceedings, the court appoints another person to make decisions for an adult who cannot make decisions for themselves (the person in need of protection) as either a full guardian (plenary guardianship) or one of limited scope. Under guardianship, the court may require the guardian to control possessions, purchases, or firearm use or explicitly remove their rights surrounding gun ownership (Kohn, 2020c). An order for guardianship would likely meet the criterion imposed by the Gun Control Act (1968) of a person who has been adjudicated with a "mental defect."

CONCLUSION

In general, older adults commit fewer of all types of crimes than does any other age group in accordance with well-investigated research on the age–crime curve. Despite this, there have been warnings of geriatric crime waves in response to anxiety around growth of the aging population, more generally. In Sacco's (2005) book *When Crime Waves*, the author asserts that crime waves are social constructs that are created by groups who benefit from the fears generated. Data trends have never confirmed a geriatric crime wave. However, the aging population has experienced its largest growth from 1920 to 2020, and data illustrate some proportional increases in arrests for less serious crimes. Perhaps this is evidence of a geriatric crime ripple? If so, as Sacco questions, who benefits from fears that older adults are committing a disproportional volume of crime?

The stereotype content model (SCM, see the Introduction to this volume) theorizes and examines how perceived social structure (cooperation and status) predicts stereotypes (warmth and competence), emotional prejudice and attitudes (pride, pity, contempt, envy), and finally, the type of discrimination (active and passive help and harm). Societies admire older adults when they are perceived as having lived life on their own terms and achieving some longitudinal form of success—"having done something with their lives" (Blaine & Brenchley,

2020, p. 180). Moreover, stereotypic warmth is based in a group's perceived cooperativeness and competitiveness and is often measured as economic interdependence and shared versus conflicting symbolic values (Fiske, 2018). As such, legal responses to older adults perceived as cooperative and financially independent will differ from legal responses directed at older adults perceived as competitive and financially dependent. In considering the intersectionality of group membership for older perpetrators of crime ("elderly" and "criminal"), the SCM predicts both groups will be perceived as low on the competence dimension; therefore, how we perceive older adults who commit crime will depend on how they are perceived according to the warmth dimension, using contextual cues of friendliness and trustworthiness.

Furthermore, perceptions of older adults are more positive when older adults act in stereotype-consistent manners; as such, older adults who are perpetrators of criminal behavior are likely perceived according to negative traits because they do not conform to warmth-based attitudes such as the "perfect grandparent" (e.g., kind, generous, family-oriented, wise) or "golden ager" (e.g., intelligent, productive, healthy, independent), which typically elicit feelings of pity or sympathy and active helping behavior. Instead, perpetrators of criminal behavior are more likely to be perceived according to low-warmth negative stereotypes such as "severely impaired" (e.g., feeble, slow thinking, senile) and "despondent" (e.g., neglected, sad, afraid, lonely), which typically elicit feelings of disgust and contempt. Warmth is fundamental because an older adult's intent is predictive of their behavior, and individual perceivers are more likely to actively help an older adult they trust and pity but passively harm an older adult they do not trust and feel contempt toward (Fiske, 2018). In other words, negative attitudes and uncertain feelings about an older person's intent lead to avoidance and more stereotyping of older adults, which in turn produces more ignorance and negative emotions.

So, who then benefits from fears conjured from an alleged geriatric crime wave? As the SCM theory predicts, those who most benefit will be the ingroup of law-abiding nonolder adults, who view "elderly criminals" as doubly financially interdependent and as having conflicting values surrounding antisocial activities. In U.S. criminal procedure, very few legal responses are based on *per se* age requirements, and all adults are presumed to be treated the same under core criminal procedure legal principles. Although systematic legal responses that treat everyone the same are thought to foster institutional ageism, individualized legal responses instead may foster interpersonal ageism. As this chapter and the chapters in Part 2 illustrate, legal responses to older adults as criminals are mostly individualized legal decisions made by legal decision makers (i.e., police officers, judges, and jurors) and, as such, are subject to influence by assumptions about older adults and assumptions about people who engage in criminal behavior.

II

AGING AND CRIMINAL LEGAL SYSTEM STAGES

6

Involvement With Law Enforcement and the Courts

The poem, "Warning," by Jenny Joseph (1961) describes an older woman wearing a red hat and encourages women to get the most out of life in older age. The poem describes spending money on frivolous items while neglecting necessary ones. The older woman is described as picking flowers from others' gardens and eating whatever she wants. The poem, which served as the inspiration for the Red Hat Society (https://redhatsociety.com), illustrates how aging can be associated with behaving differently and suggests that in aging one should act with a whisper of irrationality.

As you think about an older woman stealing flowers as the poem describes, do you find yourself smiling with delight or scowling with concern? Is that a description of petty theft? Or is it about a person with memory problems mistakenly going into someone else's yard? These are some of the questions that may arise when older adults come to the attention of legal decision makers, such as law enforcement (or other first responders), who are required to make judgments about the older adult's behavior within the given context and act accordingly. Using visual cues about the older person and the environment, police officers often make fast decisions and may rely on their assumptions about aging and older people. How might ageist beliefs be related to the officer's perceptions and subsequent behavior? If she appears "doddering, but dear," social psychologists predict that these mixed perceptions explain overhelping behavior (Fiske et al., 2002). For instance, the officer may question whether the older woman needed help and approach her, only to discover something

https://doi.org/10.1037/0000469-007
Aging and the Criminal Legal System: Community Services, Courts, Corrections, and Policy, by L. E. Wylie and E. M. Brank

that looks like a weapon. Inversely, if she appears admirable, but aloof, the officer may disregard the behavior and woman, later to discover she was reported missing by her adult daughter.

Whether an older person's behavior is typical for them or due to a behavioral health issue, cognitive disorder, or other sociostructural problem (e.g., housing, income), legal professionals working with older adults at times must screen for possible signs of diminished capacities. In some roles, legal professionals must respond based on quick decisions to balance the safety of the older adult and the public while also protecting due process rights. This is especially true of legal professionals in crisis services (sequential intercept model [SIM] Intercept 0), law enforcement, and jail staff during pretrial detention (SIM Intercept 1), who are more likely to have incomplete information. When decision makers have limited information, as social psychology theories predict, this may lead to overreliance on stereotypes. As such, legal responses to older adults during the initial stages of the criminal legal system are prone to ageist responses.

In the poem detailed at the beginning of the chapter, the woman in the red hat is described as picking some flowers from other people's gardens (Joseph, 1961). What if the woman was carrying scissors or a knife for cutting those flowers? What if she was confused due to language barriers, physical or mental health issues, medication interactions, dementia symptoms, or a combination thereof? Then what would happen if she were approached by law enforcement? The present chapter, which follows the discussion of older adults as the perpetrators of antisocial and criminal behavior in Chapter 5, describes specific legal responses by early responders, such as law enforcement officers, at prearrest and arrest stages. Afterward, we discuss legal responses by court decision makers at both the pretrial and sentencing phases of the court process, such as attorneys and judges.

INTERACTIONS WITH LAW ENFORCEMENT

Law enforcement and other first responders often encounter older adults who have gotten lost, stopped as confused shoplifters, or involved in domestic disputes. Law enforcement may also be called to nursing homes or assisted living facilities for assaultive behavior between residents or between a resident and staff. To study the legal responses to community-dwelling older adults, researchers analyzed data from the New Haven Established Populations for Epidemiologic Studies of the Elderly (Lachs et al., 2004). Data include a cohort of older adults ($n = 2{,}321$) who had regular standardized evaluations of medical, functional, and psychosocial health. Individuals in the observed cohort were matched to police records over 11 years (from 1985 to 1995) in the same catchment area. Overall, adjusting for sampling, 29% of the cohort had interactions with police during the study period, which amounted to 1,651 separate contacts. Of the cohort members with police contact, they averaged 2.4 contacts (out of a range of 1 to 35 contacts), mostly as victims (62%), but also had substantial interactions as complainants, witnesses, and perpetrators of crime. Older adults who were younger (age measured as continuous), Black, and male were more likely to have contact with the police in all roles. However, contrary to what the authors expected, older adults with fewer functional and cognitive problems had contact with the police in varied roles but fewer contacts as "older and frail" victim depicted by aging stereotypes.

Police Decision Making and Discretion

Along the earliest SIM Intercepts 0 and 1 (see Chapter 5 for review of the SIM), first responders may have to make quick decisions about the person of interest for public safety and the safety of the individual. When older adults behave contrary to societal expectations, social psychology theory on role congruity predicts prejudicial attitudes and discrimination (see the Introduction). In the first moments of an encounter with an aging person of interest, law enforcement and other first responders make informal judgments to quickly screen the person's current mental status, often relying solely on experience and contextual cues but typically lacking specialized knowledge of normative or pathological aging. Social–psychological research and studies on stereotyping indicate that these quick judgments made under *hot cognition* are the types of decisions that are most vulnerable to bias and stereotypical thinking (Wheeler & Petty, 2001). Consequently, as a product of the situation and needs for protecting the safety of all, early-system decision makers may rely on stereotypes of older adults during their—sometimes quick—legal responses. When responding to calls for which safety is a concern, decision makers may also rely on assumptions about mental illness and dangerousness.

In rural Georgia in 2018, an 87-year-old woman who was using a knife to cut dandelions in the woods near her home, not dissimilar to the flower picker in the poem described at the beginning of the current chapter, was tased and arrested following a 911 call (K. Allen, 2018). The person who called indicated that they did not think the woman was threatening, stating, "There's a lady walking on the bike trails, she has a knife, and she won't leave. . . . She told me she doesn't speak English. . . . It looks like she's walking around looking for something, vegetation to cut down or something. She has a bag too" (K. Allen, 2018, para. 3). A family member indicated she had dementia-related issues, in addition to confirming her language barrier. The charges against the woman were dropped, but the police department defended their use of force as appropriate. However, use-of-force standards should be impacted by factors such as age, height, and the presence of a weapon. In other words, the use of force appropriate for a 6-foot-tall muscular man is likely not appropriate for an 80-year-old frail woman. Although the standard of minimum necessary force for arrests is guided by Amendment VIII to the U.S. Constitution's prohibition on cruel and unusual punishment (see Chapter 1, this volume), police should be using their professional discretion to determine what amount of force is necessary. Indeed, this older woman from rural Georgia sued the police department and was awarded $150,000 in damages; moreover, the police department was required to reinforce standard de-escalation and crisis intervention training (Curtin, 2020).

There is limited research on police interactions and older adults, with most of the existing studies examining issues relevant to older adults as victims or witnesses. One study in the United Kingdom analyzed police custody data and demonstrated that older detainees had more problems with alcohol withdrawal and more cognitive impairment consistent with dementia disorders than had younger detainees (McKinnon et al., 2017). Illustrating how law enforcement screening contributes to legal responses, in the study's sample, the police officers recommended 80% of the older detainees to complete a health assessment.

Nonfatal and Fatal Injury by Police

Data demonstrate that the rates of older adults with harmful police interactions have also risen—notably so in several cases of excessive force, in which police misread confusion caused by dementia symptoms as defiance to their requests (Goel, 2023). According to the Centers for Disease Control and Prevention's web-based Injury Statistics Query and Reporting System (WISQARS), which provides national nonfatal injury data from 2015 to 2020, more than 15,000 individuals aged 60 and older were brought to the hospital emergency room for injuries caused by the responses of police or private security (Centers for Disease Control and Prevention, n.d.). Although some older individuals may be a threat to public safety, regardless of age or cognitive capacity, interactions with law enforcement can escalate when the person is confused or cannot follow an officer's instructions. In addition, behavioral health and cognitive impairment may impede communication, and officers may perceive an older adult's presentation of disorder symptoms as aggressive (Goel, 2023).

Illustrating this are numerous media accounts of nonfatal incidents involving older adults and law enforcement. For instance, in June 2020 an officer in Loveland, Colorado, arrested and then dislocated the shoulder of a 73-year-old woman with a dementia-related disorder after the older woman left the store with $13 of unpaid merchandise. During the arrest, the older woman pled with other police officers almost 50 times for medical care (Swanson, 2022). An investigation into the case found "egregious mistakes" in how they handled the situation, and in May 2022, the arresting officer was sentenced to 5 years in prison (Borden, 2022). In October 2021, a 70-year-old man in El Paso, Texas, with Parkinson's disease and dementia symptoms wandered from his home in the middle of the night (C. Thompson, 2022). Confused and agitated at 2 a.m. in front of his home, he picked up wooden blocks and threw them at a vehicle and walked away. In response, a police officer fired a stun gun at him that resulted in multiple facial fractures and bleeding around his brain. During the same month, police in Tulsa, Oklahoma, were called to a scene where a 70-year-old woman was locked in a bathroom during a mental health crisis (Querry-Thompson, 2022). After making attempts for 34 minutes, one of the officers threatened to tase the older woman, and when officers broke into the bathroom to detain her, she sustained facial injuries. Charges against her were dropped due to her mental health condition, and the woman sued the Tulsa Police Department and other government agencies for violating her rights to due process.

Sadly, there have also been news stories of fatal incidents. After her daughter called 911 for help with her mother, informing them of her mental illness and dementia, a 75-year-old woman in Las Cruces, New Mexico, was fatally shot twice by officers as she stood in her doorway holding two large kitchen knives (Garcia, 2022). The police interaction lasted only 38 seconds. Those seconds involved the officers demanding in English that she drop the knives, but in addition to her cognitive impairments, she was a native Spanish speaker. Further media investigation revealed that the officer who used the stun gun had been in the force for only 3 years but had received training on crisis intervention and handling individuals with mental impairment. Even though this jurisdiction had law enforcement teams with special training who should have responded to this call, the Las Cruces Police Department indicated that information from 911 calls is often incomplete, and it is not always clear the situation requires a specialized team (C. Thompson, 2022). Most training to date has focused on how police should respond to those with behavioral health issues, yet these examples demonstrate that training may be inadequate for the complexities of normative and pathological impacts of aging on older adults. See Box 6.1 for a case example that explores some of the factors law enforcement may use when making quick decisions for public safety.

Training for First Responders

In Chapter 3, we discussed a study that examined police knowledge of aging-related health in the San Francisco Police Department that indicated most police officers interacted with older adults monthly, but only one in three saw themselves as knowledgeable about aging-related health issues (Brown et al., 2014). The officers expressed concerns with difficulty in distinguishing between criminal activity and medical or psychiatric issues as well as needing to slow down their typical quick decision making. The Alzheimer's Association offers free online training for first responders, which is much different than the type of training officers generally receive on how best to approach individuals with cognitive disorders (Alzheimer's Association, 2019). The association has provided online training for more than 31,000 emergency responders (C. Thompson, 2022), covering such topics as dementia, wandering, driving, abuse and neglect, shoplifting, and disaster response. Their first responder training framework includes T.A.L.K. tactics to remind officers to Take it slow, Ask simple questions, Limit reality checks, and Keep eye contact when working with someone with potential cognitive issues who may be agitated or afraid (Alzheimer's Association, 2019).

BOX 6.1 | INTERACTIONS WITH LAW ENFORCEMENT IN SOUTH CAROLINA, JOSEPH JACKSON, AGED 72

Joseph Jackson, a 72-year-old man from Charleston County, South Carolina, failed to register as a sex offender—a requirement stemming from a conviction he received at age 51 (Yee, 2021). When law enforcement served an arrest warrant to his home, Jackson yelled to leave his property and fired a gun in the direction of the officers. One officer was wounded with a non-life-threatening injury. Jackson did not leave his house right away; when the SWAT team entered, Jackson was lying on the floor with injuries sustained from returned gunshots. After receiving medical care, Jackson was transported to jail and charged with one count of attempted murder and possession of a firearm during the commission of a violent crime.

What contextual cues may have impacted the officers' perceptions of Jackson and how could these cues have influenced their decision to shoot? The stereotype content model (see the Introduction, this volume) predicts that an older man will be thought of as warm, but incompetent (Fiske et al., 2002), although positive attitudes may decrease when the older adult does not conform to societal expectations of an elderly person (Cuddy et al., 2005; Eagly & Karau, 2002). As such, how may Jackson's warrant, sex-crime conviction, refusal to comply with officers, and the presence of a weapon further impact judgments? In this scenario, Jackson does not fit the elderly stereotype. Thus, although officers may have assumed Jackson's diminished capacity solely based on cues of an older person, his stereotype-inconsistent behavior could lead to negative attitudes and biased legal responses.

Jackson's intersectional membership as an older Black man with a criminal history also further explains legal responses involving quick judgments. According to psychological studies on decisions to shoot a firearm, experimental laboratory studies have found that research participants (typically undergraduate students) are more likely to "shoot" (with a computer button) an unarmed Black person than an unarmed White person (e.g., Correll et al., 2002; B. K. Payne, 2001). However, recent field studies with police officers as participants did not show a biased pattern of shooting by race and demonstrated that the officers could overcome the influence of stereotypes (Correll et al., 2014). Moreover, performance depended most on whether the environment was anxiety-provoking, such as the presence of gunfire (Nieuwenhuys et al., 2012). In Jackson's case, several factors likely influenced the officers' perceptions of dangerousness. Later media accounts suggested Jackson was exhibiting symptoms of dementia at the time of the incident. What may have happened to Jackson next? Chapter 7 describes the forensic evaluation processes as well as specific issues emerging for individuals with possible dementia-related disorders.

In recognition that law enforcement often interacts with individuals in mental health crisis, police forces have collaborated with mental health professionals to form crisis intervention teams (CITs). The CIT program trains police officers to serve as first responders to individuals experiencing a psychiatric crisis and to assist them in accessing psychological evaluation and treatment, as opposed to arrest or another punitive outcome. Several studies have identified positive outcomes for community-dwelling adults with serious mental illness (Steadman et al., 2000; Strauss et al., 2005), but there is much less research on the effectiveness of such programs with older adults (Tyuse et al., 2017). A descriptive study was conducted by Tyuse and colleagues on the types of calls a CIT program in St. Louis, Missouri, received from older adults with serious mental illness or dementia symptoms. The average age of the older adults (both men and women) in the study was 75 years, with ages ranging from 65 to 100 years. Most calls for help came from family members (25%), anonymous callers (23.9%), or the older adults themselves (21.9%). Approximately 32% of CIT calls were related to suicide (threat, 17%; attempt, 16%), with most subjects having the means to carry out the suicide attempt (e.g., medication, cutting instrument, firearms). Most of the sample of older adults had been transported to the emergency department for evaluation (70%), but 5% were arrested and taken into custody for felony assault on a family member or other person.

In the Las Cruces case described above, the police department had launched a CIT in 2019 before the shooting of the older woman on her doorstep (C. Thompson, 2022). When the media asked why they did not send the CIT to the scene, the department responded that the CIT is focused on mental health issues and not dementia disorders. Many departments do not have policies specific to dementia symptoms specifically but do have clearer legal responses toward individuals with mental health symptoms. As may be applicable to older adults experiencing diminished capacities, legal responses to calls for mental-health-related behavior indicate that agents should approach individuals calmly and use additional caution when deciding to use force based on a person's perceived age.

Screening by Law Enforcement

In cases that do not involve quick judgments or immediate concerns about safety, legal professionals may perform a short screening to determine a person's mental status using a short screening tool. Indeed, the Police–Mental Health Collaboration provides a framework and toolkit for law enforcement agencies to better respond to people with mental illness, co-occurring substance use, and/or intellectual disabilities (Bureau of Justice Assistance, n.d.). A full behavioral health and needs assessment would not be practical or feasible for officers in the field, but officers can employ short mental health screening tools to identify individuals with serious mental health disorders. Tools such as these can assist law enforcement in deciding whether it is more appropriate to transport the person to a hospital instead of arresting and detaining them in jail. A screening tool and process can also provide common language and promote collaborative approach between systems (K. M. Hoffman et al., 2016).

Individuals with dementia symptoms may exhibit behavioral problems such as wandering, indecent exposure, shoplifting, traffic violations, or violence toward others that cause safety concerns and warrant police involvement (Sun et al., 2019). Cognitive and sensory impairment may escalate police involvement during crisis, and police are often not properly trained to identify and address these health-related issues (Moll, 2013). Whether through law enforcement or crisis response teams, the timely identification of diminished capacities is essential to understanding the influence of neurocognitive decline on behavior. Early identification would also connect older adults to treatment and services, which could delay disease progression, address existing symptoms, and identify appropriate alternatives of care.

AFTER ARREST AND PRETRIAL

Once a criminal case reaches the stages of the SIM Intercepts 2 and 3 (see Chapter 5 for a review of the SIM), defendants have been charged with an offense by law enforcement, and the case is now with the court system to handle. During these stages, older adults may be detained in jail or in a community setting, depending on the seriousness of the offense, while waiting for their initial court hearing. They may be detained in jail to determine whether the case will proceed and whether they should be released or stay in jail before their trial. If they are not released, they may spend time in jail waiting for the start of their adjudication process, in which the government and defense present evidence to determine guilt, and/or while they await the case's final disposition (e.g., guilty, not guilty, incompetent, dismissed). During the pretrial phase, the government will determine whether the case should move forward or be dropped for lack of evidence. Although there is not much research on older adults in the pretrial phase, it is likely that many are released, especially when there is no public safety concern. Research on prosecutorial discretion and shoplifting, for example, found that prosecutors often consider older age when determining whether to prosecute someone for shoplifting (Adams & Cutshall, 1987). As promoted under the SIM, individuals should be screened early to avoid further court involvement and diverted at any appropriate intercept of the SIM (American Bar Association [ABA] Commission on Law and Aging, 2022; National Judicial Task Force, 2023).

SCREENING FOR CAPACITY BY ATTORNEYS AND JUDGES

As do law enforcement and other first responders, attorneys and judges have a role in screening older adults within criminal contexts. The court with jurisdiction over the case has the duty to ensure that defendants are competent throughout the case because convicting an individual who is not competent violates their constitutional right to due process (*Pate v. Robinson*, 1966). If the defendant's attorney does not raise the issue of competency to proceed and should have, that is considered a violation of the constitutional right to effective counsel (*McMann v. Richardson*, 1970) under Amendments VI and XIV to the U.S. Constitution (*State v. Johnson*, 1986). Specifically, the defendant's attorney is required to inform the court of any suspicions of diminished capacity if an attorney has reasonable doubt in their client's capacity to participate in each legal process. This means that attorneys cannot withhold that information, even if they think it is in the best interests of the defendant's case; otherwise, it is a "breach of the duty" because "the determination of competency rest[s] with the court exclusively, not with the attorney" (*State v. Johnson*, 1986, p. 215).

If competency is raised at any point in the criminal legal case (e.g., waiving of rights, confession, proceeding with a plea or trial, testifying), federal law 18 U.S.C. § 4241(a) (Determination of mental competency to stand trial, 1948) requires courts to hold a competency hearing, during which they may order a psychological or psychiatric evaluation to be filed with the court. During the hearing, the defendant is still afforded due process rights, including representation by an attorney and the ability to testify and present evidence and to subpoena and cross-examine any witnesses (18 U.S.C. § 4247(d); see Amendment to 18 U.S.C. § 4247, 1984). Following the hearing, the judge makes the ultimate legal finding of whether the defendant has diminished capacity and is legally incompetent to proceed with the criminal case before them. If an evaluation and report are ordered by the court, the judge will consider the evaluator's testimony and/or report it as evidence during the hearing, but the judge is not bound to agree with the forensic evaluator's opinion. Sometimes only one assessment is completed, and sometimes more than one assessment is conducted—one by each party to the case (the defense and prosecution). State statutes determine how forensic evaluators are appointed: Some jurisdictions employ their own court evaluators, whereas others require the parties to hire private evaluators.

Attorneys do not typically receive formal training on assessing capacity, but each time they interact with a client, they are making informal judgments about their client's capacity to participate in the various legal processes, such as whether their client can communicate effectively about their case and understand their legal options. The ABA and American Psychological Association (APA) have published guidance for attorneys in making capacity judgments with older adults in the second edition of *Assessment of Older Adults With Diminished Capacities: A Handbook for Lawyers* (ABA Commission on Law and Aging & APA, 2021). The handbook recommends that attorneys and/or judges perform the following screenings for capacity: (a) a preliminary screening to identify any initial red flags indicating diminished capacity; (b) if needed, professional consultation or referral for a formal forensic evaluation; and (c) a final legal judgment of whether they can proceed with the case at this time. Most of the guidance for attorneys and judges has focused on determining capacity in civil matters, such as executing a will or identifying need for a full or partial guardianship. Although the broad recommendation to systematically screen individuals is similar in criminal contexts, procedures and outcomes will be different because the capacities required for adjudication through a criminal case, including the respective legal standards, differ substantially in civil and criminal contexts.

ISSUES IN COMPETENCY AND RESTORATION TO COMPETENCY

As described in the Introduction, older adults go through the process of aging at varying rates, and the process is quite heterogenous. The aging process is influenced by a myriad of factors, including some individuals' intersectional role as system-involved older adults (Holman & Walker, 2021) and the associated cumulative disadvantages (e.g., Merkt et al., 2020). Issues of competency (either permanent or temporary) become more of a concern for older persons due in part to natural aging, neurocognitive concerns, possible alcohol or substance use disorders, physical health problems, and the stress of legal system interactions (Frierson & Srinivasan, 2018), and perhaps even ageism, as described in the Introduction of this book.

One issue that has emerged in appellate cases is whether the failure to conduct a competency evaluation violates defendants' due process rights. Not many cases have prevailed under this argument, and one problem is that diminished capacities vary across people; therefore, it is difficult to meet the legal standards for incompetency. A second due process issue could occur if a defendant with diminished capacity is found incompetent to stand trial (IST). Some state statutes automatically require defendants to undergo restoration if competency is questioned and narrowly prescribe that the assessment must be conducted in a state hospital. However, substantial delays can occur in a defendant's case when courts cannot use discretion to decide whether a competency evaluation is the most effective path for the defendant and court case processing. Dementia-related disorders caused by aging have a poor prognosis for improvement, and referring defendants from jail to restoration, just for them to be found unrestorable, wastes legal system resources and contributes to further mental health declines (Callahan & Pinals, 2020; Gowensmith, 2019). Despite the poor prognosis for restorability to legal competence for cognitive and dementia-related disorders, judges in many states have little discretion on how best to handle the evaluation process under some state statutes. Without legal responses allowing individualized judicial responses to defendants' incompetency, the competency evaluation process may violate due process rights as defendants await trial for substantially long times (ABA Commission on Law and Aging, 2022).

Legal Standards in Competency

Although jurisdictional rules of evidence determine an older person's capacity to testify at trial, the Federal Rules of Evidence broadly state that "every person is competent to be a witness" with limited exceptions (Federal Rule of Evidence 601, 1975; see Chapter 4, this volume). As a defendant, there are several stages in the adjudicative process in which competency may be at issue with older adult criminal defendants (Frierson & Srinivasan, 2018; Wall et al., 2018), including standing trial, waiving rights, pleading guilty, being executed, or being released from prison early—discussed in Chapters 7, 8, and 9. Older adults are presumed to be competent unless otherwise adjudicated incompetent through a formal court hearing, which requires an evaluation (see Chapter 7, this volume). The legal standard for mental competency to stand trial (also called fitness to proceed) is guided by *Dusky v. United States* (1960), which was later extended to other adjudicative constitutional rights in *Godinez v. Moran* (1993). The legal standard test for competency to stand trial is whether the defendant is able to assist their attorney in the defense of their case as well as understand concepts related to the legal proceedings.

In a criminal case, an individual's constitutional due process rights to a fair investigation, adjudication (through plea bargain or trial), sentencing, and supervision or incarceration by the government are critical; however, most case law and research have focused on issues of competency to stand trial (i.e., capacity to assist in their defense) and retroactive assessment of whether a person had the capacity for criminal responsibility at the time of the offense (i.e., the insanity defense), with very little attention paid to diminished capacity during an investigation (i.e., capacity to confess), during sentencing (i.e., capacity for incarceration or execution), or once incarcerated for release (i.e., capacity for continued incarceration; see Chapter 9).

Restoration to Competency and Dementia

Older age has frequently been documented as associated with both incompetence (Fogel et al., 2013; Schwalbe & Medalia, 2007) and nonrestorability (Toofanian Ross et al., 2015; Zapf & Roesch, 2011), even after controlling for dementia symptoms (D. R. Morris & Parker, 2009). For example, D. R. Morris and Parker (2009) studied those in restoration treatment with and without a dementia diagnosis. The researchers used regression analyses that included patient characteristics and psychiatric illness, finding that patients with dementia were significantly less likely to be restored. Moreover, although restoration is possible for some people with dementia, the likelihood of successful restoration decreased by 10% per 5-year increase in age. Older adults with concerns of a dementia-related disorder are the least likely to be restored. A meta-analysis that collectively analyzed all selected studies on restoration to competency by Pirelli and Zapf (2020) found that approximately 81% of individuals overall were eventually restored, usually within 90 to 120 days; however, additional variables could not be analyzed because the body of research was not yet suited for meta-analyses because few studies included acceptable outcome measures. Because restoration research is lacking overall, it is not surprising that even less is known about issues specific to older adults.

As courts and researchers alike work toward improving the court-competency system, one avenue for doing so is for first responders to deflect cases (at Intercepts 0 or 1) or divert cases from court processing (Intercepts 2 and 3) in which public safety risk is low, and the defendant has obvious signs of dementia symptoms that is unlikely to be restorable (ABA Commission on Law and Aging, 2022; Dubljević, 2020). As case law on competency restorability and dementia symptoms is only emerging, and research is very limited (Pirelli et al., 2011), courts have been hesitant to assume that a diagnosis of dementia-related disease is a *per se* qualification for closing a case with the disposition of "incompetent and not restorable." It is critical that research focuses on understanding how functional capacity impairments caused by dementia contribute to ability for restoration to competency. Case law points to the overwhelming need to address the cycle that defendants with dementia experience in some jurisdictions. Legal scholars recommend that states examine their statutory barriers and court standards regarding competency evaluation and services (ABA Commission on Law and Aging, 2022; Dubljević, 2020; National Judicial Task Force, 2023).

In Nevada, dementia and other cognitive disorders do not qualify under civil commitment statutes (Nev. Rev. Stat. [NRS] § 433A.310(1)(b)), and in some states, civil commitment requires a "mental illness," generally a substantive disorder of mood or thought, but which typically excludes substance use disorders, intellectual disabilities, brain injury, or dementia (Substance Abuse and Mental Health Services Administration [SAMHSA], 2019). When defendants undergo a forensic evaluation and are determined to be IST, they are committed to a psychiatric hospital for restoration services (e.g., ABA Commission on Law and Aging, 2022; *State v. Silvils*, 2022). With dementia disorders caused by aging, as opposed to a brain injury in a younger person, a person is unlikely to regain the capacity required for proceeding with their case (D. R. Morris & Parker, 2009). They may cycle from psychiatric hospital, which is not designed for dementia-related disorders, back to jail and subsequent court hearings, with additional evaluations for competency, and possibly back to the hospital before it is eventually concluded that the services for restoring someone to competency are not appropriate for dementia as they are for other serious mental illnesses. Furthermore, as we detail in Chapter 8, jails are not well-suited for older adults and especially not for those with dementia.

Other issues have materialized for IST and older adults with dementia symptoms. Some argue that defendants could be faking their symptoms of dementia, that is, *malingering*, as in the case example of Ron Jeremy Hyatt (see Box 6.2), to receive what they believe are less punitive consequences. The frequency of such occurrences may be low, and safeguards are in place to account for malingering, such as psychological tests that measure whether someone is feigning symptoms. In the D. Miller (2020) review of appellate cases that involved legal questions involving dementia, the courts identified 13 cases (14%) in which evidence of the defendant's functional ability was presented showing that the defendant was feigning symptoms of dementia.

BOX 6.2 | INCURABLE DEMENTIA AND INCOMPETENCY TO STAND TRIAL? RONALD JEREMY HYATT, AGED 69

In 2023, Ronald Jeremy Hyatt (also known by his former adult television star name, Ron Jeremy) made headlines after Los Angeles County courts found him incompetent to stand trial (IST) for multiple rape charges from the 1990s, which collectively carry a sentence of up to 300 years in prison. Hyatt was arrested in 2020 and sent to the Twin Towers Correctional Facility; just 6 weeks before the trial start in March 2022, the court paused the case so that forensic evaluators could complete psychological assessments (Patten, 2022). His behavior had started to raise concerns about his ability to assist in his case, including Hyatt's refusal to attend a hearing and his defense attorney's assertion that Hyatt was "incoherent" and refused physical assistance to court (para. 5). After a series of evaluations, the judge found Hyatt IST and "suffer[ing] from an incurable neurocognitive decline" (para. 1). Hyatt was transferred to a state psychiatric facility where he could be held for up to 2 years (Paul, 2023). The prosecutor reported that the forensic experts retained by the prosecution and defense both agreed Hyatt suffered from severe dementia with no evidence of malingering.

Early media reports indicated the court ordered Hyatt to a residential competency restoration program and then continued prosecuting the case (Kalmbacher, 2023). However, it was later reported that nine "facilities refused to take him on as a patient" (para. 13) so instead Hyatt would be released to a private residence to receive medical care. Victims who testified have since expressed public anger at the court's legal response in Hyatt's case, and prosecutors have filed motions for the court to reconsider his placement (Queally, 2023). Understandably, due to Hyatt's notoriety, this case received considerable attention. Members of the public expressed concerns Hyatt was malingering. A comment under an online news article poignantly stated, "This feels all too convenient. Either this is an act, and he has fooled the court, or he was masking his cognitive decline before these charges have revealed their true extent" (Markson, 2023). Another commenter retorted: "The only person on the planet who thinks Ron Jeremy can act" (Anonymous, 2023). Although dementia symptoms in older adults generally continue to worsen, both Hyatt and Jackson (see Box 6.1) present risk factors that contributed to accelerated processes while in jail undergoing evaluations, such as lengthier time in detention and unhealthy lifestyles. As such, it is possible Hyatt did not present symptoms at arrest, but his cognitive function deteriorated through his detention.

Research has also found that those who were determined to be feigning symptoms of incompetency, on average, had shorter psychiatric hospital stays (Broderick et al., 2020), suggesting that individuals who were feigning symptoms are detected while under competency restoration services at the hospital.

Case law and anecdotal evidence suggest that it is difficult to place older and infirm individuals in community-based facilities that have sufficient medical care and supervision (see Chapter 9), even more so for those who cannot live independently due to physical or cognitive impairments. A significant challenge for the legal system arises when older adults with violent or sex-related criminal records require care. Most nursing homes refuse to admit such individuals, which complicates court-supervised care or correctional system oversight (Clark & Mezey, 1997). Moreover, state statutes limited to individuals with a mental illness may leave few options for where to place forensic patients with dementia (e.g., Nevada). Box 6.2 presents a case example that illustrates how courts have decided cases in which a defendant's dementia symptoms are progressively worsening with no evidence of restorability to competency to stand trial.

ISSUES IN SENTENCING

Even though a judge orders the final punishment, sentencing laws are created by the legislative branch. In these state and federal sentencing guidelines, the legislative branch outlines the range of permissible sentences for crimes. Using the guidelines, the judge can use their discretion in ordering a sentence, as long as it is within those statutory guidelines. State and federal statutes, however, vary on the discretion they allow. Whereas some jurisdictions impose mandatory minimum sentences and sentencing guidelines with little judicial discretion, especially for more serious offenses, other jurisdictions allow the judge more discretion to tailor the sentence to the crime and defendant. Once a defendant is found guilty of a crime, there are two phases to sentencing. The first is the determination of guilt (i.e., guilty or not guilty), which may be determined by a judge or jury. The second is the sentencing phase, which is determined by a judge in all but six states; in those six states, the determination is made by a jury. The next section discusses legal responses to older adults convicted of a crime that were developed under federal and state statutes interpreted by judges.

Legislative Sentencing Guidelines

Although each state has its own criminal code, states may also follow federal crime laws and procedures. State criminal codes, based on legislation and court rules, define specific crimes and their punishments. However, federal laws can sometimes take precedence or provide additional guidance. First published in 1987, the U.S. Sentencing Guidelines are rules published by the U.S. Sentencing Commission (2021) to produce determinate and uniform sentences across federal court judges in an effort to reduce indeterminate and inconsistent sentencing practices (Legal Information Institute, 2023). Prior to the establishment of the U.S. Sentencing Guidelines, the U.S. federal court system primarily ordered "indeterminate" sentences that consisted of a minimum and maximum range of the number of years to be served, and then, if and once an individual was up for parole, the parole board would decide on a case-by-case basis whether the person should be released from prison. Beginning in the late 1970s, there was a movement toward sentencing guidelines and "truth in sentencing," which aimed to increase certainty in time served by abolishing parole boards at federal prisons (and in some states) and creating benchmarks for the minimum time that must be served before release from prison (K. L. Mitchell, 2017).

Although Minnesota developed guidelines prior to the federal ones, no states have fully adopted the U.S. Sentencing Guidelines. Instead, states have developed their own sentencing guidelines from legislative statutes and court rules, which vary substantially across jurisdictions, ranging from some states with strict mandatory adherence to sentencing rules to other states with rules intended to be advisory. As a result, the rules that guide each state's sentencing policies can differ on key measures such as the risk assessment tool used and how scores are applied, the availability of departures from the rules (i.e., level of discretion permitted by judges), or how sentences can be served (i.e., consecutively or concurrently), which can greatly impact a person's sentence (K. L. Mitchell, 2017). The federal and state sentencing guidelines create the parameters within which judges then exercise discretion to adjust the punishment upward for aggravating factors or downward for mitigating circumstances.

Age and physical health are two mitigating factors that judges may consider under sentencing guidelines, whereas other factors, such as race, sex, national origin, creed, and socioeconomic status, cannot be considered during sentencing (6H, U.S. Sentencing Commission, 2021). Several cases have been brought by older adult defendants challenging sentences on the grounds that judges failed to adequately consider age as a factor. In interpreting the sentencing guidelines, courts have generally held that age should be considered as a mitigating factor only when age-related circumstances are present to an exceptional degree.

International Perspectives on Life in Prison and Parole for Older Adults

Like the United States, many other countries are experiencing the graying of their prison populations, with increasing rates of older adults in prison (Prais, 2019). Beyond just the aging of society, the prevalence of life sentences contributes to the aging prison populations. Most countries allow for life sentences, and the number of individuals who are incarcerated and serving life sentences almost doubled between the years 2000 and 2014. In India, 53.7% of its individuals who are incarcerated are serving a life sentence (Penal Reform International and Thailand Institute of Justice, 2018). The rejection of the death penalty by many countries has led to more dependence on life sentences as the harshest punishment. In some countries, such as Russia, Ukraine, and Romania, the legal systems do not allow a life sentence for individuals over 65 years old. In other jurisdictions, such as Spain and France, the legal system ensures that older adults sentenced to life have the possibility of leaving prison by making them eligible for parole when they are 70 years old (Prais, 2019).

Advanced Age as a *De Facto* Life Sentence

Three U.S. Courts of Appeals cases (*United States v. Bullion*, 2006; *United States v. Brooke*, 2002; *United States v. Johnson*, 2013) have interpreted how age should be considered as a mitigating factor in sentencing decisions. In each of the cases, older men were convicted of drug-related crimes (e.g., possession, selling, distributing) while 78, 58, and 70 years old, respectively, and had a history of criminal arrests and convictions. Across all three cases, the defendants argued their sentences were a *de facto* life sentence that violates the maximum sentencing guidelines because of their ages and health conditions. In all three cases, the court's decisions rested on whether the defendant's health status and age would deter future offending—a fundamental rationale for sentence leniency—but a *per se* downward deviation was not required. The case example in Box 6.3 illustrates the court's rationale in these cases.

Judicial Discretion

Little research has examined the sentencing guidelines and how age influences downward departures. In one known study using data from the federal

BOX 6.3 | AGE ALONE IS NOT A FACTOR IN SENTENCING, *UNITED STATES V. BROOKE*, AGED 82

Illustrating legal responses to older age in sentencing cases, the following case describes whether court decision makers must consider the defendant's age as a mitigating factor. The defendant in *United States v. Brooke* (2002) was arrested for conspiracy to sell cocaine at age 82. He had several recent drug-related convictions and probation violations. He was sentenced to 60 months in prison—the maximum under the sentencing guidelines based on his criminal history. During sentencing in the lower criminal court, the defendant presented evidence in support of his physical ailments (i.e., swollen knee, stiffness in hands, chest pains, respiratory problems, and arthritis) and argued that his health conditions and age meant the judge should mitigate his punishment and not give him the maximum sentence. The court did not adjust his sentence, and the opinion stated that age can be a factor to consider in mitigation, but judges have discretion in whether and how age is weighed in their decision. Moreover, the lower court and U.S. Supreme Court decisions explained that their rationale was not based on his age or illnesses, which they agreed were factors to consider. Rather, their decision relied on a separate provision of the sentencing guidelines: that sentencing could be reduced if an alternative "form of punishment such as home confinement . . . [would] be equally efficient as . . . incarceration" (5H1.1, U.S. Sentencing Commission, 2021). For the defendant, however, the court concluded home confinement would not be appropriate because of his history of selling drugs at his home. The court also indicated that age alone would not grant a downward sentence and that health problems need to be "extraordinary," and in this case, the courts did not think they were.

sentencing commission, Burrow and Koons-Witt (2003) analyzed all cases from 1999 ($n = 25{,}333$ defendants) to investigate age and health factors influencing downward departures. The study found significant variations across circuits in the general use of downward departures as well as determined whether circuits relied on older adult status (measured as aged 50 and older for analysis) for a downward departure. In just three of the circuits, there were downward departure trends based on age. The authors concluded that one of the "most salient findings is that the jurisdictions in which a defendant is tried and sentenced significantly influence" (Burrow & Koons-Witt, 2003, p. 323) downward departures for old age, which is contrary to the intent of the sentencing guidelines. Burrow and Koons-Witt concluded that one reason for this may be the lack of a common definition for what age is considered "elderly" under sentencing guidelines and suggested adopting a uniform definition, such as the age of social security eligibility.

Older defendants differ from younger defendants in physical appearance, psychological state, and life circumstances (D. Miller, 2011). What, if any, effect does this have on judicial system legal responses to older adults in sentencing? Research on whether there is an older age bias is not clear. According to focal concerns theory (Hartley, 2014), in determining a sentence, judges generally think of three things: blameworthiness (i.e., culpability, crime severity, and criminal history), protecting the community, and practical constraints (e.g., ability to complete the sentence, health condition, special needs, costs to correctional system or family members). Because judges do not necessarily have all the information about a single defendant, social–psychological theories suggest that they may rely on physical attributes or stereotypes about the defendant to assess whether they are likely to commit future offenses and are amenable to rehabilitation (M. S. Smith & Schriver, 2018).

In considering research on beliefs, attitudes, and behavior toward older adults in social psychology research described in the Introduction, theories suggest that judges could be more lenient because they perceive an older person as being less blameworthy and the community in less need of protection (low risk of danger or recidivism), and the person has higher practical needs that make incarceration less feasible (incarceration could be harsher, financial burden to corrections). On the other hand, according to research on stereotype consistency (Cuddy et al., 2005) and role congruity (Eagly & Karau, 2002), judges may give harsher sentences because older adults involved in the criminal legal system are viewed as deviating from traditional aging stereotypes and deserving of punishment, "knowing better," or being less amenable to rehabilitation because of old age.

Limited research on age bias in actual sentencing practices, based on analyses of large-scale archival court data, suggests a trend toward leniency for older offenders. Early research typically treated age as a continuous variable and assumed linear effects, finding small or insignificant effects on sentencing (Champion, 1987; Kramer & Steffensmeier, 1993; Peterson & Hagan, 1984). However, more recent studies have indicated a curvilinear effect on sentencing, such that younger adults (under 21) and older adults (50 and older) were less likely to be incarcerated and received shorter sentences (Steffensmeier et al.,

1995, 1998). At the intersection of age and other variables, such as gender and race, Steffensmeier and Motivans (2000) found that older adults received more lenient sentences than did younger adults in a large sample of cases from Pennsylvania. However, the leniency effect diminished when examining only drug offenses. The effects of age were stronger for men than for women—older women received the most leniency. At the intersection of group membership according to age, gender, and race, older offenders still received more lenient sentences (Doerner & Demuth, 2010; Morrow-Howell et al., 2014).

Building on previous archival studies, Martha S. Smith and Schriver (2018) administered a survey to a sample of 212 trial court judges to measure age leniency in sentencing decisions, within the context of the attitudes of aging and the judge's own age. Contrary to their hypotheses, the authors found that only 31% of judges acknowledged treating older defendants with greater leniency. Of those who indicated being lenient, the most frequent factors considered were cognitive impairment and criminal history, but attitudes or the judge's age was not predictive. Although leniency effects have been illustrated in archival research, experimental methods using fictional case facts will likely not get the same results if the judges ascertain the study purpose. According to M. S. Smith and Schriver, judges are particularly sensitive about not wanting to appear as treating groups differently and want to be perceived as being impartial. As such, additional prospective methodologies should be considered in gathering data on judicial sentencing decisions.

The Death Penalty and Competency for Execution

The United States has a growing death row population of older adults, and in many circumstances, they are more likely to die from natural causes than to be executed because of the length of time they spend on death row (Death Penalty Information Center, 2025). An emerging area of case law addresses whether the death penalty is an appropriate punishment for older adults and what is the legal standard for competency to execute (Stanziani et al., 2020). Historically, the Supreme Court has limited who can be sentenced to death, each time questioning whether the goals of punishment are being achieved by the death penalty. In *Ford v. Wainwright* (1986), the court held that it was unconstitutional (i.e., cruel and unusual punishment) to execute defendants who are mentally incompetent, opining that such executions are neither a deterrent nor retributive. In the *Atkins v. Virginia* (2002) case, this rationale was extended to defendants with intellectual disabilities and low IQ (see Salekin & Wood, 2023), and in *Roper v. Simmons* (2005), the limits of the death penalty were extended to juveniles.

In 2006, an older adult who was incarcerated in prison filed for a petition in a California district court for *writ of habeas* seeking relief from his death sentence in *Allen v. Ornoski* (2006a). He contended the sentence was cruel and unusual punishment under Amendment VIII to the U.S. Constitution, arguing that he was "elderly" and "woefully infirm" from physical ailments. The lower district court did not dismiss his execution, stating

> nothing about his advanced age or his physical infirmities (chronic heart disease, diabetes, legal blindness, and inability to ambulate), affected his culpability at the time he committed the capital offenses. There is no evidence now that he does not understand the gravity and meaning of his imminent execution. (*Allen v. Ornoski*, 2006b)

After the district court of appeals denied both of Allen's petitions for *writ of habeas* prior to his scheduled execution, Allen petitioned the Supreme Court, but the court did not agree to hear the case.

Then, the Supreme Court heard *Madison v. Alabama* (2019), again attempting to develop the legal standard for competency for execution. While incarcerated for nearly 30 years on Alabama's death row and having experienced mental health issues his entire adult life, Vernon Madison had several life-threatening strokes that left him blind, with slurred speech and unable to use the toilet on his own. He was unable to walk unassisted without a walker and presented with vascular dementia that left him unable to remember the crime or circumstances that led to receiving the death penalty. The Equal Justice Initiative in Alabama, founded by civil rights attorney Bryan Stevenson, represented Madison. The court held that Amendment VIII to the U.S. Constitution does not prohibit the state from executing someone if they do not remember the crime they committed, but it does prohibit the execution of someone who does not rationally understand the reasons for his execution—whether due to dementia or psychosis. Ultimately, the courts have asserted that physical ailments and age alone would not preclude execution, but once someone loses their rational understanding of why they are being executed, that crosses the threshold into cruel and unusual punishment.

CONCLUSION

Oftentimes, law enforcement and other first responders are placed in situations in which they must make fast decisions to promote the safety of older adults suspected of criminal behavior and the public, especially when a weapon is present. Social psychology research, however, shows that under these conditions, the quick judgments of police officers can be influenced by ageism. Concerning the safety of older adults in law enforcement interactions, aging researchers advocate for better identification systems to support early screening and preventive policies. Moreover, the ABA Commission on Law and Aging (2022) recently called for more effective screening as well as training and resources to help identify those who may have cognitive impairments that could deteriorate while detained in jail or going through the court process. For example, linking law enforcement and other first responders to dementia registries could inform legal responses by police officers when they encounter older adults, so they rely less on biased assumptions of incapacity and more on the information provided. With access to this information at the time of an interaction, law enforcement could better understand and respond to the situation, potentially preventing escalation or harm (Arias & Flicker, 2020).

Without any additional information, officers who arrive in a potentially dangerous situation have core legal responses that are applicable to all individuals during arrest. For instance, restriction on the use of excessive force (Amendment VIII to the U.S. Constitution) is civil rights protection for all individuals at arrest. However, as illustrated elsewhere, this core legal response may be insufficient to protect older adults from harm when law enforcement must use force to deescalate the situation. To this end, to prevent additional harm to older adults when police officer force is necessary, legal responses specifically direct that police officers should consider age when exercising force to ensure it is not excessive. In other words, law enforcement must modify their decisions around use of force based on perceived age of the person, and whether force is considered excessive will differ by older adult status. Legal responses meant to be preventive, however, can prevent further harm only if they are applied consistently. However, decisions on the use of force are made quickly, and judgments of someone's age in dangerous environments may not be consistently applied and rely on assumptions about the abilities of older adults and other environmental cues that could impact assumptions. Although age serves as a proxy measure for physical frailty in legal responses preventing excessive force, in practice, using age as a proxy can facilitate legal responses based in interpersonal ageism between the older adult and the police officer.

Additionally, the legal responses for law enforcement at the stage of arrest also include deflection from any system involvement or diversion to a more appropriate legal response, which can protect impaired older adults' due process rights. Although ensuring older adults' due process rights is a core legal response applicable to all persons during arrest, systematic early screening of older adults around the time of arrest is a preventive response because screening results can prevent further legal system involvement for an older adult with behavioral health needs. As such, law enforcement deflection and diversion practices, when based on systematic early screening, are supportive legal responses that can connect older adults with behavioral health needs to appropriate supervision or health care (Moll, 2013).

If an older adult is arrested and continues through the court process, legal responses from court decision makers also include prosecutorial and judicial discretion. Prosecutors decide whether criminal charges will be filed, and judges decide how the charges will be disposed (i.e., guilty, not guilty, or an alternative) and what the punishment will be at sentencing. Although researchers and policymakers have urged courts to promote supportive legal responses that divert and/or dispose of cases to alternative legal system responses, these practices are not consistently applied across jurisdictions, courts, and even judges. Like many legal responses in criminal procedure that aim to treat everyone equally, alternative legal responses, such as diversion to a specialty court (e.g., drug court, mental health court, veterans' court), are supportive legal responses available to many court-involved individuals and not a specific response to older adults. Legal professionals should be informed of community resources to divert older adult offenders from further involvement in the criminal legal system (Sun et al., 2019).

Indeed, most of the legal responses for older adults involved in the court system are core legal responses based on universal due process rights and equal protection. In determining criminal responsibility (*mens rea*) and an appropriate sentence, court legal responses mostly refrain from considering older adults as requiring distinct response. For instance, there is no separate test of criminal responsibility that speaks to a different standard of intent. In this sense, older adults are assumed competent at the time of the offense, unless found to be otherwise.

In sentencing decisions, age is one factor that judges can include as a mitigating factor. Although some studies have found a leniency effect whereby older adults received less punishment than did younger adults, the research does not indicate this leniency is applied consistently. Indeed, such legal responses that require judges to make individualized decisions are prone to ageist beliefs and attitudes, and, as such, legal responses of leniency may be based on faulty assumptions and applied inconsistently. For instance, although age can be considered in sentencing, the cases presented in this chapter illustrated that during sentencing for serious crimes, judges less often make sentencing decisions on age alone and more often incorporate functional capacity and/or potential for reoffending. More specifically, although older defendants have argued for sentence reductions because their advanced age makes any lengthy sentence a *de facto* life sentence, judges have opined that age alone is not a reason to have leniency, and in the cases presented, judicial decisions have instead pointed to defendants' continued criminal behavior—despite their age. With serious crimes, judicial legal responses appear to rely less on ageist beliefs that older adults are incapable and instead are prompted by environmental cues of criminal dangerousness. In legal responses stemming from courts, the seriousness of the criminal behavior likely modifies legal responses to older adults, such that less serious offenses are more stereotype-consistent, and serious offenses are stereotype-inconsistent. Thus, legal responses may be based on negative perceptions of stereotype-inconsistent defendants, resulting in more punitive outcomes for older adults involved in more serious criminal behavior than for older adults engaging in less serious crimes.

7

Forensic Evaluation of Older Adults in Criminal Cases

Treating people with a mental disorder specially, is a two-edged sword. Failing to do so when it is appropriate is unjust, but the opposite is demeaning, stigmatizing, and paternalistic. The central normative question is when special treatment is justified. . . . Only if the person has sufficient capacity for rationality does the law leave him or her free to pursue his or her own projects unencumbered by state intervention, to bear the consequences of his or her actions, and to be treated in the process as all other responsible, autonomous agents are treated. This accords the person the greatest degree of dignity and respect.

—Morse, 2011, p. 892

Psychological evaluation of older adults occurs in a variety of legal settings and for a variety of legal questions, and the evaluation process may differ depending on the defendant and case circumstances. Take, for instance, one scenario in which an older man is arrested for taking merchandise from a store without paying, typically a misdemeanor if the merchandise is under a certain value. Compare this to an older man arrested for possessing child pornography on his computer. If both men are brought to jail and show obvious signs of dementia and alcohol abuse, how does the criminal legal system respond and handle each case? What if their mental health condition does not become apparent right away, but instead symptoms are revealed while they serve their sentences? What may differ as one man is ordered by the courts to substance abuse outpatient treatment and the other to serve years in prison?

https://doi.org/10.1037/0000469-008
Aging and the Criminal Legal System: Community Services, Courts, Corrections, and Policy, by L. E. Wylie and E. M. Brank

As discussed throughout the current book, all adults are presumed to be competent, even older adults whose behavior does not conform to cultural standards of aging or stereotypes of the "elderly." Unlike children, whose decisional incapacity is clearly outlined by a state's age of majority, legal responses for older adults do not have similar *per se* age requirements. As described in Chapter 1 and throughout Part 2 of this book, advanced age is never a lone factor in determining whether an older adult should be treated differently in legal responses to legal competencies, criminal responsibility (i.e., *mens rea*), and/or the type and length of punishment. If all adults are and should be treated the same in the criminal legal system, then why does this book include a separate chapter on older adults and forensic evaluation?

It is important to take into account unique behavioral health considerations when dealing with older adults in the criminal justice system. An individual's age can have a significant impact on legal responses during various stages, including arrest, the adjudicative process, and sentencing (see Chapters 5 and 6). These factors necessitate special attention and understanding when addressing cases involving older adults. Whereas Chapter 6 discussed informal screening by law enforcement and court legal professionals, this chapter focuses on formal evaluations completed by licensed mental health experts (e.g., psychologist, psychiatrist, social worker)—forensic evaluators—for the purpose of assisting legal actors with making better-informed decisions about system-involved individuals (Heilbrun et al., 2002). Although there may be reasons for an older witness or victim to be referred for a forensic evaluation in a criminal case, in practice, forensic evaluations are usually not conducted with older witnesses or victim–witnesses. Instead, older adults in these roles are typically informally screened for issues such as ability to participate as a reliable witness or victim–witness (see Chapters 3 and 4, this volume) and would likely not participate in the criminal investigation or trial if deemed unable to participate meaningfully (Love, 2019).

Although widespread data are not readily available on the frequency with which older adults are referred for forensic evaluations, anecdotal evidence indicates a high need for forensic screening and assessment of older adults. Indeed, legal scholars have called for more formal screening of older adults to better document referrals for assessment, especially at earlier intercepts, because the legal system is ill-equipped to address the needs of older adults with cognitive disorders and high medical needs. By not screening for cognitive issues early in the criminal legal system process, defendants may be deprived of their due process rights to a fair investigation and trial (American Bar Association [ABA], 2022).

PSYCHOLOGICAL EVALUATIONS IN THE CRIMINAL LEGAL SYSTEM

A forensic evaluation is the systematic assessment, conducted by a mental health expert, for the purpose of informing the court about a defendant's behavioral health issues relevant to the facts or legal decisions in a case. To formulate their opinion, forensic evaluators may interview the older person, administer psychological tests, and/or gather collateral information from third parties (e.g., legal or medical records, interviews with family). Historically, forensic evaluators reported their conclusions as a generic description of the examinee's clinical adjustment, functioning, and mental health diagnosis, but these descriptors suffered from a lack of legal significance to courts. Today, following decades of research to develop legally meaningful evaluation methods, evaluators use assessment tools developed specifically to measure specific functional legal abilities (e.g., competency to stand trial). Such tools that are specific to the legal capacity at issue strengthen the relevancy of the mental health expert's conclusions so that judges no longer have to make connections between a clinical opinion of functioning or diagnosis and the legal question to be answered.

Because of the differences caused by normative and pathological aging processes as well as social and psychological determinants, forensic evaluators who specialize in aging are in high demand. In a recent article published in *Clinical Psychology: Science and Practice*, a new American Psychological Association (APA) journal aimed at publishing cutting-edge issues in clinical psychology, Mast et al. (2022) stated there is "a pressing need" (p. 43) for psychologists who are specifically trained to evaluate older adults. Without practitioners skilled in geriatric forensic assessment, older adults are vulnerable to judicial and correctional legal responses that may infringe on their legal rights afforded under state and federal constitutions (Reimers, 2019). To further exacerbate the issue, most psychological tests employed in forensic assessments were not developed to specifically assess older adults and instead were created with younger forensic populations. Using assessment tools designed for one group over a different group can be problematic. In such cases, clinicians cannot accurately determine if assessment scores fall within normal ranges for the individual being evaluated. The legal issues and practical concerns mirror what research discovered—namely, that assessment tools unintentionally caused racial biases (Venner et al., 2021).

In light of the research on normative aging that indicates older adults have more in common with middle-aged or younger adults than aging stereotypes would suggest, is there a justification for the legal responses of forensic evaluators to differ by age? Building off the recognition that young people in the legal system have evaluation needs that may differ from other age groups, geropsychologists—experts in psychological practice with older adults—urge forensic psychologists to gain specialized skills to provide services to the aging population. However, forensic mental health experts have had little guidance on whether, and how, they should adjust their typical forensic evaluation process to accommodate older adults. More specifically, although the American Academy of Psychiatry and the Law (AAPL) *Practice Guideline for the Forensic Assessment* (Glancy et al., 2015) discusses how to adjust an evaluation for children, adolescents, and individuals with intellectual disability, there is no special subsection for older adults, and the topic of dementia symptoms was only briefly discussed (Reimers, 2019). The lack of guidance for forensic mental health experts is concerning, given approximately 40% of psychologists reported working with older adults but also reported little specialized training in aging (Hinrichsen & Emery-Tiburcio, 2022). Clinical experts in aging assert the "pressing need for more psychologists trained to work with older adults" (Mast et al., 2022, p. 43).

APPLYING PRACTICES FROM GEROPSYCHOLOGY TO FORENSIC EVALUATIONS

As discussed in the Introduction, older adults have distinct experiences, strengths, and developmental gains, but they can also have losses and weaknesses that accompany aging. According to the American Psychological Association (APA; 2008), geropsychology is a subspecialty of psychology that applies the knowledge and methods of psychology to understanding and helping older adults. Geropsychologists are important for forensic evaluation because they have specialized knowledge about the biological, social, and psychological determinants of aging. This specialized knowledge includes a recognition of mental disorders that uniquely affect older adults, familiarity with the biological impacts of aging and specific domains affected as people age (e.g., cognition, social, emotional, personality), and an understanding of the social factors that contribute to individualized aging processes. Equally important is the less often discussed issue of aging biases that are held about older adults in these domains (see the Introduction).

The second volume of Lichtenberg and colleagues' (2015) *APA Handbook of Clinical Geropsychology* illustrates the typical diagnostic process for older adults and common symptoms to consider. For instance: Does the older adult have dementia symptoms? Delirium? Frailty? Are there behavioral health concerns, such as severe depression, anxiety, bipolar disorder, schizophrenia, or another psychotic disorder? Is the person currently using or have they ever used substances, including alcohol, recreational drugs, and/or prescribed medications? Importantly, experts performing forensic assessments with older adults must be trained to identify whether an older adult's behavior is the product of normative aging, medical disease, behavioral health, and/or physical or social functioning (Arnold, 2015). As with other legal professionals discussed in this book, forensic mental health experts must understand how ageist beliefs, attitudes, and behaviors influence their assessment conclusions and how they communicate their conclusions to the court.

FORENSIC SCREENING AND EVALUATIONS WITH OLDER ADULTS

Once cases get to the point of requiring a forensic evaluation, some steps have likely already taken place to informally assess or screen individuals for discretionary arrest or deflection (see Chapter 6). If the case is filed in court, at the sequential intercept model (SIM) Intercept 3, the defense attorney is often the person who initiates the order for a forensic evaluation by submitting a legal motion to the judge, likely after the defense attorney informally assesses their client as having some psychological or physical issues affecting their ability to assist in their case. As discussed in Chapter 6, however, a forensic evaluation can also be ordered by the judge or by a motion to the court by another case participant, such as the prosecuting attorney or other legal professional (e.g., probation, corrections).

The clinician's role in this process is to provide the court with a summary of the individual's skills, abilities, and deficits that may relate to their overall decisional capacity. A judge would then consider this evidence, along with other relevant information, to determine a ruling concerning the individual's competency (Moberg & Shah, 2012). Although sometimes only one expert offers an opinion to the court, depending on issues of fact in the case and any state law requirements, often there is more than one expert who offers their opinion following an evaluation. In general, research on expert forensic testimony agreement suggests that when there is a single evaluator, the judge tends to agree with that expert's opinion in their ruling (Neal et al., 2022). However, when there is more than one evaluator, agreement between experts declines as the number of evaluators increases, and judges tend to agree with the expert who was hired by the prosecution or the court, termed *adversarial allegiance*.

Despite the frequency of cases involving cognitive decline and anecdotal evidence from legal system actors, criminal forensic assessment research (D. Miller, 2020) has not focused much attention on older adults, producing little guidance for forensic evaluations with older adults. Recognizing this gap, the American Bar Association's (ABA's) Commission on Law and Aging (2022) has emphasized the importance of early and effective assessment for older individuals who may have diminished capacity when arrested or detained. This approach is illustrated using the SIM Intercepts 1 and 2 (see Chapter 5). The ABA's focus addresses the limited legal responses currently available for screening and assessing older adults in these situations. Forensic practitioners have expressed similar concerns, especially for older adults with nonreversible cognitive declines. As discussed in Chapter 6, courts and mental health experts have recognized that some older defendants, exemplified by Hyatt's case in Box 6.2, may not be restorable to legal competency to proceed with their case (D. Miller, 2020). Legal professionals' concerns are highlighted by the present U.S. "competency crisis," in which some individuals are waiting in jail longer for a competency evaluation than what their sentence may have been had their competency not been at issue (Gowensmith, 2019; National Judicial Task Force, 2023).

Age-related impairments can significantly change the evaluation process for older individuals. When assessing someone with such impairments, evaluators often need to shift their approach and rely more heavily on external sources of information. This is because the older person's condition may limit their ability to provide accurate information about themselves. As a result, evaluators frequently turn to family members, friends, and caretakers for insights into the individual's condition and behavior. They also rely more heavily on medical records to gather relevant information. This multifaceted approach allows evaluators to build a more comprehensive picture of the individual's mental state and capabilities, compensating for the challenges posed by age-related impairments (Mast et al., 2022). In addition, forensic evaluators may need to adjust their typical process to accommodate loss in hearing, vision, and processing speed (Lim & Loo, 2018; Mast & Gerstenecker, 2010) or other medical conditions more common among older adults than among younger adults. Clinicians diagnose individuals with the *Diagnostic and Statistical Manual of Mental Disorders* (5th ed.; *DSM-5*; American Psychiatric Association, 2013), and although it is appropriate to use across the lifespan, knowledge in geropsychology can enhance the utility of diagnostic systems for older adults (Mast et al., 2022). A foundation in geropsychology can help forensic evaluators become familiar with how contextual factors, cultural identities, and cohort differences impact functional impairment.

TYPES OF FORENSIC EVALUATIONS

Clinicians with forensic specializations are increasingly likely to encounter older adults in pretrial settings (Frierson et al., 2002) who may require an evaluation before appearing in court (Aday & Krabill, 2012; Fogel et al., 2013). The most common forensic evaluations to which an older adult may be referred are similar to the types of evaluations that a person of any age may require, including competency to proceed (i.e., competency to stand trial) during plea bargaining or trial, expert testimony on the defendant's legal responsibility, or determination of whether their risk level poses a danger to community safety during sentencing (Lewis et al., 2006). Although research and practice have focused primarily on assessment before trial (SIM Intercept 2), the criminal legal system also requires opinions from forensic mental health experts for other court operations, such as sentencing (SIM Intercept 3; see Chapter 6) and reentry from incarceration (SIM Intercept 4; see Chapter 9).

Competency to Stand Trial and Competency to Proceed

Competency evaluations are the most frequently requested court-ordered assessments. These evaluations aim to determine whether a defendant possesses the necessary mental capacity to understand and participate in the current stage of legal proceedings. As discussed in the Introduction, capacity and competency are related but distinct constructs in the legal system. Competency refers to a legal capacity determined by a judge or other legal professional as to whether the individual has the ability under law to carry out a specific act or series of acts (Darby & Dickerson, 2017; Marson, 2001).

Whether a defendant is competent to proceed (CTP) is a legal construct and is determined by the judge. To weigh their decision, judges rely on clinical opinions presented as evidence prepared by forensic mental health experts. Before 1960, psychological testing to decide competency to proceed was not typical, and the presiding judge made decisions based on the evidence introduced by the prosecution and defense. Then in 1960, the U.S. Supreme Court heard *Dusky v. United States* (1960), which created the legal standard for determining whether someone is CTP. The *Dusky* standard requires a defendant to have "sufficient present ability to consult with his lawyer" and "rational as well as factual understanding of the proceedings" (p. 402) and standardized the legal criteria for competency to proceed. Because *Dusky* extended to state courts, each state has adopted legislative and/or court rules outlining the process for determining whether someone is CTP.

Scholars, practitioners, and courts alike have noted an exponential increase in court orders for preadjudication competency evaluations (Kois et al., 2024; S. Morris et al., 2023). Although forensic evaluators report an anecdotal increase in referrals for competency evaluations and lengthy delays to restore individuals to be CTP, there is little data on the specific characteristics of individuals court ordered for various forensic evaluations (Callahan & Pinals, 2020; Gowensmith, 2019). Since the 1970s, researchers have attempted to collect data on the frequency of competency evaluations. However, a significant problem persists: Comprehensive data, including details about case factors and defendant demographics, have been unavailable or nonexistent. Consequently, there is minimal information about who is ordered for competency evaluations and the types of cases associated with orders (Kois et al., 2024). Of the few analyses with available data, trends show that most court orders for competency evaluations are for cases with nonserious misdemeanors (Callahan & Pinals, 2020; Gowensmith, 2019), often cycling through the criminal legal system due to serious mental health and cognitive illnesses (National Judicial Task Force, 2023).

Competency to Proceed and Research With Older Adults

A meta-analysis completed by Pirelli and colleagues (2011) sought to compare CTP outcomes between age groups, among other factors. Age comparisons were not included in the meta-analysis because studies did not consistently report the age of their samples. Of the studies that did, they exclusively focused on young adults (average 33 years old, range 30–38), and extraordinarily little is known about other age groups. In general, studies have found that individual characteristics do not strongly predict orders for competency evaluations or the outcomes of the evaluation (i.e., incompetent to proceed [ITP] and CTP). However, individual characteristics are associated with the length of hospitalization while undergoing competency restoration services (Callahan & Pinals, 2020; Renner et al., 2017).

Research focusing on older defendants and competency evaluations is limited. However, the available studies show a trend similar to that observed in younger adults: Most older defendants referred for evaluations of competency to proceed are found competent to stand trial and return to court to continue with their cases. If an older defendant is determined ITP, however, then research shows that they often have dementia-related and psychotic disorders—like the case example of Joseph Jackson introduced in Chapter 6 and continued in this chapter (see Boxes 6.1 and 7.1).

One study examined whether there were demographic and case differences between older adults found CTP and ITP (Heinik et al., 1994). In a sample of court-ordered evaluations in felony cases from 1991 to 1999 ($n = 8{,}250$), the overall prevalence of older defendants (aged 65 and older) was 0.8% ($n = 66$). Of the 57 cases with sufficient data, two in three (66%) older defendants were found CTP. As compared with older defendants found CTP, older defendants found ITP tended to be older and more frequently diagnosed with a dementia-related disorder, but the rates of other diagnoses did not differ by group. Contextualizing these figures is important: Forensic evaluations typically include older adults with higher risk and higher needs, such as alcohol dependency, dementia-related disorders, antisocial personality disorders, and those with violent offenses and/or prior convictions (Lewis et al., 2006).

BOX 7.1 | DETERMINING COMPETENCY WHILE IN PRETRIAL DETENTION IN SOUTH CAROLINA: JOSEPH JACKSON, NOW AGED 74 (CONTINUED FROM BOX 6.1)

After his arrest in April 2021 for shooting at law enforcement while they served a warrant for failure to register as a sex offender, Joseph Jackson was transported to jail. In January 2023, Jackson, then aged 74, was determined to be incompetent to proceed following a forensic evaluation that diagnosed him with a delusional disorder, dementia-related disorder, and posttraumatic stress disorder. South Carolina's "Fitness to Stand Trial" standard is akin to the *Dusky* standard—a defendant is not fit to stand trial if they "lack the capacity to understand the proceedings against him or to assist in his own defense"—but further adds from the *Dusky* standard that legal competency must be "as result of a lack of mental capacity" (S.C. Code § 44-23-410(A), 2024). Media reports indicated Jackson was court ordered to a state psychiatric hospital for 60 days for restoration services. Jackson waited 4 months in jail for an available bed at the psychiatric hospital, and after 60 days, he returned to jail (Schumer, 2023)—18 months after the incident. Although 18 months is a long time, it is not an uncommon duration, according to forensic psychology experts in forensic competency evaluations (e.g., Gowensmith, 2019). What should happen with someone such as Joseph Jackson who has diminished capacity, mental illness, and dementia? Although individuals found incompetent to stand trial often have psychotic disorders such as Jackson's delusional disorder, and many have their competency restored, we know much less about the restorability of someone with a dementia-related disorder.

Incompetency to Proceed and Restoration to Competency

If the defendant is found CTP, their case proceeds to trial or other methods of disposition, such as plea bargain or deferred disposition, pending court requirements. If the defendant is found ITP, they are ordered to receive competency restoration services. While the defendant is receiving services, often in a state forensic hospital or jail, the legal case is postponed until the defendant is determined CTP by the judge (who again relies on opinions from mental health experts). Typically, competency restoration services include medication and education aimed at increasing knowledge of the court process. The purpose is not treatment for any underlying behavioral health problems but for the individual to be fit enough to proceed with the legal case. At times, the court may find that a defendant is unlikely to be restored to competency (Melton et al., 2017), often due to developmental disabilities or nonreversible cognitive-related issues. If a court determines a defendant nonrestorable, the legal procedures that follow differ according to each state. For further discussion of issues that arise in cases in which someone is found unlikely to reach CTP status, see Chapter 6 (see also Box 6.2).

In cases in which defendants are determined ITP and undergo restoration services, the trajectory of services and the legal case may be complex. In some cases, a defendant is restored within a month once they are consistently taking their mental health medications. For other defendants, their illnesses may contribute to less predictable treatment plans and outcomes, and their level of capacity can vary throughout the restoration process. A defendant may regain competency during restoration services but then digress before their trial, then return to restoration services. Such situations are challenging for evaluators and the courts alike. For instance, an evaluation conducted weeks or days apart could produce varied expert opinions. Consequently, when the case requires more than one evaluator, this can produce contradictory and confusing findings, as demonstrated in the case example in Box 7.2.

Using data from all patients admitted to a California state hospital from 2010 to 2018 under ITP orders ($n = 20{,}041$), Broderick and colleagues (2020) investigated the role of clinical and demographic factors with length of stay for patients involuntarily committed to a California state psychiatric hospital under competency statutes. The sample included individuals aged 18 and older, with a total of 4,152 study observations of those aged 50 and older (21%), indicating that a substantial proportion of older adults are undergoing competency evaluations and being found ITP. The researchers' analysis indicated that having a severe mental illness (i.e., schizophrenia) and a history of violence, as well as older age at admission, were the strongest predictors of how long a patient was hospitalized under court-ordered IST treatment. The authors concluded that because aging is related to chronic mental and medical illness, older adults are more impacted by deficiencies in cognition and learning that is required of restoration to competency services. Of note, the study included a small sample of individuals with neurocognitive disorders (2%, $n = 445$), which was not related to length of stay and demonstrates the much smaller

BOX 7.2 | **MULTIPLE EVALUATORS AND COMPETENCY TO STAND TRIAL IN DELAWARE**

In a Delaware criminal case, a 61-year-old man with a 40-year history of schizophrenia, alcohol dependence, and antisocial personality disorder was charged with stabbing his former attorney on the street (*State v. Silvils*, 2022). State law permits the presiding judge to decide whether the evidence presented satisfies Delaware's standard for "too mentally ill to stand trial" (11 Del. C. § 404(a), 2024) and to decide whether there can be multiple evaluators (hired by defense and prosecution). In the case, two mental health experts testified: the state's expert psychologist, Dr. Roberts, and the defense's expert neuropsychologist, Dr. Bell. Collectively, evaluators submitted eight reports over a 36-month period (over the COVID-19 pandemic in 2020) spanning his arrest to disposition in February 2022. During competency hearings, the two experts presented contrary opinions. In response to the different opinions, the court commented that "the two experts' opinions are best described as two ships passing in the night" (*State v. Silvils*, 2022, p. 21).

A primary reason for their differing opinions, in part, was that their evaluations of the defendant did not occur in close temporal proximity. As stated in the court opinion,

> The Court sought to schedule a competency hearing but recognized that each delay in the opposing evaluations due to "leapfrogging" expert evaluations, prevented the experts from making an apples-to-apples comparison regarding his condition. In other words, the delays in the successive evaluations left open the possibility that [the defendant] would be competent at the time of one evaluation, but then would decompensate by the time of the next evaluation. (*State v. Silvils*, 2022, p. 14)

Dr. Bell, the defense's evaluator, diagnosed the defendant with a dementia-related disorder and testified that dementia symptoms presented while he was detained; overlaid with schizophrenia, the dementia "rendered him incompetent to stand trial" (*State v. Silvils*, 2022, p. 21). Because the prosecution did not provide rebuttal evidence to the dementia diagnosis, procedurally the state did not meet its burden of proof required in criminal cases. As such, the court determined the defendant was ITP.

Dr. Bell's testimony also stated that the defendant was unlikely to regain competency following his diagnoses, which would mean he would be detained at the state hospital indefinitely receiving competency restoration services. The court chose to postpone addressing whether a dementia diagnosis should warrant not following the typical process, indicating that if the state wants to maintain that the defendant is competent, it would need to offer rebuttal to the dementia diagnosis. The court scheduled a competency hearing 6 months later, and in an effort to prevent the "leapfrogging," set a strict schedule for the competency evaluation.

number of individuals referred for ITP with only a diagnosis of cognitive illnesses rather than serious mental illness. As the judge in the example in Box 7.2 illustrated, the court systems are responsible for ensuring forensic evaluations are being completed and evidence presented to the court in a timely manner (National Judicial Taskforce, 2023). As leaders in the judicial branch, judges and court administrators must continue to identify legal responses appropriate for individuals who are assessed at lower risk but have higher needs and reserve legal system resources for the most serious cases.

Evaluation of Criminal Responsibility

Older age may also be at issue for determining criminal responsibility and presenting evidence for an insanity defense. As discussed in Chapter 1, in determining whether a defendant had criminal intent to commit the offense, it is not sufficient for the government solely to prove the *actus rea* (bad act); the defendant must also have criminal intent, *mens rea* (guilty mind), at the time of the offense. A forensic mental health expert may be called to determine whether the person lacked *mens rea* at the time of the crime, based on the state's legal standard (see Chapter 1 under the section on criminal responsibility).

Although forensic mental health experts can be called to evaluate a defendant's criminal intent, not all courts have allowed such testimony because of practical and reliability challenges. Unlike evaluations for competency to proceed, assessing for criminal responsibility requires forensic evaluators to give their opinion as to the defendant's mental state at the time of the crime—which could have been 2 days ago or 2 decades ago. Further complicating the utility of criminal intent evaluations, mental health experts must connect the defendant's mental state at the time of the offense to their behavior at the time and also account for whether the defendant is malingering or faking their symptoms in hopes of receiving lesser punishment (Ferguson & Ogloff, 2011). Indeed, forensic psychological evaluations to determine *mens rea* are challenging due to the absence of any biomarkers, low reliability between evaluators, and potential cognitive biases (Scarpazza et al., 2021). In retrospective assessments, there is typically less information, and the evaluator is drawing assumptions about a past behavior, based on the defendant before them in the present. Situations presenting less information for decision making are the most likely to introduce aging biases, as predicted by social–psychological theories of perception (see the Introduction for discussion of specific theories).

Because criminal responsibility evaluations are done much less frequently than are competency evaluations, there is much less social science research on the former than on the latter and, consequently, few recommendations. As discussed in Chapter 5, crime statistics and trends show that older adults typically commit less serious offenses more frequently than they commit serious ones. However, within the context of evaluating criminal responsibility, the types of crimes that reach the stage of trial are more serious cases. Based on criminal cases in Turkey from 2014 to 2019, a retrospective chart review of

150 older men and women (aged 65 and older) who were referred for a determination of criminal responsibility identified that two thirds of cases involved homicide, attempted homicide, or sexual offenses (Tasdemir et al., 2023). In most of these cases, the defendant was opinioned to have the requisite *mens rea* at the time of the crime (76%). In the remaining cases (24%) in which the defendant was found not to have the requisite *mens rea* at the time, the defendants were most often diagnosed with a dementia-related disorder (37%) or schizophrenia (31%) and less often diagnosed with other mood or delusional disorders.

Forensic geropsychologists have noted a significant research gap. As Heck and Vauter (2018) noted,

> Despite the fact that psychotic disorders are the most frequent threshold condition in not guilty by reason of insanity (NGRI) defenses of all ages, no literature base exists that separately addresses older adults with psychotic or affective disorders in an NGRI context. (p. 167)

Of the literature specific to older adults, most focused on cognitive issues such as delirium, Alzheimer's disease, and frontotemporal dementia.

COGNITIVE AND DEMENTIA-RELATED DISORDERS

In legal and clinical communities, interest is growing in individuals with dementia and cognitive-related disorders and their involvement in the criminal justice system. This interest spans issues of competency, criminal responsibility, and mitigation in sentencing (ABA Commission on Law and Aging, 2022). However, research in this area is just emerging. One method that researchers use to examine the impact of an issue on the criminal legal system is to conduct a systematic analysis of appellate court cases and qualitatively code cases for key variables within each case; however, case law methods are limited to appellate cases (judges in trial courts rarely write opinions to be analyzed) and do not account for cases disposed by plea bargains or cases dismissed or dropped by prosecutors before trial at Intercept 1. Moreover, the available information may underestimate the true extent of the issue. This is because older adults may be diverted from the criminal legal system through law enforcement discretion at the initial point of contact (known as Intercept 0). As a result, many cases involving older adults with dementia symptoms may never enter the formal legal system, making it difficult to accurately assess the full scope of the problem.

A recent review of case law by the ABA Commission on Law and Aging (2022) examined cases involving individuals with dementia symptoms and their ability to stand trial, criminal responsibility, and mitigation in sentencing or release from incarceration based on diminished mental capacity. Generally, ABA's review indicated that case law involving dementia disorders and questions of law were sparse, but the most frequent area was in competency to stand trial—specifically, cases wherein individuals argued that their due process rights were violated when the court failed to order a competency evaluation *sua sponte* (on its own motion). The authors concluded that in CTP cases with dementia at issue compared with those without dementia at issue, it might be more difficult to prove incompetency to proceed "due to the subtle presentation of symptoms" and "individualized rates of disease progression" (ABA Commission on Law and Aging, 2022, p. 21).

D. Miller (2020) conducted and presented a more systematic case law review to better understand how dementia symptoms and competency have appeared in U.S. appellate court cases. After searching for cases with dementia disorders and competency to proceed at issue from 2002 to 2019, researchers coded 90 cases for defendant and case factors, how the issue of competency was raised in the case, the number of independent forensic evaluations conducted in each case, indicators of dementia-related diagnoses and functional impairment, and the evaluator's (or evaluators') opinion. Defendants in these cases were almost all male; in the cases in which age could be determined, the average age was 69 years old; and about one third of the criminal charges were for violent offenses. The defense raised the issue of competency most often in three out of four cases, and the court or prosecution did so in the remainder. Just under half of the defendants (47%) in the sampled cases were determined incompetent to stand trial (Frierson et al., 2002; Heinik et al., 1994). D. Miller (2020) identified that the most common diagnosis was dementia not otherwise specified (47%), followed by Alzheimer's disease (10%) and vascular dementia (8%).

Challenges in Connecting Neurobiological Impairments to Legal Standards

Clinical and legal scholars have noted that dementia symptoms pose specific challenges for mental health experts in accurately diagnosing and specifically connecting the person's neurocognitive impairments to capacity (or lack of capacity) necessary for each legal question (ABA Commission on Law and Aging, 2022; D. Miller, 2020; *State v. Silvils*, 2022). For one, there is not a single test to identify dementia or diagnose someone with a dementia-related disorder. Currently, an evaluation includes a full medical history, mental status tests, physical and neurological exams, neuropsychological tests, laboratory and genetic tests, psychiatric evaluation, and brain imaging (Alzheimer's Association, 2019). However, diagnosing dementia disorders and understanding how they contribute to competency is not a widely held skill of evaluators. In the case example presented previously (*State v. Silvils*, 2022) involving the man charged with stabbing his former attorney on the street (see Box 7.2), one of the issues was the difference in evaluation diagnoses from the two evaluators, Dr. Bell, hired by the defense, and Dr. Roberts, the state evaluator from the Delaware Psychiatric Center. The court's legal determination for incompetency to stand trial was based on the judge's reasoning that the state had not adequately met its burden of proof to rebut a diagnosis of dementia. In his testimony, Dr. Roberts explained that neither he nor anyone at the Delaware Psychiatric Center had the expertise to evaluate dementia-related disorders and that no staff were qualified to determine the impact of dementia symptoms on the defendant's competency. If the state wanted to continue to pursue the case, the court directed the state to instead secure "an appropriate competency evaluation by a neuropsychologist or other appropriate expert" (*State v. Silvils*, 2022, p. 25) either through a change in protocol or hiring an outside evaluator. Although it is not clear from the opinion how the evaluators were hired and paid, the expertise needed to diagnose a dementia disorder confidently among experts, as well as the expense of doing so, poses a challenge to due process, especially for defendants who are indigent or lack capacity.

Second, although clinicians can identify neurocognitive symptoms and functional impairments generally consistent with dementia symptoms with a high level of certainty, accurately diagnosing the underlying disease and disease progression is more challenging with psychological tests common to forensic evaluations (D. Miller, 2020). This means that it can be difficult to determine when cognitive impairment is severe enough to be eligible for categorical protections from the law, and the challenges posed differ depending on the legal question asked. Assessing the current mental competency of someone with early dementia symptoms presents challenges. Their capacity may fluctuate over time, making it difficult to obtain an accurate evaluation. Additionally, the legal process for determining competency can be lengthy, further complicating the assessment. This poses challenges that differ from retroactively diagnosing dementia disorders and functional capacity at the time of the offense for criminal responsibility. Although neurocognitive science supports a judicial determination that dementia symptoms impede the ability to establish *mens rea*, there are practical and legal challenges for showing the defendant's dementia at the time of the offense (Arias & Flicker, 2020). First, dementia-related disorders are underdiagnosed, and many older adults with dementia symptoms have not been formally diagnosed with a specific disorder (Amjad et al., 2018). If a defendant is unaware of their diagnosis, any events leading to a criminal act could predate their diagnosis and affect criminal responsibility. Take, for example, a 65-year-old man who grabs and hits a patron at a grocery store. The store clerk calls the police, and the man is arrested for assault and battery. The incident is not typical of his behavior, so the defendant seeks out medical care and learns he has frontotemporal dementia and that the assault and battery could have been the result of the illness. Because he was not aware of the diagnosis, the defendant and legal defense would likely face challenges demonstrating that the defendant was experiencing symptoms at the time of the offense, which could mitigate his criminal responsibility.

Another issue is that dementia disorders do not clearly fall under either of the standards as qualifying for the insanity defense. For example, the *M'Naghten* test may exclude individuals with frontotemporal dementia because this type of dementia does not affect cognitive capacity or cause impairment to rationality (Mendez, 2010; Sfera et al., 2014). On the other hand, because symptoms of frontotemporal dementia may contribute to inability in controlling behavior even when an individual understands that an action is wrong, an individual with this dementia disorder may qualify for the insanity defense in states that use the American Law Institute test but not the *M'Naghten* test (Berryessa, 2016).

Forensic Neuropsychological Assessment

Traditionally, forensic evaluators have solely examined psychosocial factors, such as mental health symptoms or substance use, family or parenting status, and employment or educational experiences, and how psychosocial factors impact functional abilities using information observed or gathered through client interviews and collateral information (e.g., interviews with others and documents). With growing attention on biological and neuropsychological factors that contribute to antisocial behavior (e.g., Gao & Raine, 2010; Meldrum et al., 2018), there is a need for understanding how neurocognitive disorders affect functional abilities using neuropsychological testing with tools validated and normed on older adults (Mast et al., 2022). In part, this attention was driven by advances in technology and science, including wider availability of functional magnetic resonance imaging technology, which allows researchers to better understand the role of neurobiological factors in risky or violent behavior (van der Gronde et al., 2014). For example, we now have a better understanding of the role that traumatic brain injuries can play in criminal behavior (Kuin et al., 2019; W. H. Williams et al., 2018), and studies in brain development have identified regions of the brain responsible for specific types of behaviors (Meldrum et al., 2018). Although functional magnetic resonance imaging and other brain scan technologies have become more available to multidisciplinary research teams to study the relationship between neurobiology and functional abilities, these resources are extremely expensive and likely not at the disposal of most criminal legal systems. Furthermore, cognitive-related disorders—especially the diversity of disorders that fall under the general term *dementia*—have a myriad of causes that make diagnoses more challenging (see the Introduction) than a mental health or substance use diagnosis.

CONCLUSION

Following arrest and if an older adult is detained in jail, limited funds and other barriers may make a complete psychological, behavioral, and cognitive assessment impossible, especially for the types of assessments typically required for cognitive-related disorders—neuropsychological assessments. Because of delays in court calendars and scheduling assessments, older adults with cognitive-related disorders are at increased risk of harm (see Chapter 6). Legal decision makers and policymakers should glean insights from the competency crisis and challenges associated with restoration to competency for individuals determined to be unrestorable (Gowensmith, 2019; National Judicial Task Force, 2023). Lessons achieved in criminal legal responses for individuals with behavioral health needs can be applied to legal responses for older adults, who, as a group, will likely have the most behavioral health needs.

Within forensic evaluation, legal competency has been the most examined and discussed. The legal standards and process for older adults have essentially remained similar to other standards and processes in the adult criminal legal system. For instance, the *Dusky* legal test for competency to proceed is similarly applied to everyone, and there are no *per se* age requirements that treat older adults distinctly. Thus far, the legal responses to accommodate older adults in forensic evaluation as they apply to criminal contexts have been minimal, despite Mast and colleagues' (2022) call for psychologists to specialize in working with older adults in legal contexts. In part, this lack of accommodation is due to lack of guidance for mental health experts and lack of resources for conducting required neurobiological or neuropsychological assessments. Even though the AAPL forensic guidelines discuss forensic evaluation and older adults, the context is for guardianship in civil law, with no mention of forensic evaluations in criminal contexts for older adults. Additionally, there are no known forensic evaluation assessment tools specific to older adults, but regardless, most of this limited attention has focused on diminished capacity and/or legal competency (ABA Commission on Law and Aging & APA, 2021). Presently, that attention is directed to the complexities of assessing dementia and cognitive disorders, which also disproportionately impact people as they age, but not all people.

Although there are no approved guidelines specific to older adults in the AAPL *Practice Guideline for the Forensic Assessment*, the medical history section of the guideline alerts evaluators to "the presence of degenerative brain diseases . . . that sometimes . . . mimic psychiatric presentations" (Glancy et al., 2015, p. S17). Under the section on psychological testing, the guideline suggests that neurological testing combined with focused diagnostic testing to identify the cause of dementia symptoms may be a "better use of resources" than a battery of personality tests common to the standard forensic evaluation practice. In 2021, the APA published *APA Guidelines for the Evaluation of Dementia and Age-Related Cognitive Change*, supporting psychologists' use of specialized neuropsychological tests that can differentiate "pathophysiological dementia from age-related cognitive decline, cognitive difficulties that are depression related, and other related disorders" (APA Task Force on the Evaluation of Dementia and Age-Related Cognitive Change, 2021, p. 3).

Neuropsychological testing is not yet universally available within forensic evaluation, and such a legal response is very costly. Research has promoted the use of neuropsychological assessments to accommodate legal responses for individuals with cognitive decline, but case law examples describe the financial barriers and legal problems that such testing has already revealed (see Box 7.2 illustrating the state's inability to rebut dementia evidence). If the expense of forensic evaluations is not equitable across adversarial sides, then modifications to the standard forensic evaluation could produce unintended disparities in case outcomes.

8

Older Adults in the Correctional System

"Aging in Prison"

Katie Engelhart (2023), a *New York Times* journalist experienced in covering dementia-related stories, recalls a particularly haunting encounter from her reporting: "That of a prisoner who, as a result of cognitive impairment, no longer remembers his crimes—but is still being punished for them. We don't know exactly how many people in American prisons have dementia because nobody is counting" (section 2, para. 1). This case struck Engelhart deeply, highlighting the complex ethical issues surrounding incarceration and cognitive decline. It also underscores a significant gap in the criminal justice system's understanding and tracking of dementia among prisoners.

As she reported, dementia may go unnoticed because older adults are not routinely screened for dementia and related disorders unless they exhibit symptoms, which can go masked by the "monotony of institutional life. . . . A person can get by, for a while, just by following the man ahead of him" (Engelhart, 2023, section 2, para. 5). Brie Williams, a leading geriatric medicine scholar in aging and incarceration quoted in the Tokar (2006) article, questioned: "What do we, as a society, want to do with a prisoner who is so demented he doesn't remember his name, or who has had a stroke and is completely paralyzed?" (para. 10). As discussed in previous chapters, older adults usually prefer to remain in their homes, neighborhoods, and communities as they age, which is known in policy and research as "aging in place." Studies show improved cognition, depression, performance of activities of daily living (ADLs), and continence in participants who age in community settings, as compared with institutions (Marek et al., 2005).

https://doi.org/10.1037/0000469-009
Aging and the Criminal Legal System: Community Services, Courts, Corrections, and Policy,
by L. E. Wylie and E. M. Brank

DEFINING OLDER ADULTS WHO ARE INCARCERATED

As discussed in the Introduction and throughout this book, older age is inconsistently defined within criminal legal settings and literature involving older adults. There is even a different age cutoff that applies to older adults who are incarcerated. Geriatric medical scholars specializing in the health of older adults who are incarcerated define an older adult as 50 and older (Loeb & AbuDagga, 2006; B. A. Williams et al., 2012). In this context, the definition of *older adult* includes younger ages than do the other definitions of older age discussed in earlier chapters because individuals within correctional facilities are some of the unhealthiest individuals in the United States (Marek et al., 2005; B. A. Williams et al., 2012). This is due in part to socioeconomic issues and unhealthy lifestyles before and during incarceration but also because incarceration often exacerbates medical issues that already existed (Curran, 2000).

Geriatric medical scholars believe that incarceration modifies aging patterns and contributes to an accelerated or premature aging process, whereby functional abilities decline much faster, compared with living in the community (Brinkley-Rubinstein, 2013; M. Greene et al., 2018; Merkt et al., 2020). Prolonged and/or repeated incarceration also exacerbates cumulative disadvantages experienced early in life, especially for minoritized populations, such as untreated physical health and mental health issues; social isolation; oppression from ageism, sexism, and racism; toxic family stress; lack of access to quality education and services; and discrimination and institutional barriers (Maschi & Morgen, 2020). Consequentially, older adults who live in jails and prisons likely experience aspects of normative and pathological aging sooner (Loeb & AbuDagga, 2006).

THE NEEDS OF OLDER ADULTS IN JAILS AND PRISONS

Research with individuals in correctional facilities most often includes those sentenced to prison, with far fewer studies that examine jail populations. Jail populations tend to be more transient than those in prisons because jails usually only house individuals waiting to be prosecuted or sentenced or those sentenced to less than a year, whereas prisons include individuals sentenced for longer periods. This means that jail populations are often different than prison populations. In a retrospective analysis of electronic health records in a New York City jail between 2015 and 2019, data revealed an increase in the number of older adults 55 and up admitted to the jail each year, with several noted vulnerabilities: This age group was most likely to be unhoused; suffer from serious mental illness; carry the burden of chronic, infectious, and serious medical illnesses; be hospitalized during detainment; and die in jail custody (Bedard et al., 2022). A national survey of jails in 2005 found that most of the sample included older adults with extensive legal system involvement (70%), described in Chapter 5 (this volume) as the inveterate chronic older offender type, and a smaller proportion of the sample were more like first timers with few contacts with the legal system (30%; Kuhlmann & Ruddell, 2005). Data indicated that older adults were the least likely to be involved in problem behaviors while in jail, such as disruption or assault of other inmates or staff, but were also the most likely to be victimized and engage in self-harm and/or suicidality.

More than 203,000 people are now serving life sentences in U.S. prisons, and approximately 61,000 of them are 55 and older (Nellis, 2021). Older adults in prison mostly come from disproportionately racial/ethnic minoritized groups or communities of poverty and often suffer from issues with trauma, mental health, and substance use (Maschi & Morgen, 2020). America's prisons are experiencing what some have called the "silver tsunami" (Jefferson-Bullock, 2018), as the median age of individuals who are incarcerated has significantly increased and produced many new challenges for the correctional system. The sizable increase is mostly attributed to the "get tough on crime" policies from the 1980s and 1990s that sent more people to prison and for longer terms, including life sentences (see the Issues in Sentencing section in Chapter 6). Therefore, there has been an increase in both total admissions for older adults and a greater proportion of individuals serving longer sentences (Carson & Sabol, 2016). To illustrate, the Bureau of Justice Statistics reported a 400% increase in the number of state prisoners 55 and older during a 10-year period from 1993 to 2013 (Carson, 2020). In 2021, data revealed that 30% of the prison population were older adults (Nellis, 2021).

Most individuals aging in prison are there for violent offenses and sentenced to longer sentences (Lemieux et al., 2002)—even though most older adults coming in contact with law enforcement and the courts are more likely to be arrested for minor offenses (Feldmeyer & Steffensmeier, 2007; see Chapters 5 and 6, this volume). The profile of an aging prisoner, therefore, includes not only the three typologies outlined in Chapter 5 (i.e., the inveterate, the relapsing, and the first-time offender) but also individuals who were incarcerated at a younger age and aged in prison while they completed a long or life sentence (Fattah & Sacco, 1989). In other words, the aging of American prisons is both because the United States incarcerates people as older adults and because some people are in prison for so long that they become an older adult and likely experience accelerated aging while living in prison (Stoliker et al., 2022). Social and medical factors also contribute to the proportional increase, as the Baby Boomer generation became age 50 and up in the 1990s, and medical advances in health care continue to extend human life expectancy (Aday & Krabill, 2013; Auerhahn, 2002).

Physical Health

Older adults in jails and prisons have unique needs compared with their younger counterparts. On average, older men and women who are incarcerated have three chronic physical health conditions, such as diabetes, heart disease, and pulmonary issues (Falter, 1999; Lane et al., 2020) and require seven to 10 medications (Mai & Subramanian, 2017). Estimates suggest approximately 30% to 44% of older adults in jails or prisons present pathological impairments, including dementia disorders, traumatic brain injuries, and developmental deficits (Cipriani et al., 2017; du Toit et al., 2019; Maschi, Sutfin, & O'Connell, 2012). In addition, older adults may have mobility issues and physical ailments caused by arthritis and osteoporosis. In a sample of 238 older adults in jail, aged 55 and older, M. Greene and colleagues (2018) identified high rates of hepatitis C (50%) and HIV (12%), with many also experiencing other conditions that can contribute to poor health, including recent illegal drug use (64%), homelessness (45%), and serious mental illness (56%). Whether these conditions developed before or after incarceration, they are intensified by high chronic stress (Lin & Mathew, 2005; Munday et al., 2019).

Older adults in jails and prisons are typically less physically healthy than are older adults who are living in the community. Although some research has compared groups by the difference in prevalence of chronic health conditions (Binswanger et al., 2009; Prost et al., 2021), other research compared group differences in *geriatric conditions* that limit ADLs (see the Introduction). Consistent with the accelerated aging theory, older men in jail (aged 55 and older) had higher rates of all geriatric conditions limiting ADLs, hypertension, chronic lung disease, stroke, and arthritis than did a representative matched sample of older men living in the community. Moreover, even though the mean age of the jail-based sample was 59, their number of geriatric conditions (an average of four) was similar to those of the group of community-dwelling older adults aged 75 and up (M. Greene at al., 2018).

Mental Health and Psychological Distress

Compared with older adults in the community, older adults in jails and prisons also experience much higher rates of mental health issues. A descriptive study in Utah of 360 older adults in prison (over age 50) specified that both the rate of depression and the rate of schizophrenia were higher in older adults living in prison than in older adults in the community (Caverley, 2006). The author further explained that across all age groups, mental health problems were greater among individuals in correctional facilities because in practice, they serve as *de facto* replacements for long-term mental health care (Caverley, 2006; National Judicial Task Force, 2023). To illustrate, data suggest approximately one in five older adults (20%) in the community experience mental health issues (Volkert et al., 2013), most often depressive symptoms (Edens et al., 2012; Volkert et al., 2013). Yet, a systematic review estimated that 38.4% of older adults who are incarcerated experience at least one psychiatric disorder, most commonly depression and personality disorders (Di Lorito et al., 2018). Of the nine studies that met inclusion criteria in Di Lorito and colleagues' systematic review, six exclusively included male samples. Importantly, there is a notable absence of research estimating the prevalence of cognitive and psychiatric disorders—especially for older women—as most studies with jail and prison samples have included older men. Indeed, the prevalence of mental health disorders for incarcerated older women is higher than for incarcerated older men (Steadman et al., 2009), some have explained, because older women have greater trauma exposure than do older men (B. L. Green et al., 2016). Older women were more likely than older men (both over age 55) to report having a mental health diagnosis before incarceration and taking medication for symptoms (Lane et al., 2020).

Research has sought to better understand the adverse life experiences of the aging population (e.g., adverse childhood experiences; Messina et al., 2007). Evidence suggests that older adults who are incarcerated have experienced high levels of trauma, stress, grief, and loss. Most experienced a traumatic and stressful life event (70%) that included childhood and/or adult exposure to violence, unexpected or expected loss of a loved one, family separation, or being diagnosed with a serious physical or mental illness (Maschi et al., 2015). In addition, a review of case files demonstrated that many older males in prison have a history of sexual victimization (Haugebrook et al., 2010; Zgoba et al., 2013), which is associated with adverse mental and physical health in older adults (Lamet et al., 2008). Approximately 40% of older adults indicated exposure to violent victimization measured with the Trauma and Stressful Life Experiences Screening Inventory (Maschi, Gibson, et al., 2011). Specifically, younger adults reported more physical assaults, but older adults reported more natural disasters, life-threatening illnesses, and death of a loved one.

While incarcerated, older adults generally report experiencing poor subjective health and high psychological distress (Baidawi et al., 2016; Nijhawan, 2016) due to both individual and institutional factors. However, perspectives may be different for "older" older adults and "younger" older adults as they adjust to life in prison. For instance, in a sample of older individuals who were incarcerated aged 55 and older, the "younger" older adults reported higher levels of cumulative traumatic and stressful life events and subjective psychological distress than did the "older" older adults (Maschi, Morgen, et al., 2011). A comprehensive literature review including 19 studies between 1985 and 2010 indicated that older adults (aged 50 and older) experienced several stressors associated with prison conditions, their physical health and access to health care, housing assignments and services offered, and fear of victimization (Maschi, Morgen, et al., 2011). Experiences of aging in prison may be further complicated by suicide. Among inmate populations, older prisoners have the highest rates of suicide, consistent with suicide trends in community-dwelling populations (Barry et al., 2017; Carson, 2020). Researchers suggest that older prisoners may be at greater risk for suicidal ideation based on higher rates of chronic disease, functional disability, pain, and mood disorders (Barry et al., 2017).

The psychological stress of prison may be more harmful to older individuals than to younger ones (Caverley, 2006; Maschi, Morgen, et al., 2011). The experience of incarceration can cause damaging psychological injuries, including mental health disorders and symptoms (e.g., depression, anxiety, posttraumatic stress disorder, dissociative symptoms, anger, fear of safety) and substance use disorders (Caverley, 2006). Social work professor Tina Maschi and her colleagues have extensively studied the experiences of older adults in prisons (e.g., Maschi & Morgen, 2020) and in one study found a positive association between objective and subjective measures of trauma, stressful life events, and posttraumatic stress symptoms (Maschi, Gibson, et al., 2011; Maschi, Morgen, et al., 2011). Understanding the different types of traumas that incarcerated individuals experience as both children and adults can be used to develop or improve trauma-informed services that target needs based on age and experience.

Anxiety Surrounding Death and Dying

Perhaps the most notable stressor is death anxiety around the older adult's own death in prison and the death and loss of others. Deaths in prisons happen for several reasons, including accidents, suicides, homicides, natural causes, and, in rare cases, executions. According to mortality statistics, most individuals died in custody from illness (87% of deaths), and many of these were older adults aged 55 and older (Tofle, 2009). Consistent with trends of the increasing rate of older adults in prison, they are also accounting for a higher proportion of deaths in prison. To illustrate, in 2019 older adults accounted for 63% of all deaths in prison, but in 2001 they accounted for only 34% of deaths. More than death itself, the surroundings in which death occurs represent one of the most significant issues for people. Dying in prison is often very different from dying in the community (Dawes, 2002; M.-F. O'Connor, 2004; Ratcliff, 2005). Behind bars, a person thinks about the possibility of dying all alone and the loss of having family present for support or time for reconciliations.

Sociologist Ronald Aday (2006) compared the average death anxiety scores of 102 Black and White men aged 50 years and older living in a maximum-security prison (their average time to parole consideration was 11 years) with similar-aged community members. Findings revealed higher death anxiety among those in prison than among those in the community. The reasons underlying death anxiety for older men were influenced by death as an escape from prison and the stigma associated with incarceration. Using a comparable methodology, the researchers completed a study with a sample of 327 women aged 50 and older who were incarcerated in one of five prisons (average time left on their sentence was 17 years; Deaton et al., 2010). Like the previous sample of older incarcerated men, death anxiety was higher for women who were incarcerated than for similar women residing in the community. The reasons underlying death anxiety for women were influenced by perceived lack of health care and indifference of prison staff and other instances of harm by the penal system.

Interpersonal Relationships and Victimization

Studies have examined interpersonal relationships and social support of older prisoners and identified that relationships can be both distressing and supportive. Many older adults who are incarcerated report social trauma resulting from separation from their family and community (Maschi et al., 2015). For instance, individuals who are incarcerated for longer periods of time may no longer receive regular visits from their family and friends who are also aging and can no longer make visits. They may also have fewer stable relationships because of divorce or estrangement from family resulting from life before and during incarceration (Aday & Krabill, 2013; Flanagan, 1995; Leigey, 2010). Nonetheless, some older adults report they receive support from corrections staff during incarceration. For instance, older adults described positive interactions with staff members: They were treated with respect, and they could turn to staff with problems (Crawley & Sparks, 2005).

Inversely, a perceived lack of social support from staff and other inmates while in prison has been linked to an increase in psychological distress (Baidawi et al., 2016) and anxiety around death and dying (Aday, 2006) among older adults. More specifically, some studies have found that interactions with correctional officers and health staff can be distressing for older prisoners, especially when navigating health care systems for chronic health and mental health issues (Aday & Farney, 2014; Crawley & Sparks, 2005; Loeb & Steffensmeier, 2011; Mann, 2012). For example, a qualitative study with older women in prison described interactions as infantilizing, unresponsive, disrespectful, and degrading, which felt contrary to what the older women saw as their "place within the generational order" (Wahidin, 2004, p. 169).

Another concern is whether older adults are more vulnerable to being victimized while incarcerated. Research on the safety and victimization of older prisoners, however, has been limited, despite correctional institutions recognizing that the victimization of older adults is a serious institutional concern, with some institutions establishing specialized protective custody programs or units for older prisoners (Aday, 1994). In general, quantitative research with administrative data shows that younger adults face a higher risk of victimization than do older adults (Steiner et al., 2017). Observable signs of physical and cognitive decline could mark them as vulnerable targets and increase risk to victimization (Baidawi, 2016; Kerbs & Jolley, 2007). Similar to the general victimization concerns described in Chapter 3 of this volume, older adults who are victimized experience higher psychological distress (Baidawi, 2016) and more serious health consequences compared with younger incarcerated persons. Interactions with younger adults are commonly described by older adults as a source of distress in prisons, often described as fear of victimization, especially for those experiencing declines in physical functioning (Aday, 2003; Baidawi, 2016; Mann, 2012; Wahidin, 2004).

Are the fears of victimization from older adults who are incarcerated warranted? Kerbs and Jolley (2007) gathered administrative data on victimization and conducted follow-up surveys with a random sample of older prisoners and documented the frequency of four types of victimization: psychological, environmental, property, and physical and sexual. Administrative data revealed a high prevalence of all five types, mostly perpetrated on older prisoners by younger prisoners. Survey data identified the most common examples of each type. Psychological victimization included being cut in front of while waiting in line, verbal insults, attempted physical threats, being labeled a snitch, and verbal threats. Environmental victimization examples included excessive noise (e.g., talking loudly, screaming, and playing the radio loudly, all violations of the prison rules) as well as exposure to secondhand cigarette smoke. Examples of property victimization included being cheated out of money or having items stolen from their cell. Older adults reported that property victimization was common and believed it was because they appeared generous and vulnerable to manipulation from other prisoners. Although physical and sexual victimization was less common, some older adults reported being attacked without a weapon and/or sexually harassed verbally or physically. A small number reported being raped or sexually assaulted or repaying debts through sexual acts.

Well-Being and Coping Strategies

Older adult prisoners experienced a concerning level of trauma stemming from both the physical and mental stresses of incarceration, but researchers have identified positive coping strategies for improving well-being among older incarcerated adults. Coping strategies can be thought of as being either internal strategies that are cognitive, emotional, spiritual/philosophical, and physical or external strategies such as social support from family and friends. Internal resources, such as self-control and emotional awareness, were significantly correlated with prisoners' overall positive functioning pre- and postrelease (Day et al., 2008). External coping resources included religious activities, social and occupational functioning, social support from family and friends in the community, and peer support within the prison system.

To identify coping strategies, Maschi and colleagues (2015) surveyed 677 older adults (aged 50 and up), mostly men (96%) who were incarcerated in a Northeastern U.S. state prison. The study measured cumulative trauma from childhood through incarceration, posttraumatic stress symptoms, and whether coping strategies were associated with better well-being while incarcerated. More than half of the respondents reported experiencing current abuse and/or other stressors in prison, such as being physically or socially targeted by guards or other inmates, with the average age of the first incident in prison at age 47. Despite cumulative trauma and stress, the respondents reported relatively positive outlooks and healthy coping strategies, which served as protective factors for improving both physical and mental well-being while in prison. In another study, using qualitative interviewing techniques, 31 older adults (age 40-plus, 78% male) provided experiential narratives of incarceration, revealing experiences of past trauma and abuse; loss of family and friends on the outside; untreated medical issues; and verbal, sexual, and psychological abuse. Despite the negative experiences they recalled, they also shared positive opportunities for accessing services, refraining from substances, resting, and healing (Smoyer et al., 2019).

HOUSING FOR OLDER ADULTS

Jails and prisons are some of the most stressful, least accommodating environments and were certainly not built with an aging population in mind. The intensity of the physical and interpersonal environments, including emphasis on authority, overcrowding, lack of privacy, architectural impediments, and threats of violence and exploitation, makes prisons particularly ill-suited places for older persons (Human Rights Watch, 2012). Scholars in fields such as medicine, nursing, gerontology, social work, public health, and even anthropology have studied and recognized the harm that is exponentially caused to older adults incarcerated in restrictive institutional environments (Aday & Krabill, 2013; Danely, 2022; B. A. Williams et al., 2012). As such, there has been growing attention to the most appropriate legal responses to balance government and victim interests in punishment and retribution, with humanistic person-centered health and end-of-life care for older adults residing in correctional facilities. Facilities have developed various approaches to address the rise in incarceration rates of aging adults, including legal responses that modify policy so that more older and/or infirm adults are released (see Chapter 9) or that accommodate older adults so they can live within correctional facilities.

In prison, independence requires mastering unique functional tasks beyond traditional activities of daily living (ADLs). These prison-specific tasks, known as prison activities of daily living (PADLs), were developed by B. A. Williams et al. (2006) based on standard gerontological categories of functioning (see the Introduction, this volume). PADLs include functional activities required within prison settings, such as dropping to the floor for alarms, hearing orders, walking to the dining hall for meals, walking with handcuffs on, standing in line for medications, and climbing up and down from the top of a cell's bunk bed. Impairment in ADLs, those activities that are required for independent living (e.g., bathing, toileting, eating), is a significant predictor of depression and suicide in older adults who live in community settings (Barry et al., 2013; Conwell et al., 2010; Ormel et al., 2002). Similarly, in individuals who are incarcerated, Barry and colleagues (2013, 2017) studied older adults (aged 50 and up) in prison and found that impairments in PADLs were also significant predictors of depression and suicidality, with the impact even stronger for males than for females.

Because aging prisoners may begin to suffer impairment in both ADLs and PADLs, correctional facilities are faced with deciding how to approach accommodating loss in functional impairment. Although some legal responses have focused on designing separate facilities or wings within current facilities to accommodate older infirm adults, other responses instead keep older and infirm individuals within the general population and make accommodations and/or provide services within those existing housing units (see Box 8.1 for examples from Virginia and Nevada).

BOX 8.1 | **TWO EXAMPLES OF APPROACHES FOR AGING IN PRISON: VIRGINIA AND NEVADA**

Regardless of the approach to separate older adults or keep them integrated into the general population, special housing and services for older adults are typically stretched thin in prisons. Take, for example, Deerfield Correctional Center in Virginia, a prison where older individuals are "sent to grow old" (Sieff, 2010, para. 3), which contains a 57-bed assisted living unit for aging adults (as well as a second unit for military veterans). These beds are consistently full, with a waiting list. Also in Virginia is an 18-bed infirmary that provides hospice services for prisoners who are dying and need end-of-life care. As with most facilities, the infirmary must also have beds available for individuals with nonterminal acute issues, such as recovering from a recent surgery or other short-term medical issues needing continuous care. Since implementing its program, Deerfield Correctional Center has tightened eligibility criteria for transferring prisoners to assisted living or hospice facilities. This ensures that only inmates with the most critical needs are moved to these specialized units. In years prior, individuals would have been eligible for assisted living if they could not perform one activity of daily living such as bathing, dressing, or walking, but the prison has since limited the criteria to include an inability to perform two or three activities of daily living (Ollove, 2016). A reporter for *The Washington Post* visited the unit and interviewed prisoners, the warden, and nurses working at the facility. While there, the reporter noted that there were few lucid individuals, with most having dementia, some who were bedridden and needed assistance with rolling in their beds to avoid bedsores, and others who needed assistance with going to the bathroom (Sieff, 2010).

Another example of one state's approach is the Northern Nevada Correctional Center's True Grit Senior Structured Living Program for elderly inmates, which is available for approximately 120 prisoners aged 60 and older. The program involves daily activities for residents that are encouraged, but not required, including sporting events, performance plays, time with companion dogs, and crafts. The program encourages fellowship among aging inmates for companionship and support and was designed to enhance their physical health through activities, mental health with group and individual therapies, and spiritual health with coordinated volunteer and chaplain services (Harrison, 2006).

HEALTH CARE FOR OLDER ADULTS

With the number of chronic health conditions, including dementia and other cognitive disorders, it is important to provide adequate health care to older adults, even though it is very costly to corrections systems. Accommodations for aging prisoners constitute some of the highest expenditures for prison systems in the United States—largely attributed to the simultaneous increase in the number of aging prisoners and rising costs of care (Murolo, 2020). The Vera Institute's Center on Sentencing and Corrections reported in its publication entitled *The Price of Prisons: Examining State Spending Trends, 2010–2015* that it costs an estimated $70,000 per year per person to incarcerate someone over the age of 60, compared with $22,000 per year for younger people (Mai & Subramanian, 2017). State and federal eligibility for Medicare and Medicaid are suspended when a person is incarcerated, thus state corrections budgets foot the bill for costs.

Over time, although many states spent more money because of rising prison populations, 10 states' prison spending increased even though the prison population decreased during that time. After employment expenses, rising health care costs were the other largest expense—more than doubling between 2003 and 2013—for typical chronic health conditions that affect older adults such as dementia, mobility problems, and loss of hearing and vision (Mai & Subramanian, 2017). As prisons face rising numbers of medical issues among inmates, they may need to enhance their health care services to manage long-term costs more effectively. For instance, one of the largest expenses is contracting medical care outside of prison; thus, creating in-house services that care for chronic illnesses (e.g., dialysis) could significantly reduce costs.

When it comes to determining the most efficient housing and health care model for older adults in prison, there is debate within correctional systems and among researchers. Although some facilities have chosen to create specialized in-house units with centralized health care, away from the general population, others have consolidated older adults in housing units within the prison or used a combination of the two (Thivierge-Rikard & Thompson, 2007). Thivierge-Rikard and Thompson's analysis of Bureau of Justice Statistics data from the Census of State and Federal Adult Correctional Facilities indicated that one noted benefit of consolidated health care for older adults is that these facilities provided more general mental health services (nongeriatric); however, these facilities did not increase the availability of nongeriatric mental or physical health services. With further analyses, the researchers concluded that the presence of other programs in the facility (i.e., work, educational, and counseling/special programs) accounted for any effects of consolidated geriatric care, suggesting that the availability of programmatic resources can provide advantages similar to those found in specialized geriatric housing.

Proponents of specialized in-house accommodations suggest that these special units could alleviate some of this financial strain, improve older adults' quality of life, and minimize victimizations. Managing vulnerable groups requires consideration of functional and cognitive ability and navigating logistical obstacles such as prescription medication oversight. When individuals require similar specialized medical staff, medical equipment (e.g., dialysis machines), and mobility accommodations (e.g., wheelchair ramps, grab bars), it is less expensive for these health services to be in a common location. Opponents of separate housing for older adults argue that integrating them with the general prison population is beneficial. This integration allows them to access both age-specific services (e.g., specialized health care) and general services (e.g., recreational activities; Thivierge-Rikard & Thompson, 2007). Moreover, staying with the general population maintains long-term relationships with other incarcerated individuals, and consistency in environment and housing is important for promoting healthy aging. In Nebraska and other states, for instance, younger adults who are incarcerated work as health aides, which allows older adults to stay in units that are familiar to them and have younger peers for support. Younger adults employed as health aides for older adults may also benefit (see Box 8.2).

BOX 8.2 | **HEALTH PORTERS OR COMPANIONS: NEBRASKA, CALIFORNIA, AND MASSACHUSETTS**

Another program tried in some jurisdictions (e.g., Nebraska, California, Massachusetts) involves inmate health porters, that is, incarcerated individuals with specialized training (i.e., certified nursing assistants) who help older incarcerated individuals with health care needs. The programs were instituted to reduce the costs of hiring outside help. Inmate porters must pass a rigorous selection process before being hired. This process includes a security screening to check for recent misconduct, a review of their criminal history, a psychological evaluation, and an interview with a panel of security and medical staff. Successful candidates are paid an hourly wage significantly higher than what other prison jobs pay. Although no research to date has evaluated the programs, anecdotal communications indicate that porters feel the position allows them to gain redemption for prior mistakes and creates more meaning out of their time in prison. One inmate porter was quoted as saying, "I'm gonna die in here. I want to have a program like this available so when I need it, it is there" (Correctional News, 2014, para. 10). Inmate peer programs have also been used to positively support persons with dementia, such as California's Gold Coats program and California Men's Colony, which utilize a peer support program in which volunteer inmates provide protection and facilitate social integration for those with dementia in the correctional setting (Garavito, 2019; Maschi, Morgen, et al., 2011). Limited research exists on the effectiveness of inmate health porter or companion programs. Studies are also lacking on how participants view their roles, whether as providers or recipients of this care.

Challenges Specific to Dementia

Incarcerated populations are diagnosed with dementia disorders at a higher rate than the general population and face a series of unique challenges, given the disease process and environmental difficulties and accelerants (American Bar Association [ABA] Commission on Law and Aging, 2022; Brook et al., 2020; Maschi, Kwak, et al., 2012; M. C. Miller et al., 2023). One study compared South Carolina's registry of Alzheimer's disease and related dementias with South Carolina's Department of Corrections data (fiscal years 1992–2016) to compare the prevalence of diagnosed dementia-related disorders in incarcerated and community populations (M. C. Miller et al., 2023). In the general population, the rate of dementia-related disorders was 6.7% compared with 14.4% in the incarcerated population. Furthermore, those who were diagnosed with dementia-related disorders earlier—that is, between 55 and 65 years of age—had a significantly lower age at first incarceration compared with those diagnosed later in life (mean of 34.6 years versus 55.9 years of age at first incarceration). In other words, those incarcerated earlier in life were more likely to also be diagnosed with dementia-related disorders earlier in life.

Although most individuals enter prison as younger individuals without cognitive decline, as the aging process accelerates in prison, they begin to experience symptoms of cognitive decline throughout their sentence (see an example of decline while detained in Box 6.2). Currently, most correctional facilities do not regularly screen for dementia symptoms or other cognitive-related declines (ABA Commission on Law and Aging, 2022; Peacock et al., 2020), and dementia and related illnesses are likely underdiagnosed (Baillargeon et al., 2023). If facilities are screening, they may not occur at meaningful intervals or early enough for preventive efforts (ABA Commission on Law and Aging, 2022; see the Preface for discussion of Nebraska's screening). Dementia is progressive, and early signs may not be detected, which could be further exacerbated by inmates' inability to detect their symptoms and the desire for many inmates to reduce any appearance of vulnerability (Maschi, Kwak, et al., 2012). Because of underdiagnoses, individuals with dementia symptoms may experience heightened fear and distress and denial of access to appropriate health care, which is a violation of civil rights. The lack of understanding by correctional staff can lead to conflict between staff and inmates, restraint, and segregation that could escalate dementia-related distress (United Kingdom Ministry of Justice, 2018). As with other stages in the criminal legal system, to date, there is truly little research on aging, dementia, and corrections. A recent systematic review of research, published in the *International Journal of Prison Health*, identified only eight studies conducted internationally on dementia disorders in corrections and recognized dementia as a public health concern for correctional populations and facilities (Peacock et al., 2020).

Correctional facilities have new responsibilities for providing health and social care to older adults in jails and prisons. Importantly, to support those living with dementia in correctional settings, health and legal scholars call for enhanced screening of dementia in jails and prisons to identify dementia as early as possible. Early detection is important so that the correctional system health care team can tailor interventions to meet the needs of each inmate. Without ongoing screening, it is challenging to meet the needs of older adults in correctional facilities, and it is also difficult to know the progression of the disease to determine whether the individual is still appropriately in prison.

Recent recommendations from fieldwork suggest keeping individuals with cognitive impairment integrated into the general population for as long as possible because segregating them from other cognitively healthy inmates in the initial stages can hasten cognitive decline by way of reduced social and emotional opportunities. However, prisoners with dementia may experience episodes of wandering and agitation caused by restrictions and locked doors (Maschi, Kwak, et al., 2012). In addition, unfamiliar environments can be destabilizing as the disease progresses (Hagos, Butler, et al., 2022; Maschi, Kwak, et al., 2012). Allowing individuals with dementia to have this consistency can mitigate distress and improve prognoses; however, this must be balanced with institutional safety and policies in place to reduce the risk of injury and victimization (Hagos, Butler, et al., 2022; Maschi, Kwak, et al., 2012). As illustrated in Box 8.3, experts have proposed that integrating memory care systems into inmates' current living spaces may be the most practical way to ensure both consistency and safety (Hagos, Withall, et al., 2022). Even in the absence of specialized programs, research suggests relatively inexpensive and easy-to-implement structural changes may help maintain independence and dignity for those with dementia in prisons. These changes could include marking cell doors with assorted colors, installing handrails and nonslippery floors, placing older inmates in lower bunks, and allowing for more time to respond to stimuli such as drills (Mistry & Muhammad, 2015).

LEGAL ISSUES AND RESPONSES IN PRISON HEALTH CARE

Regardless of spiritual or moral debates, the U.S. Constitution requires that incarcerated individuals receive health care. Conversely, the right to refuse treatment while incarcerated is also constitutionally protected. Failure to meet these requirements may be a constitutional violation of Amendment VIII to the U.S. Constitution as cruel and unusual punishment. Ethically and constitutionally, legal and health care scholars have discussed the ethical balance in human rights between preserving individual human rights in aging health care and maintaining victims' rights to a fair distribution of justice. The incarceration of people with dementia, especially, poses a unique set of legal, ethical, and health-care–related questions that impact multiple social systems and demand attention (ABA Commission on Law and Aging, 2022). Within the prison context, the correctional priorities are to maintain safety, mitigate risk, and reduce vulnerability, which may be contradictory to the goals of ethical provision of health care for the sickest and most vulnerable groups (Hagos, Withall,

BOX 8.3 | **TWO EXAMPLES OF MEMORY DISORDER UNITS IN PRISON: MASSACHUSETTS AND NEW YORK**

In recognition that nursing homes are not a placement option for violent or sex offenders, the Memory Disorder Unit at the Federal Medical Center in Devens, Massachusetts, opened in 2019. It was the first for those incarcerated with a dementia diagnosis and was designed similarly to a memory care facility. The unit uses a multidisciplinary team approach (i.e., nurses, doctors, correctional staff, facilities, and executive staff) to provide medication management, therapeutic recreation, and safety modifications for up to 36 individuals in the middle stages of dementia. Policies and procedures were developed specific to the unit to employ best practices in staff safety, security, pat-down searches, communication techniques, and environmental changes to promote a calming effect. For example, most of the walls are painted a calming pale pink, and cell doors have pictures to help navigation (Engelhart, 2023). Correctional officers on the unit receive training from the National Council of Certified Dementia Practitioners to understand how symptoms of dementia progress and better understand how symptoms may look similar to noncompliance. The unit employs nonpharmacological approaches and interventions, such as exercise, music, aromatherapy, massage, pet therapy, and art programs. Moreover, there is an inmate companion program in which healthy inmates are trained as certified nurse assistants and earn $30 to $100 a month and possibly time off from their sentences (Bollinger & Gordon, 2019).

Another example is the Fishkill Correctional Facility in New York, which is a 30-bed unit for those with cognitive impairment that provides a safer environment. The staff receive training on cognitive impairments and dementia-related conditions to better recognize inmate behavior as symptoms of the disorder and not acts of hostility. Much more like an assisted living than a prison unit, the physical space in the unit provides bright lighting to elevate and stabilize mood and subdued colors for comfort, with ongoing programming from volunteers, musicians, and special needs dogs (Murolo, 2020). Although specialized units are useful for oversight of the most advanced care within prison environments, they are costly and rare.

et al., 2022; Stal, 2013). In many cultures and societies globally, death and dying are perceived as a spiritual rite of passage that should be peacefully provided to all dying individuals. However, once a person is convicted of a criminal offense, this can change how people perceive the person and whether they think the individual should have similar access to health care services and/or end-of-life palliative care while incarcerated.

Right to Treatment

Since the 1970s, the U.S. Constitution, as interpreted under the *Estelle v. Gamble* (1976) case, has required that prisons must provide incarcerated individuals with medical treatment, and if prisons are "deliberately indifferent" to inmates' medical needs, it is a constitutional violation of the cruel and unusual punishment clause of Amendment VIII to the U.S. Constitution. Because of an injury while working at his job in prison, Gamble was unable to complete his work and was placed in administrative solitary confinement for what was seen as his refusal to work. He later developed back pain and heart problems. Gamble filed a complaint asserting the correctional staff's negligence and inadequate treatment led to increased medical problems, which was unconstitutional cruel and unusual punishment. The Supreme Court did not side with Gamble, even though the case created the legal standard for deciding whether failure to provide medical treatment was a constitutional violation of cruel and unusual punishment. The court articulated the standard as whether correctional staff were deliberately indifferent to a prisoner's medical needs. In light of the evidence presented, the court did not agree the staff were deliberately indifferent based on failure to complete a specific diagnostic technique when Gamble received medical treatment on 17 occasions over a 3-month period.

Another source of law that applies to older adults who are incarcerated is the Americans With Disabilities Act (1990), as interpreted under *Pennsylvania Dept. of Corrections v. Yeskey* (1998). Similar to its application in community-dwelling individuals, the ADA requires prisons to accommodate people with disabilities. In *Yeskey*, the defendant was sentenced to complete a first-time offender's motivational boot camp; however, because of his medical history of hypertension, the Pennsylvania Department of Corrections refused to allow him to participate in the program. The court held that no public entity, including prisons, may discriminate against a qualified disabled individual due to their disability. For older or disabled individuals who are incarcerated, accommodations may include grab bars in the showers, mobility equipment, eliminating the need for stairs or installing elevators, or lower bunk assignments.

Right to Refuse Treatment

If competent to make medical decisions, under general health care law that applies to all people whether incarcerated or not, a person may refuse medical treatment, including life-sustaining medical treatment (*Cruzan v. Director, Missouri Dept. of Health*, 1990). In prison environments, inmates have limited rights to refuse medical treatment. For example, a person who is incarcerated cannot refuse antipsychotic medications if they are a danger to themselves or others and the treatment is in their best medical interest (*Washington v. Harper*, 1990). Generally, however, the courts have recognized that a competent person's interest in declining life-sustaining treatment outweighs the state's interest in preserving life, even if the person is in prison. Why may someone refuse medical treatment in prison? Incarcerated individuals may be suspicious of medical professionals employed by correctional institutions and may hold concerns about treatment being used to control or sedate them (Aday & Krabill, 2012). Some may choose not to pursue life-sustaining treatments.

In a California case involving a man sentenced to life in prison, *Thor v. Superior Court* (1993), the court was asked to decide whether the prison must provide medical care, even when the person refuses. After falling/jumping from a prison wall, the man was irreversibly injured, and he required prison staff to assist with all ADLs, including his feeding and the administration of medication. The attending physician, Dr. Thor, petitioned the court *ex parte* (without the man present) to request the court to allow him to force-feed the man through medical tubes. The court held that individuals who are incarcerated should be provided with life-sustaining treatment (under *Estelle v. Gamble*, 1976) unless they have the legal competency to waive medical treatment. The court cited long-standing principles of Anglo-American legal tradition of personal autonomy and right to self-determination within a historical Supreme Court case (*Union Pacific Railway Co. v. Botsford*, 1891):

> No right is held more sacred, or is more carefully guarded, by the common law, than the right of every individual to possession and control of his own person, free from all restraint or interference of others, unless by clear and unquestionable authority of law. . . . 'The right to one's person may be said to be a right of complete immunity: to be let alone.' (*Thor v. Superior Court*, 1993, p. 141)

Examining both philosophical and legal doctrines, the opinion recognized the difficulties for medical professionals and correctional staff alike but ultimately concluded, "Since death is the natural conclusion of all life, the precise moment may be less critical than the quality of time preceding it" (*Thor v. Superior Court*, 1993, p. 749).

Failure to Protect

Although they have typically been unsuccessful, some older individuals who are incarcerated have brought claims against prison administration for failure to separate them from the general population (*Brown v. Pattison*, 2004; *Edney v. Kerrigan*, 2004). To establish a failure to protect under Amendment VIII to the U.S. Constitution, an inmate plaintiff must satisfy a two-prong test: (a) prison conditions posed a substantial risk of serious harm and (b) prison officials were deliberately indifferent (had knowledge and disregarded the potential harm) to the plaintiff's health and safety. These are difficult prongs to meet because the plaintiff must show that prison officials had the requisite knowledge that the older adult was at high risk for attacks. In fact, some correctional officers have testified that they thought older adults would be less vulnerable to attack because of their status as an elderly inmate (*Edney v. Kerrigan*, 2004, p. 17).

Too "Old" to Confine

Relatedly, correctional systems have also dealt with whether older adults are "too old" to be confined on death row because the conditions (e.g., confinement to room, isolation) are harsh for those who are ill or infirm, and inmates often spend a considerable number of years on death row awaiting execution. Regardless of one's opinion about whether the death penalty itself is cruel and unusual punishment, some argue that the length of time that individuals sit on death row is in and of itself cruel and unusual punishment (Rapaport, 2012). Under what has been termed a "*Lackey* claim" based on *Lackey v. Texas* (1995), individuals have sought relief from execution based on the argument that the duration and conditions of death row are cruel and unusual punishment. Although *Lackey* claims have not been successful at preventing executions, proponents suggest a modified *Lackey*-for-the-elderly claim, which may be more likely to succeed (Rapaport, 2012) based on previous tests for the death penalty that have shifted due to community sentiment and an *evolving standards of decency* test for limiting the death penalty (*Trop v. Dulles*, 1958).

END-OF-LIFE AND HOSPICE CARE

The growing demand for end-of-life and hospice care in prisons stems from global advances in health care and increased life expectancy. As a result, more inmates are living longer and requiring extended periods of intensive and terminal care (Stensland & Sanders, 2016). The Louisiana State Penitentiary at Angola created a program that qualifies as hospice care and is run by prison staff and inmate volunteers (Hawryluk, 2024). Depicted in the *Angola Prison Hospice: Opening the Door* documentary (Louisiana-Mississippi Hospice and Palliative Care Organization, n.d.), the program has even been successful in reversing a state prohibition for hospice organizations to hire individuals with previous system involvement. With the prohibition lifted, those who get hospice work experience while incarcerated can be employed as hospice aides after their release from prison.

Although dementia and specialized care units in prisons remain uncommon, an increasing number of facilities such as Angola are implementing or advancing hospice and palliative care options for incarcerated individuals (H. C. Hoffman & Dickinson, 2011; Prost & Williams, 2020). Research suggests that improvements in existing prison facilities for older inmates may be more cost-effective than geriatric release programs that use private contractors (Murolo, 2020; Virginia Department of Corrections and Parole Board, 2008). Other considerations for end-of-life in prison populations include supporting spiritual and psychological wellness through chaplaincy and counseling, facilitating end-of-life advance care planning, and managing funeral arrangements and body disposition with incarcerated individuals and their family members (Cloyes et al., 2016; Gijsberts et al., 2011; Penrod et al., 2014).

Problems that arise in end-of-life care are often due to dissonance between health staff and correctional officers; for example, late-stage hospice patients require levels of care and attention exceeding the norm, which may be in discord with prison policy (Hagos, Butler, et al., 2022; Stensland & Sanders, 2016). Standard prison safety rules, such as limiting physical contact with inmates, directly conflict with providing ethical hospice care (Hagos, Withall, et al., 2022; Stensland & Sanders, 2016). Similarly, the use of medications in hospice and general palliative care, namely for pain management, can be contrary to prison safety policy (Stensland & Sanders, 2016; B. A. Williams et al., 2014). Misuse and theft of prescription medications are high in inmate populations; however, failure to make these drugs available entirely is equally problematic as it markedly decreases incarcerated individuals' quality of life (Hampton et al., 2015; Stensland & Sanders, 2016; B. A. Williams et al., 2014).

CONCLUSION

The COVID-19 pandemic brought attention to health care needs in prisons as the media covered rising death rates within prisons (Berryessa, 2020; Soucheray, 2023). COVID-19 mitigation strategies in facilities increased, and timelines for release and community reentry were accelerated to protect infirm individuals who were incarcerated, many of them older adults, from potential infection and death from the virus. During the COVID-19 pandemic, infection rates in prisons across the country significantly outnumbered those in the general population, and research found a rise in deaths of older adults incarcerated from 2019 to 2020. Among all deaths in prison during that period, older adults comprised the majority, and many of them had been positive for COVID-19 (Bolotnikov et al., 2022). However, release policies during this time were more likely to rely on health status and were not based solely on age. To this end, many legal responses in correctional facilities rely first on the core legal principles, as they apply to everyone, but make few exceptions to legal responses specific to older adults.

In addition to health concerns, older adults who are incarcerated also have considerable mental health and cognitive problems. Although some individuals with serious mental illness may be transferred to a forensic hospital, many will remain in the general prison population (Paradis et al., 2000). As such, correctional facilities and psychologists working in prison must prepare for legal responses by doing the following: offer unique assessment and treatment, adequately provide care to those who want it, and honor those who refuse treatment. A review by the Office of Justice Programs described seven legal responses important for planning for the needs of older adult who are incarcerated with mental disorders: early detection of mental illness, access to appropriate mental health treatment services, suicide prevention, programs to support coping with loss and stress, staff training and competencies, coordinated care and planning, and reentry challenges (J. F. Cox & Lawrence, 2010). However, such responses are universal and should be applied to all individuals, regardless of age, and to suggest that all older adults require special services at the expense of others may be based in ageist beliefs about the needs and capabilities of older adults.

Given the extremely high medical needs that older adults do have, legal responses in correctional facilities have also aimed at providing formal support in jails and prisons so that older adults can make autonomous, individual choices about the services they receive and endorsed ideals that older adults can be capable members in a society (i.e., within correctional facilities). In their systematic review of published studies that specifically address interventions aimed at older inmates' physical and mental health, Canada and colleagues (2020) found five such unique interventions. The interventions focused on treating depression (BE-ACTIV); increasing overall health through physical, mental, and spiritual activities (True Grit); providing trauma coping skills (Art Expression); increasing identification of health and social problems (OHSCAP); and interacting with music therapy (Good Vibrations). Although programs like these are likely necessary, such legal responses require care for older adults and turn moral decisions to provide formal supports into legal decisions to provide support. Scholars caution that removing this moral obligation can undermine positive interpersonal interactions when care is based on felt moral responsibility (Doron & Kohn, 2011).

Providing health care in prisons is an important investment and can even be cost-effective. Similar to medical advice for community dwellers, preventive medicine promotes long-term maintenance and/or improvements to health. If the incarcerated person may eventually be released into the community, releasing a healthier individual offers the community a financial benefit (see Chapter 9). When former prisoners return to the community, it is in society's best interest that they are as healthy as possible because good health has been linked to acquiring and retaining employment, reducing recidivism, and reducing costs of health care for society (Stal, 2013). The case law covered in this chapter shows that core legal protections apply to all incarcerated individuals. These protections include the right to receive accommodations under the ADA (*Yeskey*), the right to receive medical treatment (*Gamble*), and the right to refuse treatment (*Thor*). There are no special constitutional protections that are distinct for older adults.

Instead, legal responses have sought to identify whether older adults, specifically older adults with functional limitations to PADLs, require separate treatment in prison housing. As discussed, some legal responses created separate geriatric housing units and others have accommodated general housing units to meet the needs of older adults. Each of these responses carries different underlying justifications. A choice to house older adults separately may be based on paternalistic philosophies. For instance, separate units are a protective response that gives prison decision makers the authority to intervene and may undermine an older adult's autonomous choice to remain in the housing unit they prefer. Separate housing may also be a supportive response, requiring correctional facilities to care for older adults but simultaneously removing informal social support from younger individuals in general population housing units. Conversely, legal responses that aim to keep older adults in the general housing unit may be based in more autonomous philosophies and create preventive mechanisms that prepare older adults to autonomously remain in intergenerational units. Such responses may even be empowering legal responses that aim to remedy imbalances in functional ability and advocacy for older adults.

Consistent with patterns identified thus far with serious criminal behavior, legal responses to older adults on death row have not considered age specifically. Although the cases we discussed describe arguments that death row is cruel and unusual punishment, such claims have not been successful for older adults requesting relief based on age alone. To this end, legal responses associated with giving leniency after sentencing typically fall to the core legal responses universal to all. Some legal scholars have suggested legal responses such as the *Lackey*-for-the-elderly claim that seeks relief from death row and is specific to older adults, but thus far, this legal response has not been tested in the courts.

9

Reduce, Resentence, Release, and Prepare for Reentry

Legal Responses to Aging in Prison

In 1997, at age 44, Janet Carter was arrested for first-degree murder of her husband, her first offense, and she was sentenced to life in prison (Hernandez, 1998). Carter asserted that she had no part in the murder and was drugged by the men who admitted to killing her husband (a distant relative staying with them and another man). She confessed to helping to hide the murder, but said she did so because she felt threatened and under duress by the men. A year prior to the murder, Carter was assaulted while working at a storage facility and was knocked unconscious and hospitalized. Her records stated that she began to suffer memory loss after the trauma. In May 2022, at age 69, she appeared for the third time before the California parole board to decide whether she would be released on parole after 25 years in prison. During the hearing, the parole board asked what she learned in her prison programs, a question commonly asked to determine a person's rehabilitation and whether they are a risk to the public. She was unable to answer, often pausing for 30 seconds as she sat in her wheelchair and attempted to explain her memory loss. At the hearing, her lawyer presented evidence explaining the memory loss, including her Parkinson's disease, early dementia, a neurocognitive disorder, chemotherapy, and the brain injury she experienced before she was incarcerated. The commissioners denied her parole and admonished her for her inability to answer questions, stating that she was "manipulative . . . lacking in sincerity . . . and continued to pose an unreasonable risk of danger to society" (Levin, 2022, para. 3).

https://doi.org/10.1037/0000469-010
Aging and the Criminal Legal System: Community Services, Courts, Corrections, and Policy, by L. E. Wylie and E. M. Brank

This example highlights one of the legal responses to older adults seeking release from lengthy prison sentences. As do other legal decision makers discussed throughout this book, parole board members, policymakers, and judges responsible for release decisions may rely on ageist beliefs and ill-informed attitudes about normative and pathological aging. Older adults requesting release from prison may be seen only for their easily identified factors, such as age, number of prison infractions, or a 25-year-old criminal history. As described in previous chapters, ageism may consciously or unconsciously influence legal decisions about older adults, whether it be institutional ageism in policies for releasing older adults or individual ageism when individual decisions are made about the release of an aging adult. For example, at the system level, a state may have a compassionate release statute based on chronological age but fail to pass a more evidence-informed compassionate release statute based on a person's individual functional ability. Laws that designate eligibility based on chronological "old age" may contribute to institutional ageism by perpetuating assumptions that all older adults of a given age lack functional capacity. Moreover, failing to acknowledge individualized aging, especially among individuals who experience accelerated aging, could be explained by negative biases towards both "the elderly" and "criminals" (in addition to racial biases, given that many aging adults in prison are Black men). At an individual level, as Carter's case exemplifies, cognitive-related disorders could be perceived as ornery behavior and contribute to staff and parole board assumptions that a person has not been rehabilitated and should not be released. Decision makers, such as parole board members and judges, use discretion and maybe even quick decision-making processes to make release decisions. They can even cite an individual's need for mental health care as justification to keep them incarcerated (UnCommon Law, 2022).

Chapter 8 discussed the breadth and depth of the issues surrounding aging in prison. As rates for long-term incarceration and aging in prison are rising, overcrowding and the associated health care costs for treating older individuals continue to rise, and all three branches of government are tasked with identifying short- and long-term solutions to reducing the U.S. prison population of older adults. This chapter discusses law and policy to address the problem of aging in prison as well as the areas of law that can be responsible for such solutions, including legislative changes to statutes, opinions in case law interpreting statutes and constitutional issues, or administrative policies in correctional agencies.

Most of the laws and policies discussed in this chapter are at the federal level, wherein those incarcerated are under the jurisdiction of the Bureau of Prisons (BOP). Because the United States has both federal and state laws that people can break, there are federal and state court systems for sentencing and federal and state prison systems for housing individuals completing their sentences following a conviction. This means that the federal government and each state have their own specified laws and policies that govern sentencing, incarceration, parole, and other release and reentry from incarceration. Throughout this chapter, it is important to keep in mind that the federal system is just one system among many others (K. L. Mitchell, 2017) and that states can, but do not have to, model their criminal code and procedure on the federal rules. Ultimately, differences depend on jurisdiction; therefore, the optimal policy response should be tailored locally (Litwok et al., 2020).

REDUCING SENTENCES TO INCARCERATION AND RESENTENCING

As described in more detail in Chapter 6 (in the Issues in Sentencing section), the U.S. Sentencing Commission (USSC) established the Federal Sentencing Guidelines (USSC, 2021) to create definitive and uniform sentences across federal court judges (Legal Information Institute, 2023). Additionally, many states have adopted their own criminal sentencing guidelines. Sentencing guidelines establish minimum sentences for each offense, after which judges can exercise discretion during the sentencing process to adjust the punishment upward for aggravating factors or downward for mitigating circumstances.

During the time of mandatory minimums that placed long minimum sentences for crimes such as drug possession and trafficking, the criminal legal system of the 1990s was also experiencing an expansion of other punitive sentencing policies. For instance, in response to the war on drugs of the 1980s and 1990s, habitual-offender or three-strikes laws imposed harsher punishments on those with prior convictions, including laws in some states with mandatory life sentences for a third felony conviction. Washington, in 1993, and California, in 1994 were the first two states to implement such laws, with many states enacting similar laws after (Karch & Cravens, 2014). Research has found little evidence that three-strikes laws have any effect on deterring individuals from recidivating (Males & Macallair, 1999), instead finding that they have contributed to Black individuals charged with felonies receiving longer prison sentences (Sutton, 2013). Mandatory minimums and mandatory life sentences reduce the discretion of judges to weigh someone's previous convictions and current risk level when arriving at a sentence. As a result, many people who are incarcerated are repeat drug offenders who are lower risk and rehabilitated while serving their sentence but who have little or no opportunity for parole or release. In such incidences, they will age, possibly develop dementia symptoms or other terminal or chronic health conditions, and then die in prison. In some states, advocacy groups have urged the state's governor to release older adults who are serving long sentences for drug crimes using their executive power of clemency (see Box 9.1).

Nearly 2 decades following the punitive criminal justice reforms of the 1990s, the U.S. Senate overwhelmingly passed the First Step Act of 2018, with what *The New York Times* called "the most substantial changes in a generation" (Fandos, 2018, para. 1) to the tough-on-crime sentencing laws. Having had bipartisan support, the act is aimed at addressing the punitive policies of the 1980s and 1990s that disproportionally affected Black individuals (Krent &

BOX 9.1 | **GOVERNOR'S ABILITY TO RELEASE WITH CATEGORICAL CLEMENCY: NEW YORK**

Several state and national organizations advocated and inspired calls for the governor of New York to grant clemency to older people in prison. Clemency is a path for release that relies on a governor to reduce a defendant's sentences or grant a pardon (Sakala et al., 2020). Proponents called for clemency to be applied based on both age and time served—for example, for people who have reached the age of 50 and have served at least 25 years in prison. Data published by the New York State Department of Corrections and Community Supervision indicated that from 2008 to 2021, although the overall prison population and number of older adults had decreased, the proportion of older adults increased steadily through 2021 (DiNapoli, 2022). In response to these figures, Release Aging People in Prison (RAPP) focused on executive clemency in New York State. RAPP is a campaign advocacy project, founded by formerly incarcerated individuals, their families, and allies. The project's aims are to increase parole releases for individuals who are aging in prison as well as create partnerships to increase awareness nationwide (RAPP, n.d.). In New York State, the efforts began with the hashtag #CuomoLetThemGo and now #HochulBringThemHome, respectively, to urge New York governors to grant clemency to thousands of older adults who pose little risk to public safety. In 2023, under a commitment to review clemency applications on a rolling basis as opposed to once annually, Governor Hochul granted clemency to 13 individuals (10 of whom were over the age of 50), including 10 pardons and three commutations (New York State, 2023).

Rucker, 2022). The First Step Act (2018) requires the U.S. Attorney General to assess the risk and needs of all federal individuals who are incarcerated and place them in recidivism-reducing programs and productive activities to address their needs and reduce this risk. The act also seeks to improve criminal legal system outcomes, reduce the federal prison population, and maintain public safety. Concerning modifications to the sentencing guidelines, the act included a range of sentencing reforms that made the Fair Sentencing Act of 2010 retroactive, so that individuals sentenced before the 2010 reform (which established lower penalties for crack cocaine and eliminated mandatory minimums for crack cocaine possession) would be resentenced under the new laws; it also enhanced judicial discretion, reduced some mandatory minimum sentences, and modified how prior minor convictions should be considered during sentencing for subsequent convictions (Nellis & Komar, 2023). Although those who are proponents of less punitive sentencing measures were pleased with the federal government's efforts, many did not think the reform addressed all the problems that generated prison overcrowding and produced disparate treatment of people of color (Fandos, 2018). According to an annual report from the U.S. Department of Justice (2023), the 3-year recidivism rate for those released under the First Step Act was 12%, compared with the 45% recidivism rate reported for the general population.

RELEASE TO PAROLE OR REDESIGNATION OF SENTENCE

Whether someone is eligible for parole first depends on whether the state has parole as an option, as some states have removed parole boards, and there is considerable variation in the location, administration, and organization of parole boards in states that have them (National Institute of Corrections, 2024). Once someone has been sentenced to prison, their sentence may or may not include the ability to be paroled from prison (indeterminate and determinate sentences, respectively), which involves a parole board of qualified individuals (e.g., judges, psychiatrists, criminologists) or community members who decide whether a person is suitable to return to the community. The parole board generally focuses on whether the potential parolee presents a threat and assesses their current dangerousness. If a person is administratively released through the parole system, then they remain under parole supervision for the period required and are supervised by community corrections (at the Substance Abuse and Mental Health Services Administration's [2024] sequential intercept model Intercept 5; see Chapter 5, this volume, for a review).

Under punitive parole policies, individuals who are incarcerated have no opportunity for parole, even if they can demonstrate rehabilitation. As supported by the age–crime curve, recidivism for older adults is lower than for younger adults (Rakes et al., 2018). A study by Daftary-Kapur and Zottoli (2020) examined Pennsylvania juveniles who were initially sentenced to life for first- or second-degree murder. These individuals were, on average, 16 years old when sentenced. They were later released at an average age of 51, following the Supreme Court ruling in *Miller v. Alabama* (2012) that declared life sentences for juveniles unconstitutional. The research found that only 1% of these individuals were convicted of new crimes after release. This finding was based on an average postrelease period of 21 months. Daftary-Kapur and Zottoli concluded that the release of Philadelphia's juvenile lifers, to date, will result in an estimated minimum $9.5 million in savings in correctional costs for Pennsylvania over the first decade. Although more attention has been paid to compassionate release for older or aging adults (see the Compassionate Release and Elderly Parole section below), proponents state that general parole reforms could be more inclusive of all groups who have demonstrated rehabilitation (e.g., participated in vocational activities, having viable employment upon release) and advocate for removing sentence options that do not allow for parole, while also allowing older adults to have more frequent access to the parole board as they age or become ill.

Generally, the parole process is cumbersome for all, not only for the individuals who are incarcerated themselves but also for parole board members, who are often making high-pressure decisions about releasing a convicted felon with an extensive criminal history. Psychological research using experimental methods and mock parole decision making has found that decisions around parole are sometimes influenced by extralegal factors that are not typically outlined in parole release rules, such as the timing of an apology (Cunius & Miller, 2023), gender of the decision maker (Cunius & Miller, 2023; Yelderman et al., 2021), moral judgments, and attributions of blame and responsibility (Yelderman et al., 2021).

As a former parole board member, Carol Shapiro wrote about her time on the board in New York State in a column called "Life Inside" published by The Marshall Project, an online nonprofit criminal justice news outlet. In one of her writings, she stated the following:

> The problem is that these investigations were fixed in time; they could be from 30-some-odd years ago.
>
> The purpose of parole is not to focus on a static event; that is the purpose of sentencing. Parole should consider primarily who the person is today. But New York parole laws [N.Y. Comp. Codes R. & Regs., tit. 9, § 8002.2(d)(7), 2017] have a "deprecation" clause, which basically means that the seriousness of the crime justifies keeping you in prison. This gives commissioners an easy out, even when someone has been before the board three, five or seven times, or they committed the crime at 17, and they're now 70. (Shapiro & Schwartzapfel, 2022, paras. 10–11)

Research in California found that the number of parole hearings increased 745% from 1980 to 2010 due to the number of people serving life sentences with the possibility of parole, likely creating backlogs and delays in parole hearings (Weisberg et al., 2011) and requiring parole board members to make decisions under undesirable conditions. Tasked with determining if someone should be released early, parole boards differ across jurisdictions and states. In California, the parole board lists that parole suitability includes static factors such as a juvenile record, history of violent crime, crime as a result of stress, institutional behavior, a stable social history, and current age and likelihood of reoffense, with some attention to dynamic factors such as remorse and a realistic release plan (California Department of Corrections and Rehabilitation, 2024). Shapiro provides additional context to what can be a cumbersome process:

> I started to call what we were doing "conveyor belt justice," because you'd be busy preparing to lead the next interview instead of watching and listening closely to the one taking place. Then you might be writing an opinion during the next interview.
>
> And the paperwork was a huge challenge. There was a lot of it, and since it wasn't digitized, you'd have to wade through dozens of pieces of paper. The files included prisoners' . . . risk-analysis scores and the programs they completed. Then there might be letters from victims, judges and prosecutors. If the crime involved a police officer, the police union would gather hundreds of letters, saying, "Do not release this person." We had to physically sign each victim impact statement. More paper.
>
> The files for the most heinous offenses—the ones where the individuals who are incarcerated was denied parole umpteen times—were the worst. They were

> hundreds of pages, so you could end up relying on a top sheet that summed up how many years the person had been in prison, what their sentence was, and what the pre-sentence investigation said at the time. (Shapiro & Schwartzapfel, 2022, paras. 8–10)

Despite the large number of people serving life sentences in the United States, parole hearings have not been well-studied (K. M. Young & Pearlman, 2022). Of the research that exists, the results indicate that parole board members sometimes make decisions based on extralegal factors, such as race, gender of the parole board members, or the emotional expression of individuals who are incarcerated during their parole hearings. To illustrate, in 2022, sociologists coded transcripts of more than 700 parole hearings for those sentenced to life in prison with indeterminant sentences between 2007 and 2010. The findings revealed racial disparities in parole outcomes, such that Black individuals were less likely to be released than were White individuals, which were further explained by disparities in psychological assessment, behavioral judgments, and prosecutors' recommendations.

In another study, psychologists Logan Yelderman and colleagues (2021) observed and coded 205 parole hearings in one state for extralegal and legal factors. As suggested by the emotions as social information model, which proposes that emotions act as social cues in unclear situations (Van Kleef et al., 2010), Yelderman and colleagues hypothesized that parole release decisions could be impacted by the emotional situation, which can be confusing, frustrating, or disappointing. As expected, individuals with lower risk scores were more likely to be released, but incarcerated individuals' positive emotions did not relate to release decisions. Individuals expressing negative emotions were less likely to be released, even while controlling for risk score (Yelderman et al., 2021).

COMPASSIONATE RELEASE AND ELDERLY PAROLE

In the Netflix series *Orange Is the New Black* (Kohan, 2013), one of the characters, Jimmy, is depicted as an older woman who is starting to show symptoms of dementia while she is incarcerated. Although she is likely in her late 80s, she believes she's still in her 20s, is unaware that she is in prison, and sometimes forgets to shower. In the show, Jimmy is granted compassionate release and is dropped off at a bus station by the facility staff. Although the episode brought some awareness to the issue of aging and dementia in prison, outside of the television series, compassionate release is not as frequently used as one might think based on the existence of such policies and the demand for them in prison, and it certainly does not often happen in a timely manner. As some have noted, some older and infirm individuals who are incarcerated are "literally dying to get out of prison" (Corwin, 2000, p. 687) as they wait for parole boards to act and paperwork to be processed. Additionally, although a prison facility would hopefully not abandon someone needing care at a bus station, it can be challenging to design policies and procedures for placing dying individuals who are released from incarceration in appropriate community-based settings (Vera Institute of Justice, 2017).

Still, compassionate release policies, which allow people who meet certain aging or medical criteria to be released earlier than their statutory release dates, offer one promising avenue for reducing aging prison populations (Vera Institute of Justice, 2017). Such policies have both a humanistic purpose, allowing elderly or seriously ill people to spend their final months or years with their closest loved ones, and a practical one, acknowledging that correctional facilities are not equipped to care for seriously ill people. Based on the rationale that older and infirm individuals who are incarcerated pose little risk of committing more crime, compassionate or early release is one of the most discussed solutions for deincarceration efforts (e.g., Berry, 2008; B. S. Green, 2014; Maschi et al., 2016), yet federal and state policies alike are underutilized, and the proportions of those who apply who are granted release under these policies are low (Berryessa, 2020; C. Thompson, 2018). Because so few have been released due to statutory ineligibility and procedural problems, and many policies have not been implemented for long, not much research has examined whether these policies are effective at safely and significantly reducing the elderly and infirm prison population (Vera Institute of Justice, 2017), while balancing public safety.

Compassionate Release at the Federal Level

To reduce overcrowding, lessen the workload for correctional staff members, increase safety, and provide a dignified death for terminally ill individuals who are incarcerated, Congress passed the Sentencing Reform Act in 1984 and later modified it under the First Step Act (2018). More commonly known as "Compassionate Release," the law allows federal courts to release individuals who are incarcerated before the completion of their sentence for "extraordinary and compelling" medical, personal, or familial circumstances that the court could not reasonably have foreseen at the time of sentencing (18 U.S.C. § 4205(g), 2023; 18 U.S.C. §§ 3582(c)(1)(A), 2025). When the compassionate release program was first implemented, Congress included a statutory provision to test the program with a pilot study in which low-risk older adults (i.e., over age 65, having a non–life-in-prison sentence for certain nonviolent crimes, no past escapes, and low risk of reoffending) were released from prison to home detention, which could include nursing homes or other residential long-term care facilities.

Despite the pilot study, federal compassionate release suffered from serious implementation problems and effectiveness and was criticized in 2013 by the inspector general of the U.S. Department of Justice (2013). As researchers and policymakers noted, prior to modifications initiated by the First Step Act (2018), few applicants have been granted compassionate release since the program's implementation (Berryessa, 2020; C. Thompson, 2018). To illustrate, data from 2006 to 2011 indicated that over 5 years, wardens submitted

211 individuals' requests, and the BOP approved 142 of them (68%; U.S. Department of Justice, 2013). In 28 of the cases (13%), individuals died while the BOP considered their request. Although data were not gathered on the total number of requests from individuals, the number of requests was likely extremely low considering the proportion of infirm or older adults in federal prisons. Moreover, the pilot program indicated poor financial outcomes because the expenses of home detention with a private company were greater than the expenses associated with remaining in prison. Although the findings have since been criticized methodologically as missing key costs in the cost–benefit analysis of the program (e.g., construction of new prisons, certain modernization and repair projects, depreciation of its existing facilities), the report tarnished the program, and it continued to be ineffective for many older and/or infirm adults (U.S. Department of Justice, 2013).

First Step Act Modifications to Federal Compassionate Release

The First Step Act of 2018 modified the policies and procedures for compassionate release and reduction in sentences. Prior to the First Step Act, the BOP often prevented compassionate release cases from reaching the courts. Even when incarcerated individuals met the criteria for compassionate release, the BOP frequently chose not to file the necessary motions for court consideration. Therefore, compassionate release was revised to permit individuals who are incarcerated to file directly with the court after denial or neglect from the BOP, or 30 days after submission to the warden. Practices were also modified to increase awareness of compassionate release among individuals who are incarcerated as well as set time standards for terminally ill individuals by requiring specific notice and assistance for them and requiring requests to be processed within 14 days (Congressional Research Service, 2019).

Prior to the revisions, individuals seeking compassionate release were required to show their medical symptoms were *compelling and extraordinary* to warrant release, which were challenging legal standards to meet, especially within the context of accelerated aging processes (see the Introduction). The revisions allow older adults to be released if they are aged 65 and older, are experiencing physical or mental health issues due to aging, and have served 10 years or 75% of their sentence (whichever is less). Under these revisions, an older adult meeting the age and time-served eligibility need only show they are experiencing health symptoms because of aging. In addition to eligibility based on aging, the revisions expanded early release program eligibility so that people with terminal illnesses (defined as a life expectancy of 18 months or less or conditions with an end-of-life trajectory) and debilitating medical conditions (including cognitive deficits from dementia or traumatic brain injury) could be released.

The compassionate release program has seen significant activity since its inception, and the federal government must now report regular statistics on the number of motions filed, granted, and denied. From October 2019 through June 2024, approximately 33,301 motions were filed, and 5,311 motions were granted (15.9%; USSC, 2024). In the first 6 months of 2024 alone, 230 motions were granted. Data trends reveal that in the few months after implementation in late 2019, there were very few requests for release. However, in April 2020, at the start of the COVID-19 pandemic, the total number of monthly requests substantially increased through mid-2021, ranging from approximately 1,000 to 2,000 each month (peaking in September 2020). Although the frequency of approvals also increased during the pandemic months, approvals for release were not granted to the extent of the requests. Since September 2021, the number of motions granted each month averages about 50. Data are now published by the USSC, updated monthly, in an online dashboard (https://www.ussc.gov/research/data-reports/compassionate-release-data-reports).

Compassionate Release and Federal Sentencing With "Old Law" Defendants

The federal sentencing reduction processes have distinct criteria, depending on the date someone was sentenced. As they have been called informally and formally, "old law" individuals in federal prison are serving sentences for offenses committed prior to November 1, 1987, before the Federal Sentencing Guidelines went into effect and parole was eliminated at the federal level in 1984, and are the oldest, sickest, and most vulnerable cohort of people incarcerated in the federal system currently. Unlike individuals sentenced under the guidelines, old-law individuals are barred from seeking compassionate release under the First Step Act and must use the U.S. Parole Commission (and criteria from the USSC), which will consider when people convicted under the federal old law become eligible for parole.

If parole is denied to a person who is in custody for an old-law offense, the USSC must hold interim hearings every 2 years thereafter until the individual is released (U.S. Parole Commission, 2010). Given this statutory duty, it is critical for the agency to know about and track all of the old-law individuals in custody who are eligible for parole. There has been ongoing discussion about the issue (e.g., Berman, 2021) and efforts by the American Civil Liberties Union and The Sentencing Project to urge the federal government, specifically the U.S. Parole Commission, to provide fair processes for several hundred 'old law' people within federal jurisdiction (American Civil Liberties Union & Sentencing Project, 2020). Importantly, for some older adults still sentenced under outdated federal law, prison wardens and judges also make life-altering decisions about older adults' release (see Box 9.2 for a case example).

Compassionate Release in the States

In addition to federal policy, almost all states have some form of release or parole in their legislative statutes or administrative law parole board rules to allow for medical or compassionate release from prison. Most recently, in 2021, Illinois passed its first compassionate release law, the Joe Coleman Medical Release Act (2022). In a report published by a sentencing advocacy group and

BOX 9.2 | FEDERAL "OLD LAW" AND CHALLENGES TO RELEASE: RICHARD JOSEPH, AGE 73

Richard Joseph, age 73, serving a 150-year sentence in federal prison, was granted release to home confinement in May 2022 (*United States v. Joseph*, 2022). Joseph was convicted in 1986 under the USSC's "old law" and prior to the elimination of federal parole. Joseph served 35 years and was eligible for parole after serving 40 years. For 2 years, Joseph made several requests to the warden for release, followed by motions to the court stating his medical conditions made prison unsafe during the spread of COVID-19. The procedural history of this case demonstrates the complexities of early release, especially for individuals caught in the kerfuffle of the old-law sentences, and the role of legal decision makers in legal responses to older adults applying for early release.

Following the procedures for the Bureau of Prisons (BOP) compassionate release under the Sentencing Reform Act (1984), Joseph made his first request to the warden for redesignation to home confinement in 2020, amid all the requests during the COVID-19 pandemic (see the Conclusion in Chapter 8). The warden denied his request, citing his condition was "stable," "not terminal," and his "life expectancy [was] normal for [his] age" (*United States v. Joseph*, 2022, p. 3). After his first request to the warden was denied, the next procedural step, which was added by the First Step Act (2018), allowed Joseph to motion the original sentencing court for redesignation to home confinement. The court recommended redesignation in September 2020; however, the court's decision was not binding because federal release decisions rest with the BOP warden (*Tapia v. U.S.*, 2011, p. 828). Again, the warden rejected the redesignation. In 2021 as his health continued to decline, Joseph filed additional motions to the court *pro se* (without an attorney), requesting compassionate release because his medical conditions were considered "extraordinary and compelling." After reviewing nine pages of medical evidence, the sentencing court did not agree with Joseph's claim, stating that medical conditions must be "serious and advanced . . . with an end-of-life trajectory" (*United States v. Joseph*, 2022, p. 6). Again, the court recommended redesignation to home confinement but not release from his sentence. Modifying his legal approach and now represented by an attorney, Joseph cited the updated 2021 U.S. Sentencing Commission Guidelines, which now allowed release based on the age of the defendant (§1B1.13, Application Notes, 1B1.1; see U.S. Sentencing Commission, 2021). The court again recommended redesignation, noting evidence presented showing Joseph's recent sharp health decline and strong family support outlined in his release plan. Again, the final decision still rests with the BOP warden. As of 2024, Joseph is still in federal prison and set to be released in 2083, when he would be 125 years old—what some have argued is a *de facto* life sentence.

appropriately referring to compassionate release in the title as being "Everywhere and Nowhere," Iowa was identified as the only state without explicit rules allowing for medical or compassionate release (Price, 2018), and, in fact, the Iowa Board of Parole explicitly states on its website that it "does not grant paroles due to medical reasons or for family hardship cases" (Iowa Board of Parole, 2024, "Does the Board consider offenders for a 'hardship' or 'medical parole'?").

Boxes 9.3 and 9.4 illustrate how jurisdictions vary considerably in terms of the eligibility and ineligibility criteria for release and the process for applying for release (Price, 2018; Wylie, Knutson, & Greene, 2018). Most states require an individual to have a chronic illness and/or a terminal illness to be eligible for release (see Box 9.5), and some allow release based on mental health reasons. Approximately one third allow eligibility criteria based on age—with some of the states specifying an age (ranging from 45 to 70 years old) and other states not indicating a specific age criterion. Although state laws focus mostly on the

BOX 9.3 | **CALIFORNIA'S PAROLE PROCESS FOR OLDER ADULTS**

In 2015, a class action lawsuit in California argued that overcrowding was causing constitutionally inadequate mental health care in prisons (i.e., *Coleman v. Newsom*, 2020). Following this, California courts and then the California legislature created rules to expand eligibility based on age, called the Elderly Parole Program (AB 1448), which also later added rules requiring that the parole board consider dynamic factors when assessing risk for violence in the community, which are believed to be more indicative of current risk level than are static measures of criminal history (Andrews & Bonta, 2003; K. S. Douglas & Skeem, 2005; Fass et al., 2008). When first introduced, the criteria included older adults aged 60 or older and having served a minimum of 25 years. However, in 2021, eligibility was further expanded to individuals aged 50 or older who have served 20 years or more of continuous incarceration (Cal. Penal Code § 3055, subd. (a), 2024).

Eligible older adults who are not currently in the parole board's hearing cycle, such as those sentenced under a determinate sentence (parole ineligible) or sentenced under an indeterminate sentence (but not yet parole eligible), are notified 6 months before their elderly parole eligibility date for a suitability hearing. The parole board reviews evidence, including forensic evaluation reports, assessing for unreasonable risk of danger to society (see Chapter 7) At elderly parole hearings, the board is required to consider whether age, time served, or any diminished physical condition has reduced their risk of violence (California Department of Corrections and Rehabilitation, 2022). If an individual is granted elderly parole, release is still dependent on review by the board and the governor (which can take up to 5 months). If they are denied elderly parole, they are denied parole for 3 to 15 years (Cal. Penal Code § 3041.5, subd. (b)(3), 2016).

BOX 9.4 | **VIRGINIA'S ELDERLY PAROLE STATUTE**

As with the federal "old law" issue, states that eliminated parole also face complexities. Virginia, for example, removed discretionary parole in 1995 in favor of truth-in-sentencing policies that required defendants to complete their entire sentences without early parole. Due to rising costs to incarcerate aging adults in Virginia, the financial committee of the state legislature passed the Senate Budget Bill of 2014, requiring all older individuals (defined as 65 years and older) sentenced under truth-in-sentencing policies to have a parole board review within 1 year of eligibility (under Va. Code § 53.1-40.01), when previously only individuals under geriatric conditional release had parole reviews. Analysis conducted by Virginia projected that state corrections could save up to $6.6 million if 62 individuals—just 15% of the population eligible—were released (Ollove, 2016).

To assess whether compassionate release outcomes differed after the law change in 2014, Murolo (2022) examined publicly available parole decision data from before and after the law change in Virginia. Comparisons from before and after the law change revealed an insignificant increase in the number of reviews conducted by the state parole board and no change in the number of approved releases. Contrary to the researcher's expectations, the population of Virginia's older incarcerated individuals actually increased from 171 individuals before the law change to 583 individuals after the law change. Murolo concluded the increase was due to the eligibility expansion, which increased the population of eligible individuals, whereas the requests for review and/or release did not proportionally increase.

condition of the person being released, some indicate eligibility for release if the state will incur *exorbitant expenses* (e.g., Rhode Island (RI) Medical Parole Act: RI Gen L § 13–8.1–1, 2024), and some require that, prior to being released, the individual demonstrate they have a proper residential and medical care plan outside of the facility (e.g., Delaware). State laws also have categorical exclusionary criteria such as ineligibility from violent convictions, specific types of offenses (i.e., sex offenses and murder), type of sentencing structure (e.g., life or death sentence, mandatory minimums, sentences without parole), or the proportion of time served required for application (Price, 2018; Wylie, Knutson, & Greene, 2018).

Continued Efforts at Expanding Eligibility for Medical Release

Efforts in the federal and state systems are ongoing, often with legislatures attempting to draft laws that define or further refine eligibility criteria so that the correct population is targeted, while also recognizing that the legal system must create bright-line rules for interpretation. For example, Virginia's law changed in 2014 to reflect a correction to allow all individuals meeting the

BOX 9.5 | NEBRASKA'S MEDICAL RELEASE STATUTE

Nebraska's medical release statute allows release based on terminal illness or permanent incapacitation, with the exception of individuals sentenced to death or life in prison (Nebraska Revised Statute 83-1,110.02). Echoing criticisms nationwide, the Office of Inspector General of the Nebraska Correctional System called Nebraska's existing program "impracticable" (p. 44)—as evidenced by only three people being approved to go to the parole board in 22 years of the policy being in place and the board granting release for only two of them (Alamdari, 2022). The Nebraska Office of Inspector General suggested that the legislature provide for emergency processes with shorter notice and allow powers of attorney to appear in place of the applicant (Office of Inspector General of the Nebraska Correctional System, 2021). Just as in the federal system, paperwork is often difficult and time-consuming, especially for someone who is dying. Many individuals die before anyone can review their paperwork or before they have had the chance to appear before the board. Take, for example, a woman's letter requesting assistance from the state ombudsman after she learned her life sentence prevented her eligibility for medical parole:

> I am unsure if the next route is to file a commutation, sadly, we know how long that could take. I feel as though my institutional record can help immensely. I have completed almost every program/class offered. I have graduated from York College with an Associate's Degree. I also volunteer with Domesti-pups. . . . I am a peer mentor. I came in at a young age with somewhat of a tainted past. Therefore, I understand the younger generation and try to help them gain the tools they need to become successful. I have had 58 misconduct reports since 1999. However, I have not received one since May 3, 2016. I have not incurred any violent misconduct reports. I also have a residence already in place and a strong family, friends, and religious support system to help me with any medical, mental health, etc. needs that will come along the way. (Office of Inspector General of the Nebraska Correctional System, 2021, pp. 43-44)

After sending this letter, she died 1 month later from terminal cancer. To address the rise in cost associated with incarcerating older and infirm adults, in 2022 the Nebraska legislature debated a criminal justice reform bill, which, among several other changes to criminal justice processes, included a geriatric parole clause expanding eligibility to include age and time served, instead of allowing release only for a terminal illness. Although the geriatric parole section was supported by lawmakers more than were other parts of the bill, it failed to pass due to lack of overall bill support. As one of the few states that has not enacted compassionate release reform, Nebraska has seen its prison population continue to increase (Alamdari, 2022).

age and medical requirements to be eligible, even if they were sentenced under outdated state sentencing policy (Va. Code § 53.1–40.01). Other efforts have sought to expand eligibility to allow advanced age, in addition to or in place of demonstrating a medical need for release (e.g., federal law, Virginia state law). Some states have sought to define terms such as *life expectancy* (e.g., Georgia, which uses the criteria "reasonably expected to die in 12 months") or significant debilitating illness (e.g., New York) as a means for identifying the eligible target population (GA Code § 42-9-43, 2013; NY Exec. L. 259-s, 2024). Other states have recognized a need for expedited processes in some circumstances (see Box 9.5 for an example of one such state, Nebraska). The compassionate release process is fraught with irony and challenges. Many incarcerated individuals may not even be aware of its existence or understand how to apply. For those who do, the application and approval process can be agonizingly slow. Ironically, this process often takes longer than the very life expectancy requirements it's meant to address. As a result, some applicants may not survive long enough to benefit from the program they desperately need. The time it takes to process applications has always been a problem, as demonstrated by the examples throughout this chapter. To speed up the review process in the federal system, the First Step Act of 2018 added a provision that applications from individuals who are terminally ill must be processed within 14 days to reduce waiting times.

Most recently, release policies for aging adults have been criticized because they fail to allow the release of individuals with sentences for violent criminal convictions—the population most likely to benefit from medical release—as they are the group most likely to age in prison as they serve long or life sentences in prison. To effectively reduce the number of sick people in prison, medical release laws must reduce obstacles for releasing individuals with violent convictions (O'Leary, 2021). Although few states have attempted to use assessed or measured risk for release decisions (Wylie, Knutson, & Greene, 2018), these too may restrict older adults who are no longer a danger to public safety if they rely on risk as it relates to the crime(s) originally committed. In decisions for parole and reentry, if static measures of risk such as criminal history are the only factors in making decisions about risk, then convictions or even prison infractions in the distant past could inappropriately classify someone as high risk for release, even if they are no longer a public safety risk and/or are terminally ill.

One practical limitation of medical release policies is that the defendant must proactively file an application or court motion to request the release, which requires both general knowledge of the program and procedures in addition to the ongoing knowledge and stamina needed to proceed through several steps in the application, review, and release process. Some research suggests that education for those incarcerated will expand the impact of release policies by increasing knowledge and subsequent access. Of 46 male patients in two state prisons and one large urban jail who were surveyed on the minimum knowledge required to apply for early medical release—the existence of such policy and who to speak with about applying—a small proportion demonstrated the knowledge they would need to apply (Kanbergs et al., 2019). Most of the respondents were older, with chronic conditions, but fewer than half demonstrated the knowledge required to apply for medical release, and about one in five demonstrated no relevant knowledge. As mentioned earlier in this chapter, the federal statute revisions in the First Step Act of 2018 acknowledged these limitations and now require individuals who are incarcerated federally to be informed of the policy, also allowing others to apply on their behalf if they are unable to do so for themselves.

At the federal level, modifications continue to be proposed for releasing individuals who are incarcerated federally, which has the secondary purpose of modeling to the states how to revise policies. In April 2023, under the 118th Congress, bipartisan senators introduced three bills in furtherance of the First Step Act of 2018, including the Safer Detention Act of 2023 that would modify the Elderly Home Detention Pilot Program to clarify time-served calculations, increase eligibility to include nonviolent offenses with 50% of the sentence served, correct the old-law issue for individuals who are incarcerated federally and were sentenced before the change in parole law, and provide judicial review of elderly home detention eligibility. Although the Safer Detention Act had not yet passed at the time of the writing of this book, the bill's legislative history can be tracked online using GovTrack, a website that allows the public to view bills introduced to the U.S. Congress (visit https://govtrack.us/congress/bills/118/s1248).

Perceptions of Compassionate Release

Some films and television shows (such as *Orange Is the New Black* [Kohan, 2013], discussed earlier in this chapter) suggest that compassionate release is a simple and common occurrence. Despite continued federal attention, this release mechanism is used much less often than one would expect given the problems that prison systems are facing with their aging and infirm populations. One reason for this may be due to perceived or actual lack of support of these policies by the public or by prison officials, either because they fear risking public safety (incapacitation and deterrence) or they believe that individuals should complete the punishment they have received (retribution). After all, many of the individuals who are dying in prison have committed heinous crimes, and victim's rights are also a consideration, even if the person is no longer a danger to public safety. Indeed, early surveys asking about general attitudes toward compassionate release found marginal support for releasing individuals who are incarcerated early due to negative attitudes toward those individuals (e.g., Boothby & Overduin, 2007; General Assembly of the Commonwealth of Pennsylvania, 2005). However, at the time these studies were conducted, less was known about overreliance on prison and its impact on aging individuals and systems not built for them.

More recent surveys conducted within the climate of sentencing and incarceration reform, using methods known to elicit more empathetic attitudes, have alternatively found greater support for releasing aging and infirm adults. Using a more specific vignette methodology that described an individual requesting compassionate release, Wylie, Knutson, and Greene (2018) found that the public and wardens alike support the use of medical or compassionate release. Recently, social work researchers Kaushik and Currin-McCulloch (2023) systematically reviewed all the published research studies on the topic of compassionate release laws and policies with qualitative or quantitative data. Summarizing the findings of the 20 studies published between 1999 and 2021 meeting their criteria, their review identified four primary themes to explain underutilization of compassionate release, including vague, inconsistent, and overly complex medical and legal language; narrow and complex eligibility criteria; an overreliance on prognosis and terminal requirements despite the difficulty in mortality estimation; and negative attitudes toward punishment and older adults.

REENTRY AND REINTEGRATION TO THE COMMUNITY

The impact of incarceration on older adults is not limited to their time in prison, because once released, they face unique challenges that younger individuals who are incarcerated may not experience. Finding employment, other financial support, housing, and other government benefits may pose more difficulties for older adults who are released compared with younger adults. Accelerated aging before and while in prison (see Chapter 8) means that most will have physical and psychological health problems or chronic diseases that make navigating life more challenging as they encounter new physical, psychological, and social situations outside of prison as an aging person. They may encounter difficulties in physical decline in unfamiliar or unsafe surroundings, have multiple health conditions with limited access to medical care, and experience adverse effects from polypharmacy as multiple medications are prescribed for various health conditions (B. Williams & Abraldes, 2007), often requiring medication management that younger adults reintegrating do not require (Substance Abuse and Mental Health Services Administration, 2020). Despite these unique challenges, very little research has been conducted on reentry and reintegration to the community with older adults, and not much is known about effective reentry planning for this population.

A qualitative study interviewing 26 older adults who were previously incarcerated about their experiences reentering the community from prison found that older adults experience complicated emotions and can face difficulty in reintegrating into family or social support (C. Clarke, 2017). A theme revealed in the interviews is that older adults reentering the community after prison express general feelings of despair over lost opportunities and a life wasted to crime (especially those with lengthy or multiple incarcerations), guilt for stress caused to their family, and an overall sense of hopelessness for the future. Some may feel negative emotions from leaving the prison because it was a familiar home with people they lived with for possibly decades (B. Williams & Abraldes, 2007). Older adults who were isolated during long prison terms may need help rejoining their family and/or other social services support, which can help with feelings of wanting to remain crime-free to avoid disappointing others caring for them (C. Clarke, 2017) and give them a sense of purpose. Similar to the character in the 1994 film *The Shawshank Redemption*, in which Morgan Freeman plays the character "Red," who is paroled after 40 years of incarceration (Darabont, 1994), some older adults will struggle to adapt to life outside of prison. Mental health symptoms are prevalent in older adults, especially depression (B. Williams & Abraldes, 2007), and formerly incarcerated adults report symptoms of depression, posttraumatic stress disorder, and anger management issues after release (C. Clarke, 2017). Despite this, they had little insight into their own mental health issues or possible need for mental health services.

Release from jail is not as simple as heading home with $200 and a bus ticket. Reentry, for all individuals who are incarcerated, is complex and difficult and requires addressing many personal and societal issues that are not currently addressed specifically to older adults (Doyle et al., 2022; Onyeali et al., 2023; Ritvo, 2018). Older adults released from prison have expressed a desire for prerelease planning specific to the needs of elderly ex-offenders, with permanent housing identified as the highest barrier in reintegration (C. Clarke, 2017). Some may need additional assistance with residential support through assisted living or nursing homes; however, placing this population can present challenges (Burke et al., 2022).

If released, older adults may experience financial insecurity in the community. Although some formerly incarcerated older adults report receiving training while incarcerated, they indicate that many of the vocational training programs were obsolete because they learned to work on machines or programs that were no longer relevant in a community setting (C. Clarke, 2017). As such, older adults likely have outdated job skills at reentry, which hinders employment opportunities. For instance, one man interviewed reported having trained for air conditioning and refrigeration, but when he was released, everything had been computerized. A woman indicated that women had fewer opportunities and could choose cosmetology without the opportunity for licensure or the print shop that used old-fashioned methods of mimeography (such as carbon printing). They may also experience challenges accessing public benefits and services due to lack of identification (Ritvo, 2018) or state laws barring participation in certain benefit programs (e.g., food stamps, housing, financial aid) for those convicted of a felony or experience gaps in coverage as they wait weeks for health coverage benefits (C. Clarke, 2017). If they have spent most of their lives incarcerated, they may not be eligible for social security benefits that are accessible only once someone has worked for at least 10 years, or 40 credits (Bae, 2020).

At the federal level, the First Step Act of 2018 expanded prison and reentry programming to reduce recidivism among individuals who were incarcerated federally and released to the community, mostly directing the attorney general to enhance and improve reentry programs, policies, and guidelines. Most of the planning and programming around reentry is most often aimed at younger people and ensuring they have adequate skills upon release by assessing their skills upon entry, developing a plan, and assessing adherence to their plan while in prison.

At the state level, although most states do not include assessed risk in their release statutes, California began using a static actuarial risk assessment tool (i.e., Correctional Offender Management Profiling for Alternative Sanctions; COMPAS) to target rehabilitation based on needs on a periodic basis (Fass et al., 2008; Zhang et al., 2014). In 2020, federal law began requiring risk and needs assessment for those sentenced to incarceration of their skills upon entry, and the Bureau of Prisons has developed a risk tool (i.e., PATTERN; BOP, 2024), which is still in the process of validation. Neither of these assessment tools for release and reentry planning were intended and normed for a younger healthier population who were incarcerated for much less time. Although federal law requires validating the tool annually to evaluate predictive and dynamic validity as well as racial and ethnic neutrality, age is not a factor discussed, despite evidence that the needs of reentering older adults are quite different from younger adults (BOP, 2024). As such, even though there is recent movement toward developing release and reentry assessment tools, the attention is on younger individuals, and the need for older adult specialized assessment tools remains.

Reentry and Reintegration Programs for Older Adults

Federal and state funding for reentry programs to support the growing need of aging adults in the criminal legal system is not enough for what experts believe is needed to address the problem, but a growing number of correctional administrators, criminal justice agencies, and social service providers have worked to meet the needs of older adults reentering the community. For instance, the Senior Ex-Offender Program in San Francisco, California, was the first reentry program in the United States to focus on adults aged 50 and older, providing wraparound services before and after release with assistance through counseling, referrals, and social support (Shelter Tech, 2024).

Following federal initiatives by the U.S. attorney general and the Federal Interagency Reentry Council, several federal agencies created initiatives to reduce reentry barriers for all individuals released. A network of agencies specific to older adults, the Area Agencies on Aging are state-designated agencies to address the needs and concerns of older people regionally and locally. In response to federal attention to reentry issues, the National Association of Area Agencies on Aging (2017) surveyed 231 state AAAs to assess their capacity to assist aging adults who are reentering from jails or prisons. Overall, only 9% of the responding agencies had a program to serve aging individuals who were incarcerated or released. Of those that did exist, most were chronic disease self-management education programs for older adults and adults with disabilities. Although most were not yet providing specialized services to the older adult reentry population, 74% were interested in a pilot program to serve this population but unable to because of insufficient staff time and/or not having the budget for such programming.

Other potential solutions are reintegration programs that assist older adults (and all individuals who are incarcerated) for release into the community to increase success upon release. As Box 9.6 illustrates, older adults who are released from prison often have several sociostructural needs, including housing. Services may include applying for government services or providing subsidized housing for those who do not qualify for other programs. Programs such as the Project for Older Prisoners, originating at George Washington University, can legally assist in obtaining early release for older individuals who are incarcerated and pose little threat to society. Law student volunteers at the Project for Older Prisoners conduct background investigations on older individuals who are incarcerated, review prison records and medical history, and gather collateral information from victims to support the older adult's case. If the individual is successfully released from incarceration, the student volunteers serve as case workers and assist the older person in reentering the community (George Washington University, 1991).

Release to Community Facilities

Compassionate release and medical parole are a means to provide individuals with physical and cognitive declines with more appropriate health care in the community (Garavito, 2019; Pro & Marzell, 2017); however, release and reentry policies are limited in practice because suitable housing or facilities for released individuals are often lacking. Whether released after completing their sentence or through a compassionate or medical release program, there is a

BOX 9.6 | HOUSING INSTABILITY AFTER RELEASE: JANET CARTER, AGED 69 (CONTINUED FROM CHAPTER OPENING)

After release in May 2022, Janet Carter returned home after serving 25 years at the Central California Women's Facility (Paratore, 2023). Although it was reported on a GoFundMe page created by her attorney Lilli Paratore (2023), director of legal services at UnCommon Law, that she has a "safe, supportive place to live," it was also noted that "she paroled with very little and needs help as she enters this new chapter of her life" (para. 2). According to the page, the funds raised "will be used to purchase essentials for Janet's daily life" (Paratore, 2023, para. 2). An update posted in 2023 indicated Janet was facing possible housing instability.

scarcity of geriatric-focused reentry programs, especially those specialized for individuals with dementia (ABA Commission on Law and Aging, 2022; Ahalt & Williams, 2015). Because they often lack ability to complete activities of daily living and instrumental activities of daily living (see the Introduction), they cannot live independently and must identify to parole boards who will be their caregiver upon release. As described in Chapter 8, many are estranged from their families and do not have alternative social support, which means that they will need some sort of institutional placement such as a nursing home. However, system-involved individuals are often stigmatized, impacting the ability to place them in short- or long-term care facilities, which are often hesitant to accept patients with a criminal record (Pro & Marzell, 2017). For those who were convicted of sexual offenses or who are perceived to pose a threat to care staff, studies report that it is nearly impossible to find institutional placements (Mistry & Muhammad, 2015; see also Box 6.2). In one Virginia case, a formerly incarcerated person who was wheelchair-bound was living in a hotel with a daily visit from a nurse because they could not find appropriate housing (Ollove, 2016).

With respect to dementia disorders, it can be impossible to find memory care, skilled nursing care, or dementia care for a person with dementia and a history of violent or sexual acts, even without a prior conviction. Even seeking placement for people who are very sick and near the end of life is challenging, unless a family member is willing to become a caregiver (ABA Commission on Law and Aging, 2022). Innovative health care models are emerging for high-risk, hard-to-place individuals in both correctional and community settings. These include specialized care units within prisons and dedicated facilities in the community. However, research on the effectiveness of these new approaches is still lacking. One potential solution proposed in the United Kingdom has been the implementation of crisis response/resolution teams that aim to reduce the number of inpatient hospitalizations for individuals with mental health problems. However, systematic reviews in the United Kingdom on the effectiveness of crisis response teams in cases involving older adults with dementia have found a lack of evidence to support that crisis response teams are reducing hospital admissions for people with dementia (Streater et al., 2017).

Another complication is that many individuals cannot financially support themselves after medical release and will need to be supported by government programs, including Medicaid or Medicare and other subsidies and services. As an example of one state's efforts to support older paroled individuals, Connecticut contracted with a private nursing home in 2012 to specifically accept elderly and infirm individuals who are deemed not to be a public safety risk and have been granted parole from the Department of Corrections (Wisnieski, 2017). However, this model nursing home for paroled individuals, which was the first facility in the country to win approval from the Centers for Medicare & Medicaid Services, has faced several setbacks, including legal battles with the federal government in 2015 over whether the facility qualified for Medicare or Medicaid reimbursement. Although the court originally ruled that the facility was not eligible for reimbursement because paroled individuals do not meet federal guidelines, the court reversed the rejection, making the facility eligible to receive federal funding. Medicaid, funded jointly by federal and state governments, pays for half of the costs of care when an individual is in a facility that is a true nursing home and covers nothing when someone is incarcerated, which will save the state corrections budget about $5 million annually.

To this end, opponents to early release programs argue that it does not really reduce costs but rather shifts costs from one state or federal budget to another (M. M. Holland et al., 2020). Instead of the cost of care coming from corrections' budgets while incarcerated, it comes from Medicaid or Medicare health care budgets. Scholars in gerontology also suggest, however, that with end-of-life palliative services now available in prisons (see Chapter 8), it may be more humanitarian for individuals to die in prison hospice care, instead of being released to the community with fewer supports and inability to navigate their medical care (M. M. Holland et al., 2020). There is much left to understand and explore in this area and a need for much better coordination between systems within states and between the states and federal systems.

CONCLUSION

There are several ways to address the overcrowding and aging of individuals in U.S. prisons. Generally, legal responses aim to reduce the number of people who are sentenced to prison initially, using diversion and sentencing strategies at sequential intercept model Intercepts 0 through 3. One legal response is to reduce lengthy sentences that developed out of the tough-on-crime era because life sentences or longer-than-life-expectancy sentences have resulted in the incarceration of many older and infirm adults. However, these responses are directed to all individuals and not older adults specifically, though in practice may be more applicable to older adults than to younger ones. By resentencing individuals based on current community standards, which has been successful within juvenile law reform (i.e., resentencing of mandatory life without parole), prisons could drastically reduce the number of older adults incarcerated. A notable practical difference, however, is that resentencing young people within the juvenile justice system happens within the context of *per se* distinctions that make juveniles (under age 18) automatically eligible for resentencing after *Miller v. Alabama* (2012), which was retroactively applied to cases in *Montgomery v. Louisiana* (2016). The same does not hold true for adults in the criminal legal system in which responses default to the core legal principles universal to everyone.

A second legal response is to revise release policies and practices so that eligibility and processes are more effective at releasing older adults who are lower risk to reoffend, even if their time has not been fully served. These preventive legal responses aim to reduce the prison population to prevent further harm from overcrowding and may also empower older adults to realize their rights and advocate for their release. Such legal responses include increased frequency of parole board hearings (see Box 9.3), state and federal laws justifying release based on health status (see Box 9.5), and/or state and federal laws justifying release based on age (see Box 9.4). Legal responses include processes that foster an older adult's autonomy to make choices about their release. However, as with other preventive and empowering legal responses, only older adults aware of the tools available will be able to successfully engage in such planning. Reform to compassionate release under the First Step Act (2018) created mechanisms for increasing awareness to older adults who are incarcerated of such legal responses. These legal responses also require legal decision makers to enforce such responses. So even though there are laws allowing release, such legal responses require enforcement by courts and BOP wardens, which, as the case law presented shows, does not always occur.

Reentry legal responses come with either sentence reductions or release. For many older adult individuals who are incarcerated, they have spent most, if not all, of their adult lives institutionalized within a prison. Not only will that impact the way they will interact with the outside world, but it will also inevitably impact their social support. Although still an emerging area, legal responses to older adults reentering the community may best fall under supportive and empowering legal responses that promote older adults as capable members of the community to reduce the impact of structural and internalized ageism.

10

Next Steps

Expanding Legal Responses to Older Adults

In the Preface, we asked why you picked up this book. We questioned whether you selected it based on your interests or because your professor assigned it. Either way, you must be curious about older adults in our legal system. We asked you to consider why that was. No matter your reasons for initially flipping or scrolling through the pages, we hope that as you reach this final chapter, you have new insights into the criminal legal responses to the aging population. Most important, we hope that you share your knowledge with others and bring awareness that older adult issues are everyone's issues. Even more than any new or confirmed insights, we are excited to learn about your new lists of research questions or legal areas to explore.

Despite extensive campaigns to optimize aging in public discourse, such as the popular slogan "60 is the new 40," negative aging stereotypes and ageist discrimination remain pervasive (Diehl et al., 2020; Officer et al., 2020). In the context of law and aging, there are complex perceptions, attitudes, and treatment of older adults. Society holds both positive and negative stereotypes about aging, which influences feelings about older adults and highlights the mixed legal responses to older adults in the U.S. criminal legal system. Legal responses may be based on assumptions about aging and older adults or their intersection in another outgroup—for instance, the way we differently view an older woman who is a judge versus one who is on death row or an older defendant who is Black versus one who is White. Ageism may consciously or unconsciously influence legal responses to older adults. For instance,

https://doi.org/10.1037/0000469-011
Aging and the Criminal Legal System: Community Services, Courts, Corrections, and Policy, by L. E. Wylie and E. M. Brank

institutional ageism may motivate systematic policies that respond to older adults as a distinct group or based on a specified age, such as the *per se* legal responses presented throughout. Interpersonal ageism may influence individualized legal responses, which are typically directed to a specific older adult. Consequently, legal responses based on assumptions about older age may contribute to internalized ageism, in which older adults may adopt ageist beliefs about themselves in accordance with those assumptions. This is especially true with aging adults who have ample experience and context to consider. Aging occurs within subpopulations that experience varying degrees of physical and mental health disparities, which accumulate over a lifetime (LaVeist, 2000). Further complicating this issue is the challenge of explaining differences between older and younger groups. These differences could be attributed to various influences that come with aging, such as biological changes, age-related development, or generational shifts.

RESTRUCTURING LEGAL SYSTEMS AND PROCESSES FOR OLDER ADULTS

Movements within corrections systems and court systems are working to change structural components of the legal system to better address the needs of older adults. Some changes are physical updates to courtrooms and correctional facilities to make them more accessible. Other changes are systemic and aim to address underlying processes and practices within the system and increase service availability for older adults as legal responses to system involvement.

Deflection to Community Supports and Diversion to Alternative Legal Responses

The distinct challenges faced by older adults warrant increased attention to both the causes of their involvement in the criminal legal system and the system's responses to them. This includes examining older adults' experiences during arrest and throughout their interaction with the criminal justice process. Court systems have backlogs of cases, and prisons are overcrowded, so legal decision makers must find solution-focused legal responses that deflect and divert from formal legal system processing for low-risk older adults, especially for individuals with dementia-related disorders at all system points.

The Substance Abuse and Mental Health Services Administration's (2024) sequential intercept model (SIM) is a strategic planning tool that helps communities better understand the gaps and resources they have in helping those with mental illness or substance use disorders who are in the criminal justice system (see Chapter 5, this volume, for a review). Although the SIM was developed for individuals with behavioral health needs, the model illustrates best practices for effective and efficient processing through the criminal legal system for individuals believed to be less appropriate (i.e., in terms of behavioral health and level of risk) for full case processing through courts and corrections. The SIM's objective is to reduce unintentional consequences of system involvement in favor of more appropriate community services and reserve criminal legal system resources for more serious crimes and higher-risk individuals (Munetz & Griffin, 2006). Because many older adults who are system involved have behavioral health and/or cognitive issues, the SIM can inform community-based and alternative legal responses to include deflection and diversion from the criminal legal system, referral to specialty courts commonly serving older adults (e.g., elder courts, veterans treatment courts, DUI courts), or special services in corrections or at reentry. To identify individuals eligible for alternative legal responses, the American Bar Association (ABA; 2022) recommends targeted training and systematic screening to identify older adults with behavioral health needs and cognitive decline.

Physical Accommodations

Legal systems must consider whether their buildings and facilities are accessible for older adults (Love, 2019; Rothman & Dunlop, 2005) to ensure effective access to the criminal legal system, given that most core legal structures were designed with younger and healthier individuals at the forefront. Physical issues may need to be accommodated for an older person to effectively participate in their case within the requirements of courtrooms and hearings. For instance, an older defendant may need physical accommodation if they have difficulty with hearing, vision, or mobility (Aday & Krabill, 2012; Love, 2019; Rothman & Dunlop, 2005). Other solutions may involve the use of technology, which has become more commonplace in courtrooms following the COVID-19 pandemic (Pew Research, 2021). Even thinking about how to get older adults to the courtroom is important and requires a focus on public transportation, ample accessible parking, and no stairs to enter or climb once inside the building (Eglit, 2005).

Stetson University's Eleazer Courtroom is the first courtroom specifically designed to be aging-friendly and includes hearing amplification devices, colored borders on the carpet to indicate courtroom pathways, a flat touchscreen panel outside of the courtroom that displays the courtroom and key players, nonglare lighting, and a witness box located on the floor (Center for Elders and the Courts, n.d.). Other accommodations may include specialized justice centers. For example, the 13th Judicial Circuit Court of Florida implemented an Elder Justice Center, which assists those aged 60 and older involved in either criminal or civil matters by offering accessible buildings, information and support, help with navigating the court system, and referrals to appropriate legal and social services (Elder Justice Center, 2023).

Elder Specialty Courts and Centers

Following the first "elder court" in the nation in Alameda County, California (Banks et al., 2014), Cook County, Illinois, also developed a special court focused on the holistic needs of older adults similar to other specialty courts such as juvenile, drug, veteran, homeless, and mental health courts. Unlike other specialty courts, however, elder courts are focused on older adults as victims rather than as perpetrators of crime. The Cook County Elder Law Division was established in 2010 and, through multidisciplinary efforts, handles cases in abuse and neglect, powers of attorney, domestic violence, and general crimes toward older adults (Banks, 2012, 2017). The critical components of the court include education and training on older adult issues for staff and judges and developing bench card summary resources for judges (Banks, 2017). The bench card provides definitions from the Adult Protective Services Act (2013), explanations of important concepts (e.g., capacity), relevant statutes, signs of elder abuse or neglect (e.g., unkempt appearance, despondency), and how to report elder abuse (Circuit Court of Cook County Illinois, 2014). The bench card also provides helpful tips for case management such as avoiding unnecessary delays, understanding capacity fluctuations, and providing procedures that memorialize the older adult's testimony (e.g., recording depositions).

Although elder courts have grown in popularity (Grattan, 2013), they come with challenges that include securing the additional funding (Van Duizend & Uekert, 2014) and investments needed to support these specialty courts (Banks et al., 2014). Beyond simple monetary support, the elder courts also must garner the trust of victims. A court can be successful only if older adults trust the courts to handle their needs and requests. Furthermore, they need the buy-in of the judges to be open to the new way of handling all of an individual's issues rather than separating their issues into different courts (Rothman & Dunlop, 2006). Some jurisdictions have implemented centers that provide services rather than elder courts, such as the aforementioned Elder Justice Centers in Florida (Grattan, 2013). According to the website of the Elder Justice Center in Hillsborough County, the centers "address the inevitable fear, confusion, uncertainty, lack of confidence experienced by many elders confronting the courts for perhaps the first time, especially those with dementia or mental health issues" for adults 60 years of age and older (Elder Justice Center, 2023; Grattan, 2013).

In light of the ABA Commission on Law and Aging's (2022) concerns about dementia symptoms in the criminal legal system, the ABA has suggested dementia courts modeled after other established diversion courts (National Judicial Task Force, 2023). Existing diversion courts serve court-involved individuals with behavioral health challenges and, similarly, courts for system-involved individuals with dementia-related disorders could include a collaborative, nonadversarial team to link participants to appropriate services in the community and hold defendants accountable for court requirements (Dubljević, 2020). However, because dementia is progressive and incurable, treatment options the court may impose are limited, and how to finance alternative dispositions must be considered (Kapp, 2020).

Services in Jails and Prisons

Very little literature addresses specific services for older adults or systematic evaluations of services for older adults in jails and prisons, and scholars in social work have called for additional research to determine whether interventions are having an impact on physical and mental health during and after incarceration (Canada et al., 2020). In a review of published studies that specifically address interventions aimed at older inmates' physical and mental health, Canada and colleagues found five such unique interventions. The interventions focused on treating depression (Behavioral Activities Intervention; BE-ACTIV); increasing overall health through physical, mental, and spiritual activities (True Grit); providing trauma coping skills (Art Expression); increasing identification of health and social problems (Older Prisoner Health and Social Care Assessment and Plan; OHSCAP); and interacting with music therapy (Good Vibrations). Because the five interventions relied mostly on anecdotes and qualitative methodologies, the researchers were unable to make generalizable conclusions. Moreover, because of sample limitations (e.g., small samples, attrition from death or dropout), rigorous research studies on the limited programming that exists are challenging.

INCREASING RESEARCH WITH OLDER ADULTS

As stated throughout the book, there is an absence of older adults as research participants, which some claim is a substantial source of structural ageism (Chang et al., 2020). In addition to the absence of older samples generally, studies infrequently include diverse groups of older adults, including older adults of varied age groups. Moreover, the study of legal responses to aging issues is best approached through broad collaboration across disciplines, which can ensure behavioral science research, both basic and applied, is legally meaningful. Importantly, researchers have called to expand the study of aging to diverse populations, specifically to the intersectionality of ageism and other isms (e.g., ableism, classism, sexism, racism, heterosexism). Although growing, research involving the unique experiences of older adults who experience ageism and stigma from multiple identities is limited (S. R. Levy et al., 2022). We suggest researchers intentionally recruit diverse samples of older adults. To encourage the researcher, we describe an example of the authors' efforts to recruit older adults to participate in behavioral science research. This section ends with suggestions for researchers to ensure ageist language is avoided in written materials.

Researching and Writing: Attention to Ageist Language

Conducting research on and with older adults has taught us a great deal about ageism and confronting our own biases about aging—we hope this book has helped the reader begin that same journey. As one of the most socially condoned and institutionalized forms of discrimination (isms) in the United States (J. O. Allen, 2016; Angus & Reeve, 2006), and despite 20 or more years of age bias research in social psychology, ageism is still referred to as a "worldwide crisis," especially after "exacerbated hate speech, intergenerational resentment, and human rights violations" (S. R. Levy et al., 2022, p. 743) became dominant following the COVID-19 pandemic. Our research and teaching experiences have mirrored S. R. Levy and colleagues' assertion. Consistent with interpersonal ageism within social interactions, we get mixed reactions when we explain that we conduct research with older adults. Much like the stereotype content model predicts, some reactions have been positive but oftentimes with patronizing connotations (e.g., "cute, I bet they're fun"). Other reactions are more negative and offered with polite disgust (e.g., "I see. Yeah, I don't really like old people"). Consistent with institutional ageism, there have been very few aging-focused presentations at the annual American Psychology-Law conference, and when we have attended or presented at them, the sessions have had very few in attendance. Moreover, when we describe teaching efforts in aging and the law or mention writing this book, many respond with astonished eyes, having little reference to the topics covered. As we both continue to age, we have experienced opportunities to reflect on our own aging biases and potential internalized ageist beliefs about ourselves.

Reading interdisciplinary research on aging and collaborating with gerontologists has revealed our own anxieties surrounding the aging process and attitudes around death. Observing gerontologists who so comfortably discuss death and dying as a normative process that we all should be so fortunate to achieve has been refreshing and eye-opening. Collecting data with older adults has also confronted our perceptions of aging. Much like the recommendations for training to reduce racial biases, being around the outgroup can promote positive beliefs, attitudes, and behaviors toward them (i.e., the contact hypothesis; Allport, 1954; Paluck et al., 2019). In developing an older adult participant pool to recruit more older adults living independently in the community for research, in contrast to samples of convenience in nursing homes, we have observed the heterogeneity in older adults' functional abilities and the diversity of their experiences.

As in other areas of inquiry, language use has shifted over time. In law, legal scholars rebranded the subfield "elder law" to "aging and the law" to reflect its universal nature (Doron, 2020; Kohn, 2020b). Furthermore, when populations of interest involve those who have been involved in the criminal legal system, criminal justice scholars encourage the use of people-first language that focuses attention to the person rather than what they have done, or allegedly done (A. Cox, 2020). Identifying the pervasiveness and impact of ageist messages, even when inadvertent and well-intentioned, the National Institute on Aging (NIA) and the American Psychological Association (APA) recommend avoiding ageist language in writing. In addition to describing the population specifically, the NIA and APA recommend using neutral terms such as "older adults," "older populations," and "people over the age of [specific age]" instead of words with negative connotations such as "elderly," "the aged," or "Boomers" (APA, 2023; Morrison, 2023). Supporting social psychology theory on self and intergroup relations (Perdue et al., 1990), the NIA also recommends that, where appropriate, writers use "we" and "us" instead of "they" and "them," embracing that "we are all aging, and many issues that affect older adults also affect younger populations" (Morrison, 2023, para. 4).

Developing Theory and Expanding Methods: Collaboration Across Disciplines

Legal and gerontology scholars agree their fields have done little collaboration and would benefit from research collaboration and cross-disciplinary teaching (Kohn et al., 2019). Approximately 15 years ago, survey responses from attorneys and law professors indicated they believed elder law practice and education had positively grown (Kohn & Spurgeon, 2014). However, more recently, scholars have expressed concerns that the study of aging and the law has become stagnant, exacerbated by the retirement of several key elder law scholars (Doron, 2020). To invigorate and advance the study of older adult issues in the legal system, scholars assert that the field should expand to generating and testing theories using empirical social science methods and statistical analyses (Doron, 2020; Kohn, 2020b). Despite these calls and the breadth of novel topics yet to be investigated, research in aging and the law remains an understudied area in law-psychology. Nonetheless, law-psychology researchers and practitioners have expertise and skills in rigorous applied research and evidence-based clinical practice and, in collaboration with scholars from gerontology, medicine, and social work, are well suited to answer the calls of aging and the law theorists.

Operationalizing Samples: Age and Intersectional Group Membership

Of course, one of the first steps in conducting research in this area is determining what is meant by "older adult." As detailed in the Introduction, there remains a kerfuffle about what age someone enters the older adult category—is it over 45 (Nyman et al., 2019), over 50 (Kelly et al., 2017), over 60 (X. Q. Dong, 2015), over 65 (A. M. O'Connor et al., 2022), or some other age? If the researcher is studying compassionate release and age (see Chapter 9), then using a younger age to define older adults may make sense, given a comparison to the average age of inmates (approximately 39 years of age; Beatty & Snell, 2021). Conversely, if a researcher is studying the age of lawmakers or other legal actors (see Chapter 2), then we might expect older age to be defined as a higher number, given the average age of those professionals. Some scholars have also suggested multiple subgroups within the larger age group of older adults to allow for more nuanced categorization such as the "young old" (65–74 years of age), the "aged" (75–84 years of age), and the "old old" (85 years of age and older; Addington, 2013).

Furthermore, as is the case with many research areas, it is important to measure older adults and their intersectionality across group membership. Medical scholars urge intersectionality in aging research; however, despite growing racial and ethnic diversity among U.S. older adults, little aging research has included minoritized populations (Gilmore-Bykovskyi et al., 2022; Thomas Tobin et al., 2023). Conventional research practices (i.e., study design, structural factors, and social determinants of health on participation) fail to address barriers to study participation that may disproportionately reduce participation by minoritized populations (e.g., language, logistics), thus increasing distrust by these groups and introducing problematic study selection biases (Gilmore-Bykovskyi et al., 2022).

Recruiting Samples: Participant Pools for Older Adults

An older adult's group intersectionality will certainly generate differences in how older adults influence and experience the criminal legal system. As such, it is important to recruit older adults into research studies who have diverse characteristics and backgrounds, functional and mobility abilities, and residential status, to name just a few. It is important to keep in mind that when recruiting participants for studies or surveys, not all potential participants will identify as an older adult or even as an aging person. How age is measured, therefore, is also dependent on how the sample participants self-identify (Hall, 2009).

A primary reason for the limited research on older adults may be recruitment challenges, as social psychology studies have traditionally relied on easily accessible undergraduate student samples (Brank, 2007). To increase access for older adults wanting to participate in research studies, one method is to develop and maintain a database of individuals—a participant pool. Recruitment to an ongoing and well-maintained participant pool should provide opportunities for both community-dwelling and institution-dwelling (i.e., assisted living facilities) volunteers. For older adults who do not live independently, researchers will need to take precautions to ensure older adults are legally able to consent to participate in research. With regard to study topics related to older adults who are living in correctional facilities like those discussed in Chapters 8 and 9, research will require special Institutional Review Board approvals because additional requirements must be met to include prisoners in research as a distinct category of vulnerable adults (Office for Human Research Protections, n.d.). Although this subsection is wholly anecdotal, and we have no systematic evidence to support our participant pool development efforts, we share them here to encourage innovative recruitment efforts to include diverse populations of older adults and highlight some of the barriers we identified and how we addressed them.

With the move to the University of Nebraska–Lincoln described earlier, the authors discovered they needed to make efforts to build an older adult participant pool. Although online participant pools such as Prolific Academic and Amazon's Mechanical Turk are possible to use for older adult research, they are generally limited to more educated, tech-savvy, and healthy individuals (Turner et al., 2021). Through advertisements in a newspaper for adults aged 55 and over, flyers in doctors' offices and assisted living facilities, and direct recruitment at events (e.g., Osher Lifelong Learning Institute events and courses, City of Lincoln Aging Partners), in 1 year the authors developed a database of 189 adults over the age of 60 who were interested in participating in research. The Participant Volunteer Network (PVN), as it was called, provided an organized way to contact older adults about research opportunities. Other researchers such as psychology scholar Sarah Barber and her colleagues (2019), as they described in their study on stereotype threat, have used similar recruitment tactics (e.g., Osher Lifelong Learning Institute courses), which afforded them opportunities to study older adults in their research.

Some practices we established involved annual updates to the database that included postage-paid postcards the participants could return to update their contact information as needed and indicate if they were no longer interested in being contacted about research opportunities. A dedicated phone line and email address also helped provide clarity that the contacts were coming from the PVN. Furthermore, a clear website linked to the university's main website was crucial for further increasing trust. We provided multiple opportunities for contact—some were internet-based, such as an online form, and others were more basic, such as postage-paid envelopes. The variety was meant to encourage all to engage, whether tech-savvy or not, given we knew other older adult participation pools often contained more highly educated individuals than those generally found in participation pools (A. K. Thomas et al., 2020). As new generations move into the older adult category, technology use will likely increase by older adults even if there is always a divide between younger and older adults' technology use (Lee & Coughlin, 2015).

When researchers solicited participants from the PVN, we suggested in-person data collection in a public place most comfortable to the older person or in their homes. To ensure researcher and participant safety and accountability, two researchers traveled to any off-campus data collection. Another reason (quiet) public places and homes were selected is because the standard university laboratory rooms and offices generally proved unworkable because of the limited number of accessible spaces, walking distances between the spaces and the campus buildings, and the general unfamiliar nature of university campuses to nonstudents. Therefore, in-person data collection was encouraged to take place in public places such as libraries, restaurants, or aging agencies. Others have certainly also created older adult participant pools, and we encourage developing one. For example, cognitive science scholar Lauren Richmond maintains an older adult participant pool for the Stony Brook University geographical area (Stony Brook University, n.d.).

DEVELOPING SKILLS IN FORENSIC EVALUATIONS WITH OLDER ADULTS

Due to differences caused by normative and pathological aging processes as well as social and psychological determinants, forensic evaluators who specialize in aging are in high demand. In a recent article published in *Clinical Psychology: Science and Practice*, an APA journal aimed at publishing cutting-edge issues in clinical psychology, Mast and colleagues (2022) stated there is "a pressing need" (p. 43) for psychologists who are specifically trained to evaluate older adults. Without practitioners skilled in geriatric forensic assessment, older adults are vulnerable to judicial and correctional legal responses that may infringe on their legal rights afforded under state and federal constitutions (Reimers, 2019).

Forensic Evaluations and Older Adults

Currently, forensic psychologists look to the guidelines published by two of the leading national organizations that guide the practice of forensic psychology: the APA and the American Academy of Psychiatry and the Law (AAPL). The *AAPL Practice Guideline for the Forensic Assessment* (2015) is intended for forensic evaluators who provide expert opinion in legal contexts, such as evaluations for competency and criminal responsibility, risk and dangerousness, and civil proceedings. Although AAPL's guidelines discuss how to adjust an evaluation for children, adolescents, and individuals with intellectual disability, there is no special subsection for older adults, and dementia is only briefly discussed (Reimers, 2019). APA's (2013) *Specialty Guidelines for Forensic Psychology*, which were developed with APA Division 41 American Psychology–Law Society to provide recommendations for psychological practice in legal systems, are not specific to populations. APA (2014) has current guidelines around psychological practice with older adults, developed by APA Divisions 12 (Society of Clinical Geropsychology) and 20 (Adult Development and Aging). These guidelines focus on the general practice of treating older adults in community settings but do not have specific recommendations for forensic contexts.

Although guidance on assessing older adults in criminal legal contexts is sparse overall, Bush and Heck's (2018) *Forensic Geropsychology: Practice Essentials* is one of the few resources that address competency in both criminal and civil contexts. In the criminal contexts, Bush and Heck focus on how forensic practitioners should approach assessing older adults for competency to stand trial, competency to be executed, the insanity defense, and treatment for individuals who are incarcerated. Historically, resources have focused on evaluation in civil contexts. Indeed, key resources often state that examples in criminal contexts are beyond the scope of their work. For instance, in *Assessing Capacities of Older Adults: A Casebook to Guide Difficult Decisions* (Moye, 2020), the topics include assessing capacities for civil contexts such as financial exploitation, undue influence, sexual consent, and medical aid in dying. There is no mention of criminal contexts in which an older adult's competency could be in question.

Forensic Assessment Instruments and Age

Psychological tests, diagnostic instruments, and decision-making heuristics are most effective when applied to individuals who closely resemble the population for which these tools were developed and validated. An instrument's fit and applicability to the individual being evaluated will predict the reliability and validity of the evaluation (Heilbrun et al., 2002). As such, forensic evaluators should know whether the tool selected in an evaluation is appropriate for the population they are assessing, including age (typically juvenile or adult), clinical status (presence or type of disorder), and legal status (legally involved or not), and whether the instrument was developed and validated with a comparable sample. As illustrated with a major theme of this book, there is no clear age when someone becomes "elderly," and deficits may occur at different rates within subpopulations. The appropriateness of an assessment instrument should be evaluated based on developmental factors, including the person's understanding, reasoning ability, level of autonomy, communication skills, and psychosocial judgment (e.g., Steinberg & Cauffman, 1996).

Historically, assessment tools were not normed with an aging older adult population. Over the past 2 decades, however, this has improved as most cognitive and some mood and personality tests have been validated with older adults (Lichtenberg, 2010; Lichtenberg et al., 2015). Aging may be further impacted by other factors such as language, culture, ethnicity, socioeconomic status, and reading level for diagnostic tests (Mast et al., 2022). APA's general practice guidelines encourage psychologists to understand possible methodological problems such as population and equivalence of measures and "consequences of inadequately developed instruments when cultural factors are not considered" (APA, 2014, p. 48; see also Okazaki & Sue, 1995). In general, because of the small proportion of older adults in the criminal legal system, it may be challenging to produce validation statistics for older adults. Accordingly, forensic assessment experts Heilbrun et al. (2002) asserted that "when there is no empirical evidence about the applicability and interpretation of results in a different population, it is usually preferable to avoid using that instrument to evaluate someone from a different population" (p. 17). Legal system decision makers will increasingly expect forensic evaluation processes and assessment tools to be scientifically validated for system-involved older adults.

Epilogue

In 2013, on her fifth attempt and at age 64, Diana Nyad swam 110 miles from Havana, Cuba, to Key West, Florida, a journey most thought the sexagenarian could not endure because the swimming conditions included challenges such as jellyfish and sharks, winds that could set her off course, eating and drinking over the few days, and extreme sun and water exposure. Most of all, many were concerned about the strength it would take to swim for hours without stopping. Most thought she was "too old" to complete the swim, let alone the training it would require beforehand. When questioned about whether she really wanted to spend her aging years training for such a feat, Nyad's response was, "But for each of us, isn't life about determining your own finish line?" (ABC News, 2011, para. 3). As we have illustrated throughout this book, the aging process differs for each person, and whether someone is "too old" for the given task at hand—swimming, testifying in court, sitting on the bench, or living in prison—may be in the eye of the beholder. On the other hand, if "old age" is a social construct that is self-defined and based on "embodied experiences of aging" (Hall, 2009, p. 2), how and when to define "too old" will continue to be a central question and moving target.

Nyad completed her infamous swim in 53 hours, but she did not do it alone. During the swim, more than 30 people on her team sailed beside her. As she swam, there were individuals responsible for driving the boat, navigating the ocean and wind, and making sure she was hydrated and fed. As depicted in the Netflix movie *Nyad* (Chin & Vasarhelyi, 2023), her lifelong friend and

https://doi.org/10.1037/0000469-012
Aging and the Criminal Legal System: Community Services, Courts, Corrections, and Policy, by L. E. Wylie and E. M. Brank

trainer Bonnie Stoll cheered, motivated, and cried with Nyad the whole way, but Nyad, despite her weathered skin and mental exhaustion from the external conditions and her internal strength, was always in command. At moments when she appeared to be losing consciousness, her team was there to support her and jump in if there was a safety concern. Legal responses to aging could operate in the same manner. Regardless of the substantive area of law or sequential intercept in the criminal legal system process, what if legal responses used individualized approaches and support systems as the default core legal principle, before responding with legal interventions that determine someone else's finish line?

One undeniable fact: Both we, the authors, and you, the readers, are older now than when we began writing this book. Growing older is a privilege—however it is defined—and an achievement in stamina and strength. In the words of Diana Nyad, "endurance is not a young person's game. I thought I might even be better at 60 than I was at 30. You have a body that's almost as strong, but you have a much better mind" (Weil, 2011, para. 8). To echo Jimmy Buffet (France, 2023), "growing old is not for sissies, [we] promise you."

SUGGESTED FURTHER READING

We could fill another book with book recommendations, but we will focus on just a few. We discuss each recommendation here and provide a list at the end. First, Atul Gawande's (2015) *Being Mortal: Medicine and What Matters in the End* should be required reading for everyone, but especially those who consider the inevitable end-of-life issues that are present with older adults. Similarly, Sherwin Nuland's (1995) *How We Die: Reflections on Life's Final Chapter* also serves as a good reminder that death will find all of us, and the sooner we embrace that, the sooner we can more fully live. For a comedic yet poignant take on caring for older adult family members, we recommend Meg Federico's (2009) autobiographical tale of her own mother's caregiving and death in *Welcome to the Departure Lounge: Adventures in Mothering Mother*. As mentioned in Chapter 3 (this volume), Arthur Brooks's (2022) *From Strength to Strength: Finding Success, Happiness, and Deep Purpose in the Second Half of Life* permits one to move into the next phase of life without the same goals from the previous phases by embracing one's aging as it relates to their career and priorities. Finally, made popular through a movie by the same title, Lisa Genova's (2009) *Still Alice* tells the story of a successful 50-year-old professor who has early-onset Alzheimer's. The story humanizes cognitive disorders. Defying ageist stereotypes, Doris Payne's (2019) memoir *Diamond Doris* follows her jewel capers over 6 decades. These are just a few books that helped shape our perspectives and drew us toward studying, thinking about, and understanding research on older adults.

Brooks, A. C. (2022). *From strength to strength: Finding success, happiness, and deep purpose in the second half of life*. Portfolio/Penguin.

Federico, M. (2009). *Welcome to the departure lounge: Adventures in mothering mother.* Random House.

Gawande, A. (2015). *Being mortal: Medicine and what matters in the end* (13th ed.). Picador.

Genova, L. (2009). *Still Alice.* Gallery Books.

Nuland, S. B. (1995). *How we die: Reflections on life's final chapter.* Vintage.

Payne, D. (2019). *Diamond Doris: The true story of the world's most notorious jewel thief.* Amistad.

REFERENCES

AARP. (2024). *What is AARP?* https://www.aarp.org/membership

ABC News. (2011). *Diana Nyad ends swim from Cuba to Florida after two man-of-war stings.* https://abcnews.go.com/US/diana-nyad-ends-cuba-florida-swim-man-war/story?id=14601794

Abrams, D. S., & Yoon, A. H. (2007). The luck of the draw: Using random case assignment to investigate attorney ability. *The University of Chicago Law Review, 74*(4), 1145–1177. https://doi.org/10.2307/20141859

Achenbaum, A. (2015). A history of ageism since 1969. *Generations: Journal of the American Society on Aging, 39*(3), 10–16. https://www.jstor.org/stable/26556123

Achenbaum, W. (1978). *Old age in the new land.* Johns Hopkins University Press. https://doi.org/10.1353/book.72152

Acierno, R., Hernandez, M. A., Amstadter, A. B., Resnick, H. S., Steve, K., Muzzy, W., & Kilpatrick, D. G. (2010). Prevalence and correlates of emotional, physical, sexual, and financial abuse and potential neglect in the United States: The National Elder Mistreatment Study. *American Journal of Public Health, 100*(2), 292–297. https://doi.org/10.2105/AJPH.2009.163089

Adams, K., & Cutshall, C. R. (1987). Refusing to prosecute minor offenses: The relative influence of legal and extralegal factors. *Justice Quarterly, 4*(4), 595–609. https://doi.org/10.1080/07418828700089541

Adams-Price, C. E., Dalton, W. T., III, & Sumrall, R. (2004). Victim blaming in young, middle-aged, and older adults: Variations on the severity effect. *Journal of Adult Development, 11*(4), 289–295. https://doi.org/10.1023/B:JADE.0000044532.83720.74

Aday, R. H. (1994). Golden years behind bars—Special programs and facilities for elderly inmates. *Federal Probation, 58*(2), 47–54.

Aday, R. H. (2003). *Aging prisoners: Crisis in American corrections.* Praeger. https://doi.org/10.5040/9798216956211

Aday, R. H. (2006). Aging prisoners' concerns toward dying in prison. *Omega: Journal of Death and Dying, 52*(3), 199–216. https://doi.org/10.2190/CHTD-YL7T-R1RR-LHMN

Aday, R., & Farney, L. (2014). Malign neglect: Assessing older women's health care experiences in prison. *Journal of Bioethical Inquiry, 11*(3), 359–372. https://doi.org/10.1007/s11673-014-9561-0

Aday, R. H., & Krabill, J. J. (2012). Aging offenders in the criminal justice system. *Marquette Elder's Advisor,* 7(2), 237–258.

Aday, R. H., & Krabill, J. J. (2013). Older and geriatric offenders: Critical issues for the 21st century. In L. Gideon (Ed.), *Special needs offenders in correctional institutions* (pp. 203–232). Sage Publications. https://doi.org/10.4135/9781452275444.n7

Addington, L. A. (2013). Who you calling old? Measuring "elderly" and what it means for homicide research. *Homicide Studies, 17*(2), 134–153. https://doi.org/10.1177/1088767912461784

Administrative Office of the U.S. Courts. (n.d.-a). *About federal judges.* https://www.uscourts.gov/judges-judgeships/about-federal-judges

Administrative Office of the U.S. Courts. (n.d.-b). *FAQs: Federal judges.* https://www.uscourts.gov/faqs-federal-judges

Adult Protective Services Act, 320 Ill. Comp. Stat. 20 (2013). https://www.ilga.gov/legislation/ilcs/ilcs3.asp?ActID=1452&ChapterID=31

Age Discrimination in Employment Act of 1967, 29 U.S.C. §§ 621–634.

Age Discrimination in Employment Act Amendments of 1978, Pub. L. No. 95-256, 92 Stat. 189.

Age Discrimination in Employment Act Amendments of 1986, Pub. L. No. 99-592, 92 Stat. 1559.

Ahalt, C., & Williams, B. (2015, February 25). How can criminal justice systems from police to probation address the medical and social care needs of elderly prisoners? *Penal Reform International.* https://www.penalreform.org/blog/declining-health-advancing-years-prison-call-policy-oriented

Aizpurua, A., García-Bajos, E., & Migueles, M. (2011). False recognition and source attribution for actions of an emotional event in older and younger adults. *Experimental Aging Research, 37*(3), 310–329. https://doi.org/10.1080/0361073X.2011.568829

Alamdari, N. (2022, November 4). "Waiting on death": Nebraska prisoners are getting older, and it's costing taxpayers. *Flatwater Free Press.* https://flatwaterfreepress.org/waiting-on-death-nebraska-prisoners-are-getting-older-and-its-costing-taxpayers

Alizadehsani, R., Abdar, M., Roshanzamir, M., Khosravi, A., Kebria, P. M., Khozeimeh, F., Nahavandi, S., Sarrafzadegan, N., & Acharya, U. R. (2019). Machine learning-based coronary artery disease diagnosis: A comprehensive review. *Computers in Biology and Medicine, 111,* 103346. https://doi.org/10.1016/j.compbiomed.2019.103346

Allen, J. O. (2016). Ageism as a risk factor for chronic disease. *The Gerontologist, 56*(4), 610–614. https://doi.org/10.1093/geront/gnu158

Allen, J. O., & Sikora, N. (2023). Aging stigma and the health of US adults over 65: What do we know? *Clinical Interventions in Aging, 18,* 2093–2116. https://doi.org/10.2147/CIA.S396833

Allen, K. (2018). *Police use taser on 87-year-old woman cutting dandelions with a knife.* CNN. https://www.cnn.com/2018/08/16/us/georgia-police-taser-woman-dandelions-knife/index.html

Allen v. Ornoski, No. CIV. S-06-64 FCD/DAD (E.D. Cal. Jan. 12, 2006a).

Allen v. Ornoski, No. CCV-00064-FCD-DAD (E.D. Cal. Jan. 15, 2006b).

Allport, F. H. (1954). The structuring of events: Outline of a general theory with applications to psychology. *Psychological Review, 61*(5), 281–303. https://doi.org/10.1037/h0062678

Alvord, K. (2024, February 28). Mitch McConnell, 82, to step down as Republican Senate leader after reaching historic milestone. *People*. https://people.com/mitch-mcconnell-resigning-senate-leadership-8601632

Alzheimer's Association. (2019, December 16). *Legislation to require first responders to get dementia training needed for those who wander*. https://alz.org/nwohio/news/legislation-to-require-first-responders-to-get-dem

Alzheimer's Association. (2024). *2024 Alzheimer's disease facts and figures*. https://www.alz.org/getmedia/76e51bb6-c003-4d84-8019-e0779d8c4e8d/alzheimers-facts-and-figures.pdf

Amendment to 18 U.S.C. § 4247, Pub. L. No. 98-473, 98 Stat. 2057 (1984).

American Academy of Psychiatry and the Law. (2015). *AAPL Practice Guideline for the Forensic Assessment*. https://aapl.org/docs/pdf/Forensic_Assessment.pdf

American Association for Geriatric Psychiatry. (n.d.). *History*. https://aagponline.org/about-aagp/history

American Bar Association. (2023). *Profile of the legal profession 2023*. https://www.americanbar.org/content/dam/aba/administrative/news/2023/potlp-2023.pdf

American Bar Association Commission on Law and Aging. (2022, May). *Persons living with dementia in the criminal legal system: Final report*. https://www.americanbar.org/content/dam/aba/administrative/law_aging/2022-dementia-crim-just-rpt.pdf

American Bar Association Commission on Law and Aging & American Psychological Association. (2021). *Assessment of older adults with diminished capacities: Handbook for lawyers* (2nd ed.). ABA Book Publishing.

American Civil Liberties Union & Sentencing Project. (2020, April 21). *Call for urgent action: Technical Amendment to the First Step Act to give "old law" federal prisoners equal access to compassionate release* [Letter]. https://www.aclu.org/documents/compassionate-release-technical-amendment-coalition-letter-support

American Law Institute. (1962). *Model penal code*.

American Psychiatric Association. (2013). *Diagnostic and statistical manual of mental disorders* (5th ed.). https://doi.org/10.1176/appi.books.9780890425596

American Psychiatric Association. (2022). *Diagnostic and statistical manual of mental disorders* (5th ed., text rev.). https://doi.org/10.1176/appi.books.9780890425787

American Psychological Association. (2008). *Geropsychology*. https://www.apa.org/ed/graduate/specialize/geropsychology

American Psychological Association. (2013). Specialty guidelines for forensic psychology. *The American Psychologist, 68*(1), 7–19. https://doi.org/10.1037/a0029889

American Psychological Association. (2014). Guidelines for psychological practice with older adults. *The American Psychologist, 69*(1), 34–65. https://doi.org/10.1037/a0035063

American Psychological Association. (2023). *Inclusive language guide*. https://www.apa.org/about/apa/equity-diversity-inclusion/language-guidelines

American Psychological Association. (2024, July 8). *Elder abuse: How to spot warning signs, get help, and report mistreatment*. https://www.apa.org/topics/aging-older-adults/elder-abuse

American Psychological Association Task Force on the Evaluation of Dementia and Age-Related Cognitive Change. (2021). *APA guidelines for the evaluation of dementia and age-related cognitive change.* https://www.apa.org/practice/guidelines/guidelines-dementia-age-related-cognitive-change.pdf

American Psychology–Law Society. (n.d.). *Our mission.* https://ap-ls.org/about

Americans With Disabilities Act of 1990, as amended by ex. ord. no. 13217 (2001), 42 U.S.C. § 12131–12134.

Amjad, H., Roth, D. L., Sheehan, O. C., Lyketsos, C. G., Wolff, J. L., & Samus, Q. M. (2018). Underdiagnosis of dementia: An observational study of patterns in diagnosis and awareness in US older adults. *Journal of General Internal Medicine, 33,* 1131–1138. https://doi.org/10.1007/s11606-018-4377-y

Andrews, D. A., & Bonta, J. (2003). *The psychology of criminal conduct* (3rd ed.). Anderson.

Anetzberger, G. J. (2005). The reality of elder abuse. *Clinical Gerontologist, 28*(1–2), 1–25. https://doi.org/10.1300/J018v28n01_01

Angus, J., & Reeve, P. (2006). Ageism: A threat to "aging well" in the 21st century. *Journal of Applied Gerontology, 25*(2), 137–152. https://doi.org/10.1177/0733464805285745

Anonymous. (2023, January 17). The only person on the planet who thinks Ron Jeremy can act [Comment on the webpage *Ron Jeremy Escapes Rape Trial Due To "Incurable Neurocognitive Decline," Judge Says; Ex-Porn Star Faced Over 300 Years Behind Bars If Found Guilty*]. Deadline. https://deadline.com/2023/01/porn-ron-jeremy-dementia-rape-trial-la-da-1235225388/comment-page-2/#comments

Anwar, S., Bayer, P., & Hjalmarsson, R. (2014). The role of age in jury selection and trial outcomes. *The Journal of Law & Economics, 57*(4), 1001–1030. https://doi.org/10.1086/675257

Aprile, J. V., II. (2012). Defending the elderly. *GPSolo, 29*(5), 70–71.

Arias, J. J. (2013). A time to step in: Legal mechanisms for protecting those with declining capacity. *American Journal of Law & Medicine, 39*(1), 134–159. https://doi.org/10.1177/009885881303900103

Arias, J. J., & Flicker, L. S. (2020). A matter of intent: A social obligation to improve criminal procedures for individuals with dementia. *Journal of Law, Medicine & Ethics, 48*(2), 318–327. https://doi.org/10.1177/1073110520935345

Armstrong, B., Gallant, S. N., Li, L., Patel, K., & Wong, B. I. (2017). Stereotype threat effects on older adults' episodic and working memory: A meta-analysis. *The Gerontologist, 57*(Suppl. 2), S193–S205. https://doi.org/10.1093/geront/gnx056

Arnold, M. (2015). Psychopharmacology and polypharmacy. In P. A. Lichtenberg, B. T. Mast, B. D. Carpenter, & J. Loebach Wetherell (Eds.), *APA handbook of clinical geropsychology: History and status of the field and perspectives on aging* (Vol. 1, pp. 587–605). American Psychological Association. https://doi.org/10.1037/14458-025

Ash, E., & MacLeod, W. B. (2020). *Mandatory retirement for judges improved performance on U.S. State Supreme Courts* (Working Paper 28025). National Bureau of Economic Research. https://doi.org/10.3386/w28025

Atkins v. Virginia, 536 U.S. 304 (2002).

Auerhahn, K. (2002). Selective incapacitation, three strikes, and the problem of aging prison populations: Using simulation modeling to see the future. *Criminology & Public Policy, 1*(3), 353–388. https://doi.org/10.1111/j.1745-9133.2002.tb00097.x

Ayalon, L., Lev, S., Green, O., & Nevo, U. (2016). A systematic review and meta-analysis of interventions designed to prevent or stop elder maltreatment. *Age and Ageing, 45*(2), 216–227. https://doi.org/10.1093/ageing/afv193

Babb v. Wilkie, Secretary of Veterans Affairs, 589 U.S. ___ (2020).

Bachand, D. J. (1984, November 6–November 9). *Increased criminal behavior by the elderly: Concerns for the justice system* [Paper presentation]. American Society of Criminology Annual Meeting, Cincinnati, Ohio, United States. https://files.eric.ed.gov/fulltext/ED253829.pdf

Baddeley, A. D., & Hitch, G. (1974). Working memory. In G. H. Bower (Ed.), *Psychology of learning and motivation* (Vol. 8, pp. 47–89). Academic Press. https://doi.org/10.1016/S0079-7421(08)60452-1

Bae, S. S. (2020). *The barriers to reentry of formerly incarcerated elderly individuals that can ultimately lead to homelessness: A policy document analysis* [Capstone paper]. UCLA Center for Community Engagement. https://escholarship.org/uc/item/3cr7h8t5

Baidawi, S. (2016). Older prisoners: Psychological distress and associations with mental health history, cognitive functioning, socio-demographic, and criminal justice factors. *International Psychogeriatrics, 28*(3), 385–395. https://doi.org/10.1017/S1041610215001878

Baidawi, S., Trotter, C., & Flynn, C. (2016). Prison experiences and psychological distress among older inmates. *Journal of Gerontological Social Work, 59*(3), 252–270. https://doi.org/10.1080/01634372.2016.1197353

Baillargeon, J., Linthicum, L. C., Murray, O. J., Raji, M. A., Kuo, Y.-F., Pulvino, J. S., Milani, S. A., Williams, B., Baillargeon, G. R., Blair, P. A., Kristen Peek, M., & Penn, J. V. (2023). The prevalence of cognitive impairment and dementia in incarcerated older adults. *The Journals of Gerontology: Series B, 78*(12), 2141–2146. https://doi.org/10.1093/geronb/gbad136

Banks, P. (2012). A new age and a new court for older litigants. *Experience, 22*, 12–22.

Banks, P. (2017). Elder protection courts: Responding to the now, anticipating the future. *Court Review, 53*, 62–63.

Banks, P., Conger, J., & Cram, J. M. (2014). Elder protection courts: Judicial perspective, holistic approach. *Experience, 24*(1), 12–30.

Barak, Y., Perry, T., & Elizur, A. (1995). Elderly criminals: A study of the first criminal offence in old age. *International Journal of Geriatric Psychiatry, 10*(6), 511–516. https://doi.org/10.1002/gps.930100611

Baral, S. P., Prasad, P., & Raghuvamshi, G. (2022). Mental health awareness and generation gap. *Indian Journal of Psychiatry, 64*(Suppl. 3), S636. https://doi.org/10.4103/0019-5545.341859

Barbaree, H. E., Blanchard, R., & Langton, C. M. (2003). The development of sexual aggression through the life span: The effect of age on sexual arousal and recidivism among sex offenders. *Annals of the New York Academy of Sciences, 989*(1), 59–71. https://doi.org/10.1111/j.1749-6632.2003.tb07293.x

Barber, C. R., & DeChalus, C. (2022, September 27). Alzheimer's disease, retirement "pacts," and serving until you're 104 years old: Inside the federal judiciary's reckoning with age. *Business Insider*. https://www.businessinsider.com/gerontocracy-federal-judges-red-white-and-gray-courts-supreme-2022-8

Barber, S. J., Seliger, J., Yeh, N., & Tan, S. C. (2019). Stereotype threat reduces the positivity of older adults' recall. *The Journals of Gerontology: Series B, 74*(4), 585–594. https://doi.org/10.1093/geronb/gby026

Barker, D. T., & Clark, R. L. (1980). Mandatory retirement and labor-force participation of respondents in the retirement history study. *Social Security Bulletin, 43*(11), 20–29, 55.

Barker, H. (2021, May 11). 'A preventable mess': How dementia takes toll on aging lawyers. *Bloomberg Law.* https://news.bloomberglaw.com/us-law-week/a-preventable-mess-how-dementia-takes-toll-on-aging-lawyers

Barnes, C. (2008). Time to go. Helping lawyers retire with dignity. *Bar Leader, 32*(6). https://www.americanbar.org/groups/bar-leadership/publications/bar_leader/2007_08/3206/dignity/

Barrett, A. E., & Cantwell, L. E. (2007). Drawing on stereotypes: Using undergraduates' sketches of elders as a teaching tool. *Educational Gerontology, 33*(4), 327–348. https://doi.org/10.1080/03601270701198950

Barry, L. C., Soulos, P. R., Murphy, T. E., Kasl, S. V., & Gill, T. M. (2013). Association between indicators of disability burden and subsequent depression among older persons. *The Journals of Gerontology: Series A, 68*(3), 286–292. https://doi.org/10.1093/gerona/gls179

Barry, L. C., Wakefield, D. B., Trestman, R. L., & Conwell, Y. (2017). Disability in prison activities of daily living and likelihood of depression and suicidal ideation in older prisoners. *International Journal of Geriatric Psychiatry, 32*(10), 1141–1149. https://doi.org/10.1002/gps.4578

Bartels, S. J., & Naslund, J. A. (2013). The underside of the silver tsunami—Older adults and mental health care. *The New England Journal of Medicine, 368*(6), 493–496. https://doi.org/10.1056/NEJMp1211456

Bartlett, J. C., & Memon, A. (Eds.). (2007). Eyewitness memory in young and older eyewitnesses. In R. C. L. Lindsay, D. F. Ross, J. D. Read, & M. P. Toglia (Eds.), *The handbook of eyewitness psychology: Memory for people* (Vol. 2, pp. 309–338). Erlbaum. https://doi.org/10.4324/9780203936368

Baruch, B. (n.d.). Bernard Baruch: Quotes. *Britannica.* https://www.britannica.com/quotes/Bernard-Baruch

Batson v. Kentucky, 476 U.S. 79 (1986).

Beatty, L. G., & Snell, T. L. (2021). *Survey of prison inmates: Profile of prison inmates, 2016* (NCJ No. 255037). U.S. Department of Justice, Office of Justice Programs, Bureau of Justice Statistics.

Bedard, R., Huxley-Reicher, Z., Burke, K., MacDonald, R., & Yang, P. (2022). Aging in jail: Retrospective analysis of older patients in New York City's jail system, 2015–19. *Health Affairs, 41*(5), 732–740. https://doi.org/10.1377/hlthaff.2021.01518

Berman, D. A. (2021, May 11). "Old law" federal prisoners provide new reminder that parole does not cure all ills. *Sentencing Law and Policy*. https://sentencing.typepad.com/sentencing_law_and_policy

Berry, W. W., III. (2008). Extraordinary and compelling: A re-examination of the justifications for compassionate release. *Maryland Law Review, 68*(4), 850–888.

Berryessa, C. M. (2016). Behavioral and neural impairments of frontotemporal dementia: Potential implications for criminal responsibility and sentencing. *International Journal of Law and Psychiatry, 46*, 1–6. https://doi.org/10.1016/j.ijlp.2016.02.020

Berryessa, C. M. (2020). Compassionate release as a "right" in the age of COVID-19. *The American Journal of Bioethics, 20*(7), 185–187. https://doi.org/10.1080/15265161.2020.1777348

Bessey, B. L., & Ananda, S. M. (1991). Age discrimination in employment: An interdisciplinary review of the ADEA. *Research on Aging, 13*(4), 413–457. https://doi.org/10.1177/0164027591134002

Bhutto, A., & Morley, J. E. (2008). The clinical significance of gastrointestinal changes with aging. *Current Opinion in Clinical Nutrition and Metabolic Care, 11*(5), 651–660. https://doi.org/10.1097/MCO.0b013e32830b5d37

Binswanger, I. A., Krueger, P. M., & Steiner, J. F. (2009). Prevalence of chronic medical conditions among jail and prison inmates in the USA compared with the general population. *Journal of Epidemiology and Community Health, 63*(11), 912–919. https://doi.org/10.1136/jech.2009.090662

Blaine, B. E., & Brenchley, K. J. M. (2020). *Understanding the psychology of diversity.* Sage Publications.

Blazina, C., & Desilver, D. (2023, January 30). *House gets younger, Senate gets older: A look at the age and generation of lawmakers in the 118th Congress.* Pew Research Center. https://www.pewresearch.org/short-reads/2023/01/30/house-gets-younger-senate-gets-older-a-look-at-the-age-and-generation-of-lawmakers-in-the-118th-congress

Bliss, M. (1999). *William Osler: A life in medicine.* Oxford University Press.

Block, C. R. (2013). Homicide against or by the elderly in Chicago 1965–2000. *Homicide Studies, 17*(2), 154–183. https://doi.org/10.1177/1088767913478596

Boettger, S., Bergman, M., Jenewein, J., & Boettger, S. (2016). Advanced age and decisional capacity: The effect of age on the ability to make health care decisions. *Archives of Gerontology and Geriatrics, 66,* 211–217. https://doi.org/10.1016/j.archger.2016.06.011

Bolkan, C., Teaster, P. B., & Ramsey-Klawsnik, H. (2023). The context of elder maltreatment: An opportunity for prevention science. *Prevention Science, 24*(5), 911–925. https://doi.org/10.1007/s11121-022-01470-5

Bollinger, S. S., & Gordon, L. (2019). *Caring for inmates in a specialized dementia unit in a correctional setting!* National Council of Certified Dementia Practitioners. https://portal.nccdp.org/resources/caring-for-inmates-in-a-specialized-dementia-unit-in-a-correctional-setting.pdf

Bolotnikov, J., Soble, J., & Raiji, V. (2022). 313 Aging in Illinois prisons in the time of COVID-19. *Annals of Emergency Medicine, 80*(4), S134. https://doi.org/10.1016/j.annemergmed.2022.08.341

Boni-Saenz, A. A. (2022). Legal age. *Boston College Law Review, 63*(2), 521–570.

Booth, B. D. (2016). Elderly sexual offenders. *Current Psychiatry Reports, 18*(4), 34. https://doi.org/10.1007/s11920-016-0678-1

Boothby, J. L., & Overduin, L. Y. (2007). Attitudes regarding the compassionate release of terminally ill offenders. *The Prison Journal, 87*(4), 408–415. https://doi.org/10.1177/0032885507306518

Borden, A. (2022, November 4). *Officers involved in the arrest of 73-year-old Karen Garner violated key Loveland Police Department policies, report finds.* Colorado Public Radio News. https://www.cpr.org/2022/11/04/loveland-police-department-karen-garner-report

Bornstein, B. H., Witt, C. J., Cherry, K. E., & Greene, E. (2000). The suggestibility of older witnesses. In M. B. Rothman, B. D. Dunlop, & P. Entzel (Eds.), *Elders, crime, and the criminal justice system: Myth, perceptions, and reality in the 21st century* (pp. 149–161). Springer.

Bosman, J., Smith, M., McKinley, J., & Root, J. (2023, April 19). Hundreds of miles apart, separate shootings follow wrong turns. *The New York Times*. https://www.nytimes.com/2023/04/19/us/yarl-gillis-shooting-missouri-ny.html

Boss, G. R., & Seegmiller, J. E. (1981). Age-related physiological changes and their clinical significance. *The Western Journal of Medicine, 135*(6), 434–440.

Bottoms, B. L., Kovera, M. B., & McAuliff, B. D. (Eds.). (2002). *Children, social science, and the law*. Cambridge University Press. https://doi.org/10.1017/CBO9780511500114

Bourns, W. F. (2000). Police gerontology services for the elderly: A policy guide. *The Justice Professional, 13*(2), 179–192. https://doi.org/10.1080/1478601X.2000.9959583

Brandl, B., & Raymond, J. A. (2012). Policy implications of recognizing that caregiver stress is not the primary cause of elder abuse. *Generations: Journal of American Society on Aging, 36*(3), 32–39.

Brank, E. M. (2007). Elder research: Filling an important gap in psychology and law. *Behavioral Sciences & the Law, 25*(5), 701–716. https://doi.org/10.1002/bsl.780

Brank, E. M. (2011). Baby boomers at work: Growing older and working more. In R. L. Wiener & S. L. Willborn (Eds.), *Disability and aging discrimination: Perspectives in law and psychology* (pp. 93–105). Springer. https://doi.org/10.1007/978-1-4419-6293-5_5

Brank, E. M. (2019). *The psychology of family law*. New York University Press. https://doi.org/10.18574/nyu/9781479865413.001.0001

Brank, E. M., & Weisz, V. (2004). Paying for the crimes of their children: Public support of parental responsibility. *Journal of Criminal Justice, 32*(5), 465–475. https://doi.org/10.1016/j.jcrimjus.2004.06.010

Brank, E., Williams, A., Weisz, V., & Ray, R. (2001). Parental compliance: Its role in termination of parental rights cases. *Nebraska Law Review, 80*(2), Article 5. https://digitalcommons.unl.edu/nlr/vol80/iss2/5

Brank, E. M., & Wylie, L. E. (2016). Differing perspectives on older adult caregiving. *Journal of Applied Gerontology, 35*(7), 698–720. https://doi.org/10.1177/0733464813517506

Brank, E. M., & Wylie, L. E. (2021). Legal responsibility among the young and the elderly. *Annual Review of Law and Social Science, 17*(1), 93–108. https://doi.org/10.1146/annurev-lawsocsci-021721-091626

Brank, E. M., Wylie, L. E., & Hamm, J. A. (2012). Potential for self-reporting of older adult maltreatment: An empirical examination. *Elder Law Journal, 19*, 351–384.

Braun, J. A., & Frolik, L. A. (2000). Legal aspects of chemical restraint use in nursing homes. *Marquette Elder's Advisor, 2*(2), 21–31.

Brickley, J. A., Lu, S. F., & Wedig, G. J. (2022). Are firms with 'deep pockets' more responsive to tort liability? Evidence from nursing homes. *Health Economics, 31*(8), 1590–1617. https://doi.org/10.1002/hec.4528

Brimacombe, C. A. E., Quinton, N., Nance, N., & Garrioch, L. (1997). Is age irrelevant? Perceptions of young and old adult eyewitnesses. *Law and Human Behavior, 21*(6), 619–634. https://doi.org/10.1023/A:1024808730667

Brinkley-Rubinstein, L. (2013). Incarceration as a catalyst for worsening health. *Health & Justice, 1*(1), 3. https://doi.org/10.1186/2194-7899-1-3

Brittain, B., & Raymond, N. (2023, September 21). *Suspended US appeals judge warns her treatment could erode confidence in judiciary*. Reuters. https://www.reuters.

com/legal/litigation/suspended-us-appeals-judge-warns-her-treatment-could-erode-confidence-judiciary-2023-09-21

Broderick, C., Azizian, A., & Warburton, K. (2020). Length of stay for inpatient incompetent to stand trial patients: Importance of clinical and demographic variables. *CNS Spectrums, 25*(5), 734–742. https://doi.org/10.1017/S1092852920001273

Brook, R. D., Levy, P., & Rajagopalan, S. (2020). Cardiometabolic risk factor control during times of crises and beyond. *Circulation: Cardiovascular Quality and Outcomes, 13*(7), 382–385. https://doi.org/10.1161/CIRCOUTCOMES.120.006815

Brooks, A. C. (2022). *From strength to strength: Finding success, happiness, and deep purpose in the second half of life* (1st ed.). Portfolio/Penguin.

Brown, R. T., Ahalt, C., Steinman, M. A., Kruger, K., & Williams, B. A. (2014). Police on the front line of community geriatric health care: Challenges and opportunities. *Journal of the American Geriatrics Society, 62*(11), 2191–2198. https://doi.org/10.1111/jgs.13093

Brown v. Pattison, 2:01-CV-0411 (N.D. Texas, March 4, 2004).

Brownie, S., & Nancarrow, S. (2013). Effects of person-centered care on residents and staff in aged-care facilities: A systematic review. *Clinical Interventions in Aging, 8*, 1–10. https://doi.org/10.2147/CIA.S38589

Bryan, C. S. (2018). Osler goes viral: "The Fixed Period" revisited. *Baylor University Medical Center Proceedings, 31*(4), 550–553. https://doi.org/10.1080/08998280.2018.1493322

Budd, K. M., & Liddic, M. A. (2021). Incidents of sexual assault against older adults: A comparison study. *Sexual Abuse, 33*(6), 654–677. https://doi.org/10.1177/1079063220940298

Bugental, D. B., & Hehman, J. A. (2007). Ageism: A review of research and policy implications. *Social Issues and Policy Review, 1*(1), 173–216. https://doi.org/10.1111/j.1751-2409.2007.00007.x

Bureau of Justice Assistance. (n.d.). *Police–Mental Health Collaboration Toolkit*. Office of Justice Programs, U.S. Department of Justice. https://bja.ojp.gov/program/pmhc

Bureau of Prisons. (2024). *PATTERN Risk Assessment*. https://www.bop.gov/inmates/fsa/pattern.jsp

Burgess, A. W., Commons, M. L., Safarik, M. E., Looper, R. R., & Ross, S. N. (2007). Sex offenders of the elderly: Classification by motive, typology, and predictors of severity of crime. *Aggression and Violent Behavior, 12*(5), 582–597. https://doi.org/10.1016/j.avb.2007.02.006

Burgess, A. W., & Phillips, S. L. (2006). Sexual abuse, trauma and dementia in the elderly: A retrospective study of 284 cases. *Victims & Offenders, 1*(2), 193–204. https://doi.org/10.1080/15564880600663935

Burke, G., Prunhuber, P., Phan, T., & Takshi, S. (2022). *Reducing barriers to reentry for older adults leaving incarceration* [Issue brief]. Justice in Aging. https://justiceinaging.org/wp-content/uploads/2022/05/Reducing-Barriers-to-Reentry-for-Older-Adults-Leaving-Incarceration.pdf.

Burnes, D., Henderson, C. R., Jr., Sheppard, C., Zhao, R., Pillemer, K., & Lachs, M. S. (2017). Prevalence of financial fraud and scams among older adults in the United States: A systematic review and meta-analysis. *American Journal of Public Health, 107*(8), e13–e21. https://doi.org/10.2105/AJPH.2017.303821

Burnes, D., Pillemer, K., Caccamise, P. L., Mason, A., Henderson, Jr., C. R., Berman, J., Cook, A. M., Shukoff, D., Brownell, P., Powell, M., Salamone, A., & Lachs, M. S. (2015). Prevalence of and risk factors for elder abuse and neglect in the community: A population-based study. *Journal of the American Geriatrics Society, 63*(9), 1906–1912. https://doi.org/10.1111/jgs.13601

Burnight, K., & Mosqueda, L. (2011). *Theoretical model development in elder mistreatment* [Technical report]. U.S. Department of Justice.

Burrow, J. D., & Koons-Witt, B. A. (2003). Elderly status, extraordinary physical impairments and intercircuit variation under the federal sentencing guidelines. *The Elder Law Journal, 11*(2), 273–328.

Bush, S. S., & Heck, A. L. (Eds.). (2018). *Forensic geropsychology: Practice essentials.* American Psychological Association. https://doi.org/10.1037/0000082-000

Butler, R. N. (2009). Combating ageism. *International Psychogeriatrics, 21*(2), 211. https://doi.org/10.1017/S104161020800731X

Butts, J. A. (2019, November 11). *Older adults responsible for total growth in drug arrests* [Data brief]. Jon Jay College of Criminal Justice Research and Evaluation Center. https://johnjayrec.nyc/2019/11/11/databits201902

California Department of Corrections and Rehabilitation. (2022, March). *Elderly parole fact sheet.* https://www.cdcr.ca.gov/bph/wp-content/uploads/sites/161/2022/03/Elderly-Parole-Fact-Sheet3_18-1.pdf

California Department of Corrections and Rehabilitation. (2024, March). *The California parole hearing process handbook.* https://www.cdcr.ca.gov/bph/wp-content/uploads/sites/161/2024/03/pv-CA-Parole-Hearing-Process-Handbook-For-Publication-03-08-24.pdf

Callahan, L., & Pinals, D. A. (2020). Challenges to reforming the competence to stand trial and competence restoration system. *Psychiatric Services, 71*(7), 691–697. https://doi.org/10.1176/appi.ps.201900483

Cal. Penal Code § 3041.5, subd. (b)(3) (2016).

Cal. Penal Code § 3055, subd. (a) (2024).

Canada, K. E., Barrenger, S. L., Robinson, E. L., Washington, K. T., & Mills, T. (2020). A systematic review of interventions for older adults living in jails and prisons. *Aging & Mental Health, 24*(7), 1019–1027. https://doi.org/10.1080/13607863.2019.1584879

Capitano, F. (1986). Age discrimination and police employment practices. *Hofstra Labor & Employment Law Journal, 4*(1), 153–180.

Caplan, Z. (2023). *U.S. older population grew from 2010 to 2020 at fastest rate since 1880 to 1890.* U.S. Census Bureau. https://www.census.gov/library/stories/2023/05/2020-census-united-states-older-population-grew.html

Carson, E. A. (2020). *Prisoners in 2020 – statistical tables* (NCJ No. 302776). U.S. Department of Justice, Office of Justice Programs, Bureau of Justice Statistics. https://bjs.ojp.gov/content/pub/pdf/p20st.pdf

Carson, E. A., & Sabol, W. J. (2016). *Aging of the state prison population, 1993–2013* (NCJ No. 248766). U.S. Department of Justice, Office of Justice Programs, Bureau of Justice Statistics. https://bjs.ojp.gov/content/pub/pdf/aspp9313.pdf

Carter, P. M., Losman, E., Roche, J. S., Malani, P. N., Kullgren, J. T., Solway, E., Kirch, M., Singer, D., Walton, M. A., Zeoli, A. M., & Cunningham, R. M. (2022). Firearm ownership, attitudes, and safe storage practices among a nationally representative sample of older U.S. adults age 50 to 80. *Preventive Medicine, 156,* 106955. https://doi.org/10.1016/j.ypmed.2022.106955

Castelli, L., Macrae, C. N., Zogmaister, C., & Arcuri, L. (2004). A tale of two primes: Contextual limits on stereotype activation. *Social Cognition, 22*(2), 233–247. https://doi.org/10.1521/soco.22.2.233.35462

Caverley, S. J. (2006). Older mentally ill inmates: A descriptive study. *Journal of Correctional Health Care, 12*(4), 262–268. https://doi.org/10.1177/1078345806295546

Ceci, S. J., & Bruck, M. (1995). *Jeopardy in the courtroom: A scientific analysis of children's testimony*. American Psychological Association. https://doi.org/10.1037/10180-000

Center on Budget and Policy Priorities. (2024, July 18). *Policy basics: Where do our federal tax dollars go?* https://www.cbpp.org/research/federal-budget/where-do-our-federal-tax-dollars-go

Center for Elders and the Courts. (n.d.). *The role of the courts*. https://www.eldersandcourts.org/aging/the-role-of-the-courts

Centers for Disease Control and Prevention. (n.d.). *CDC Wisqars™*. U.S. Department of Health & Human Services. https://www.cdc.gov/injury/wisqars/index.html

Champion, D. J. (1987). Elderly felons and sentencing severity: Interregional variations in leniency and sentencing trends. *Criminal Justice Review, 12*(2), 7–14. https://doi.org/10.1177/073401688701200203

Chan, J. C. K., Thomas, A. K., & Bulevich, J. B. (2009). Recalling a witnessed event increases eyewitness suggestibility: The reversed testing effect. *Journal of Psychological Science, 20*(1), 66–73. https://doi.org/10.1111/j.1467-9280.2008.02245.x

Chang, E.-S., Kannoth, S., Levy, S., Wang, S.-Y., Lee, J. E., & Levy, B. R. (2020). Global reach of ageism on older persons' health: A systematic review. *PLoS One, 15*(1), e0220857. https://doi.org/10.1371/journal.pone.0220857

Chapman, N. S., & Yoshino, K. (n.d.). *The Fourteenth Amendment Due Process Clause: Common interpretation*. National Constitution Center. https://constitutioncenter.org/the-constitution/amendments/amendment-xiv/clauses/701

Chasteen, A. L., Schwarz, N., & Park, D. C. (2002). The activation of aging stereotypes in younger and older adults. *The Journals of Gerontology: Series B, 57*(6), P540–P547. https://doi.org/10.1093/geronb/57.6.P540

Chen, J. I.-Z., & Hengjinda, P. (2021). Early prediction of coronary artery disease (CAD) by machine learning method—A comparative study. *Journal of Artificial Intelligence and Capsule Networks, 3*(1), 17–33. https://doi.org/10.36548/jaicn.2021.1.002

Chin, J., & Vasarhelyi, E. C. (2023). *Nyad* [Film]. Black Bear, Mad Chance, & Zurich Avenue.

Chonody, J. M., & Teater, B. (2016). Why do I dread looking old?: A test of social identity theory, terror management theory, and the double standard of aging. *Journal of Women & Aging, 28*(2), 112–126. https://doi.org/10.1080/08952841.2014.950533

Chopik, W. J., Bremner, R. H., Johnson, D. J., & Giasson, H. L. (2018). Age differences in age perceptions and developmental transitions. *Frontiers in Psychology, 9*. https://doi.org/10.3389/fpsyg.2018.00067

Chopin, J., & Beauregard, E. (2021). Sexual abuse of elderly victims investigated by the police: From motives to crime characteristics. *Journal of Interpersonal Violence, 36*(13–14), 6722–6744. https://doi.org/10.1177/0886260518821456

Chu, L. D., & Kraus, J. F. (2004). Predicting fatal assault among the elderly using the national incident-based reporting system crime data. *Homicide Studies, 8*(2), 71–95. https://doi.org/10.1177/1088767903262396

Chua, J., Cheung, G., Friedman, S. H., & Taylor, S. (2018). What are the characteristics of first time older sexual offenders? *International Psychogeriatrics, 30*(5), 647–662. https://doi.org/10.1017/S1041610217002186

Cipriani, G., Danti, S., Carlesi, C., & Di Fiorino, M. (2017). Old and dangerous: Prison and dementia. *Journal of Forensic and Legal Medicine, 51*, 40–44. https://doi.org/10.1016/j.jflm.2017.07.004

Cipriani, G., Lucetti, C., Danti, S., Carlesi, C., & Nuti, A. (2016). Violent and criminal manifestations in dementia patients. *Geriatrics & Gerontology International, 16*(5), 541–549. https://doi.org/10.1111/ggi.12608

Circuit Court of Cook County Illinois. (2014, September 2). *Elder abuse and neglect benchcard*. https://www.nawj.org/uploads/files/annual_conference/session_materials/aging/elder_abuse_and_neglect_benchcard.pdf

Civil Rights Act of 1964, 42 U.S.C. § 2000e-2.

Civil Rights Act of 1991, 42 U.S.C. § 2000e-2(m).

Civil Service Retirement Act, 5 U.S.C. § 8331 (1947). https://uscode.house.gov/view.xhtml?req=(title:5%20section:8331%20edition:prelim)#shorttitle-amendment-note

Clackamas Gastroenterology Associates, PC v. Wells, 538 U.S. 440 (2003).

Clark, C., & Mezey, G. (1997). Elderly sex offenders against children: A descriptive study of child sex abusers over the age of 65. *Journal of Forensic Psychiatry, 8*(2), 357–369. https://doi.org/10.1080/09585189708412017

Clarke, A., Williams, J., & Wydall, S. (2016). Access to justice for victims/survivors of elder abuse: A qualitative study. *Social Policy and Society, 15*(2), 207–220. https://doi.org/10.1017/S1474746415000202

Clarke, C. (2017). *Reentry experiences of elderly ex-offenders: Wasted lives* (No. 10275276) [Doctoral dissertation, State University of New York at Stony Brook]. ProQuest Dissertations and Theses Global.

Cloyes, K. G., Rosenkranz, S. J., Berry, P. H., Supiano, K. P., Routt, M., Shannon-Dorcy, K., & Llanque, S. M. (2016). Essential elements of an effective prison hospice program. *The American Journal of Hospice & Palliative Care, 33*(4), 390–402. https://doi.org/10.1177/1049909115574491

Cohen, G., & Faulkner, D. (1989). Age differences in source forgetting: Effects on reality monitoring and on eyewitness testimony. *Psychology and Aging, 4*(1), 10–17. https://doi.org/10.1037/0882-7974.4.1.10

Coleman v. Newsom, No. 2:90-cv-0520 KJM DB P (E.D. Cal. Sep. 2, 2020).

Collins, T. A., Dumas, T. L., & Moyer, L. P. (2017). Intersecting disadvantages: Race, gender, and age discrimination among attorneys*. *Social Science Quarterly, 98*(5), 1642–1658. https://doi.org/10.1111/ssqu.12376

Compassionate Release, 18 U.S.C. §§ 4205(g) (2023).

Congressional Research Service. (2019). *The First Step Act of 2018: An overview* (No. R45558). https://crsreports.congress.gov/product/pdf/R/R45558

Conlie Shaw, M. M. (1998). Nursing home resident abuse by staff: Exploring the dynamics. *Journal of Elder Abuse & Neglect, 9*(4), 1–21. https://doi.org/10.1300/J084v09n04_01

Conrad, K. J., Iris, M., Ridings, J. W., Rosen, A., Fairman, K. P., & Anetzberger, G. J. (2011). Conceptual model and map of psychological abuse of older adults. *Journal of Elder Abuse & Neglect, 23*(2), 147–168. https://doi.org/10.1080/08946566.2011.558784

Constitution Arms. (2024). *Palm Pistol.* https://constitutionarms.com/palm-pistol

Conwell, Y., Duberstein, P. R., Hirsch, J. K., Conner, K. R., Eberly, S., & Caine, E. D. (2010). Health status and suicide in the second half of life. *International Journal of Geriatric Psychiatry, 25*(4), 371–379. https://doi.org/10.1002/gps.2348

Correctional News. (2014, January 22). *Top 5 corrections stories of 2013.* https://correctionalnews.com/2014/01/22/top-5-corrections-stories-2013

Correll, J., Hudson, S. M., Guillermo, S., & Ma, D. S. (2014). The police officer's dilemma: A decade of research on racial bias in the decision to shoot. *Social and Personality Psychology Compass, 8*(5), 201–213. https://doi.org/10.1111/spc3.12099

Correll, J., Park, B., Judd, C. M., & Wittenbrink, B. (2002). The police officer's dilemma: Using ethnicity to disambiguate potentially threatening individuals. *Journal of Personality and Social Psychology, 83*(6), 1314–1329. https://doi.org/10.1037/0022-3514.83.6.1314

Corwin, P. S. (2000). Senioritis: Why elderly federal inmates are literally dying to get out of prison. *Journal of Contemporary Health Law & Policy, 17*(2), 687–714.

Covey, H. C. (1992). The definitions of the beginning of old age in history. *International Journal of Aging & Human Development, 34*(4), 325–337. https://doi.org/10.2190/GBXB-BE1F-1BU1-7FKK

Cowan, N. (2008). What are the differences between long-term, short-term, and working memory? *Progress in Brain Research, 169,* 323–338. https://doi.org/10.1016/S0079-6123(07)00020-9

Cox, A. (2020). The language of incarceration. *Incarceration: An International Journal of Imprisonment, Detention and Coercive Confinement, 1*(1). https://doi.org/10.1177/2632666320940859

Cox, J. F., & Lawrence, J. E. (2010). Planning services for elderly inmates with mental illness. *Corrections Today, 72,* 52–57.

Coxon, P., & Valentine, T. (1997). The effects of the age of eyewitnesses on the accuracy and suggestibility of their testimony. *Applied Cognitive Psychology, 11*(5), 415–430. https://doi.org/10.1002/(SICI)1099-0720(199710)11:5<415::AID-ACP469>3.0.CO;2-A

Crawley, E., & Sparks, R. (2005). Hidden injuries? Researching the experiences of older men in English prisons. *Howard Journal of Criminal Justice, 44*(4), 345–356. https://doi.org/10.1111/j.1468-2311.2005.00380.x

Crenshaw, K. (1989). Demarginalizing the intersection of race and sex: A Black feminist critique of antidiscrimination doctrine, feminist theory and antiracist politics. *University of Chicago Legal Forum, 1989*(1), 139–167.

Crenshaw, K. (2016, October). *Kimberlé Crenshaw: The urgency of intersectionality* [Video]. TED Conferences. https://www.ted.com/talks/kimberle_crenshaw_the_urgency_of_intersectionality

Criminal Code of 2022, 720 Ill. Comp. Stat. 5., Sec. 12-4.4a(e). https://www.ilga.gov/legislation/ilcs/fulltext.asp?DocName=072000050K12-4.4a

Crockett, C., Brandl, B., & Dabby, F. C. (2015). Survivors in the margins: The invisibility of violence against older women. *Journal of Elder Abuse & Neglect, 27*(4–5), 291–302. https://doi.org/10.1080/08946566.2015.1090361

Crookes, R. L., Tramontano, C., Brown, S. J., Walker, K., & Wright, H. (2022). Older individuals convicted of sexual offenses: A literature review. *Sexual Abuse, 34*(3), 341–371. https://doi.org/10.1177/10790632211024244

Crosby, F. J., & Dovidio, J. F. (2008). Discrimination in America and legal strategies for reducing it. In E. Botgida & S. T. Fiske (Eds.), *Beyond common sense: Psychological science in the courtroom* (pp. 22–43). Blackwell Publishing.

Cruzan v. Director, Missouri Dept. of Health, 497 U.S. 261 (1990).
Cuddy, A. J. C., & Fiske, S. T. (2002). Doddering but dear: Process, content, and function in stereotyping of older persons. In T. D. Nelson (Ed.), *Ageism: Stereotyping and prejudice against older persons* (pp. 3–26). Massachusetts Institute of Technology Press. https://doi.org/10.7551/mitpress/1157.003.0004
Cuddy, A. J. C., Norton, M. I., & Fiske, S. T. (2005). This old stereotype: The pervasiveness and persistence of the elderly stereotype. *Journal of Social Issues, 61*(2), 267–285. https://doi.org/10.1111/j.1540-4560.2005.00405.x
Cumming, M. E. (1964). New thoughts on the theory of disengagement. In R. Kastenbaum (Ed.), *New thoughts on old age* (pp. 3–18). Springer. https://doi.org/10.1007/978-3-662-38534-0_1
Cunius, M. K., & Miller, M. K. (2023). The effects of an apology's timing and type on parole board decision-making. *Criminal Justice Studies, 36*(1), 83–100. https://doi.org/10.1080/1478601X.2023.2182302
Curran, N. (2000). Blue hairs in the bighouse: The rise in the elderly inmate population, its effect on the overcrowding dilemma and solutions to correct it. *New England Journal on Criminal and Civil Confinement, 26*(2), 225–264.
Curry, J. M., & Haydon, M. R. (2018). Lawmaker age, issue salience, and senior representation in Congress. *American Politics Research, 46*(4), 567–595. https://doi.org/10.1177/1532673X18754557
Curtice, M., Parker, J., Schembri Wismayer, F., & Tomison, A. (2003). The elderly offender: An 11-year survey of referrals to a regional forensic psychiatric service. *Journal of Forensic Psychiatry & Psychology, 14*, 253–265. https://doi.org/10.1080/1478994031000077989
Curtin, K. (2020, January 24). *Chatsworth Police settle with woman officers used a stun gun on in 2018.* Channel 9 News. https://newschannel9.com/news/local/settlement-chatsworth-police-promise-more-training-after-syrian-immigrant-stun-gun-case
Cutshall, C. R., & Adams, K. (1983). Responding to older offenders: Age selectivity in the processing of shoplifters. *Criminal Justice Review, 8*(2), 1–8.
da Costa, J. P., Vitorino, R., Silva, G. M., Vogel, C., Duarte, A. C., & Rocha-Santos, T. (2016). A synopsis on aging—Theories, mechanisms and future prospects. *Ageing Research Reviews, 29*, 90–112. https://doi.org/10.1016/j.arr.2016.06.005
Daftary-Kapur, T., & Zottoli, T. (2020). *Resentencing of juvenile lifers: The Philadelphia experience.* Montclair State University. https://doi.org/10.21428/cb6ab371.2cd702e3
Dando, C. J., Gabbert, F., & Hope, L. (2020). Supporting older eyewitnesses' episodic memory: The self-administered interview and sketch reinstatement of context. *Memory, 28*(6), 712–723. https://doi.org/10.1080/09658211.2020.1757718
Danely, J. (2022). What older prisoners teach us about care and justice in an aging world. *Anthropology & Aging, 43*(1), 58–65. https://doi.org/10.5195/aa.2022.395
Dannefer, D. (2003). Cumulative advantage/disadvantage and the life course: Cross-fertilizing age and social science theory. *The Journals of Gerontology: Series B, 58*(6), S327–S337. https://doi.org/10.1093/geronb/58.6.S327
Darabont, F. (1994). *The Shawshank redemption* [Film]. Castle Rock Entertainment.
Darby, R. R., & Dickerson, B. C. (2017). Dementia, decision making, and capacity. *Harvard Review of Psychiatry, 25*(6), 270–278. https://doi.org/10.1097/HRP.0000000000000163
Dau-Schmidt, K., Lardent, E., Glazer, R., & Ressmeyer, K. (2009). "Old and making hay": The results of the Pro Bono Institute Firm Survey on the viability of a

"second acts" program to transition attorneys to retirement through pro bono work. *Cardozo Public Law, Policy, and Ethics Journal*, 7, 321–342. https://www.repository.law.indiana.edu/facpub/56

Davis, M. (2022, November 21). *Despite pandemic, percentage of older adults who want to age in place stays steady*. AARP. https://www.aarp.org/home-family/your-home/info-2021/home-and-community-preferences-survey.html

Dawes, J. (2002). Dying with dignity: Prisoners and terminal illness. *Illness, Crises, and Loss, 10*(3), 188–203. https://doi.org/10.1177/105413730201000302

Day, A., Davey, L., Wanganeen, R., Casey, S., Howells, K., & Nakata, M. (2008). Symptoms of trauma, perceptions of discrimination, and anger: A comparison between Australian indigenous and nonindigenous prisoners. *Journal of Interpersonal Violence, 23*(2), 245–258. https://doi.org/10.1177/0886260507309343

Death Penalty Information Center. (2025). *Growing elderly population on death row*. https://deathpenaltyinfo.org/growing-elderly-population-on-death-row

Deaton, D., Aday, R. H., & Wahidin, A. (2010). The effect of health and penal harm on aging female prisoners' views of dying in prison. *Omega: Journal of Death and Dying, 60*(1), 51–70. https://doi.org/10.2190/OM.60.1.c

DeLamater, J. (2012). Sexual expression in later life: A review and synthesis. *Journal of Sex Research, 49*(2–3), 125–141. https://doi.org/10.1080/00224499.2011.603168

Del. C. 11 § 404(a) (2024). https://law.justia.com/codes/delaware/title-11/chapter-4/section-404/

Delgado, J. M. (1982). Animal and human emotionality. *Behavioral and Brain Sciences, 5*(3), 425–427.

Demontiero, O., Vidal, C., & Duque, G. (2012). Aging and bone loss: New insights for the clinician. *Therapeutic Advances in Musculoskeletal Disease, 4*(2), 61–76. https://doi.org/10.1177/1759720X11430858

DePrince, A. P., Olomi, J. M., Lee, M. S., Hasche, L. K., Casparian, A. M., & Pettit, L. L. (2020). Exploring an emerging measurement issue in older adult maltreatment: Exploitation of older adults' residences. *Journal of Trauma & Dissociation, 21*(2), 158–171. https://doi.org/10.1080/15299732.2020.1692406

De Tavernier, W., Naegele, L., & Hess, M. (2019). A critical perspective on ageism and modernization theory. *Social Inclusion, 7*(3), 54–57. https://doi.org/10.17645/si.v7i3.2371

Determination of competency to stand trial, 18 U.S.C. § 4241 (1948).

Devine, D. J., & Caughlin, D. E. (2014). Do they matter? A meta-analytic investigation of individual characteristics and guilt judgments. *Psychology, Public Policy, and Law, 20*(2), 109–134. https://doi.org/10.1037/law0000006

Diehl, M., Smyer, M. A., & Mehrotra, C. M. (2020). Optimizing aging: A call for a new narrative. *American Psychologist, 75*(4), 577–589. https://doi.org/10.1037/amp0000598

Diekman, A. B., & Hirnisey, L. (2007). The effect of context on the silver ceiling: A role congruity perspective on prejudiced responses. *Personality and Social Psychology Bulletin, 33*(10), 1353–1366. https://doi.org/10.1177/0146167207303019

Di Lorito, C., Völlm, B., & Dening, T. (2018). Psychiatric disorders among older prisoners: A systematic review and comparison study against older people in the community. *Aging & Mental Health, 22*(1), 1–10. https://doi.org/10.1080/13607863.2017.1286453

DiNapoli, T. P. (2022). *New York State's aging prison population: Share of older adults keeps rising*. Office of the New York State Comptroller. https://www.osc.ny.gov/files/reports/pdf/aging-prison-population-2022.pdf

District of Columbia v. Heller, 554 U.S. 570 (2008).

Dix, D. (2021). *The lived experiences of elderly jury members in determining verdicts* [Doctoral dissertation, Walden University]. Scholar Works. https://scholarworks.waldenu.edu/dissertations/10032

Dodson, C. S., & Krueger, L. E. (2006). I misremember it well: Why older adults are unreliable eyewitnesses. *Psychonomic Bulletin & Review, 13*(5), 770–775. https://doi.org/10.3758/BF03193995

Dodson, C. S., Powers, E., & Lytell, M. (2015). Aging, confidence, and misinformation: Recalling information with the cognitive interview. *Psychology and Aging, 30*(1), 46–61. https://doi.org/10.1037/a0038492

Doerner, J. K., & Demuth, S. (2010). The independent and joint effects of race/ethnicity, gender, and age on sentencing outcomes in U.S. Federal Courts. *Justice Quarterly, 27*(1), 1–27. https://doi.org/10.1080/07418820902926197

Dominguez, L. J., & Barbagallo, M. (2016). Ageing and sexuality. *European Geriatric Medicine, 7*(6), 512–518. https://doi.org/10.1016/j.eurger.2016.05.013

Dong, X. Q. (2015). Elder abuse: Systematic review and implications for practice. *Journal of the American Geriatrics Society, 63*(6), 1214–1238. https://doi.org/10.1111/jgs.13454

Dong, X. Q. (2017). Elder self-neglect: Research and practice. *Clinical Interventions in Aging, 12,* 949–954. https://doi.org/10.2147/CIA.S103359

Dong, X. & Simon, M. A. (2011). Enhancing national policy and programs to address elder abuse. *Journal of the American Medical Association, 305,* 2460–2461. https://doi.org/10.1001/jama.2011.835

Doron, I. (2009a). A multi-dimensional model of elder law. In I. Doron (Ed.), *Theories on law and ageing: The jurisprudence of elder law* (pp. 59–74). Springer. https://doi.org/10.1007/978-3-540-78954-3_5

Doron, I. (2009b). Preface. In I. Doron (Ed.), *Theories on law and ageing: The jurisprudence of elder law* (pp. v–x). Springer. https://doi.org/10.1007/978-3-540-78954-3_5

Doron, I. (2018). Re-thinking old age: Time for ageivism. *Human Rights Defender, 27*(1), 33–35.

Doron, I. (2020). 25 years of elder law: An integrative and historical account of the field of law and aging. *Theoretical Inquiries in Law, 21*(1), 1–24. https://doi.org/10.1515/til-2020-0002

Doron, I., & Kohn, N. A. (2011). Aging and law: Using a multi-dimensional model to understand the legal response to aging. In S. Chen & J. L. Powell (Eds.), *Aging in perspective and the case of China: Issues and approaches* (pp. 71–86). Nova Science Publishers.

Douglas, K. S., & Skeem, J. L. (2005). Violence risk assessment: Getting specific about being dynamic. *Psychology, Public Policy, and Law, 11*(3), 347–383. https://doi.org/10.1037/1076-8971.11.3.347

Douglas, S. J. (2020, September 8). The forgotten history of the radical 'elders of the tribe.' *The New York Times*. https://www.nytimes.com/2020/09/08/opinion/sunday/gray-panthers-maggie-kuhn.html

Doyle, C., Yates, S., Bartels, L., Hopkins, A., & Taylor, H. (2022). 'Just a bunch of what ifs and unknowns': The post-prison service provision experiences of people in Canberra, Australia. *International Journal of Law, Crime and Justice, 70,* 100546.

Dubljević, V. (2020). The principle of autonomy and behavioural variant frontotemporal dementia. *Journal of Bioethical Inquiry, 17*(2), 271–282. https://doi.org/10.1007/s11673-020-09972-z

Dunlap, E. E., Golding, J. M., Hodell, E. C., & Marsil, D. F. (2007). Perceptions of elder physical abuse in the courtroom: The influence of hearsay witness testimony. *Journal of Elder Abuse & Neglect, 19*(3–4), 19–39. https://doi.org/10.1300/J084v19n03_02

Dusky v. United States, 362 U.S. 402 (1960).

du Toit, S. H. J., Withall, A., O'Loughlin, K., Ninaus, N., Lovarini, M., Snoyman, P., Butler, T., Forsyth, K., & Surr, C. A. (2019). Best care options for older prisoners with dementia: A scoping review. *International Psychogeriatrics, 31*(8), 1081–1097. https://doi.org/10.1017/S1041610219000681

Eagly, A. H., & Karau, S. J. (2002). Role congruity theory of prejudice toward female leaders. *Psychological Review, 109*(3), 573–598. https://doi.org/10.1037/0033-295X.109.3.573

Eastley, R. J., MacPherson, R., Richards, H., & Mian, I. H. (1993). Assaults on professional carers of elderly people. *British Medical Journal, 307*(6908), 845.

Edemekong, P. F., Bomgaars, D. L., Sukumaran, S., & Schoo, C. (2023). Activities of daily living. In *StatPearls*. https://www.ncbi.nlm.nih.gov/books/NBK470404

Eden, J., Maslow, K., Le, M., & Blazer, D. (Eds.). (2012). *The mental health and substance use workforce for older adults: In whose hands?* National Academies Press.

Edney v. Kerrigan, 00 Civ. 2240 (GBD) (JCF) (S.D.N.Y. 2004).

EEOC v. Sidley Austin Brown & Wood, 315 F.3d 696 (7th Cir. 2002).

EEOC v. Wyoming, 460 U.S. 226 (1983).

Eglit, H. (1986). The Age Discrimination in Employment Act's forgotten affirmative defense: The reasonable factors other than age exception. *Boston University Law Review, 66*(2), 155–228.

Eglit, H. C. (2004). *Elders on trial: Age and ageism in the American legal system*. University Press of Florida.

Eglit, H. (2005). Ageism and the American legal system. *Generations Journal, 29*(3), 59–65.

El-Bawab, N. (2023, September 21). *Why a 96-year-old judge was just banned from the bench for a year*. ABC News. https://abcnews.go.com/US/96-year-judge-banned-bench-year/story?id=103383531

Elder Justice Center. (2023). *About Elder Justice Center*. https://www.fljud13.org/CourtPrograms/ElderJusticeCenter/AboutElderJusticeCenter.aspx

Engelhart, K. (2023). Opinion: I've reported on dementia for years, and one image of a prisoner keeps haunting me. *The New York Times*. https://www.nytimes.com/2023/08/11/opinion/dementia-prisons.html

Erber, J. T. (1989). Young and older adults' appraisal of memory failures in young and older adult target persons. *Journal of Gerontology, 44*(6), P170–P175. https://doi.org/10.1093/geronj/44.6.P170

Erber, J. T., Etheart, M. E., & Szuchman, L. T. (1992). Age and forgetfulness: Perceivers' impressions of targets' capability. *Psychology and Aging, 7*(3), 479–483. https://doi.org/10.1037/0882-7974.7.3.479

Erber, J. T., Szuchman, L. T., & Etheart, M. E. (1993). Age and forgetfulness: Young perceivers' impressions of young and older neighbors. *International Journal of Aging & Human Development, 37*(2), 91–103. https://doi.org/10.2190/2966-K1WN-0J00-P6FA

Erickson, W. B., Lampinen, J. M., & Moore, K. N. (2016). Eyewitness identifications by older and younger adults: A meta-analysis and discussion. *Journal of Police and Criminal Psychology, 31*(2), 108–121. https://doi.org/10.1007/s11896-015-9176-3

Erikson, E., & Erikson, J. (1998). *The life cycle completed*. W.W. Norton & Company.

Eshima, S., & Smith, D. M. (2022). Just a number? Voter evaluations of age in candidate-choice experiments. *The Journal of Politics, 84*(3), 1856–1861. https://doi.org/10.1086/719005

Estelle v. Gamble, 429 U.S. 97 (1976).

Evans, H. (1998, August 13). Older and violent: Attacks by people over 60 on rise. *Newsday*, A5, 38.

Exemptions for police and firefighters under the Age Discrimination in Employment Act: Hearing before the Committee on Education and Labor, 99th Cong. (1986). https://www.ojp.gov/pdffiles1/Digitization/103277NCJRS.pdf

Fagan, A. A., & Western, J. (2005). Escalation and deceleration of offending behaviours from adolescence to early adulthood. *Australian and New Zealand Journal of Criminology, 38*(1), 59–76. https://doi.org/10.1375/acri.38.1.59

Fair Sentencing Act of 2010, Pub. L. No. 111-220, 124 Stat. 2372.

Faklis, L. (2018). Can they still decide at 75? Increasing the jury duty opt-out age from 70 to 75. *The Elder Law Journal, 26*(1), 189–226.

Falk, E., & Hoffman, N. (2014). The role of capacity assessments in elder abuse investigations and guardianships. *Clinics in Geriatric Medicine, 30*(4), 851–868. https://doi.org/10.1016/j.cger.2014.08.009

Falter, R. G. (1999). Selected predictors of health services needs of inmates over age 50. *Journal of Correctional Health Care, 6*(2), 149–175. https://doi.org/10.1177/107834589900600202

Family and Medical Leave Act of 1993, 29 U.S.C. §§ 2601–2654.

Fandos, N. (2018, December 19). Senate passes bipartisan criminal justice bill. *The New York Times*. https://www.nytimes.com/2018/12/18/us/politics/senate-criminal-justice-bill.html

Farnsworth, E. A. (2010). *An introduction to the legal system of the United States* (4th ed.). Oxford University Press.

Farrington, D. P. (1986). Age and crime. *Crime and Justice, 7*, 189–250. https://doi.org/10.1086/449114

Fass, T. L., Heilbrun, K., DeMatteo, D., & Fretz, R. (2008). The LSI-R and the Compas: Validation data on two risk-needs tools. *Criminal Justice and Behavior, 35*(9), 1095–1108. https://doi.org/10.1177/0093854808320497

Fattah, E. A., & Sacco, V. F. (1989). Offences the elderly commit and their explanations. In E. A. Fattah & V. F. Sacco (Eds.), *Crime and victimization of the elderly* (pp. 34–68). Springer. https://doi.org/10.1007/978-1-4613-8888-3_3

Fazel, S., & Grann, M. (2002). Older criminals: A descriptive study of psychiatrically examined offenders in Sweden. *International Journal of Geriatric Psychiatry, 17*(10), 907–913. https://doi.org/10.1002/gps.715

Fazel, S., Hope, T., O'Donnell, I., & Jacoby, R. (2002). Psychiatric, demographic and personality characteristics of elderly sex offenders. *Psychological Medicine, 32*(2), 219–226. https://doi.org/10.1017/S0033291701005153

Fazel, S., Sjöstedt, G., Långström, N., & Grann, M. (2006). Risk factors for criminal recidivism in older sexual offenders. *Sexual Abuse, 18*(2), 159–167. https://doi.org/10.1177/107906320601800204

Federal Rules of Evidence, 28 U.S.C. App (1975).

Federal Rules of Evidence, Pub. L. 93-595, 88 Stat. (1975). https://www.congress.gov/bill/93rd-congress/house-bill/5463/text

Federico, M. (2009). *Welcome to the departure lounge: Adventures in mothering mother*. Random House.

Feldmeyer, B., & Steffensmeier, D. (2007). Elder crime: Patterns and current trends, 1980–2004. *Research on Aging, 29*(4), 297–322. https://doi.org/10.1177/0164027507300802

Fenequito, A. C., Robles, C. F., Santos, A. F., & Valencia, K. B. C. (2023). Effects of caregiver burden to the psychosocial adjustment and quality of life of caregivers of older people with debilitating diseases. *Globus, 12*(1), 41–53.

Ferguson, M., & Ogloff, J. R. P. (2011). Criminal responsibility evaluations: Role of psychologists in assessment. *Psychiatry, Psychology, and Law, 18*(1), 79–94. https://doi.org/10.1080/13218719.2010.482952

Fernández-Ballesteros, R., Sánchez-Izquierdo, M., Olmos, R., Huici, C., Ribera Casado, J. M., & Cruz Jentoft, A. (2019). Paternalism vs. autonomy: Are they alternative types of formal care? *Frontiers in Psychology, 10,* 1460. https://doi.org/10.3389/fpsyg.2019.01460

Fetterman, M. (2023, November 10). *The future of aging in place . . . is moving?* AARP. https://www.aarp.org/home-family/your-home/info-2023/future-of-aging-in-place.html

Fettig, N., Mitchell, H., Gassoumis, Z., Nizam, Z., Whittier Eliason, S., & Cory, S. (2024). Adult maltreatment risk factors: Adding community-level factors to an individual-level field. *Trauma, Violence & Abuse, 25*(1), 5–21. https://doi.org/10.1177/15248380221137659

First Responder Fair RETIRE Act of 2021, Pub. L. No. 117-225.

First Step Act of 2018, Pub. L. No. 115-391, 132 Stat. 5194.

Fisk, J. E., & Sharp, C. A. (2003). The role of the executive system in visuo-spatial memory functioning. *Brain and Cognition, 52*(3), 364–381. https://doi.org/10.1016/S0278-2626(03)00183-0

Fiske, S. T. (1993). Controlling other people. The impact of power on stereotyping. *American Psychologist, 48*(6), 621–628. https://doi.org/10.1037/0003-066X.48.6.621

Fiske, S. T. (2018). Stereotype content: Warmth and competence endure. *Current Directions in Psychological Science, 27*(2), 67–73. https://doi.org/10.1177/0963721417738825

Fiske, S. T., Cuddy, A. J. C., & Glick, P. (2007). Universal dimensions of social cognition: Warmth and competence. *Trends in Cognitive Sciences, 11*(2), 77–83. https://doi.org/10.1016/j.tics.2006.11.005

Fiske, S. T., Cuddy, A. J. C., Glick, P., & Xu, J. (2002). A model of (often mixed) stereotype content: Competence and warmth respectively follow from perceived status and competition. *Journal of Personality and Social Psychology, 82*(6), 878–902. https://doi.org/10.1037/0022-3514.82.6.878

Flanagan, T. J. (1995). *Long-term imprisonment: Policy, science, and corrrectional practice.* Sage Publications. https://doi.org/10.4135/9781483327228

Fleming, K. C., Evans, J. M., & Chutka, D. S. (2003). A cultural and economic history of old age in America. *Mayo Clinic Proceedings, 78*(7), 914–921. https://doi.org/10.4065/78.7.914

Fogel, M. H., Schiffman, W., Mumley, D., Tillbrook, C., & Grisso, T. (2013). Ten year research update (2001–2010): Evaluations for competence to stand trial (adjudicative competence). *Behavioral Sciences & the Law, 31*(2), 165–191. https://doi.org/10.1002/bsl.2051

Ford, A. B., Haug, M. R., Stange, K. C., Gaines, A. D., Noelker, L. S., & Jones, P. K. (2000). Sustained personal autonomy: A measure of successful aging. *Journal of Aging and Health, 12*(4), 470–489. https://doi.org/10.1177/089826430001200402

Ford v. Wainwright, 477 U.S. 399 (1986).

Forde, A. T., Crookes, D. M., Suglia, S. F., & Demmer, R. T. (2019). The weathering hypothesis as an explanation for racial disparities in health: A systematic review. *Annals of Epidemiology, 33,* 1–18.e3. https://doi.org/10.1016/j.annepidem.2019.02.011

Fozard, J. L., & Gordon-Salant, S. (2001). Changes in vision and hearing with aging. In J. E. Birren & K. W. Schaie (Eds.), *Handbook of the psychology of aging* (5th ed., pp. 241–266). Academic Press.

France, L. R. (2023, May 19). *Jimmy Buffett hospitalized, postpones show.* CNN. https://www.boston25news.com/news/local/growing-old-is-not-sissies-jimmy-buffett-hospitalized-boston/CLAEG5FRENAMRBL2VEDL2APSI4

Friedman, L. S., Avila, S., Tanouye, K., & Joseph, K. (2011). A case-control study of severe physical abuse of older adults. *Journal of the American Geriatrics Society, 59*(3), 417–422. https://doi.org/10.1111/j.1532-5415.2010.03313.x

Frierson, R. L., Shea, S. J., & Shea, M. E. (2002). Competence-to-stand-trial evaluations of geriatric defendants. *Journal of the American Academy of Psychiatry and the Law Online, 30*(2), 252–256.

Frierson, R. L., & Srinivasan, S. (2018). Evaluation of elderly persons in the criminal justice system. In J. C. Holzer, R. Kohn, J. M. Ellison, & P. R. Recupero (Eds.), *Geriatric forensic psychiatry: Principles and practice* (pp. 163–169). Oxford University Press.

Frolik, L. A. (2009). Later life legal planning. In I. Doron (Ed.), *Theories on law and ageing: The jurisprudence of elder law* (pp. 11–30). Springer. https://doi.org/10.1007/978-3-540-78954-3_2

Frolik, L. A., & Barnes, A. M. (2015). *Elder law: Cases and materials* (6th ed.). LexisNexis.

Frumkin, L. A., & Stone, A. (2020). Not all eyewitnesses are equal: Accent status, race and age interact to influence evaluations of testimony. *Journal of Ethnicity in Criminal Justice, 18*(2), 123–145. https://doi.org/10.1080/15377938.2020.1727806

GA Code § 42-9-43 (2013).

Gallione, C., Dal Molin, A., Cristina, F. V. B., Ferns, H., Mattioli, M., & Suardi, B. (2017). Screening tools for identification of elder abuse: A systematic review. *Journal of Clinical Nursing, 26*(15-16), 2154–2176. https://doi.org/10.1111/jocn.13721

Gallup. (2020, November 13). *What percentage of Americans own guns?* https://news.gallup.com/poll/264932/percentage-americans-own-guns.aspx

Galluzzi, K., & Warner-Maron, I. (2018). Guns and older adults: The physician's role. *Journal of Osteopathic Medicine, 118*(12), 775–780. https://doi.org/10.7556/jaoa.2018.169

Gao, Y., & Raine, A. (2010). Successful and unsuccessful psychopaths: A neurobiological model. *Behavioral Sciences & the Law, 28*(2), 194–210. https://doi.org/10.1002/bsl.924

Garavito, D. M. N. (2019). The prisoner's dementia: Ethical and legal issues regarding dementia and healthcare in prison. *Cornell Journal of Law and Public Policy, 29,* 211–235.

Garcia, J. (2022, May 12). "Amelia Baca was executed": Baca family, attorneys demand murder charge in police killing. *Las Cruces Sun-News.* https://www.lcsun-news.com/story/news/crime/2022/05/13/amelia-baca-family-attorneys-demand-murder-charge-police-killing/9752745002

García-Bajos, E., Migueles, M., & Aizpurua, A. (2012). Bias of script-driven processing on eyewitness memory in young and older adults. *Applied Cognitive Psychology, 26*(5), 737–745. https://doi.org/10.1002/acp.2854

Gavisk, M., & Greene, E. (2007). Guardianship determinations by judges, attorneys, and guardians. *Behavioral Sciences & the Law, 25*(3), 339–353. https://doi.org/10.1002/bsl.772

Gawande, A. (2015). *Being mortal: Medicine and what matters in the end* (13th ed.). Picador.

Gawrylowicz, J., Memon, A., Scoboria, A., Hope, L., & Gabbert, F. (2014). Enhancing older adults' eyewitness memory for present and future events with the Self-Administered Interview. *Psychology and Aging, 29*(4), 885–890. https://doi.org/10.1037/a0038048

Geiselman, R. E., Fisher, R. P., Cohen, G., Holland, H., & Surtes, L. (1986). Eyewitness responses to leading and misleading questions under the cognitive interview. *Journal of Police Science and Administration, 14*, 31–39.

General Assembly of the Commonwealth of Pennsylvania. (2005). *Report of the Advisory Committee on Geriatric and Seriously Ill Inmates*. Joint State Government Commission. https://jsg.legis.state.pa.us/resources/documents/ftp/publications/2005-40-INMATES%20REPORT.pdf

Genova, L. (2009). *Still Alice*. Gallery Books.

George Washington University. (1991). *Project for older prisoners* (NCJ No. 132249).

Geronimus, A. T. (1992). The weathering hypothesis and the health of African-American women and infants: Evidence and speculations. *Ethnicity & Disease, 2*(3), 207–221.

GF v. Department of Human Services, No. CAAP-14-0000890 (Haw. Intermediate Ct. App., June 20, 2017).

Ghantous, Z., Ahmad, V., & Khoury, R. (2022). Illicit drug use in older adults: An invisible epidemic? *Clinics in Geriatric Medicine, 38*(1), 39–53. https://doi.org/10.1016/j.cger.2021.07.002

Ghossoub, E., & Khoury, R. (2021). Characteristics of older adult first-time sex offenders: Insights from the Missouri registry. *The American Journal of Geriatric Psychiatry, 29*(3), 230–238. https://doi.org/10.1016/j.jagp.2020.06.020

Gibson, S. C., & Greene, E. (2013). Assessing knowledge of elder financial abuse: A first step in enhancing prosecutions. *Journal of Elder Abuse & Neglect, 25*(2), 162–182. https://doi.org/10.1080/08946566.2013.751820

Gijsberts, M.-J. H. E., Echteld, M. A., van der Steen, J. T., Muller, M. T., Otten, R. H. J., Ribbe, M. W., & Deliens, L. (2011). Spirituality at the end of life: Conceptualization of measurable aspects-a systematic review. *Journal of Palliative Medicine, 14*(7), 852–863. https://doi.org/10.1089/jpm.2010.0356

Giles, H., & Reid, S. A. (2005). Ageism across the lifespan: Towards a self-categorization model of ageing. *Journal of Social Issues, 61*(2), 389–404. https://doi.org/10.1111/j.1540-4560.2005.00412.x

Gilmore-Bykovskyi, A., Croff, R., Glover, C. M., Jackson, J. D., Resendez, J., Perez, A., Zuelsdorff, M., Green-Harris, G., & Manly, J. J. (2022). Traversing the aging research and health equity divide: Toward intersectional frameworks of research justice and participation. *The Gerontologist, 62*(5), 711–720. https://doi.org/10.1093/geront/gnab107

Glancy, G. D., Ash, P., Bath, E. P., Buchanan, A., Fedoroff, P., Frierson, R. L., Harris, V. L., Hatters Friedman, S. J., Hauser, M. J., Knoll, J., Norko, M., Pinals, D., Price, M., Recupero, P., Scott, C. L., & Zonana, H. V. (2015). AAPL Practice

Guideline for the Forensic Assessment. *Journal of the American Academy of Psychiatry and the Law, 43*(2 Suppl.), S3–S53. https://www.aapl.org/docs/pdf/Forensic_Assessment.pdf

Glick, P., & Fiske, S. T. (2001). An ambivalent alliance. Hostile and benevolent sexism as complementary justifications for gender inequality. *American Psychologist, 56*(2), 109–118. https://doi.org/10.1037/0003-066X.56.2.109

Glück, J., & Scherpf, A. (2022). Intelligence and wisdom: Age-related differences and nonlinear relationships. *Psychology and Aging, 37*(5), 649–666. https://doi.org/10.1037/pag0000692

Godefroy, O., Azouvi, P., Robert, P., Roussel, M., LeGall, D., Meulemans, T., & Groupe de Réflexion sur l'Evaluation des Fonctions Exécutives Study Group. (2010). Dysexecutive syndrome: Diagnostic criteria and validation study. *Annals of Neurology, 68*(6), 855–864. https://doi.org/10.1002/ana.22117

Godfrey, D. (2023, March 10). *New ABA policy on dementia and the criminal justice system.* American Bar Association. https://www.americanbar.org/groups/law_aging/publications/bifocal/vol44/vol44issue4/newabapolicyondementia

Godinez v. Moran, 509 U.S. 389 (1993).

Godsey, M. (2017). *Blind injustice: A former prosecutor exposes the psychology and politics of wrongful convictions* (1st ed.). University of California Press. https://doi.org/10.1525/9780520962958

Goel, R. (2023). Grandma got arrested: Police, excessive force, and people with dementia. *University of Richmond Law Review, 57*(2), 335–379. https://scholarship.richmond.edu/lawreview/vol57/iss2/3/

Golding, J. M., Allen, J., Yozwiak, J. A., Marsil, D. F., & Kinstle, T. S. (2004). Perceptions of elder neglect in the courtroom. *Journal of Elder Abuse & Neglect, 16*(1), 23–46. https://doi.org/10.1300/J084v16n01_02

Golding, J. M., Yozwiak, J. A., Kinstle, T. L., & Marsil, D. F. (2005). The effect of gender in the perception of elder physical abuse in court. *Law and Human Behavior, 29*(5), 605–614. https://doi.org/10.1007/s10979-005-6831-8

Gowensmith, W. N. (2019). Resolution or resignation: The role of forensic mental health professionals amidst the competency services crisis. *Psychology, Public Policy, and Law, 25*(1), 1–14. https://doi.org/10.1037/law0000190

Grady, C. L., McIntosh, A. R., & Craik, F. I. (2005). Task-related activity in prefrontal cortex and its relation to recognition memory performance in young and old adults. *Neuropsychologia, 43*(10), 1466–1481. https://doi.org/10.1016/j.neuropsychologia.2004.12.016

Graebner, W. (1984). Help wanted: Age discrimination in Buffalo, New York, 1895–1935. *New York History, 65*, 349–365.

Grafman, J., Schwab, K., Warden, D., Pridgen, A., Brown, H. R., & Salazar, A. M. (1996). Frontal lobe injuries, violence, and aggression: A report of the Vietnam Head Injury Study. *Neurology, 46*(5), 1231–1238. https://doi.org/10.1212/WNL.46.5.1231

Gramlich, J. (2023, October 4). *Most Americans favor maximum age limits for federal elected officials, Supreme Court justices.* Pew Research Center. https://www.pewresearch.org/short-reads/2023/10/04/most-americans-favor-maximum-age-limits-for-federal-elected-officials-supreme-court-justices

Grattan, H. S. (2013). The elder law and miscellaneous remedies division: A unique opportunity to serve as a model court for the nation. *The Elder Law Journal, 20*(2), 521–564.

Green, B. L., Dass-Brailsford, P., Hurtado de Mendoza, A., Mete, M., Lynch, S. M., DeHart, D. D., & Belknap, J. (2016). Trauma experiences and mental health among incarcerated women. *Psychological Trauma: Theory, Research, Practice, and Policy, 8*(4), 455–463. https://doi.org/10.1037/tra0000113

Green, B. S. (2014). As the pendulum swings: The reformation of compassionate release to accommodate changing perceptions of corrections. *University of Toledo Law Review, 46*(1), 123–163.

Greenberg, J., Schimel, J., & Martens, A. (2002). Ageism: Denying the face of the future. In T. D. Nelson (Ed.), *Ageism: Stereotyping and prejudice against older persons* (pp. 27–48). The MIT Press.

Greene, E., Bornstein, B. H., & Dietrich, H. (2007). Granny, (don't) get your gun: Competency issues in gun ownership by older adults. *Behavioral Sciences & the Law, 25*(3), 405–423. https://doi.org/10.1002/bsl.766

Greene, E. L. (2008). Deciding to let others decide—Judging the need for guardianship and conservatorship. *Probate & Property, 22*(1), 47–50.

Greene, M., Ahalt, C., Stijacic-Cenzer, I., Metzger, L., & Williams, B. (2018). Older adults in jail: High rates and early onset of geriatric conditions. *Health & Justice, 6*(1), Article 3. https://doi.org/10.1186/s40352-018-0062-9

Greene, N. R., & Naveh-Benjamin, M. (2022). Adult age differences in specific and gist associative episodic memory across short- and long-term retention intervals. *Psychology and Aging, 37*(6), 681–697. https://doi.org/10.1037/pag0000701

Greenwood, M. (2023). *Nikki Haley calls for 'mental competency tests' for politicians over 75*. The Hill. https://thehill.com/homenews/campaign/3859468-haley-calls-for-mental-competency-tests-for-politicians-over-75

Gregory v. Ashcroft, 501 U.S. 452 (1991).

Greve, W. (1998). Fear of crime among the elderly: Foresight, not fright. *International Review of Victimology, 5*(3–4), 277–309. https://doi.org/10.1177/026975809800500405

Grisso, T. (2002). *Evaluating competencies: Forensic assessments and instruments* (2nd ed.). Springer.

Grisso, T., & Appelbaum, P. S. (1998). *Assessing competence to consent to treatment: A guide for physicians and other health professionals*. Oxford University Press. https://doi.org/10.1093/oso/9780195103724.001.0001

Gross v. FBL Financial Services, Inc., 557 U.S. 167 (2009).

Gudjonsson, G. H., & Grisso, T. (2008). Legal competencies in relation to confession evidence. In A. Felthous & H. Sa (Eds.), *The international handbook of psychopathic disorders and the law* (Vol. II, pp. 177–187). John Wiley & Sons. https://doi.org/10.1002/9780470772973.ch12

Gun Control Act of 1968, Pub. L. No. 90-618, 82 Stat.

Gunther, J. (2023, June 27). *The scope of elder financial exploitation: What it costs victims*. AARP Public Policy Institute. https://doi.org/10.26419/ppi.00194.001

Hagos, A. K., Butler, T. G., Howie, A., & Withall, A. L. (2022). Optimizing the care and management of older offenders: A scoping review. *The Gerontologist, 62*(9), e508–e519. https://doi.org/10.1093/geront/gnab104

Hagos, A. K., Withall, A., Ginnivan, N. A., Snoyman, P., & Butler, T. (2022). Barriers and enablers to health and social services for older prisoners transitioning to community. *International Journal of Prisoner Health, 18*(2), 124–137. https://doi.org/10.1108/IJPH-08-2021-0088

Hall, M. I. (2009). Equity theory: Responding to the material exploitation of the vulnerable but capable. In I. Doron (Ed.), *Theories on law and ageing: The jurisprudence of elder law* (pp. 107–119). Springer. https://doi.org/10.1007/978-3-540-78954-3_8

Hall, M. I. (2014). "Old age" (or, do we need a critical theory of law and aging?). *Windsor Review of Legal and Social Issues, 35*, 1–21.

Hamby, S., Smith, A., Mitchell, K., & Turner, H. (2016). Poly-victimization and resilience portfolios: Trends in violence research that can enhance the understanding and prevention of elder abuse. *Journal of Elder Abuse & Neglect*, 28(4–5), 217–234. https://doi.org/10.1080/08946566.2016.1232182

Hampton, S., Blomgren, D., Roberts, J., Mackinnon, T., & Nicholls, G. (2015). Prescribing for people in custody. *Australian Prescriber, 38*(5), 160–163. https://doi.org/10.18773/austprescr.2015.057

Han, B., Gfroerer, J. C., Colliver, J. D., & Penne, M. A. (2009). Substance use disorder among older adults in the United States in 2020. *Addiction, 104*(1), 88–96. https://doi.org/10.1111/j.1360-0443.2008.02411.x

Han, S. D., & Mosqueda, L. (2020). Elder abuse in the COVID-19 era. *Journal of the American Geriatrics Society, 68*(7), 1386–1387. https://doi.org/10.1111/jgs.16496

Hanson, R. K. (1997). *The development of a brief actuarial risk scale for sexual offense recidivism (Cat. No. JS4-1/1997-4E)*. Solicitor General of Canada. https://publications.gc.ca/pub?id=9.614094&sl=0

Hanson, R. K. (2002). Recidivism and age: Follow-up data from 4,673 sexual offenders. *Journal of Interpersonal Violence, 17*(10), 1046–1062. https://doi.org/10.1177/088626002236659

Hanson, R. K., & Bussiere, M. T. (1998). Predicting relapse: A meta-analysis of sexual offender recidivism studies. *Journal of Consulting and Clinical Psychology, 66*(2), 348–362. https://doi.org/10.1037/0022-006X.66.2.348

Hareven, T. K. (1976). The last stage: Historical adulthood and old age. *Daedalus, 105*(4), 13–27.

Harris, A. J. R., & Hanson, R. K. (2004). *Sex offender recidivism: A simple question*. Public Safety and Emergency Preparedness Canada.

Harrison, M. T. (2006). True grit: An innovative program for elderly inmates. *Corrections Today, 68*(7), 46–49.

Hart, M. (2008). The geriatric sex offender: Senile or pedophile. *Law & Psychology Review, 32*, 153–162.

Hartley, R. D. (2014). Focal concerns theory. In J. M. Miller (Ed.), *The encyclopedia of theoretical criminology* (pp. 1–5). John Wiley & Sons. https://doi.org/10.1002/9781118517390.wbetc148

Hastings, D. (2023, November 21). *Elderly man charged in wife's shooting death may have been "overwhelmed by being caregiver": Police*. Inside Edition. https://www.insideedition.com/elderly-alabama-man-charged-in-wifes-shooting-death-may-have-been-overwhelmed-by-being-caregiver

Haugebrook, S., Zgoba, K. M., Maschi, T., Morgen, K., & Brown, D. (2010). Trauma, stress, health, and mental health issues among ethnically diverse older adult prisoners. *Journal of Correctional Health Care, 16*(3), 220–229. https://doi.org/10.1177/1078345810367482

Havard, C., Laybourn, P., & Klecha, B. (2017). The mystery man can increase the reliability of eyewitness identifications for older adult witnesses. *Journal of Police and Criminal Psychology, 32*(3), 214–224. https://doi.org/10.1007/s11896-016-9214-9

Hawryluk, M. (2024, February 19). *Death and redemption in an American prison.* NPR news. https://www.npr.org/sections/health-shots/2024/02/19/1231119824/prison-hospice-angola-louisiana-quilting

Hayes, A. J. (2017). Aging inside: Older adults in prison. In B. S. Elger, C. Ritter, & H. Stöver (Eds.), *Emerging issues in prison health* (pp. 1–12). Springer. https://doi.org/10.1007/978-94-017-7558-8_1

Heck, A. L., & Vauter, R. (2018). The insanity defense with older adults. In S. S. Bush & A. L. Heck (Eds.), *Forensic geropsychology: Practice essentials* (pp. 167–187). American Psychological Association. https://doi.org/10.1037/0000082-009

Heilbrun, K., Rogers, R., & Otto, R. K. (2002). Forensic assessment: Current status and future directions. In J. R. P. Ogloff (Ed.), *Taking psychology and law into the twenty-first century* (Vol. 14, pp. 119–146). Springer.

Heinik, J., Kimhi, R., & Hes, J. P. (1994). Dementia and crime: A forensic psychiatry unit study in Israel. *International Journal of Geriatric Psychiatry, 9*(6), 491–494. https://doi.org/10.1002/gps.930090608

Heisler, C. (2015, July). *Working with elder abuse clients: How an FJC can help* [Webinar]. Retrieved from https://attendee.gotowebinar.com/recording/9029781392749009154

Heisler, C. J. (2017). Elder abuse forensics: The intersection of law and science. In X. Dong (Ed.), *Elder abuse forensics: The intersection of law and science* (pp. 387–416). Springer, Cham. https://doi.org/10.1007/978-3-319-47504-2_18

Hendricks, J. (1982). The elderly in society: Beyond modernization. *Social Science History, 6*(3), 321–345.

Henkel, L. A. (2014). Do older adults change their eyewitness reports when re-questioned? *The Journals of Gerontology: Series B, 69*(3), 356–365. https://doi.org/10.1093/geronb/gbt071

Hernandez, G. (1998, July 10). Wife, lover convicted of killing husband. *Los Angeles Times.* https://www.latimes.com/archives/la-xpm-1998-jul-10-me-2463-story.html

Hertzog, C., Lineweaver, T. T., & McGuire, C. L. (1999). Beliefs about memory and aging. In T. M. Hess & F. Blanchard-Fields (Eds.), *Social cognition and aging* (pp. 43–68). Academic Press. https://doi.org/10.1016/B978-012345260-3/50004-5

Hess, U., Adams, R. B., Jr., & Kleck, R. E. (2004). Facial appearance, gender, and emotion expression. *Emotion, 4*(4), 378–388. https://doi.org/10.1037/1528-3542.4.4.378

Higgins, P. L., Heath, W. P., & Grannemann, B. D. (2007). How type of excuse defense, mock juror age, and defendant age affect mock jurors' decisions. *The Journal of Social Psychology, 147*(4), 371–392. https://doi.org/10.3200/SOCP.147.4.371-392

Hindley, N., & Gordon, H. (2000). The elderly, dementia, aggression and risk assessment. *International Journal of Geriatric Psychiatry, 15*(3), 254–259. https://doi.org/10.1002/(SICI)1099-1166(200003)15:3<254::AID-GPS103>3.0.CO;2-T

Hinrichsen, G. A., & Emery-Tiburcio, E. E. (2022). Introduction to special issue: Foundational knowledge competencies in geropsychology.*Clinical Psychology: Science and Practice, 29*(1), 1–3. https://doi.org/10.1037/cps0000066

Hirschi, T., & Gottfredson, M. (1983). Age and the explanation of crime. *American Journal of Sociology, 89*(3), 552–584. https://doi.org/10.1086/227905

Hirschi, T., & Gottfredson, M. (1993). Commentary: Testing the general theory of crime. *Journal of Research in Crime and Delinquency, 30*(1), 47–54. https://doi.org/10.1177/0022427893030001004

Hochschild, A. R. (1975). Disengagement theory: A critique and proposal. *American Sociological Review, 40*(5), 553–569. https://doi.org/10.2307/2094195

Hoffman, H. C., & Dickinson, G. E. (2011). Characteristics of prison hospice programs in the United States. *The American Journal of Hospice & Palliative Care, 28*(4), 245–252. https://doi.org/10.1177/1049909110381884

Hoffman, K. M., Trawalter, S., Axt, J. R., & Oliver, M. N. (2016). Racial bias in pain assessment and treatment recommendations, and false beliefs about biological differences between blacks and whites. *Proceedings of the National Academy of Sciences of the United States of America, 113*(16), 4296–4301. https://doi.org/10.1073/pnas.1516047113

Holland, M. M., Prost, S. G., Hoffmann, H. C., & Dickinson, G. E. (2020). U.S. Department of Corrections compassionate release policies: A content analysis and call to action. *Omega: Journal of Death and Dying, 81*(4), 607–626. https://doi.org/10.1177/0030222818791708

Holland, S. (2023, November 21). *Biden turns 81 as worries about his age weigh on re-election prospects.* Reuters. https://www.reuters.com/world/us/biden-turns-81-worries-about-his-age-weigh-re-election-prospects-2023-11-20

Holliday, R. E. (2003). Reducing misinformation effects in children with cognitive interviews: Dissociating recollection and familiarity. *Child Development, 74*(3), 728–751. https://doi.org/10.1111/1467-8624.00565

Holliday, R. E., Humphries, J. E., Milne, R., Memon, A., Houlder, L., Lyons, A., & Bull, R. (2012). Reducing misinformation effects in older adults with cognitive interview mnemonics. *Psychology and Aging, 27*(4), 1191–1203. https://doi.org/10.1037/a0022031

Holman, D., & Walker, A. (2021). Understanding unequal ageing: Towards a synthesis of intersectionality and life course analyses. *European Journal of Ageing, 18*(2), 239–255. https://doi.org/10.1007/s10433-020-00582-7

Holzer, K. J., AbiNader, M. A., Vaughn, M. G., Salas-Wright, C. P., & Oh, S. (2022). Crime and violence in older adults: Findings from the 2002 to 2017 National Survey on Drug Use and Health. *Journal of Interpersonal Violence, 37*(1–2), 764–781. https://doi.org/10.1177/0886260520913652

Hoyt, J. (n.d.). *The Baby Boomer generation.* SeniorLiving.Org. https://www.seniorliving.org/life/baby-boomers

Hughes, R. B., Lund, E. M., Gabrielli, J., Powers, L. E., & Curry, M. A. (2011). Prevalence of interpersonal violence against community-living adults with disabilities: A literature review. *Rehabilitation Psychology, 56*(4), 302–319. https://doi.org/10.1037/a0025620

Hullinger, Z. (2020). Are judges policymakers? A constitutional rebuff to judicial reform. *University of Cincinnati Law Review, 89*(1), 157–175.

Human Rights Watch. (2012). *Old behind bars: The aging prison population in the United States.* https://www.hrw.org/report/2012/01/28/old-behind-bars/aging-prison-population-united-states

Hummert, M. L. (1993). Age and typicality judgments of stereotypes of the elderly: Perceptions of elderly vs. young adults. *International Journal of Aging & Human Development, 37*(3), 217–226. https://doi.org/10.2190/L01P-V960-8P17-PL56

Hummert, M. L. (2011). Age stereotypes and aging. In K. W. Schaie & S. L. Willis (Eds.), *Handbook of the psychology of aging* (7th ed., pp. 249–262). Academic Press. https://doi.org/10.1016/B978-0-12-380882-0.00016-4

Iida, R., & Itsukushima, Y. (2021). Content vs. age: Perceived credibility of older and young adult eyewitnesses with confidence inflation. *Psychology, Crime & Law, 27*(5), 476–493. https://doi.org/10.1080/1068316X.2020.1818239

Imposition of a sentence of Imprisonment, 18 U.S.C. §§ 3582(c)(1)(A) (2025).

Innocence Project. (2020). *Minnesota adopts landmark eyewitness ID law.* https://innocenceproject.org/minnesota-adopts-landmark-eyewitness-id-law

Iowa Board of Parole. (2024). *General FAQs.* https://bop.iowa.gov/general-faqs

Jackson, S. L. (2016). All elder abuse perpetrators are not alike: The heterogeneity of elder abuse perpetrators and implications for intervention. *International Journal of Offender Therapy and Comparative Criminology, 60*(3), 265–285. https://doi.org/10.1177/0306624X14554063

Jackson, S. L. (2018). *Understanding elder abuse: A clinician's guide.* American Psychological Association. https://doi.org/10.1037/0000056-000

Jackson, S. L., & Hafemeister, T. L. (2012). Pure financial exploitation vs hybrid financial exploitation co-occurring with physical abuse and/or neglect of elderly persons. *Psychology of Violence, 2*(3), 285–296. https://doi.org/10.1037/a0027273

James, D., & Glaze, L. (2006). *Mental health problems of prison and jail inmates* (NCJ No. 213600). U.S. Department of Justice, Office of Justice Programs, Bureau of Justice Statistics. https://bjs.ojp.gov/content/pub/pdf/mhppji.pdf

Jameson, J. M., Riesen, T., Polychronis, S., Trader, B., Mizner, S., Martinis, J., & Hoyle, D. (2015). Guardianship and the potential of supported decision making with individuals with disabilities. *Research and Practice for Persons with Severe Disabilities, 40*(1), 36–51. https://doi.org/10.1177/1540796915586189

J.E.B. v. Alabama, 511 U.S. 127 (1994).

Jefferson-Bullock, J. (2018). Quelling the silver tsunami: Compassionate release of elderly offenders. *The Ohio State Law Journal, 79,* 937–988. https://www.semanticscholar.org/paper/Quelling-the-Silver-Tsunami%3A-Compassionate-Release-Jefferson-Bullock/e7656f71e7d1a1b7d2a3ac9b504ec2f72f3c60b3

Joe Coleman Medical Release Act, Ill. Gen. Assembly Public Act 102-0494 (2022).

Johnson, M. K., Hashtroudi, S., & Lindsay, D. S. (1993). Source monitoring. *Psychological Bulletin, 114*(1), 3–28. https://doi.org/10.1037/0033-2909.114.1.3

Joseph, J. (1961). *Warning.* Scottish Poetry Library. https://www.scottishpoetrylibrary.org.uk/poem/warning

Jylhävä, J., Pedersen, N. L., & Hägg, S. (2017). Biological age predictors. *EBioMedicine, 21,* 29–36. https://doi.org/10.1016/j.ebiom.2017.03.046

Kalmbacher, C. (2023). *Court pauses Ron Jeremy prosecution over mental competency.* Law & Crime. https://lawandcrime.com/crime/ron-jeremy-sexual-assault-trial-halted-indefinitely-as-judge-says-state-and-defense-experts-agree-ex-porn-star-suffers-from-an-incurable-neurocognitive-decline

Kanbergs, A., Ahalt, C., Cenzer, I. S., Morrison, R. S., & Williams, B. A. (2019). "No one wants to die alone": Incarcerated patients' knowledge and attitudes about early medical release. *Journal of Pain and Symptom Management, 57*(4), 809–815. https://doi.org/10.1016/j.jpainsymman.2018.12.335

Kapler, R. A. (Ed.). (1996). Predictions of coming juvenile crime wave challenged. *NCJA Justice Bulletin, 16*(6), 4–7. https://www.ojp.gov/ncjrs/virtual-library/abstracts/predictions-coming-juvenile-crime-wave-challenged

Kapp, M. B. (2009). A therapeutic approach. In I. Doron (Ed.), *Theories on law and ageing: The jurisprudence of elder law* (pp. 31–44). Springer. https://doi.org/10.1007/978-3-540-78954-3_3

Kapp, M. B. (2020). Dementia-related behaviors: A matter of public health, not criminal prosecution. *The Journal of Law, Medicine & Ethics, 48*(2), 328–330. https://doi.org/10.1177/1073110520935346

Kappes, C., Greve, W., & Hellmers, S. (2013). Fear of crime in old age: Precautious behaviour and its relation to situational fear. *European Journal of Ageing, 10*(2), 111–125. https://doi.org/10.1007/s10433-012-0255-3

Karberg, J. C., & James, D. J. (2005, July). *Substance dependence, abuse, and treatment of jail inmates, 2002* (NCJ No. 209588). U.S. Department of Justice, Office of Justice Programs, Bureau of Justice Statistics.

Karch, A., & Cravens, M. (2014). Rapid diffusion and policy reform: The adoption and modification of three strikes laws. *State Politics & Policy Quarterly, 14*(4), 461–491.

Karni, A. (2023, September 8). Here are the 20 oldest members of Congress. *The New York Times*. https://www.nytimes.com/2023/09/08/us/politics/oldest-members-of-congress.html

Karpel, M. E., Hoyer, W. J., & Toglia, M. P. (2001). Accuracy and qualities of real and suggested memories: Nonspecific age differences. *The Journals of Gerontology: Series B, 56*(2), P103–P110. https://doi.org/10.1093/geronb/56.2.P103

Kaushik, S., & Currin-McCulloch, J. (2023). Dying for a change: A systematic review of compassionate release policies. *International Journal of Prisoner Health, 19*(1), 47–62. https://doi.org/10.1108/IJPH-11-2021-0110

Kelly, M. E., Duff, H., Kelly, S., McHugh Power, J. E., Brennan, S., Lawlor, B. A., & Loughrey, D. G. (2017). The impact of social activities, social networks, social support and social relationships on the cognitive functioning of healthy older adults: A systematic review. *Systematic Reviews, 6*(1), 259. https://doi.org/10.1186/s13643-017-0632-2

Kerbs, J. J., & Jolley, J. M. (2007). Inmate-on-inmate victimization among older male prisoners. *Crime & Delinquency, 53*(2), 187–218.

Kingman, D. (2017, February 5). Ancient Sparta—a perfect gerontocracy? *Intergenerational Foundation*. https://www.if.org.uk/2017/02/05/ancient-sparta-a-perfect-gerontocracy

Kinstle, T. L., Hodell, E. C., & Golding, J. M. (2008). The impact of juror characteristics and victim health status on the perception of elder physical abuse. *Journal of Interpersonal Violence, 23*(9), 1143–1161. https://doi.org/10.1177/0886260508314294

Kite, M. E., & Johnson, B. T. (1988). Attitudes toward older and younger adults: A meta-analysis. *Psychology and Aging, 3*(3), 233–244. https://doi.org/10.1037/0882-7974.3.3.233

Kite, M. E., & Wagner, L. S. (2002). Attitudes toward older adults. In T. D. Nelkson (Ed.), *Ageism: Stereotyping and prejudice against older persons* (pp. 129–161). The MIT Press. https://doi.org/10.7551/mitpress/1157.003.0009

Knepper, P., & Ystehede, P. J. (Eds.). (2012). *The Cesare Lombroso handbook*. Routledge. https://doi.org/10.4324/9780203083369

Knight, P. (2016, November 11). Letter: Quote from Humphrey, not Gandhi. *The Columbian*. https://www.columbian.com/news/2016/nov/11/letter-quote-from-humphrey-not-gandhi

Kohan, J. (2013–2019). *Orange is the new black* [TV series]. Tilted Productions; Lionsgate Television.

Kohn, N., Brown, M., & Doron, I. (2019). Building bridges between gerontology and elder law. *Gerontology, 65*(1), 98–102. https://doi.org/10.1159/000489883

Kohn, N. A. (2020a). *Elder law: Practice, policy, and problems* (2nd ed.). Wolters Kluwer.

Kohn, N. A. (2020b). A framework for theoretical inquiry into law and aging. *Theoretical Inquiries in Law, 21*(1), 187–205. https://doi.org/10.1515/til-2020-0009

Kohn, N. A. (2020c). How the guardianship system can help address gun violence. *The Journal of Law, Medicine & Ethics, 48*(4 Suppl.), 133–136. https://doi.org/10.1177/1073110520979413

Kohn, N. A., & Spurgeon, E. D. (2014). A call to action on elder law education: An assessment and recommendations based on a national survey. *The Elder Law Journal, 21*(2), 345–374.

Kois, L. E., Potts, H., Cox, J., & Zapf, P. (2024). Court-reported competence to proceed data across the United States. *Law and Human Behavior, 48*(3), 182–202. https://doi.org/10.1037/lhb0000565

Kong, J. (2018). Effect of caring for an abusive parent on mental health: The mediating role of self-esteem. *The Gerontologist, 58*(3), 456–466. https://doi.org/10.1093/geront/gnx053

Kong, J., Kunze, A., Goldberg, J., & Schroepfer, T. (2021). Caregiving for parents who harmed you: A conceptual review. *Clinical Gerontologist, 44*(5), 507–519. https://doi.org/10.1080/07317115.2021.1920531

Kramer, J., & Steffensmeier, D. (1993). Race and imprisonment decisions. *The Sociological Quarterly, 34*(2), 357–376. https://doi.org/10.1111/j.1533-8525.1993.tb00395.x

Kratcoski, P. C. (1990). Circumstances surrounding homicides by older offenders. *Criminal Justice and Behavior, 17*(4), 420–430. https://doi.org/10.1177/0093854890017004003

Kratcoski, P. C., & Edelbacher, M. (2016). Trends in criminality and victimization of the elderly. *Federal Probation, 80*(1), 58–63.

Krent, H. J., & Rucker, R. (2022). The First Step Act—Constitutionalizing prison release policies. *Rutgers University Law Review, 74*(2), 631–676.

Krieger, N. (2014). Discrimination and health inequities. *International Journal of Health Services, 44*(4), 643–710. https://doi.org/10.2190/HS.44.4.b

Kuerbis, A., Sacco, P., Blazer, D. G., & Moore, A. A. (2014). Substance abuse among older adults. *Clinics in Geriatric Medicine, 30*(3), 629–654. https://doi.org/10.1016/j.cger.2014.04.008

Kuhlmann, R., & Ruddell, R. (2005). Elderly jail inmates: Problems, prevalence and public health. *Californian Journal of Health Promotion, 3*(2), 49–60. https://doi.org/10.32398/cjhp.v3i2.1763

Kuin, N. C., Scherder, E. J., Gijsbers, H., & Masthoff, E. D. (2019). Traumatic brain injury in prisoners: Relation to risky decision-making, aggression and criminal behavior. *Journal of Behavioral and Brain Science, 9*(7), 289–299. https://doi.org/10.4236/jbbs.2019.97021

Kwong See, S. T., Hoffman, H. G., & Wood, T. L. (2001). Perceptions of an old female eyewitness: Is the older eyewitness believable? *Psychology and Aging, 16*(2), 346–350. https://doi.org/10.1037/0882-7974.16.2.346

Lachs, M., Bachman, R., Williams, C., Kossack, A., Bove, C., & O'Leary, J. (2004). Older adults as crime victims, perpetrators, witnesses, and complainants: A population-based study of police interactions. *Journal of Elder Abuse & Neglect, 16*(4), 25–40. https://doi.org/10.1300/J084v16n04_02

Lachs, M., Bachman, R., Williams, C. S., & O'Leary, J. R. (2007). Resident-to-resident elder mistreatment and police contact in nursing homes: Findings from a population-based cohort. *Journal of the American Geriatrics Society, 55*(6), 840–845. https://doi.org/10.1111/j.1532-5415.2007.01195.x

Lachs, M. S., & Pillemer, K. A. (2015). Elder abuse. *The New England Journal of Medicine, 373*(20), 1947–1956. https://doi.org/10.1056/NEJMra1404688

Lackey v. Texas, 52 F.3d 98 (5th Cir. 1995).

Lamet, A., Szuchman, L., Perkel, L., & Walsh, S. (2008). Risk factors, resilience, and psychological distress among holocaust and nonholocaust survivors in the post-9/11 environment. *Educational Gerontology, 35*(1), 32–46. https://doi.org/10.1080/03601270802349403

Lamont, R. A., Swift, H. J., & Abrams, D. (2015). A review and meta-analysis of age-based stereotype threat: Negative stereotypes, not facts, do the damage. *Psychology and Aging, 30*(1), 180–193. https://doi.org/10.1037/a0038586

Lane, C., Bratina, M. P., & Antonio, M. E. (2020). Inmates' self-reported physical and mental health problems: A comparison by sex and age. *Journal of Correctional Health Care, 26*(4), 338–348. https://doi.org/10.1177/1078345820953421

La Rooy, D., Brubacher, S. P., Aromäki-Stratos, A., Cyr, M., Hershkowitz, I., Korkman, J., Myklebust, T., Naka, M., Peixoto, C. E., Roberts, K. P., Stewart, H., & Lamb, M. E. (2015). The NICHD protocol: A review of an internationally-used evidence-based tool for training child forensic interviewers. *Journal of Criminological Research, Policy and Practice, 1*(2), 76–89. https://doi.org/10.1108/JCRPP-01-2015-0001

LaVeist, T. A. (2000). On the study of race, racism, and health: A shift from description to explanation. *International Journal of Health Services: Planning, Administration, Evaluation, 30*(1), 217–219. https://doi.org/10.2190/LKDF-UJQ5-W1KU-GLR1

LaVeist, T., Pollack, K., Thorpe Jr, R., Fesahazion, R., & Gaskin, D. (2011). Place, not race: Disparities dissipate in southwest Baltimore when Blacks and Whites live under similar conditions. *Health Affairs, 30*(10), 1880–1887. https://doi.org/10.1377/hlthaff.2011.0640

Lee, C., & Coughlin, J. F. (2015). Perspective: Older adults' adoption of technology: An integrated approach to identifying determinants and barriers. *Journal of Product Innovation Management, 32*(5), 747–759. https://doi.org/10.1111/jpim.12176

Legal Information Institute. (2020). *M'naghten rule*. Cornell Law School. https://www.law.cornell.edu/wex/m%27naghten_rule

Legal Information Institute. (2023). *Federal sentencing guidelines.* Cornell Law School. https://www.law.cornell.edu/wex/federal_sentencing_guidelines

Legal Information Institute. (2024). *Strict scrutiny*. Cornell Law School. https://www.law.cornell.edu/wex/strict-scrutiny

Le Grand, A. M., Jenkins, B. D., Golding, J. M., & Pals, A. M. (2021). Elder neglect in civil versus criminal court: Legal decision-making in cases of overmedication. *Psychology, Crime & Law, 27*(10), 956–972. https://doi.org/10.1080/1068316X.2020.1867133

Leigey, M. E. (2010). For the longest time: The adjustment of inmates to a sentence of life without parole. *The Prison Journal, 90*(3), 247–268. https://doi.org/10.1177/0032885510373490

Lemieux, C. M., Dyeson, T. B., & Castiglione, B. (2002). Revisiting the literature on prisoners who are older: Are we wiser? *The Prison Journal, 82*(4), 440–458. https://doi.org/10.1177/0032885502238680

Levin, S. (2022, December 19). An elderly woman in prison is losing her memory. Why won't California release her? *The Guardian.* https://www.theguardian.com/us-news/2022/dec/19/california-elderly-prison-losing-memory-release

Levy, B. (2009). Stereotype embodiment: A psychosocial approach to aging. *Current Directions in Psychological Science, 18*(6), 332–336. https://doi.org/10.1111/j.1467-8721.2009.01662.x

Levy, B. R., Hausdorff, J. M., Hencke, R., & Wei, J. Y. (2000). Reducing cardiovascular stress with positive self-stereotypes of aging. *The Journals of Gerontology: Series B, 55*(4), P205–P213. https://doi.org/10.1093/geronb/55.4.P205

Levy, M. (2023, December 27). *As pandemic unfolded, deaths of older adults in Pennsylvania rose steeply in abuse or neglect cases.* AP News. https://apnews.com/article/older-adult-deaths-abuse-neglect-pennsylvania-covid-c9e76aa9852dc1071eb5190e5961d391

Levy, S. R., Lytle, A., & Macdonald, J. (2022). The worldwide ageism crisis. *Journal of Social Issues, 78*(4), 743–768. https://doi.org/10.1111/josi.12568

Levy, S. R., & Macdonald, J. L. (2016). Progress on understanding ageism. *Journal of Social Issues, 72*(1), 5–25. https://doi.org/10.1111/josi.12153

Lewis, C. F., Fields, C., & Rainey, E. (2006). A study of geriatric forensic evaluees: Who are the violent elderly? *Journal of the American Academy of Psychiatry and the Law, 34*(3), 324–332.

Lichtenberg, P. A. (Ed.). (2010). *Handbook of assessment in clinical gerontology.* Academic Press.

Lichtenberg, P. A., Mast, B. T., Carpenter, B. D., & Loebach Wetherell, J. (Eds.). (2015). *APA handbook of clinical geropsychology, Vol. 2. Assessment, treatment, and issues of later life.* American Psychological Association. https://doi.org/10.1037/14459-000

Liederbach, J., & Stelle, C. (2010). Policing a graying population: A study of police contacts with older adults. *Journal of Crime and Justice, 33*(1), 37–68. https://doi.org/10.1080/0735648X.2010.9721279

Liljegren, M., Landqvist Waldö, M., & Englund, E. (2018). Physical aggression among patients with dementia, neuropathologically confirmed post-mortem. *International Journal of Geriatric Psychiatry, 33*(2), e242–e248. https://doi.org/10.1002/gps.4777

Lim, M. Y. L., & Loo, J. H. Y. (2018). Screening an elderly hearing impaired population for mild cognitive impairment using Mini-Mental State Examination (MMSE) and Montreal Cognitive Assessment (MoCA). *International Journal of Geriatric Psychiatry, 33*(7), 972–979. https://doi.org/10.1002/gps.4880

Lin, J. T., & Mathew, P. (2005). Cancer pain management in prisons: A survey of primary care practitioners and inmates. *Journal of Pain and Symptom Management, 29*(5), 466–473. https://doi.org/10.1016/j.jpainsymman.2004.08.015

Lindt, N., van Berkel, J., & Mulder, B. C. (2020). Determinants of overburdening among informal carers: A systematic review. *BMC Geriatrics, 20,* Article 304. https://doi.org/10.1186/s12877-020-01708-3

Litwok, D., Cutler, C., & Luallen, J. (2020). Causes of aging in the federal prison population and a comparison to states. *Criminal Justice Review, 45*(1), 129–142. https://doi.org/10.1177/0734016819876337

Löckenhoff, C. E., De Fruyt, F., Terracciano, A., McCrae, R. R., De Bolle, M., Costa, P. T., Jr., Aguilar-Vafaie, M. E., Ahn, C. K., Ahn, H. N., Alcalay, L., Allik, J., Avdeyeva, T. V., Barbaranelli, C., Benet-Martínez, V., Blatný, M., Bratko, D., Cain, T. R., Crawford, J. T., Lima, M. P., . . . Yik, M. (2009). Perceptions of aging across 26 cultures and their culture-level associates. *Psychology and Aging, 24*(4), 941–954. https://doi.org/10.1037/a0016901

Loeb, S. J., & AbuDagga, A. (2006). Health-related research on older inmates: An integrative review. *Research in Nursing & Health, 29*(6), 556–565. https://doi.org/10.1002/nur.20177

Loeb, S. J., & Steffensmeier, D. (2011). Older inmates' pursuit of good health: A focus group study. *Research in Gerontological Nursing, 4*(3), 185–194. https://doi.org/10.3928/19404921-20100730-01

Loftus, E. F. (1975). Reconstructing memory: The incredible eyewitness. *Jurimetrics Journal, 15*(3), 188–193.

Loftus, E. F., Loftus, G. R., & Messo, J. (1987). Some facts about "weapon focus." *Law and Human Behavior, 11*(1), 55–62. https://doi.org/10.1007/BF01044839

Loftus, E. F., Miller, D. G., & Burns, H. J. (1978). Semantic integration of verbal information into a visual memory. *Journal of Experimental Psychology: Human Learning and Memory, 4*(1), 19–31. https://doi.org/10.1037/0278-7393.4.1.19

Lombroso, C. (2006). *Criminal man* (Gibson & Rafter, Trans.). Duke University Press Books. (Original work published 1876)

Louisiana-Mississippi Hospice and Palliative Care Organization. (n.d.). *Prison Support Project*. https://www.lmhpco.org/prison-support-project

Love, H. (2015). Aging witnesses: Exploring difference, inspiring change. *The International Journal of Evidence & Proof, 19*(4), 210–227. https://doi.org/10.1177/1365712715591462

Love, H. (2019). Seniors on the stand: Accommodating older witnesses in adversarial trials. *The Canadian Bar Review, 97*(2), 240–274.

Lowe, T. A., de Haas, B., Osborne, T., & Meijering, L. (2022). Older adults' adaptations to life events: A mobility perspective. *Ageing and Society*, 1–19. https://doi.org/10.1017/S0144686X22001283

Lu, P., & Shelley, M. (2021). Comparing older adult and child protection policy in the United States of America. *Ageing and Society, 41*(2), 273–293. https://doi.org/10.1017/S0144686X19000990

Lussier, P., & Healey, J. (2009). Rediscovering quetelet, again: The "aging" offender and the prediction of reoffending in a sample of adult sex offenders. *Justice Quarterly, 26*(4), 827–856. https://doi.org/10.1080/07418820802593360

Lutz, E. (2022, April 14). Report: California Senator Dianne Feinstein's memory is "rapidly deteriorating." *Vanity Fair*. https://www.vanityfair.com/news/2022/04/report-dianne-feinstein-memory-rapidly-deteriorating

Mackenzie, C. S., Scott, T., Mather, A., & Sareen, J. (2008). Older adults' help-seeking attitudes and treatment beliefs concerning mental health problems. *The American Journal of Geriatric Psychiatry, 16*(12), 1010–1019. https://doi.org/10.1097/JGP.0b013e31818cd3be

Madison v. Alabama, 586 U.S. 265 (2019).

Mai, C., & Subramanian, R. (2017). *The price of prisons: Examining state spending trends, 2010–2015*. Vera Institute of Justice. https://www.vera.org/price-of-prisons-2015

Males, M. A., & Macallair, D. (1999). Analysis of curfew enforcement and juvenile crime in California. *Western Criminology Review, 1*(2), 1–20.

Mann, N. (2012). *Doing harder time? The experiences of an ageing male prison population in England and Wales*. Routledge. https://doi.org/10.4324/9781315577906

Manson v. Brathwaite, 432 U.S. 98 (1977).

Marcolina, K., & Pond, M. (Directors). (2013). *The life and crimes of Doris Payne* [Film]. Treehouse Moving Images.

Marek, K. D., Popejoy, L., Petroski, G., Mehr, D., Rantz, M., & Lin, W.-C. (2005). Clinical outcomes of aging in place. *Nursing Research, 54*(3), 202–211. https://doi.org/10.1097/00006199-200505000-00008

Margoni, F., Geipel, J., Hadjichristidis, C., & Surian, L. (2018). Moral judgment in old age: Evidence for an intent-to-outcome shift. *Psychology, 65*(2), 105–114. https://doi.org/10.1027/1618-3169/a000395

Mark, V. H., & Ervin, F. R. (1970). *Violence and the brain*. Harper & Row.

Markson, J. (2023, January 17). This feels all too convenient. Either this is an act and he has fooled the court, or he was masking [Comment on the webpage *Ron Jeremy Escapes Rape Trial Due To "Incurable Neurocognitive Decline," Judge Says; Ex-Porn Star Faced Over 300 Years Behind Bars If Found Guilty*]. Deadline. https://deadline.com/2023/01/porn-ron-jeremy-dementia-rape-trial-la-da-1235225388/comment-page-2/#comments

Marquart, J. W., Merianos, D. E., & Doucet, G. (2000). The health-related concerns of older prisoners: Implications for policy. *Ageing & Society, 20*(1), 79–96. https://doi.org/10.1017/S0144686X99007618

Marson, D. C. (2001). Loss of competency in Alzheimer's disease: Conceptual and psychometric approaches. *International Journal of Law and Psychiatry, 24*(2–3), 267–283. https://doi.org/10.1016/S0160-2527(01)00064-4

Maschi, T., Gibson, S., Zgoba, K. M., & Morgen, K. (2011). Trauma and life event stressors among young and older adult prisoners. *Journal of Correctional Health Care, 17*(2), 160–172. https://doi.org/10.1177/1078345810396682

Maschi, T., Kwak, J., Ko, E., & Morrissey, M. B. (2012). Forget me not: Dementia in prison. *The Gerontologist, 52*(4), 441–451. https://doi.org/10.1093/geront/gnr131

Maschi, T., Leibowitz, G., Rees, J., & Pappacena, L. (2016). Analysis of US compassionate and geriatric release laws: Applying a human rights framework to global prison health. *Journal of Human Rights and Social Work, 1*, 165–174. https://doi.org/10.1007/s41134-016-0021-0

Maschi, T., & Morgen, K. (2020). *Aging behind prison walls: Studies in trauma and resilience*. Columbia University Press.

Maschi, T., Morgen, K., Zgoba, K., Courtney, D., & Ristow, J. (2011). Age, cumulative trauma and stressful life events, and post-traumatic stress symptoms among older adults in prison: Do subjective impressions matter? *The Gerontologist, 51*(5), 675–686. https://doi.org/10.1093/geront/gnr074

Maschi, T., Sutfin, S. L., & O'Connell, B. (2012). Aging, mental health, and the criminal justice system: A content analysis of the literature. *Journal of Forensic Social Work, 2*, 162–185. https://doi.org/10.1080/1936928X.2012.750254

Maschi, T., Viola, D., Morgen, K., & Koskinen, L. (2015). Trauma, stress, grief, loss, and separation among older adults in prison: The protective role of coping resources on physical and mental well-being. *Journal of Crime and Justice, 38*(1), 113–136. https://doi.org/10.1080/0735648X.2013.808853

Mast, B. T., Fiske, A., & Lichtenberg, P. A. (2022). Assessment: A foundational geropsychology knowledge competency. *Clinical Psychology: Science and Practice, 29*(1), 43–58. https://doi.org/10.1037/cps0000055

Mast, B. T., & Gerstenecker, A. (2010). Screening instruments and brief batteries for dementia. In P. A. Lichtenberg (Ed.), *Handbook of assessment in clinical gerontology* (2nd ed., pp. 503–530). Elsevier Academic Press. https://doi.org/10.1016/B978-0-12-374961-1.10019-3

Matter of Nunziata v. Nancy K., 72 Misc. 3d 529 (N.Y. Sup. Ct., Nassau County 2021).

Mazerolle, M., Smith, A. M., Torrance, M., & Thomas, A. K. (2021). Understanding older adults' memory distortion in the light of stereotype threat. *Frontiers in Psychology, 12,* 628696. https://doi. org/10.3389/fpsyg.2021.628696

McHugh, D., & Gil, J. (2018). Senescence and aging: Causes, consequences, and therapeutic avenues. *The Journal of Cell Biology, 217*(1), 65–77. https://doi.org/10.1083/jcb.201708092

McKinnon, I., Hayes, A., & Grubin, D. (2017). Health characteristics of older police custody detainees in London, UK. *Journal of Forensic Psychiatry & Psychology, 28*(3), 331–340. https://doi.org/10.1080/14789949.2017.1280071

McMann v. Richardson, 397 U.S. 759 (1970).

McNeal, M. H., & Brown, M. (2019). Elder restorative justice. *Cardozo Journal of Conflict Resolution, 21*(1), 91–143.

Meissner, C. A., & Brigham, J. C. (2001). Thirty years of investigating the own-race bias in memory for faces: A meta-analytic review. *Psychology, Public Policy, and Law, 7*(1), 3–35. https://doi.org/10.1037/1076-8971.7.1.3

Meissner, C. A., Sporer, S. L., & Schooler, J. W. (2007). Person descriptions as eyewitness evidence. In R. C. Lindsay, D. Ross, J. D. Read, & M. Toglia, *Handbook of eyewitness psychology: Vol. 2. Memory for people* (pp. 3–34). Lawrence Erlbaum & Associates. https://www.researchgate.net/publication/241837945

Meldrum, R. C., Trucco, E. M., Cope, L. M., Zucker, R. A., & Heitzeg, M. M. (2018). Brain activity, low self-control, and delinquency: An fMRI study of at-risk adolescents. *Journal of Criminal Justice, 56,* 107–117.

Mello, E. W., & Fisher, R. P. (1996). Enhancing older adult eyewitness memory with the cognitive interview. *Applied Cognitive Psychology, 10*(5), 403–417. https://doi.org/10.1002/(SICI)1099-0720(199610)10:5<403::AID-ACP395>3.0.CO;2-X

Melton, G. B., Petrila, J., Poythress, N. G., Slobogin, C., Otto, R. K., Mossman, D., & Condie, L. O. (2017). *Psychological evaluations for the courts: A handbook for mental health professionals and lawyers.* Guilford Press.

Memon, A., Gabbert, F., & Hope, L. (2004). The ageing eyewitness. In J. Adler (Ed.), *Forensic psychology: Concepts, debates and practice* (pp. 96–112). Willan. https://doi.org/10.4324/9781843924494

Memon, A., Hope, L., & Bull, R. (2003). Exposure duration: Effects on eyewitness accuracy and confidence. *British Journal of Psychology, 94*(3), 339–354. https://doi.org/10.1348/000712603767876262

Mendez, M. F. (2010). The unique predisposition to criminal violations in frontotemporal dementia. *The Journal of the American Academy of Psychiatry and the Law, 38*(3), 318–323.

Mendez, M. F., Shapira, J. S., & Saul, R. E. (2011). The spectrum of sociopathy in dementia. *The Journal of Neuropsychiatry and Clinical Neurosciences, 23*(2), 132–140. https://doi.org/10.1176/jnp.23.2.jnp132

Merkt, H., Haesen, S., Meyer, L., Kressig, R. W., Elger, B. S., & Wangmo, T. (2020). Defining an age cut-off for older offenders: A systematic review of literature. *International Journal of Prisoner Health, 16*(2), 95–116. https://doi.org/10.1108/IJPH-11-2019-0060

Merriam-Webster. (n.d.). Capacity. In *Merriam-Webster.com dictionary.* Retrieved January 4, 2024, from https://www.merriam-webster.com/dictionary/capacity

Mertens, B., & Sorenson, S. B. (2012). Current considerations about the elderly and firearms. *American Journal of Public Health, 102*(3), 396–400. https://doi.org/10.2105/AJPH.2011.300404

Messina, N., Grella, C., Burdon, W., & Prendergast, M. (2007). Childhood adverse events and current traumatic distress: A comparison of men and women drug-dependent prisoners. *Criminal Justice and Behavior, 34*(11), 1385–1401. https://doi.org/10.1177/0093854807305150

Miller, B. L., Darby, A., Benson, D. F., Cummings, J. L., & Miller, M. H. (1997). Aggressive, socially disruptive and antisocial behaviour associated with fronto-temporal dementia. *The British Journal of Psychiatry, 170,* 150–154. https://doi.org/10.1192/bjp.170.2.150

Miller, D. (2011). Sentencing elderly criminal offenders. *NAELA Journal, 7*(2), 221–248.

Miller, D. (2020). *Dementia and competency in United States Courtrooms: A case law review* [Master's thesis, City University of New York]. CUNY Academic Works. https://academicworks.cuny.edu/jj_etds/156

Miller, G. A., Galanter, E., & Pribram, K. H. (1960). *Plans and the structure of behavior.* Henry Holt. https://doi.org/10.1037/10039-000

Miller, M. C., Bayakly, R., Schreurs, B. G., Flicker, K. J., Adams, S. A., Ingram, L. A., Hardin, J. W., Lohman, M., Ford, M. E., McCollum, Q., McCrary-Quarles, A., Ariyo, O., Levkoff, S. E., & Friedman, D. B. (2023). Highlighting the value of Alzheimer's disease-focused registries: Lessons learned from cancer surveillance. *Frontiers in Aging, 4,* Article 1179275. https://doi.org/10.3389/fragi.2023.1179275

Miller, R. A. (1999). Kleemeier award lecture: Are there genes for aging? *The Journals of Gerontology: Series A, 54*(7), B297–B307. https://doi.org/10.1093/gerona/54.7.B297

Miller v. Alabama, 567 U.S. 460 (2012).

Milner, C. (2021). Seeking change: A vision from the past points the way to the future. *Journal on Active Aging, 20*(1), 60–68. https://www.icaa.cc/membership/pdf/seeking%20change%20.pdf

Minn. Stat. § 626.8433 (2020).

Mion, L. C., & Momeyer, M. A. (2019). Elder abuse. *Geriatric Nursing, 40*(6), 640–644. https://doi.org/10.1016/j.gerinurse.2019.11.003

Miss. Code § 13-5-25 (1972).

Mistry, P., & Muhammad, L. (2015). Dementia in the incarcerated: Ready or not? *Corrections Forum, 24*(5), 8–12.

Mitchell, K. J., Johnson, M. K., & Mather, M. (2003). Source monitoring and suggestibility to misinformation: Adult age-related differences. *Applied Cognitive Psychology, 17*(1), 107–119. https://doi.org/10.1002/acp.857

Mitchell, K. L. (2017). State sentencing guidelines: A garden full of variety. *Federal Probation, 81*(2), 28–36.

Moberg, P. J., & Shah, S. (2012). Ethical issues in capacity and competency evaluations. In G. J. Demakis (Ed.), *Civil capacities in clinical neuropsychology: Research findings and practical applications* (pp. 264–289). Oxford University Press.

Mojtabai, R. (2007). Americans' attitudes toward mental health treatment seeking: 1990–2003. *Psychiatric Services, 58*(5), 642–651. https://doi.org/10.1176/ps.2007.58.5.642

Moll, A. (2013). *Losing track of time: Dementia and the ageing prison population: Treatment challenges and examples of good practice.* Mental Health Foundation. https://www.choiceforum.org/docs/lto.pdf

Monahan, J., & Loftus, E. F. (1982). The psychology of law. *Annual Review of Psychology, 33*(1), 441–475. https://doi.org/10.1146/annurev.ps.33.020182.002301

Monahan, J., Skeem, J., & Lowenkamp, C. (2017). Age, risk assessment, and sanctioning: Overestimating the old, underestimating the young. *Law and Human Behavior, 41*(2), 191–201. https://doi.org/10.1037/lhb0000233

Montgomery v. Louisiana, 577 U.S. 190 (2016).

Morris, D. R., & Parker, G. F. (2009). Effects of advanced age and dementia on restoration of competence to stand trial. *International Journal of Law and Psychiatry, 32*(3), 156–160. https://doi.org/10.1016/j.ijlp.2009.02.009

Morris, S., Hadgkiss, M., David, A., Guinness, J., & Frewin, C. (2023). We're making a list and we're checking it twice, gonna find out what makes digital forensic examiners suffice. *Wiley Interdisciplinary Reviews: Forensic Science, 5*(5), e1487.

Morrison, S. (2023, December 27). Don't call me "old": Avoiding ageism when writing about aging. *Inside NIA: A blog for researchers*. https://www.nia.nih.gov/research/blog/2023/12/dont-call-me-old-avoiding-ageism-when-writing-about-aging

Morrow-Howell, N., Putnam, M., Lee, Y. S., Greenfield, J. C., Inoue, M., & Chen, H. (2014). An investigation of activity profiles of older adults. *The Journals of Gerontology: Series B, 69*(5), 809–821. https://doi.org/10.1093/geronb/gbu002

Morse, S. J. (2011). Mental disorder and criminal law. *Journal of Criminal Law and Criminology, 101*(3), 885–968.

Moye, J. (2020). Innovative interprofessional approaches to improving well being for older adults with interacting mental and physical health concerns. *Clinical Gerontologist, 43*(4), 363–364. https://doi.org/10.1080/07317115.2020.1761103

Moye, J., & Marson, D. C. (2009). Assessment of decision-making capacity in older adults: An emerging area of practice and research. *Focus: The Journal of Lifelong Learning in Psychiatry, 7*(1), 88–97. https://doi.org/10.1176/foc.7.1.foc88

Mueller-Johnson, K., & Ceci, S. J. (2004). Memory and suggestibility in older adults: Live event participation and repeated interview. *Applied Cognitive Psychology, 18*(8), 1109–1127. https://doi.org/10.1002/acp.1078

Mueller-Johnson, K., Toglia, M. P., Sweeney, C. D., & Ceci, S. J. (2007). The perceived credibility of older adults as witnesses and its relation to ageism. *Behavioral Sciences & the Law, 25*(3), 355–375. https://doi.org/10.1002/bsl.765

Munday, D., Leaman, J., O'Moore, É., & Plugge, E. (2019). The prevalence of non-communicable disease in older people in prison: A systematic review and meta-analysis. *Age and Ageing, 48*(2), 204–212. https://doi.org/10.1093/ageing/afy186

Munetz, M. R., & Griffin, P. A. (2006). Use of the sequential intercept model as an approach to decriminalization of people with serious mental illness. *Psychiatric Services, 57*(4), 544–549. https://doi.org/10.1176/ps.2006.57.4.544

Münsterberg, H. (1908). *On the witness stand: Essays on psychology*. McClure. https://www.loc.gov/item/42027601/

Muram, D., Miller, K., & Cutler, A. (1992). Sexual assault of the elderly victim. *Journal of Interpersonal Violence, 7*(1), 70–76. https://doi.org/10.1177/088626092007001006

Murman, D. L. (2015). The impact of age on cognition. *Seminars in Hearing, 36*(3), 111–121. https://doi.org/10.1055/s-0035-1555115

Murolo, A. S. (2020). Geriatric inmates: Policy and practice. *Journal of Correctional Health Care, 26*(1), 4–16. https://doi.org/10.1177/1078345819898465

Murolo, A. S. (2022). *Aging on parole: An empirical analysis of reentry, reintegration, and life satisfaction* [Doctoral dissertation, City University of New York]. CUNY Academic Works. https://academicworks.cuny.edu/gc_etds/5086

Myers, M. A. (1988). Social background and the sentencing behavior of judges. *Criminology, 26*(4), 649–676. https://doi.org/10.1111/j.1745-9125.1988.tb00858.x

Myhre, J., Saga, S., Malmedal, W., Ostaszkiewicz, J., & Nakrem, S. (2020). Elder abuse and neglect: An overlooked patient safety issue. A focus group study of nursing home leaders' perceptions of elder abuse and neglect. *BMC Health Services Research, 20*(1), 199. https://doi.org/10.1186/s12913-020-5047-4

Nagel, S., & Gagliano, F. (1965). Attorney characteristics and courtroom results. *Nebraska Law Review, 44*(3), 599–613.

National Academies of Sciences, Engineering, and Medicine. (2016). *Families caring for an aging America* (R. Schulz & J. Eden, Eds.). National Academies Press. https://doi.org/10.17226/23606

National Academies of Sciences, Engineering, and Medicine. (2018). *Future directions for the demography of aging: Proceedings of a workshop*. National Academies Press. https://doi.org/10.17226/25064

National Association of Area Agencies on Aging. (2017). *Supporting America's aging prisoner population: Opportunities & challenges for area agencies on aging*. https://www.usaging.org/Files/n4a_AgingPrisoners_23Feb2017REV%20(2).pdf

National Center for State Courts. (2023, December). *State judicial retirement plans.* https://www.ncsc.org/salarytracker/special-reports/retirement-map-and-states

National Conference of State Legislatures. (2023). *Elderly financial exploitation legislation.* https://www.ncsl.org/financial-services/elderly-financial-exploitation-legislation

National Firearms Act, 26 U.S.C. § 5849 (1934).

National Institute of Corrections. (2024). *Parole.* https://nicic.gov/resources/resources-topics-and-roles/topics/parole

National Institute on Aging. (2021). *Aging and your eyes.* National Institutes of Health. https://www.nia.nih.gov/health/vision-and-vision-loss/aging-and-your-eyes

National Institute on Drug Abuse. (2020, July 9). *Substance use in older adults DrugFacts.* https://nida.nih.gov/publications/drugfacts/substance-use-in-older-adults-drugfacts

National Judicial Task Force to Examine State Courts' Response to Mental Illness. (2023). *State courts leading change: Report and recommendations* (Rev. ed.). National Center for State Courts. https://www.ncsc.org/__data/assets/pdf_file/0031/84469/MHTF_State_Courts_Leading_Change.pdf

N.D. Cent. Code, § 27-17-01 (2023). https://ndlegis.gov/general-information/north-dakota-century-code/index.html

Neal, T., Lienert, P., Denne, E., & Singh, J. P. (2022). A general model of cognitive bias in human judgment and systematic review specific to forensic mental health. *Law and Human Behavior, 46*(2), 99–120. https://doi.org/10.1037/lhb0000482

Nellis, A. (2021). Using data to achieve justice reform. *Federal Sentencing Reporter, 33*(4), 265–268. https://doi.org/10.1525/fsr.2021.33.4.265

Nellis, A., & Komar, L. (2023, August 22). *The First Step Act: Ending mass incarceration in federal prisons.* The Sentencing Project. https://www.sentencingproject.org/policy-brief/the-first-step-act-ending-mass-incarceration-in-federal-prisons

Nelson, T. D. (Ed.). (2002). *Ageism: Stereotyping and prejudice against older persons.* MIT Press. https://doi.org/10.7551/mitpress/1157.001.0001

Nelson, W. R., & Roberts, R. N. (1986). Mandatory retirement and police employment. *Journal of Police Science and Administration, 14,* 6–7.

New York State. (2023). *Governor Hochul grants clemency to thirteen individuals.* https://www.governor.ny.gov/news/governor-hochul-grants-clemency-thirteen-individuals-0

Nguyen, H., Haeney, O., & Galletly, C. (2021). The characteristics of older homicide offenders: A systematic review. *Psychiatry, Psychology, and Law, 29*(3), 413–430. https://doi.org/10.1080/13218719.2021.1910589

Nicholaichuk, T. P., Olver, M. E., Gu, D., & Wong, S. C. P. (2014). Age, actuarial risk, and long-term recidivism in a national sample of sex offenders. *Sexual Abuse, 26*(5), 406–428. https://doi.org/10.1177/1079063213492340

Nieuwenhuys, A., Savelsbergh, G. J. P., & Oudejans, R. R. D. (2012). Shoot or don't shoot? Why police officers are more inclined to shoot when they are anxious. *Emotion, 12*(4), 827–833. https://doi.org/10.1037/a0025699

Nijhawan, A. E. (2016). Infectious diseases and the criminal justice system. *The American Journal of the Medical Sciences, 352*(4), 399–407. https://doi.org/10.1016/j.amjms.2016.05.020

North, B. J., & Sinclair, D. A. (2012). The intersection between aging and cardiovascular disease. *Circulation Research, 110*(8), 1097–1108. https://doi.org/10.1161/CIRCRESAHA.111.246876

North, M. S., & Fiske, S. T. (2012). An inconvenienced youth? Ageism and its potential intergenerational roots. *Psychological Bulletin, 138*(5), 982–987. https://doi.org/10.1037/a0027843

Norton, A. L., Chen, A. Z., & Tan, T. X. (2022). Firearms in clients' homes. *Psychotherapy & Politics International, 20*(3), 1–18.

Nev. Rev. Stat. (NRS) 433A.310. https://www.leg.state.nv.us/nrs/nrs-433a.html#NRS433ASec310

Nuland, S. B. (1995). *How we die: Reflections on life's final chapter*. Vintage.

Nunez, N., McCoy, M. L., Clark, H. L., & Shaw, L. A. (1999). The testimony of elderly victim/witnesses and their impact on juror decisions: The importance of examining multiple stereotypes. *Law and Human Behavior, 23*(4), 413–423. https://doi.org/10.1023/A:1022308014652

Nursing Home Reform Act of 1987, 42 U.S.C. § 1395i-3. (2025). https://uscode.house.gov/view.xhtml?req=granuleid:USC-prelim-title42-section1395i-3a&num=0&edition=prelim

N.Y. Comp. Codes R. & Regs., tit. 9, § 8002.2(d)(7) (2017).

NY Exec. L. 259-s (2024).

Nyman, T. J., Antfolk, J., Lampinen, J. M., Korkman, J., & Santtila, P. (2020). Eyewitness identifications after witnessing threatening and non-threatening scenes in 360-degree virtual reality (or 2D) from first and third person perspectives. *PLoS One, 15*(9), 238292. https://doi.org/10.1371/journal.pone.0238292

Nyman, T. J., Lampinen, J. M., Antfolk, J., Korkman, J., & Santtila, P. (2019). The distance threshold of reliable eyewitness identification. *Law and Human Behavior, 43*(6), 527–541. https://doi.org/10.1037/lhb0000342

O'Brien, L. T., & Hummert, M. L. (2006). Memory performance of late middle–aged adults: Contrasting self–stereotyping and stereotype threat accounts of assimilation to age stereotypes. *Social Cognition, 24*(3), 338–358. https://doi.org/10.1521/soco.2006.24.3.338

O'Connor, A. M., & Evans, A. D. (2020). Perceptions of older adult jurors: The influence of aging stereotypes and jury laws. *Psychology, Crime & Law, 26*(7), 648–666. https://doi.org/10.1080/1068316X.2019.1708358

O'Connor, A. M., Lyon, T. D., & Evans, A. D. (2019). Younger and older adults' lie-detection and credibility judgments of children's coached reports. *Psychology, Crime & Law, 25*(9), 925–944. https://doi.org/10.1080/1068316X.2019.1597092

O'Connor, A. M., Lyon, T. D., Wiens, M., & Evans, A. D. (2022). Use of global trait cues helps to explain older adults' decrements in detecting children's lies. *Legal and Criminological Psychology, 27*(1), 48–62. https://doi.org/10.1111/lcrp.12196

O'Connor, M. (1987). Disturbed behaviour in dementia—psychiatric or medical problem? *Medical Journal of Australia, 147*(10), 481–485.

O'Connor, M.-F. (2004). Finding boundaries inside prison walls: Case study of a terminally ill inmate. *Death Studies, 28*(1), 63–76. https://doi.org/10.1080/07481180490249274

Office for Human Research Protections. (n.d.). *Prisoner research FAQs*. U.S. Department of Health and Human Services. https://www.hhs.gov/ohrp/regulations-and-policy/guidance/faq/prisoner-research/index.html

Office of Inspector General of the Nebraska Correctional System. (2021). *2021 Annual Report*. https://nebraskalegislature.gov/FloorDocs/107/PDF/Agencies/Inspector_General_of_the_Nebraska_Correctional_System/600_20210914-140850.pdf

Officer, A., Thiyagarajan, J. A., Schneiders, M. L., Nash, P., & De la Fuente-Núñez, V. (2020). Ageism, healthy life expectancy and population ageing: How are they related? *International Journal of Environmental Research and Public Health, 17*(9), 3159. https://doi.org/10.3390/ijerph17093159

Oh, S.-J., Lee, J. K., & Shin, O. S. (2019). Aging and the immune system: The impact of immunosenescence on viral infection, immunity and vaccine immunogenicity. *Immune Network, 19*(6), e37. https://doi.org/10.4110/in.2019.19.e37

Okazaki, S., & Sue, S. (1995). Methodological issues in assessment research with ethnic minorities. *Psychological Assessment, 7*(3), 367–375. https://doi.org/10.1037/1040-3590.7.3.367

Older Americans Act of 1965, 42 U.S.C. § 3001 et seq.

Older Americans Act Amendments of 1992, Pub. L. No. 102-375, 106 Stat. 1195.

O'Leary, R. (2021). Compassionate release and decarceration in the States. *Iowa Law Review, 107*(2), 621.

Ollove, M. (2016, March 17). *Elderly inmates burden state prisons*. Stateline. https://stateline.org/2016/03/17/elderly-inmates-burden-state-prisons

Omnibus Budget Reconciliation Act of 1987, Pub. L. No. 100-203, 101 Stat. 1330. https://www.congress.gov/bill/100th-congress/house-bill/3545

Onyeali, R., Howell, B. A., McInnes, D. K., Emerson, A., & Williams, M. E. (2023). The case for transitional services and programs for older adults reentering society: A narrative review of US departments of correction and recommendations. *International Journal of Prisoner Health, 19*(1), 4–19. https://doi.org/10.1108/IJPH-08-2021-0073

Opeskin, B. (2015). Models of judicial tenure: Reconsidering life limits, age limits and term limits for judges. *Oxford Journal of Legal Studies, 35*(4), 627–663. https://doi.org/10.1093/ojls/gqu029

Ormel, J., Rijsdijk, F. V., Sullivan, M., van Sonderen, E., & Kempen, G. I. J. M. (2002). Temporal and reciprocal relationship between IADL/ADL disability and depressive symptoms in late life. *The Journals of Gerontology: Series B, 57*(4), P338–P347. https://doi.org/10.1093/geronb/57.4.P338

Overshott, R., Rodway, C., Roscoe, A., Flynn, S., Hunt, I. M., Swinson, N., Appleby, L., & Shaw, J. (2012). Homicide perpetrated by older people. *International Journal of Geriatric Psychiatry, 27*(11), 1099–1105. https://doi.org/10.1002/gps.2739

Palmore, E. (2015). Ageism comes of age. *The Journals of Gerontology: Series B, 70*(6), 873–875. https://doi.org/10.1093/geronb/gbv079

Paluck, E. L., Green, S. A., & Green, D. P. (2019). The contact hypothesis re-evaluated. *Behavioural Public Policy, 3*(2), 129–158. https://doi.org/10.1017/bpp.2018.25

Paradis, C., Broner, N., Maher, L. M., & O'Rourke, T. (2000). Mentally ill elderly jail detainees: Psychiatric, psychosocial and legal factors. *Journal of Offender Rehabilitation, 31*(1–2), 77–86.

Paratore, L. (2023). *Freedom & reentry fund for Janet Carter*. https://www.gofundme.com/f/freedom-reentry-fund-for-janet-carter

Parkin, A. J., & Walter, B. M. (1992). Recollective experience, normal aging, and frontal dysfunction. *Psychology and Aging, 7*(2), 290–298. https://doi.org/10.1037/0882-7974.7.2.290

Parrott, J. M., Houben, F. R., Visser, R. C., & Macines, D. L. (2019). Mental health and offending in older people: Future directions for research. *Criminal Behaviour and Mental Health, 29*(4), 218–226. https://doi.org/10.1002/cbm.2121

Pate v. Robinson, 383 U.S. 375 (1966).

Patten, D. (2022). Ron Jeremy rape case put on hold as judge orders psychiatric evaluations for "incoherent." *Deadline*. https://deadline.com/2022/03/ron-jeremy-rape-case-suspended-psychiatric-evaluations-1234981368

Paul, L. (2023, February 8). Ron Jeremy declared "not competent" to stand trial for rape, committed to mental health facility. *Rolling Stone*. https://www.rollingstone.com/culture/culture-news/ron-jeremy-committed-mental-health-facility-1234675977

Pavlou, M. P., & Lachs, M. S. (2008). Self-neglect in older adults: A primer for clinicians. *Journal of General Internal Medicine, 23*(11), 1841–1846. https://doi.org/10.1007/s11606-008-0717-7

Payne, B. K. (2001). Prejudice and perception: The role of automatic and controlled processes in misperceiving a weapon. *Journal of Personality and Social Psychology, 81*(2), 181–192. https://doi.org/10.1037/0022-3514.81.2.181

Payne, D. (2019). *Diamond Doris: The true story of the world's most notorious jewel thief.* Amistad.

Peacock, S., Burles, M., Hodson, A., Kumaran, M., Macrae, R., Peternelj-Taylor, C., & Holtslander, L. (2020). Older persons with dementia in prison: An integrative review. *International Journal of Prisoner Health, 16*(1), 1–16. https://doi.org/10.1108/IJPH-01-2019-0007

Penal Reform International and Thailand Institute of Justice. (2018). *Global prison trends 2018.* https://cdn.penalreform.org/wp-content/uploads/2018/04/PRI_Global-Prison-Trends-2018_EN_WEB.pdf

Pennington, N., & Hastie, R. (1992). Explaining the evidence: Tests of the story model for juror decision making. *Journal of Personality and Social Psychology, 62*(2), 189–206. https://doi.org/10.1037/0022-3514.62.2.189

Pennsylvania Dept. of Corrections v. Yeskey, 524 U.S. 206 (1998).

Penrod, J., Loeb, S. J., & Smith, C. A. (2014). Administrators' perspectives on changing practice in end-of-life care in a state prison system. *Public Health Nursing, 31*(2), 99–108. https://doi.org/10.1111/phn.12069

Perdue, C. W., Dovidio, J. F., Gurtman, M. B., & Tyler, R. B. (1990). Us and them: Social categorization and the process of intergroup bias. *Journal of Personality and Social Psychology, 59*(3), 475–486. https://doi.org/10.1037/0022-3514.59.3.475

Perls, T. T. (2004). Anti-aging medicine: The legal issues: Anti-aging quackery: Human growth hormone and tricks of the trade—More dangerous than ever. *The Journals of Gerontology: Series A, 59*(7), B682–B691. https://doi.org/10.1093/gerona/59.7.B682

Perry v. New Hampshire, 565 U.S. 228 (2012).

Peterson, R. D., & Hagan, J. (1984). Changing conceptions of race: Towards an account of anomalous findings of sentencing research. *American Sociological Review, 49*(1), 56–70. https://doi.org/10.2307/2095557

Petrow, S. (2019, June 17). An ageless question: When is someone 'old'? *The Washington Post.* https://www.washingtonpost.com/health/an-ageless-question-when-is-someone-old/2019/06/14/9ecad1f4-87ad-11e9-98c1-e945ae5db8fb_story.html

Pew Charitable Trusts. (2021, December 1). *How courts embraced technology, met the pandemic challenge, and revolutionized their operations.* https://pew.org/3CK3VaD

Pew Research. (2021). *How courts embraced technology, met the pandemic challenge, and revolutionized their operations.* https://www.pewtrusts.org/-/media/assets/2021/12/how-courts-embraced-technology.pdf

Pickel, K. L. (1998). Unusualness and threat as possible causes of "weapon focus." *Memory, 6*(3), 277–295. https://doi.org/10.1080/741942361

Pirelli, G., Gottdiener, W. H., & Zapf, P. A. (2011). A meta-analytic review of competency to stand trial research. *Psychology, Public Policy, and Law, 17*(1), 1–53. https://doi.org/10.1037/a0021713

Pirelli, G., & Zapf, P. A. (2020). An attempted meta-analysis of the competency restoration research: Important findings for future directions. *Journal of Forensic Psychology Research and Practice, 20*(2), 134–162. https://doi.org/10.1080/24732850.2020.1714398

Policastro, C., Gainey, R., & Payne, B. K. (2015). Conceptualizing crimes against older persons: Elder abuse, domestic violence, white-collar offending, or just regular 'old' crime. *Journal of Crime and Justice, 38*(1), 27–41. https://doi.org/10.1080/0735648X.2013.767533

Polzer, E. R., Nearing, K. A., Knoepke, C. E., Matlock, D. D., & Betz, M. E. (2022). Firearm access and dementia: A qualitative study of reported behavioral disturbances and responses. *Journal of the American Geriatrics Society, 70*(2), 439–448. https://doi.org/10.1111/jgs.17496

Posner, R. A. (1995). *Aging and old age.* University of Chicago Press.

Prais, V. (2019, August 23). *Elderly life-sentenced prisoners: A forgotten and "invisible" group.* Penal Reform International. https://www.penalreform.org/blog/elderly-life-sentenced-prisoners-a-forgotten-and-invisible

Price, M. (2018). *Everywhere and nowhere: Compassionate release in the states.* Families Against Mandatory Minimums. https://famm.org/wp-content/uploads/2023/12/Exec-Summary-Report.pdf

Price Waterhouse v. Hopkins, 490 U.S. 228 (1989).

Pro, G., & Marzell, M. (2017). Medical parole and aging prisoners: A qualitative study. *Journal of Correctional Health Care, 23*(2), 162–172. https://doi.org/10.1177/1078345817699608

Prost, S. G., Archuleta, A. J., & Golder, S. (2021). Older adults incarcerated in state prison: Health and quality of life disparities between age cohorts. *Aging & Mental Health, 25*(2), 260–268. https://doi.org/10.1080/13607863.2019.1693976

Prost, S. G., & Williams, B. (2020). Strategies to optimize the use of compassionate release From US prisons. *American Journal of Public Health, 110*(S1), S25–S26. https://doi.org/10.2105/AJPH.2019.305434

Putkonen, H., Weizmann-Henelius, G., Repo-Tiihonen, E., Lindberg, N., Saarela, T., Eronen, M., & Häkkänen-Nyholm, H. (2010). Homicide, psychopathy, and aging—A nationwide register-based case-comparison study of homicide offenders aged 60 years or older. *Journal of Forensic Sciences, 55*(6), 1552–1556. https://doi.org/10.1111/j.1556-4029.2010.01488.x

Queally, J. (2023). Ron Jeremy's alleged victims share fury, acceptance after latest twist in court case. *Los Angeles Times*. https://www.latimes.com/california/story/2023-11-28/ron-jeremys-alleged-victims-share-confusion-acceptance-after-latest-twist-in-court-case

Querry-Thompson, K. (2022). *Tulsa woman sues police for civil rights violations after viral arrest.* Oklahoma's News4. https://kfor.com/news/local/tulsa-woman-sues-police-for-civil-rights-violations-after-viral-arrest

Raftery, B. (2023, December 14). *FAQ: Which states have mandatory judicial retirement ages?* National Center for State Courts. https://www.ncsc.org/information-and-resources/trending-topics/trending-topics-landing-pg/faq-which-states-have-mandatory-judicial-retirement-ages

Raine, A. (2002). Biosocial studies of antisocial and violent behavior in children and adults: A review. *Journal of Abnormal Child Psychology, 30*(4), 311–326. https://doi.org/10.1023/A:1015754122318

Rakes, S., Prost, S. G., & Tripodi, S. J. (2018). Recidivism among older adults: Correlates of prison re-entry. *Justice Policy Journal, 15*(1). https://www.cjcj.org/media/import/documents/recidivism_among_older_adults_correlates_of_prison_reentry.pdf

Rando, T. A., & Chang, H. Y. (2012). Aging, rejuvenation, and epigenetic reprogramming: Resetting the aging clock. *Cell, 148*(1–2), 46–57. https://doi.org/10.1016/j.cell.2012.01.003

Rapaport, E. (2012). A modest proposal: The aged of death row should be deemed too old to execute. *Brooklyn Law Review, 77*(3), 1089–1132. https://brooklynworks.brooklaw.edu/cgi/viewcontent.cgi?article=1152&context=blr

Rasmussen, A. (n.d.). Ice queen: The story of the notorious jewel thief Doris Payne. *Grazia*. https://graziamagazine.com/us/articles/jewel-thief-doris-payne

Ratcliff, E. (2005). Is this bad form? *Australasian Psychiatry, 13*(3), 311–312. https://doi.org/10.1080/j.1440-1665.2005.2208_2.x

Reimers, K. (2019). *The clinician's guide to geriatric forensic evaluations*. Academic Press.

Release Aging People in Prison. (n.d.). *Our mission*. https://rappcampaign.com/about/#our-mission

Renner, M., Newark, C., Bartos, B. J., McCleary, R., & Scurich, N. (2017). Length of stay for 25,791 California patients found incompetent to stand trial. *Journal of Forensic and Legal Medicine, 51*, 22–26. https://doi.org/10.1016/j.jflm.2017.07.006

Retirement on salary; retirement in senior status, Pub. L. No. 98-353, 98 Stat. 350 (1984). https://uscode.house.gov/view.xhtml?path=/prelim@title28/part1/chapter17&edition=prelim

Rhodes, M. G., & Anastasi, J. S. (2012). The own-age bias in face recognition: A meta-analytic and theoretical review. *Psychological Bulletin, 138*(1), 146–174. https://doi.org/10.1037/a0025750

Richard-Devantoy, S., Gallarda, T., Annweiler, C., Dorey, J.-M., Mesu, C., Garré, J.-B., Le Gall, D., & Beauchet, O. (2010). Homicide and dementia in older adults:

The key role of dysexecutive function. *The Journal of Clinical Psychiatry, 71*(10), 1402–1403. https://doi.org/10.4088/JCP.10l06029oli

Risen, C. B. (2016). The sexual narrative: A story waiting to be told. In S. B. Levine, C. B. Risen, & S. E. Althof (Eds.), *Handbook of clinical sexuality for mental health professionals* (3rd ed., pp. 8–20). Routledge.

Ritvo, D. (2018). The leftover: Where do elderly prisoners go when released? *The Elder Law Journal,* 26(1), 227–261.

Roberto, K. A. (2016). The complexities of elder abuse. *American Psychologist, 71*(4), 302–311. https://doi.org/10.1037/a0040259

Roberto, K. A., & Teaster, P. B. (2017). Theorizing elder abuse. In X. Dong (Ed.), *Elder abuse* (pp. 21–41). Springer International Publishing. https://doi.org/10.1007/978-3-319-47504-2_2

Roberts, A. W., Ogunwole, S. U., Blakeslee, L., & Rabe, M. A. (2018). *The population 65 years and older in the United States: 2016* (ACS-38). U.S. Census Bureau.

Roberts, D. C., & Wolak, J. (2022). Do voters care about the age of their elected representatives? *Political Behavior, 45,* 1959–1978. https://doi.org/10.1007/s11109-022-09802-5

Robins, L. M., Lee, D. A., Bell, J. S., Srikanth, V., Möhler, R., Hill, K. D., & Haines, T. P. (2021). Definition and measurement of physical and chemical restraint in long-term care: A systematic review. *International Journal of Environmental Research and Public Health, 18*(7), 3639. https://doi.org/10.3390/ijerph18073639

Robinson, C. (2023, November 21). *Elderly Alabama man charged in wife's death 'overwhelmed by being her caregiver,' family told police.* AL.com. https://www.al.com/news/2023/11/elderly-alabama-man-charged-in-wifes-death-overwhelmed-by-being-her-caregiver-family-told-police.html

Rodriguez, M., Boyce, P., & Hodges, J. (2017). A neuropsychological study of older adult first-time sex offenders. *Neurocase, 23*(2), 154–161. https://doi.org/10.1080/13554794.2017.1334802

Rodríguez-Rodero, S., Fernández-Morera, J. L., Menéndez-Torre, E., Calvanese, V., Fernández, A. F., & Fraga, M. F. (2011). Aging genetics and aging. *Aging and Disease, 2*(3), 186–195.

Roe, B., Beynon, C., Pickering, L., & Duffy, P. (2010). Experiences of drug use and ageing: Health, quality of life, relationship and service implications. *Journal of Advanced Nursing, 66*(9), 1968–1979. https://doi.org/10.1111/j.1365-2648.2010.05378.x

Roediger, H. L., III, & Geraci, L. (2007). Aging and the misinformation effect: A neuropsychological analysis. *Journal of Experimental Psychology: Learning, Memory, and Cognition, 33*(2), 321–334. https://doi.org/10.1037/0278-7393.33.2.321

Rogers, M. M., & Storey, J. E. (2019). Elder homicide: A systematic literature review. *Aggression and Violent Behavior, 48,* 141–151. https://doi.org/10.1016/j.avb.2019.08.008

Roper v. Simmons, 543 U.S. 551 (2005).

Ross, D. F., Dunning, D., Toglia, M. P., & Ceci, S. J. (1990). The child in the eyes of the jury: Assessing mock jurors' perceptions of the child witness. *Law and Human Behavior, 14*(1), 5–23. https://doi.org/10.1007/BF01055786

Rothke, S. E., Demakis, G. J., & Amsbaugh, H. M. (2019). State statutes regarding the role of psychologists in performing capacity evaluations for guardianship determinations. *Professional Psychology, Research and Practice, 50*(4), 228–239. https://doi.org/10.1037/pro0000240

Rothman, M. B., & Dunlop, B. D. (2005). Judicial responses to an aging America. *Court Review: The Journal of the American Judges Association, 42*(1), 8–19. https://digitalcommons.unl.edu/ajacourtreview/42

Rothman, M. B., & Dunlop, B. D. (2006). Elders and the courts: Judicial policy for an aging America. *Journal of Aging & Social Policy, 18*(2), 31–46. https://doi.org/10.1300/J031v18n02_03

Rothman, M. B., Dunlop, B. D., & Hirt, G. M. (2000). Jury selection in aging America: The new discrimination? *Marquette Elder's Advisor, 2*(2), 69–80.

Ruiz, P., Strain, E. C., & Langrod, J. (2007). *The substance abuse handbook*. Lippincott Williams & Wilkins.

Ryan, E. B., Giles, H., Bartolucci, G., & Henwood, K. (1986). Psycholinguistic and social psychological components of communication by and with the elderly. *Language & Communication, 6*(1–2), 1–24. https://doi.org/10.1016/0271-5309(86)90002-9

Saadi, A., Choi, K. R., Takada, S., & Zimmerman, F. J. (2020). The impact of gun violence restraining order laws in the U.S. and firearm suicide among older adults: A longitudinal state-level analysis, 2012-2016. *BMC Public Health, 20,* Article 334. https://doi.org/10.1186/s12889-020-08462-6

Sacco, V. (2005). *When crime waves*. Sage Publications. https://doi.org/10.4135/9781483328799

Safer Detention Act, 34 U.S.C. § 60541(g) (2023).

Sakala, L., Taylor, R., Marcellin, C., & Matei, A. (2020). *How governors can use categorical clemency as a corrective tool*. Urban Institute.

Salekin, K. L., & Wood, M. E. (2023). 23 adults with developmental disabilities in the criminal justice system. In A. D. Redich & J. A. Quas (Eds.), *The Oxford handbook of developmental psychology and the law* (pp. 449–476). Oxford University Press.

Sampson, R. J., & Laub, J. H. (2003). Life-course desisters? Trajectories of crime among delinquent boys followed to age 70. *Criminology, 41*(3), 555–592. https://doi.org/10.1111/j.1745-9125.2003.tb00997.x

Sanderson, W. C., & Scherbov, S. (2019). *Prospective longevity: A new vision of population aging*. Harvard University Press. https://doi.org/10.4159/9780674243316

Scarpazza, C., Zampieri, I., Miolla, A., Melis, G., Pietrini, P., & Sartori, G. (2021). A multidisciplinary approach to insanity assessment as a way to reduce cognitive biases. *Forensic Science International, 319,* 110652. https://doi.org/10.1016/j.forsciint.2020.110652

S. 354, 125th Gen. Assemb., Reg. Sess. (S.C. 2023). https://www.scstatehouse.gov/sess125_2023-2024/bills/354.htm

S.C. Code § 44-23-410(A). (2024). https://www.scstatehouse.gov/code/t44c023.php

Schachter, H. L. (2013). Constructing age through bona fide occupational qualifications: De jure discrimination's last stand? *Public Administration Quarterly, 37*(3), 373–392.

Schaller, M., Park, J. H., & Mueller, A. (2003). Fear of the dark: Interactive effects of beliefs about danger and ambient darkness on ethnic stereotypes. *Personality and Social Psychology Bulletin, 29*(5), 637–649. https://doi.org/10.1177/0146167203029005008

Scheb, J. M., & Sharma, H. (2023). *An introduction to the American legal system* (6th ed.). Aspen Publishing.

Schiff, M. (1993). The age discrimination in employment act: Whither the bona fide occupational qualification and law enforcement exemptions. *St. John's Law Review, 67*(1), 13–54.

Schmidt, W. C. (2009). Law and aging: Mental health theory approach. In I. Doron (Ed.), *Theories on law and ageing: The jurisprudence of elder law* (pp. 121–143). Springer. https://doi.org/10.1007/978-3-540-78954-3_9

Schoenborn, C. A., Vickerie, J. L., Powell-Griner, E., & Centers for Disease Control and Prevention National Center for Health Statistics. (2006). Health characteristics of adults 55 years of age and over: United States, 2000–2003. *Advance Data, 370*, 1–31.

Schulz, R., Beach, S. R., Czaja, S. J., Martire, L. M., & Monin, J. K. (2020). Family caregiving for older adults. *Annual Review of Psychology, 71*(1), 635–659. https://doi.org/10.1146/annurev-psych-010419-050754

Schumer, E. M. (2023, January 31). Elderly man accused of shooting Charleston deputy found unfit for trial. *The Post and Courier*. https://www.postandcourier.com/news/elderly-man-accused-of-shooting-charleston-deputy-found-unfit-for-trial/article_7323b180-a0c5-11ed-a36d-bffb373df3f1.html

Schwalbe, E., & Medalia, A. (2007). Cognitive dysfunction and competency restoration: Using cognitive remediation to help restore the unrestorable. *The Journal of the American Academy of Psychiatry and the Law, 35*(4), 518–525.

Schwartzapfel, B. (2016, January 25). *The secret hints for winning parole*. The Marshall Project. https://www.themarshallproject.org/2016/01/25/the-secret-hints-for-winning-parole

Schwertner, E., Zelic, R., Secnik, J., Johansson, B., Winblad, B., Eriksdotter, M., & Religa, D. (2021). Biting the bullet: Firearm ownership in persons with dementia. A registry-based observational study. *Journal of Alzheimer's Disease, 81*(1), 179–188. https://doi.org/10.3233/JAD-201365

Searcy, J., Bartlett, J. C., & Memon, A. (2000). Influence of post-event narratives, line-up conditions and individual differences on false identification by young and older eyewitnesses. *Legal and Criminological Psychology, 5*(2), 219–235. https://doi.org/10.1348/135532500168100

Searcy, J. H., Bartlett, J. C., Memon, A., & Swanson, K. (2001). Aging and lineup performance at long retention intervals: Effects of metamemory and context reinstatement. *Journal of Applied Psychology, 86*(2), 207–214. https://doi.org/10.1037/0021-9010.86.2.207

Sentencing Reform Act of 1984, 18 U.S.C. § 3582.

Setterlund, D., Tilse, C., Wilson, J., Mccawley, A.-L., & Rosenman, L. (2007). Understanding financial elder abuse in families: The potential of routine activities theory. *Ageing and Society, 27*(4), 599–614. https://doi.org/10.1017/S0144686X07006009

Sevi, S. (2022). Too old to be president? *American Politics Research, 50*(6), 752–756. https://doi.org/10.1177/1532673X221118344

Sfera, A., Osorio, C., Gradini, R., & Price, A. (2014). Neurodegeneration behind bars: From molecules to jurisprudence. *Frontiers in Psychiatry, 5*, 115. https://doi.org/10.3389/fpsyt.2014.00115

Shapiro, C., & Schwartzapfel, B. (2022, June 17). *I joined the parole board to make a difference. Now I call it 'conveyor belt justice.'* The Marshall Project. https://www.themarshallproject.org/2022/06/17/i-joined-the-parole-board-to-make-a-difference-now-i-call-it-conveyor-belt-justice

Sharps, M. J. (2021, July 30). Memory and the aging eyewitness. *Psychology Today.* https://www.psychologytoday.com/us/blog/the-forensic-view/202107/memory-and-the-aging-eyewitness

Shawon, R. A., Adhia, A., DeCou, C., & Rowhani-Rahbar, A. (2021). Characteristics and patterns of older adult homicides in the United States. *Injury Epidemiology, 8*(1), 5. https://doi.org/10.1186/s40621-021-00299-w

Shelter Tech. (2024). *Senior ex-offender program.* https://www.sfserviceguide.org/services/1561

Shen, F. X. (2020). Aging judges. *Ohio State Law Journal, 81*(2), 235–314.

Shichor, D. (1985). Male–female differences in elderly arrests: An exploratory analysis. *Justice Quarterly, 2*(3), 399–414.

Shover, N. (1996). *Great pretenders: Pursuits and careers of persistent thieves.* Routledge.

Sieff, K. (2010, September 8). Virginia's prison system struggles to handle the surge in elderly inmates. *The Washington Post.* https://www.washingtonpost.com/wp-dyn/content/article/2010/09/07/AR2010090706514.html

Smith, D. (2023, February 19). Gerontocracy: The exceptionally old political class that governs the US. *The Guardian.* https://www.theguardian.com/us-news/2023/feb/19/us-congress-presidency-gerontocracy

Smith, M. S., & Schriver, J. L. (2018). Judges' sentencing decisions with older offenders. *Psychology, Crime & Law, 24*(2), 105–116. https://doi.org/10.1080/1068316X.2017.1390117

Smoyer, A. B., Madera, J. E., & Blankenship, K. M. (2019). Older adults' lived experience of incarceration. *Journal of Offender Rehabilitation, 58*(3), 220–239. https://doi.org/10.1080/10509674.2019.1582574

Smyth, G. E. (2011). Mediation in cases of elder abuse and mistreatment: The case of University of Windsor mediation services. *Windsor Review of Legal and Social Issues, 30,* 121–141.

Snell, K. (2023, August 31). *Politicians now tend to be older than they've been historically. It's causing issues.* NPR. https://www.npr.org/2023/08/31/1197084257/politicians-now-tend-to-be-older-than-theyve-been-historically-its-causing-issue

Snow, M. D., Wyman, J., Malloy, L. C., Brubacher, S. P., & Warren, K. L. (2023). Police perspectives on interviewing older adult victims and witnesses: Preliminary findings and call for future research. *Journal of Forensic Psychology Research and Practice, 23*(5), 438–458. https://doi.org/10.1080/24732850.2022.2044714

Social Security Administration. (n.d.). *Benefits planner.* Retrieved January 15, 2024, from https://www.ssa.gov/benefits/retirement/planner/1960.html

Soucheray, S. (2023, December 4). *Excess deaths soared in US prisons during first year of COVID-19.* Center for Infectious Disease Research & Policy. https://www.cidrap.umn.edu/covid-19/excess-deaths-soared-us-prisons-during-first-year-covid-19

Span, P. (2018, May 25). In elderly hands, firearms can be even deadlier. *The New York Times.* https://www.nytimes.com/2018/05/25/health/elderly-guns-suicide-dementia.html

Stal, M. (2013). Treatment of older and elderly inmates within prisons. *Journal of Correctional Health Care, 19*(1), 69–73. https://doi.org/10.1177/1078345812458245

Stamatel, J. P., & Mastrocinque, J. M. (2011). Using National Incident-Based Reporting System (NIBRS) data to understand financial exploitation of the elderly: A research note. *Victims & Offenders, 6*(2), 117–136. https://doi.org/10.1080/15564886.2011.557321

Stampacchia, S., Pegg, S., Hallam, G., Smallwood, J., Lambon Ralph, M. A., Thompson, H., & Jefferies, E. (2019). Control the source: Source memory for semantic, spatial and self-related items in patients with LIFG lesions. *Cortex, 119*, 165–183. https://doi.org/10.1016/j.cortex.2019.04.014

Stanziani, M., Cox, J., Bownes, E., Carden, K. D., & DeMatteo, D. S. (2020). Marking the progress of a "maturing" society: Madison v. Alabama and competency for execution evaluations. *Psychology, Public Policy, and Law, 26*(2), 145–153. https://doi.org/10.1037/law0000228

State v. Johnson, 24 Ohio St. 3d 87 (1986).

State v. Rodriguez, 251 Ariz. 90 (Ariz. Ct. App. Division 2, March 22, 2021).

State v. Silvils, No. 1907008254 (Del. Super. Ct. Dec. 8, 2022).

Steadman, H. J., Deane, M. W., Borum, R., & Morrissey, J. P. (2000). Comparing outcomes of major models of police responses to mental health emergencies. *Psychiatric Services, 51*(5), 645–649. https://doi.org/10.1176/appi.ps.51.5.645

Steadman, H. J., Osher, F. C., Robbins, P. C., Case, B., & Samuels, S. (2009). Prevalence of serious mental illness among jail inmates. *Psychiatric Services, 60*(6), 761–765. https://doi.org/10.1176/ps.2009.60.6.761

Steblay, N. M. (1997). Social influence in eyewitness recall: A meta-analytic review of lineup instruction effects. *Law and Human Behavior, 21*(3), 283–297. https://doi.org/10.1023/A:1024890732059

Steblay, N., Dysart, J., Fulero, S., & Lindsay, R. C. L. (2001). Eyewitness accuracy rates in sequential and simultaneous lineup presentations: A meta-analytic comparison. *Law and Human Behavior, 25*(5), 459–473. https://doi.org/10.1023/A:1012888715007

Steele, C. M. (2010). *Whistling Vivaldi: How stereotypes affect us and what we can do*. W. W. Norton.

Steffensmeier, D., & Allan, E. (2000). Gender, age, and crime. In J. Sheley (Ed.), *Criminology: A contemporary handbook* (pp. 67–93). Wadsworth.

Steffensmeier, D. J., & Harer, M. D. (1987). Is the crime rate really falling? An "aging" US population and its impact on the nation's crime rate, 1980-1984. *Journal of Research in Crime and Delinquency, 24*(1), 23–48.

Steffensmeier, D., Kramer, J., & Ulmer, J. (1995). Age differences in sentencing. *Justice Quarterly, 12*(3), 583–602. https://doi.org/10.1080/07418829500096151

Steffensmeier, D., & Motivans, M. (2000). Older men and older women in the arms of criminal law: Offending patterns and sentencing outcomes. *The Journals of Gerontology: Series B, 55*(3), S141–S151. https://doi.org/10.1093/geronb/55.3.S141

Steffensmeier, D., Ulmer, J., & Kramer, J. (1998). The interaction of race, gender, and age in criminal sentencing: The punishment cost of being young, Black, and male. *Criminology, 36*(4), 763–798. https://doi.org/10.1111/j.1745-9125.1998.tb01265.x

Steinberg, L., & Cauffman, E. (1996). Maturity of judgment in adolescence: Psychosocial factors in adolescent decision making. *Law and Human Behavior, 20*(3), 249–272. https://doi.org/10.1007/BF01499023

Steiner, B., Ellison, J. M., Butler, H. D., & Cain, C. M. (2017). The impact of inmate and prison characteristics on prisoner victimization. *Trauma, Violence & Abuse, 18*(1), 17–36. https://doi.org/10.1177/1524838015588503

Stensland, M., & Sanders, S. (2016). Detained and dying: Ethical issues surrounding end-of-life care in prison. *Journal of Social Work in End-of-Life & Palliative Care, 12*(3), 259–276. https://doi.org/10.1080/15524256.2016.1200517

Steuerle, C. E., & Smith, K. E. (2022). Social Security and Medicare lifetime benefits and taxes: 2021. Urban Institute. https://www.urban.org/sites/default/files/2022-02/social-security-medicare-lifetime-benefits-and-taxes-2021.pdf

Stevenson, B. A., & Stinneford, J. F. (n.d.). *The Eighth Amendment: Common interpretation*. National Constitution Center. https://constitutioncenter.org/the-constitution/amendments/amendment-viii/clauses/103

Stockemer, D., & Sundström, A. (2023). Age inequalities in political representation: A review article. *Government and Opposition, 2023*, 1–18. https://doi.org/10.1017/gov.2023.11

Stoliker, B. E., Kerodal, A. G., Jewell, L. M., Brown, K., Kent-Wilkinson, A., Peacock, S., O'Connell, M. E., & Wormith, J. S. (2022). Older people in custody in a forensic psychiatric facility, prevalence of dementia, and community reintegration needs: An exploratory analysis. *Health & Justice, 10*(1), 3. https://doi.org/10.1186/s40352-022-00168-8

Stony Brook University. (n.d.). *The CAM (Cognitive Aging and Memory) Lab*. https://cogagingandmemorylab.weebly.com/research-request-for-oa-participant-pool-contacts.html

Strauss, G., Glenn, M., Reddi, P., Afaq, I., Podolskaya, A., Rybakova, T., Saeed, O., Shah, V., Singh, B., Skinner, A., & El-Mallakh, R. S. (2005). Psychiatric disposition of patients brought in by crisis intervention team police officers. *Community Mental Health Journal, 41*(2), 223–228. https://doi.org/10.1007/s10597-005-2658-5

Streater, A., Coleston-Shields, D. M., Yates, J., Stanyon, M., & Orrell, M. (2017). A scoping review of crisis teams managing dementia in older people. *Clinical Interventions in Aging, 12*, 1589–1603. https://doi.org/10.2147/CIA.S142341

Substance Abuse and Mental Health Services Administration. (2019). *Civil commitment and the mental health care continuum: Historical trends and principles for law and practice*. U.S. Department of Health and Human Services. https://www.samhsa.gov/sites/default/files/civil-commitment-continuum-of-care.pdf

Substance Abuse and Mental Health Services Administration. (2020). *Treating substance use disorder in older adults, updated 2020* (Treatment Improvement Protocol No. 26). https://store.samhsa.gov/sites/default/files/tip-26-pep20-02-01-011.pdf

Substance Abuse and Mental Health Services Administration. (2024, May 24). *The Sequential Intercept Model (SIM)*. https://www.samhsa.gov/criminal-juvenile-justice/sim-overview

Sun, T., Gaut, A., Tang, S., Huang, Y., ElSherief, M., Zhao, J., Mirza, D., Belding, E., Chang, K.-W., & Wang, W. Y. (2019). Mitigating gender bias in natural language processing: literature review. *Proceedings of the 57th Annual Meeting of the Association for Computational Linguistics* (pp. 1630–1640). Association for Computational Lingustics. https://doi.org/10.18653/v1/P19-1159

Sundakov-Krumins, T. E., Lubbe, S., & Wand, A. P. F. (2022). Homicide and dementia: A systematic review. *Dementia and Geriatric Cognitive Disorders, 51*(1), 1–17. https://doi.org/10.1159/000521878

Supporting Older Americans Act of 2020, Pub. L. No. 116-131, 134 Stat. 240.

Supreme Court of the United States. (2024). *Current members*. https://www.supremecourt.gov/about/biographies.aspx

Surtees, D. (2009). What can elder law learn from disability law? In I. Doron (Ed.), *Theories on law and ageing: The jurisprudence of elder law* (pp. 93–105). Springer. https://doi.org/10.1007/978-3-540-78954-3_7

Sutton, J. R. (2013). Structural bias in the sentencing of felony defendants. *Social Science Research, 42*(5), 1207–1221. https://doi.org/10.1016/j.ssresearch.2013.04.003

Swanson, S. (2022). Former Loveland officer accepts plea deal agreement despite objection from Karen Garner's family. *Coloradoan*. https://www.coloradoan.com/story/news/2022/03/02/former-loveland-colorado-police-officer-plea-deal-karen-garner-update-arrest/6983413001

Syme, M. L., & Cohn, T. J. (2020). Elder sexual abuse and implicit agism: Examining the warm-incompetent bias among mock jurors. *Journal of Elder Abuse & Neglect, 32*(1), 1–26. https://doi.org/10.1080/08946566.2019.1695696

Tajfel, H., & Turner, J. C. (1979). An integrative theory of intergroup conflict. In W. G. Austin & S. Worchel (Eds.), *The social psychology of intergroup relations* (pp. 33–47). Brooks/Cole.

Tajfel, H., & Turner, J. C. (2004). The social identity theory of intergroup behavior. In J. T. Jost & J. Sidanius (Eds.), *Political psychology* (pp. 276–293). Psychology Press. https://doi.org/10.4324/9780203505984-16

Tapia v. U.S., 564 U.S. 319 (2011).

Tapp, S. N., & Coen, E. J. (2024). *Criminal Victimization, 2023* (NCJ No. 309335). U.S. Department of Justice, Office of Justice Programs, Bureau of Justice Statistics. https://bjs.ojp.gov/document/cv23.pdf

Tasdemir, I., Cesur, E., Mengus, A., Asliyüksek, H., & Karamustafalioglu, K. O. (2023). Sociodemographic, psychiatric and criminal characteristics of elderly offenders under evaluation for criminal responsibility in Turkey. *International Journal of Law and Psychiatry, 88*, 101888. https://doi.org/10.1016/j.ijlp.2023.101888

Taylor, E. (2011). Elderly sex offenders: What should be done? *The Elder Law Journal, 18*(2), 419–455.

Taylor, M. H., & Grossberg, G. T. (2012). The growing problem of illicit substance abuse in the elderly: A review. *The Primary Care Companion for CNS Disorders, 14*(4). https://doi.org/10.4088/PCC.11r01320

Teaster, P. B. (2017). A framework for polyvictimization in later life. *Journal of Elder Abuse & Neglect, 29*(5), 289–298. https://doi.org/10.1080/08946566.2017.1375444

Teaster, P. B., & Chamberlain, S. (2020). Public guardianship: Policy and practice. *Journal of Elder Policy, 1*(1), 155–174. https://doi.org/10.18278/jep.1.1.8

Teitelbaum, J. C. (2006). Age and tenure of the justices and productivity of the U.S. Supreme Court: Are term limits necessary? *Florida State University Law Review, 34*(1), 161–182.

Thane, P. (2003). Social histories of old age and aging. *Journal of Social History, 37*(1), 93–111. https://doi.org/10.1353/jsh.2003.0163

Thivierge-Rikard, R. V., & Thompson, M. S. (2007). The association between aging inmate housing management models and non-geriatric health services in state correctional institutions. *Journal of Aging & Social Policy, 19*(4), 39–56. https://doi.org/10.1300/J031v19n04_03

Thomas, A. K., & Dubois, S. J. (2011). Reducing the burden of stereotype threat eliminates age differences in memory distortion. *Psychological Science, 22*(12), 1515–1517. https://doi.org/10.1177/0956797611425932

Thomas, A. K., Smith, A. M., & Mazerolle, M. (2020). The unexpected relationship between retrieval demands and memory performance when older adults are faced with age-related stereotypes. *The Journals of Gerontology: Series B, 75*(2), 241–250. https://doi.org/10.1093/geronb/gby031

Thomas, M. L., Kaufmann, C. N., Palmer, B. W., Depp, C. A., Martin, A. S., Glorioso, D. K., Thompson, W. K., & Jeste, D. V. (2016). Paradoxical trend for improvement in mental health with aging: A community-based study of 1,546 adults aged 21-100 years. *The Journal of Clinical Psychiatry*, 77(8), e1019–1025. https://doi.org/10.4088/JCP.16m10671

Thomas, P. A. (2011). Trajectories of social engagement and limitations in late life. *Journal of Health and Social Behavior, 52*(4), 430–443. https://doi.org/10.1177/0022146511411922

Thomas, W. H. (2004). *What are old people for? How Elders will save the world.* Vanderwyk & Burnham.

Thomas Tobin, C. S., Gutiérrez, Á., Farmer, H. R., Erving, C. L., & Hargrove, T. W. (2023). Intersectional approaches to minority aging research. *Current Epidemiology Reports, 10*(1), 33–43. https://doi.org/10.1007/s40471-022-00317-5

Thompson, A., & Tapp, S. (2023). *Criminal victimization, 2022* (NCJ No. 307089). U.S. Department of Justice, Office of Justice Programs, and Bureau of Justice Statistics. https://bjs.ojp.gov/document/cv22.pdf

Thompson, C. (2018, March 7). Frail, old and dying, but their only way out of prison is a coffin. *The New York Times*. https://www.nytimes.com/2018/03/07/us/prisons-compassionate-release-.html

Thompson, C. (2022, November 22). As police arrest more seniors, those with dementia face deadly consequences. *USA Today*. https://www.usatoday.com/in-depth/news/investigations/2022/11/22/police-arrests-elderly-unique-risks-dementia-alzheimers/10455567002

Thomsen, J., Goudsward, A., & Brittain, B. (2023, April 21). *Probe of federal appeals judge tests aging US courts*. Reuters. https://www.reuters.com/legal/government/probe-federal-appeals-judge-tests-aging-us-courts-2023-04-21

Thor v. Superior Court, 855 P.2d 375 (1993).

Tierney, J. (2004, December 26). Adultescent. *The New York Times*. https://www.nytimes.com/2004/12/26/weekinreview/adultescent.html

Title 28, Judiciary and Judicial Procedure, Pub. L. No. 773, 62 Stat. (1948).

Tittle, C. R., & Paternoster, R. (2000). *Social deviance and crime: An organizational and theoretical approach*. Oxford University Press.

Tofle, R. B. (2009). Creating a place for dying: Gerontopia. *Journal of Housing for the Elderly, 23*(1–2), 66–91. https://doi.org/10.1080/02763890802664646

Tokar, S. (2006, March 10). *Geriatric inmates face challenges unique to prison*. https://www.ucsf.edu/news/2006/03/97827/geriatric-inmates-face-challenges-unique-prison#:~:text=What%20do%20we%2C%20as%20a%20society%2C%20want,also%20have%20a%20reasonable%20system%20of%20incarceration.%E2%80%9D

Toofanian Ross, P., Padula, C. B., Nitch, S. R., & Kinney, D. I. (2015). Cognition and competency restoration: Using the RBANS to predict length of stay for patients deemed incompetent to stand trial. *The Clinical Neuropsychologist, 29*(1), 150–165. https://doi.org/10.1080/13854046.2015.1005678

Trollope, A. (1882). *The fixed period*. William Blackwood and Sons.

Trop v. Dulles, 356 U.S. 86 (1958).

Turner, A. M., Engelsma, T., Taylor, J. O., Sharma, R. K., & Demiris, G. (2021). Recruiting older adult participants through crowdsourcing platforms: Mechanical

Turk versus Prolific Academic. *AMIA Annual Symposium Proceedings, 2020*, 1230–1238.

Tutella, F. (2023, August 3). *Q&A: What does an aging Congress mean for a much younger nation?* Penn State University. https://www.psu.edu/news/research/story/qa-what-does-aging-congress-mean-much-younger-nation

Tyler, T. R., & Lind, E. A. (2001). Procedural justice. In J. Sanders & V. L. Hamilton (Eds.), *Handbook of justice research in law* (pp. 65–92). Kluwer Academic.

Tyuse, S. W., Cooper-Sadlo, S., & Underwood, S. E. (2017). Descriptive study of older adults encountered by crisis intervention team (CIT) law enforcement officers. *Journal of Women & Aging, 29*(4), 281–293. https://doi.org/10.1080/08952841.2016.1174513

Ulmer, J. T., & Steffensmeier, D. (2014). The age and crime relationship: Social variation, social explanations. In K. M. Beaver, J. C. Barnes, & B. B. Boutwell (Eds.), *The nurture versus biosocial debate in criminology: On the origins of criminal behavior and criminality* (pp. 377–396). Sage Publications. https://doi.org/10.4135/9781483349114.n24

UnCommon Law. (2022). *2022 annual report.* https://www.uncommonlaw.org/reports

Union Pacific Railway Co. v. Botsford, 141 U.S. 250 (1891).

United Air Lines, Inc. v. McMann, 434 U.S. 192 (1977)

United Kingdom Ministry of Justice. (2018, October). *A review of self-inflicted deaths in prison custody in 2016.* https://www.parliament.uk/globalassets/documents/commons-committees/Justice/correspondence/Edward-Argar-self-inflicted-deaths-custody-17-19.pdf

United Nations Department of Economic and Social Affairs. (2019, October 10). *Our world is growing older: UN DESA releases new report on ageing.* https://www.un.org/development/desa/en/news/population/our-world-is-growing-older.html

United Nations Department of Economic and Social Affairs. (2023). *World Elder Abuse Awareness Day.* https://www.un.org/en/observances/elder-abuse-awareness-day/background

United States v. Brooke, 308 F.3d 17 (D.C. Cir. 2002).

United States v. Bullion, 466 F.3d 574 (7th Cir. 2006).

United States v. Doran, 328 F. Supp. 1261 (S.D.N.Y. 1971).

United States v. Johnson, 703 F.3d 464 (8th Cir. 2013).

United States v. Joseph, No. 1: 86-cr-00322-RAR (S.D. Fla. May 16, 2022).

United States v. Sweig, 316 F. Supp. 1148 (S.D.N.Y. 1970).

University of Nebraska Omaha. (2017, February 17). *Faculty Focus: Julie Masters.* UNO News. https://www.unomaha.edu/news/2017/02/faculty-focus-julie-masters.php

University of Texas Southwestern Medical Center v. Nassar, 570 U.S. 338 (2013)

U.S. Administration for Community Living. (2021). *Adult maltreatment report.* U.S. Department of Health and Human Services. https://pfs2.acl.gov/strapib/assets/2021%20Adult%20Maltreatment%20Report_Ready%20for%20508_ADA.pdf

U.S. Administration for Community Living. (2024). *The National Adult Maltreatment Reporting System.* U.S. Department of Health and Human Services. https://namrs.acl.gov/home#gsc.tab=0

U.S. Census Bureau. (2018). Older people projected to outnumber children for first time in U.S. history. https://www.census.gov/newsroom/press-releases/2018/cb18-41-population-projections.html

U.S. Census Bureau. (2023, April). *2020 Census Demographic and Housing Characteristics File (DHC): 2020 Census of Population and Housing.* U.S. Department of Commerce. https://www2.census.gov/programs-surveys/decennial/2020/technical-documentation/complete-tech-docs/demographic-and-housing-characteristics-file-and-demographic-profile/2020census-demographic-and-housing-characteristics-file-and-demographic-profile-techdoc.pdf

U.S. Const. amend. I–X.

U.S. Const. amend. II.

U.S. Const. amend. V.

U.S. Const. amend. VI.

U.S. Const. amend. VIII.

U.S. Const. amend. X

U.S. Const. amend. XIV.

U.S. Const. art. I, § 2

U.S. Const. art. I, § 3

U.S. Const. art. II, § 1.

U.S. Department of Justice. (2013). *The Federal Bureau of Prisons' Compassionate Release Program* (No. I-2013-006). Office of the Inspector General. https://oig.justice.gov/reports/2013/e1306.pdf

U.S. Department of Justice. (2023). *First Step Act annual report*. Office of the Attorney General. https://www.ojp.gov/first-step-act-annual-report-april-2023

U.S. Equal Employment Opportunity Commission. (n.d.). *How to file a charge of employment discrimination*. https://www.eeoc.gov/how-file-charge-employment-discrimination

U.S. Equal Employment Opportunity Commission. (2007, October 5). *$27.5 million consent decree resolves EEOC age bias suit against Sidley Austin* [Press release]. https://www.eeoc.gov/newsroom/275-million-consent-decree-resolves-eeoc-age-bias-suit-against-sidley-austin-0

U.S. Office of Personnel Management. (n.d.). *Voluntary early retirement authority*. https://www.opm.gov/policy-data-oversight/workforce-restructuring/voluntary-early-retirement-authority

U.S. Parole Commission. (2010). *U.S. Parole Commission Rules & Procedures Manual*. U.S. Justice Department. https://www.justice.gov/sites/default/files/uspc/legacy/2010/08/27/uspc-manual111507.pdf

U.S. Sentencing Commission. (2021). *2021 guidelines manual annotated*. https://www.ussc.gov/guidelines/guidelines-archive/2021-guidelines-manual-annotated

U.S. Sentencing Commission. (2024, October). *Compassionate release data report*. https://www.ussc.gov/sites/default/files/pdf/research-and-publications/federal-sentencing-statistics/compassionate-release/FY24Q4-Compassionate-Release.pdf

Va. Code § 53.1–40.01 (2024).

Valentine, T., Pickering, A., & Darling, S. (2003). Characteristics of eyewitness identification that predict the outcome of real lineups. *Applied Cognitive Psychology, 17*(8), 969–993. https://doi.org/10.1002/acp.939

van der Gronde, T., Kempes, M., van El, C., Rinne, T., & Pieters, T. (2014). Neurobiological correlates in forensic assessment: A systematic review. *PloS One, 9*(10), e110672. https://doi.org/10.1371/journal.pone.0110672

Van Duizend, R., & Uekert, B. K. (2014). Elder abuse and exploitation: How courts can take leadership in developing effective responses. *Experience, 24*(1).

Van Kleef, G. A., C. K. W. De Dreu, & A. S. R. Manstead. (2010). An interpersonal approach to emotion in social decision making: The emotions as social information model. *Advances in Experimental Social Psychology, 42*, 45–96. https://doi.org/10.1016/S0065-2601(10)42002-X

Van Ostrand, L. A. (2009). A close look at ADEA mixed-motives claims and gross v. FBL Financial Services, Inc. *Fordham Law Review, 78*(1), 399–452.

Velick, M. D. (1995). Mandatory reporting statutes: A necessary yet underutilized response to elder abuse note. *Elder Law Journal, 3*(1), 165–190.

Venner, S., Sivasubramaniam, D., Luebbers, S., & Shepherd, S. M. (2021). Cross-cultural reliability and rater bias in forensic risk assessment: A review of the literature. *Psychology, Crime & Law, 27*(2), 105–121. https://doi.org/10.1080/1068316X.2020.1775829

Vera Institute of Justice. (2017). *Aging out: Using compassionate release to address the growth of aging and infirm prison populations.* https://www.vera.org/downloads/publications/Using-Compassionate-Release-to-Address-the-Growth-of-Aging-and-Infirm-Prison-Populations%E2%80%94Fact-Sheet.pdf

Virginia Department of Corrections and Parole Board. (2008). *A balanced approach: Assisted living facilities for geriatric inmates* (General Assembly Report 387-B). https://rga.lis.virginia.gov/Published/2008/RD240/PDF

Volkert, J., Schulz, H., Härter, M., Wlodarczyk, O., & Andreas, S. (2013). The prevalence of mental disorders in older people in Western countries—A meta-analysis. *Ageing Research Reviews, 12*(1), 339–353. https://doi.org/10.1016/j.arr.2012.09.004

Von Kaenel v. Armstrong Teasdale, LLP, 943 F.3d 1139 (8th Cir. 2019).

Wahidin, A. (2004). *Older women in the criminal justice system: Running out of time.* Jessica Kingsley.

Wall, B. W., Ash, P., Keram, E., Pinals, D. A., & Thompson, C. H. (2018). AAPL practice resource for the forensic psychiatric evaluation of competence to stand trial. *The Journal of the American Academy of Psychiatry and the Law, 46*(3 Suppl.), S4–S79. https://www.jaapl.org/content/46/3_Supplement

Wasarhaley, N. E., & Golding, J. M. (2017). Ageism in the courtroom: Mock juror perceptions of elder neglect. *Psychology, Crime & Law, 23*(9), 874–898. https://doi.org/10.1080/1068316X.2017.1338699

Washington v. Harper, 494 U.S. 210 (1990).

Weil, E. (2011, December 1). Marathon swimmer Diana Nyad takes on the demons of the sea. *The New York Times.* https://www.nytimes.com/2011/12/04/magazine/marathon-swimmer-diana-nyad.html

Weinrath, M., & Gartrell, J. (1996). Victimization and fear of crime. *Violence and Victims, 11*(3), 187–197. https://doi.org/10.1891/0886-6708.11.3.187

Weir, K. (2023, March 1). Ageism is one of the last socially acceptable prejudices. Psychologists are working to change that. *Monitor on Psychology, 54*(2), 36. https://www.apa.org/monitor/2023/03/cover-new-concept-of-aging

Weisberg, R., Mukamal, D. A., & Segall, J. D. (2011). *Life in limbo: An examination of parole release for prisoners serving life sentences with the possibility of parole in California.* Stanford Criminal Justice Center. https://law.stanford.edu/publications/life-in-limbo-an-examination-of-parole-release-for-prisoners-serving-life-sentences-with-the-possibility-of-parole-in-california

Weissberger, G. H., Goodman, M. C., Mosqueda, L., Schoen, J., Nguyen, A. L., Wilber, K. H., Gassoumis, Z. D., Nguyen, C. P., & Han, S. D. (2020). Elder abuse characteristics based on calls to the National Center on Elder Abuse resource line. *Journal of Applied Gerontology, 39*(10), 1078–1087. https://doi.org/10.1177/0733464819865685

Wells, G. L., Kovera, M. B., Douglass, A. B., Brewer, N., Meissner, C. A., & Wixted, J. T. (2020). Policy and procedure recommendations for the collection and preservation of eyewitness identification evidence. *Law and Human Behavior, 44*(1), 3–36. https://doi.org/10.1037/lhb0000359

Wells, G. L., Small, M., Penrod, S., Malpass, R. S., Fulero, S. M., & Brimacombe, C. A. E. (1998). Eyewitness identification procedures: Recommendations for lineups and photospreads. *Law and Human Behavior, 22*(6), 603–647. https://doi.org/10.1023/A:1025750605807

West, R. L., & Stone, K. R. (2014). Age differences in eyewitness memory for a realistic event. *The Journals of Gerontology: Series B, 69*(3), 338–347. https://doi.org/10.1093/geronb/gbt014

Wexler, D. (2001). Therapeutic jurisprudence: An overview. *Thomas M. Cooley Law Review, 17*, 125–134.

Wexler, D. B., & Winick, B. J. (1991). *Essays in therapeutic jurisprudence*. Carolina Academic Press.

Wheeler, S. C., & Petty, R. E. (2001). The effects of stereotype activation on behavior: A review of possible mechanisms. *Psychological Bulletin, 127*, 797.

White House Conference on Aging. (2015). *Final report: 2015 White House Conference on Aging*. https://whitehouseconferenceonaging.gov/2015-WHCOA-Final-Report.pdf

Wiebe, D. J. (2003). Homicide and suicide risks associated with firearms in the home: A national case-control study. *Annals of Emergency Medicine, 41*(6), 771–782. https://doi.org/10.1067/mem.2003.187

Wiener, R. L., & Farnum, K. S. (2016). How old is old in allegations of age discrimination? The limitations of existing law. *Law and Human Behavior, 40*(5), 536–550. https://doi.org/10.1037/lhb0000199

Wilcock, R., & Bull, R. (2014). Improving the performance of older witnesses on identification procedures. In M. P. Toglia, D. F. Ross, J. Pozzulo, & E. Pica (Eds.), *The elderly eyewitness in court* (pp. 118–134). Psychology Press. https://doi.org/10.4324/9781315813936

Wilcock, R. A., Bull, R., & Vrij, A. (2007). Are old witnesses always poorer witnesses? Identification accuracy, context reinstatement, own-age bias. *Psychology, Crime & Law, 13*(3), 305–316. https://doi.org/10.1080/10683160600822212

Wilford, M. M., & Wells, G. L. (2013). Eyewitness system variables: Revisiting the system-variable concept and the transfer of system variables to the legal system. In B. L. Cutler (Ed.), *Reform of eyewitness identification procedures* (pp. 23–43). American Psychological Association. https://doi.org/10.1037/14094-002

Williams, B., & Abraldes, R. (2007). Growing older: Challenges of prison and reentry for the aging population. In R. B. Greifinger (Ed.), *Public health behind bars: From prisons to communities* (pp. 56–72). Springer. https://doi.org/10.1007/978-0-387-71695-4_5

Williams, B. A., Ahalt, C., Stijacic-Cenzer, I., Smith, A. K., Goldenson, J., & Ritchie, C. S. (2014). Pain behind bars: The epidemiology of pain in older jail inmates in a county jail. *Journal of Palliative Medicine, 17*(12), 1336–1343. https://doi.org/10.1089/jpm.2014.0160

Williams, B. A., Goodwin, J. S., Baillargeon, J., Ahalt, C., & Walter, L. C. (2012). Addressing the aging crisis in U.S. criminal justice health care. *Journal of the American Geriatrics Society, 60*(6), 1150–1156. https://doi.org/10.1111/j.1532-5415.2012.03962.x

Williams, B. A., Lindquist, K., Sudore, R. L., Strupp, H. M., Willmott, D. J., & Walter, L. C. (2006). Being old and doing time: Functional impairment and adverse experiences of geriatric female prisoners. *Journal of the American Geriatrics Society, 54*(4), 702–707. https://doi.org/10.1111/j.1532-5415.2006.00662.x

Williams, W. H., Chitsabesan, P., Fazel, S., McMillan, T., Hughes, N., Parsonage, M., & Tonks, J. (2018). Traumatic brain injury: A potential cause of violent crime? *The Lancet Psychiatry, 5*(10), 836–844. https://doi.org/10.1016/S2215-0366(18)30062-2

Willis, C. C. (2020, Spring). Age is just a number; Not a reason to force retirement. *Journal of Comparative and International Aging Law & Policy, 11*, 67–104.

Wilson, R. S., Wang, T., Yu, L., Bennett, D. A., & Boyle, P. A. (2020). Normative cognitive decline in old age. *Annals of Neurology, 87*(6), 816–829. https://doi.org/10.1002/ana.25711

Winick, B. J. (1997). The jurisprudence of therapeutic jurisprudence. *Psychology, Public Policy, and Law, 3*(1), 184–206. https://doi.org/10.1037/1076-8971.3.1.184

Wirtz, W. W. (1965, June). *The older American worker—age discrimination in employment.* U.S. Equal Employment Opportunity Commission. https://www.eeoc.gov/reports/older-american-worker-age-discrimination-employment

Wisnieski, A. (2017, April 25). *'Model' nursing home for paroled inmates to get federal funds.* Connecticut Health Investigative Team. https://c-hit.org/2017/04/25/model-nursing-home-for-paroled-inmates-to-get-federal-funds

Wixted, J. T., & Mickes, L. (2022). Eyewitness memory is reliable, but the criminal justice system is not. *Memory, 30*(1), 67–72. https://doi.org/10.1080/09658211.2021.1974485

Wolff, J. L., Mulcahy, J., Huang, J., Roth, D. L., Covinsky, K., & Kasper, J. D. (2018). Family caregivers of older adults, 1999-2015: Trends in characteristics, circumstances, and role-related appraisal. *The Gerontologist, 58*(6), 1021–1032. https://doi.org/10.1093/geront/gnx093

World Health Organization. (2017, June 14). *Abuse of older people on the rise – 1 in 6 affected.* https://www.who.int/news/item/14-06-2017-abuse-of-older-people-on-the-rise-1-in-6-affected

World Health Organization. (2021). *Ageism is a global challenge: UN.* https://www.who.int/news/item/18-03-2021-ageism-is-a-global-challenge-un

World Health Organization. (2022). *World Health Statistics 2022: Monitoring health for the SDGs.* https://www.who.int/publications/i/item/9789240051157

Wright, A. M., & Holliday, R. E. (2005). Police officers' perceptions of older eyewitnesses. *Legal and Criminological Psychology, 10*(2), 211–223. https://doi.org/10.1348/135532505X37001

Wu, L.-T., & Blazer, D. G. (2011). Illicit and nonmedical drug use among older adults: A review. *Journal of Aging and Health, 23*(3), 481–504. https://doi.org/10.1177/0898264310386224

Wylie, L., Bergt, S., Haby, J., Brank, E., & Bornstein, B. (2015). Age and lineup type differences in the own-race bias. *Psychology, Crime & Law, 21*(5), 490–506. https://doi.org/10.1080/1068316X.2014.989173

Wylie, L. E., & Brank, E. M. (2009). Assuming elder care responsibility: Am I a caregiver?: Assuming elder care responsibility. *Journal of Empirical Legal Studies, 6*(4), 899–924. https://doi.org/10.1111/j.1740-1461.2009.01164.x

Wylie, L. E., Brank, E. M., & Bornstein, B. H. (2015). "Now dear, what do you remember?" Patronizing communication and older eyewitnesses' memory performance. *American Journal of Forensic Psychology, 33*(4), 37–66.

Wylie, L. E., Hazen, K. P., Hoetger, L. A., Haby, J. A., & Brank, E. M. (2018). Four decades of the journal *Law and Human Behavior*: A content analysis. *Scientometrics, 115*(2), 655–693. https://doi.org/10.1007/s11192-018-2685-y

Wylie, L. E., Knutson, A. K., & Greene, E. (2018). Extraordinary and compelling: The use of compassionate release laws in the United States. *Psychology, Public Policy, and Law, 24*(2), 216–234. https://doi.org/10.1037/law0000161

Wylie, L. E., Patihis, L., McCuller, L. L., Davis, D., Brank, E. M., Loftus, E. F., & Bornstein, B. H. (2014). Misinformation effect in older versus younger adults: A meta-analysis and review. In M. P. Toglia, D. F. Ross, J. Pozzulo, & E. Pica (Eds.), *The elderly eyewitness in court* (pp. 38–66). Psychology Press. https://doi.org/10.4324/9781315813936

Yang, Y., & Raine, A. (2009). Prefrontal structural and functional brain imaging findings in antisocial, violent, and psychopathic individuals: A meta-analysis. *Psychiatry Research: Neuroimaging, 174*(2), 81–88. https://doi.org/10.1016/j.pscychresns.2009.03.012

Yarmey, A. D. (2001). Expert testimony: Does eyewitness memory research have probative value for the courts? *Canadian Psychology, 42*(2), 92–100. https://doi.org/10.1037/h0086883

Yarnell, S., Li, L., MacGrory, B., Trevisan, L., & Kirwin, P. (2020). Substance use disorders in later life: A review and synthesis of the literature of an emerging public health concern. *The American Journal of Geriatric Psychiatry, 28*(2), 226–236. https://doi.org/10.1016/j.jagp.2019.06.005

Yee, G. (2021, May 5). Man who wounded Charleston County sheriff's deputy in shootout charged. *The Post and Courier.* https://www.postandcourier.com/news/man-who-wounded-charleston-county-sheriffs-deputy-in-shootout-charged/article_d4775e24-ade1-11eb-affa-dfdbaea0d8df.html

Yelderman, L. A., Lawrence, T. I., Lyons, C. E., & DeVault, A. (2021). Actor–observer asymmetry in perceptions of parole board release decisions. *Psychiatry, Psychology, and Law, 28*(5), 623–644. https://doi.org/10.1080/13218719.2020.1821826

Yon, Y., Mikton, C. R., Gassoumis, Z. D., & Wilber, K. H. (2017). Elder abuse prevalence in community settings: A systematic review and meta-analysis. *The Lancet, 5*(2), e147–e156. https://doi.org/10.1016/S2214-109X(17)30006-2

Young, K. M., & Pearlman, J. (2022). Racial disparities in lifer parole outcomes: The hidden role of professional evaluations. *Law & Social Inquiry, 47*(3), 783–820. https://doi.org/10.1017/lsi.2021.37

Young, L. M. (2014). Elder physical abuse. *Clinics in Geriatric Medicine, 30*(4), 761–768. https://doi.org/10.1016/j.cger.2014.08.005

Yu, M., Wang, W., Gu, L., & Ramachandran, H. J. (2023). Perspectives and experiences of living with self-neglect among older adults: A systematic review and meta-synthesis. *Journal of Nursing Scholarship, 55*(4), 771–781. https://doi.org/10.1111/jnu.12854

Zapf, P. A., & Roesch, R. (2011). Future directions in the restoration of competency to stand trial. *Current Directions in Psychological Science, 20*(1), 43–47. https://doi.org/10.1177/0963721410396798

Zaval, L., Li, Y., Johnson, E. J., & Weber, E. U. (2015). Complementary contributions of fluid and crystallized intelligence to decision making across the life span. In T. M. Hess, J. Strough, & C. E. Löckenhoff (Eds.), *Aging and decision making: Empirical and applied perspectives* (pp. 149–168). Academic Press. https://doi.org/10.1016/B978-0-12-417148-0.00008-X

Zevitz, R. G., & Gurnack, A. M. (1991). Factors related to elderly crime victims' satisfaction with police service: The impact of Milwaukee's "Gray Squad." *The Gerontologist, 31*(1), 92–101. https://doi.org/10.1093/geront/31.1.92

Zgoba, K., Jennings, W. G., Maschi, T., & Reingle, J. M. (2013). An exploration into the intersections of early and late sexual victimization and mental and physical health among an incarcerated sample of older male offenders. *Best Practices in Mental Health, 8*(2), 82–98.

Zhang, S. X., Roberts, R. E. L., & Farabee, D. (2014). An analysis of prisoner reentry and parole risk using COMPAS and traditional criminal history measures. *Crime and Delinquency, 60*(2), 167–192. https://doi.org/10.1177/0011128711426544

Ziminski Pickering, C. E., & Rempusheski, V. F. (2014). Examining barriers to self-reporting of elder physical abuse in community-dwelling older adults. *Geriatric Nursing, 35*(2), 120–125. https://doi.org/10.1016/j.gerinurse.2013.11.002

INDEX

A

ABOUT THE AUTHORS

Lindsey E. Wylie, JD, PhD, is a senior court research associate at the National Center for State Courts and adjunct faculty at the University of Nebraska Omaha. Her research evaluates the (un)intended consequences of legal system involvement for special populations to inform state courts in developing practical and innovative evidence-informed practices, processes, and policies.

Eve M. Brank, JD, PhD, is the Aaron Douglas Professor of Psychology, courtesy professor of law, and director of the Center on Children, Families, and the Law at the University of Nebraska–Lincoln. Her research focuses primarily on the way the law intervenes (and sometimes interferes) in family and personal decision making.